8° G.
738.

VIEW FROM FOOT-BRIDGE OVER CARREI,
MENTONE.

WINTERING IN THE RIVIERA

WITH

NOTES OF TRAVEL IN ITALY AND FRANCE

AND

PRACTICAL HINTS TO TRAVELLERS

BY

WILLIAM MILLER, S.S.C.
EDINBURGH

With Illustrations

LONDON:
LONGMANS, GREEN, AND CO.
1879.

MORRISON AND GIBB, EDINBURGH,
PRINTERS TO HER MAJESTY'S STATIONERY OFFICE.

THIS VOLUME,

CONTAINING MEMORIES OF HIS BELOVED DAUGHTER'S LAST JOURNEYINGS,

IS INSCRIBED TO

CHRISTOPHER GODWIN, ESQ., J.P.,
STOKE BISHOP, BRISTOL.

CONTENTS.

	PAGE
PREFACE, ...	x

I.

CONTINENTAL TRAVELLING.

Former and Present Times—Bugbears—Language—Passports—Impedimenta—Guide-Books—Hotels—Money and Exchange—Routes to Paris—Cook's and Gaze's Railway Tickets—*Voyages circulaires*—Supplementary Billets—Customs Examination—Time—Railway Arrangements—Billets—*Salle d'attente*—Guards and Porters—Carriages—*Dames seules*—Smoking—Carriage Windows—Speed—Train Peculiarities—Stations—Omnibuses—*Petite vitesse*, . . 1

II.

HOTEL AND PENSION LIFE.

Hotels—Railway Results—Construction—Lifts—Charges—Bougies—Service—Rooms—Meals—Breakfast—Lunch—*Table-d'hôte* Dinner—Supplies—Wine—Dining *à la Carte*—Foreign Practices—Life at Table—Pension—Charges—Extras—Fires—Gratuities—Bills—Cook's and Gaze's Coupons—Amusements—Tarantala Dance—Remuneration to Performers—Charades—Readings—Plays—Amateur Performances—Musical Bands—Furnished Villas—Cost—Servants, ... 43

III.

LOCAL MEANS OF CONVEYANCE.

Private Carriages—Horses—Carriages for Hire—Whip-Cracking—Cruelty to Horses—Italian Cabs and Cabmen—Horse Bells—Fares—*Pour boire* and *buono mano*—Drives beyond Town—Crossing Swiss Passes—Diligences—Steamboat Travelling—Omnibuses—Tramways, 82

IV.

POSTAL ARRANGEMENTS.

Post Rates for Letters—Underpaid Letters—Newspapers—Registration—Letters for Interior—Post Cards—Delivery—*Poste restante*—Pillars—Postmen, ... 98

V.

SUNDAY ABROAD.

As observed by Natives—English Influence—Public Music—Museums, etc. — Carnival — Fêtes — Elections — Post Delivery — Dinner—Evening Engagements—Sunday Books—Roman Catholic Service—Protestantism—Native Protestant Churches—France—Mentone—Italy—Switzerland—Protestant Churches for English—Presbyterian—The Chapels—Ministers—English Episcopal—Ritualism abroad—Hours of Service—Growing Liberality of Feeling—A Practical Suggestion—Conclusion of Service, ... 105

FIRST WINTER IN THE RIVIERA.

VI.

LONDON TO SOUTH OF FRANCE.

Folkestone—Passage—*Paris*—Railway Journey from Paris—*Fontainebleau* — *Dijon* — *Macon* — The Rhone — *Avignon* — *Nismes* — *Marseilles*, ... 127

VII.

CANNES.

Arrival—Description of Cannes—The Bays—Estrelles—Grasse—Lord Brougham—Duke of Vallombrosa's Villa—the Eucalyptus—Croix de Garde—Promenade—Bathing Places—Drains—Garden of the Hesperides—Arbutus—Croisette—California—S. Marguerite—Fort Monterey—Use of Marble—Mosquitoes, Snakes, and Lizards, . 144

VIII.

NICE.

Cannes to Nice—Appearance of—The Chateau—The Paillon Torrent Bed—Nice as a Health Resort—Hotels and Public Places—Nice to Mentone, ... 159

IX.

MENTONE.

First Impression—Old Town—Mountain Shelter—West Bay—Tideless Sea — Drains — Olive Terraces — Valleys — Rivers — Rurality — Quarters — Doctors — The Hotels — Pension Charges — Furnished Houses or Rooms—Helvetia—Churches—School and Classes—Public Institutions — Newspapers — Guide-Books — Mentone by Night—Donkey Excursions—Castellar—Rain and Storm—Gorge of St. Louis—The Carrei Valley—View from Bridge—Boirigo Valley

CONTENTS.

—St. Agnes—Castle—Monastery of S. Annunciata and Chapel—The Gorbio Valley—Gorbio—Rochebrune—Cape Martin—Red Rocks and Caves—The Fossil Skeleton—Hanging Gardens—Belinda—Grimaldi—Promenade du Midi—Life on the Promenade—French Attire and Customs—*Monte Carlo*—Gaming Tables—the Garden—Pigeon-shooting—*Monaco*—Mentone Villas—Gardens—Shops—Circulating Libraries—Industrial Occupations—Washing Clothes—Fishing—Sheep-keeping—Donkey-letting—Woodwork—Town and Rural Labourers—Animal Labour—Birds—Mosquitoes—Deaths—Funerals—Cemetery—the Evenings—Red-letter Days—Christmas Day—New Year's Day—Conscription Day—Carnival—Corsica—Weather during Winter, ... 166

ITALY.

X.

SAN REMO AND GENOA.

Cross Frontier—The *douane*—*Ventimiglia*—*Bordighera*—*San Remo*—Climate—San Remo described—Excursions—Hotels and Pensions—Visitors—Doctors—Churches—Industries—The Women—Photographs—San Remo to Genoa—Italian Money—Fares—Coast Towns—Savona—Pegli—*Genoa*—Position and Appearance—Statue of Columbus—Hotel Rooms—Drive through Town—S. Maria di Carignano—The Streets—Palaces—Churches—Public Park—Campo Santo, ... 237

XI.

SPEZIA, PISA, SIENNA.

Railway to Spezia—Hotel—Cold Weather—*Spezia*, a Summer Place—Described—Carrara Marble Quarries—*Pisa*—Leaning Tower—Cathedral Baptistery—Campo Santo—The Town—Drive to *Lucca*—*Sienna*—Position—Collegio Tolomei—Cathedral—Its Library—Frescoes—Piazza Vittorio Emanuele—Town Hall and other Places—Citadel—Italian Soldiers, ... 263

XII.

ROME.

Quarters—Piazza di Spagna—Carriages—The seeing Rome—First Sunday—Scotch Church—Castle of St. Angelo—St. Peter's—Piazza—Interior—Apostle Peter in Rome—St. Peter's Aisles and Altars—Mosaics—Ascent of Dome—Palm Sunday—The Vatican—Sculptures—Pictures—Sistine Chapel—Preliminary Drive through Town—The Streets, Buildings, etc.—Lecturers on Rome—The Colosseum—Rome's Birthday Illuminations—Arches of Constantine and Titus—Old Roman Roads—Forum Romanum—The Capitol—Church of Ara Cœli—The Museums—Palatine Hill—Palace of the

CONTENTS.

PAGE

Cæsars—Temple of Vesta—Cloaca Maxima—Monumental Pillars, Trajan's—M. Aurelius—The Obelisks—Aqueducts—Baths of Caracalla—Columbaria—Catacombs of Calixtus—Appian Way—The Churches—Pantheon—S. Pietro in Vincoli—Jesuit Church—Capuccini—S. Clemente—S. Cosmo e Damiano—The Lateran—Santa Scala—S. Maria Maggiore—S. Paolo fuori le mura—The Palaces—Contents of Galleries—Engravings and Photographs of Pictures—Copying Pictures—The Rospigliosi—Guido's Aurora—The Barberini—Beatrice Cenci—Other Galleries and Studios—The Royal Palace—Borghese Grounds and Casino—Pincian Hill Gardens—Drive to Tivoli—The Campagna—Hadrian's Villa—*Tivoli*—S. Lorenzo fuori le mura—Shop Purchases—Photographs—Mosaic Jewellery—Bronzes—Copies of Paintings—Old Rome as it was, . 275

XIII.

NAPLES, POMPEII, SORRENTO.

Naples, Drive through—Cabs and Cabmen—Population—Thieving—Bay of Naples—Town described—Cathedral—Hotels—Museum—Chiaja—Aquarium—Photographs—Bijouterie—*Castellamare*—*Pompeii*—Museum—Excavations—Old City—Public Buildings—Private Dwellings—Streets—Shops—*Sorrento*—Excursions—Capri Blue Grotto—Sorrento Woodwork—Beggars—Return to Naples—*Puteoli*—Amphitheatre—Solfatara, ... 322

XIV.

FLORENCE AND BOLOGNA.

Florence—Situation—Lung' Arno—Florence described—Bridges—S. Miniato—Piazza Michel Angelo—Fiesole—The Streets—Cascine—Historical Associations—Churches—Cathedral—Campanile—Baptistery—Misericordia—S. Croce—Chapel and Tombs of the Medici—Museum of S. Marco—S. Spirito—Piazza della Signoria—Loggia—Palazzo Vecchio—House of Michael Angelo—Uffizi Gallery—Pitti Gallery—Artists copying—National Museum—Palazzo Corsini—Academia delle Belle Arti—Association for Encouragement of Fine Arts—Florentine Marbles and Mosaics—Italian Lungs—*Bologna*—Drive through Town—Leaning Towers—Museum and Library—S. Petronio—Villa Reale—Campo Santo—S. Domenico—S. Pietro—Academia delle Belle Arti, . . 343

XV.

VENICE AND VERONA.

Venice—Railway Station—Hotel Danieli—Bridge of Sighs—S. Marco—The Presbyterio—Clock Tower—Piazza and its Shops—Venetian Glass—Gondola—Island of S. Georgio—La Guidica—Churches of Venice—Palaces—Doge's Palace—S. Marco—Whitsunday—Mosaics—Campanile—Ponte di Rialto—Museo Correr—Academia delle Belle Arti—Arsenal—Lido—Moonlight—Is Venice healthy?

CONTENTS.

Grand Canal—*Verona*—Drive through Town—Market-Place—Piazza dei Signori—Tombs of Scaligers—Arena—S. Zenone—Other Churches—Tomb and Window of Juliet, ... 361

XVI.

MILAN AND THE ITALIAN LAKES.

Milan—Cathedral—Ceremonies—Ascent—Piazza—Galleria—Drive about Town—Piazza d'Armi—Arco della Pace—Amphitheatre—S. Ambrogio—S. Lorenzo—Public Park—Novel Mode of Watering—Temperature—*Italian Lakes*—Arona—*Maggiore*—Baveno—*Lugano*—S. Salvatore—Luini's Frescoes—*Bellaggio*—Hotel Grand Bretagne—*Lake Como*—Villa Serbelloni—Villa Carlotta—Villa Melzi—Sail to *Como*—St. Giovanni—Hot Days, ... 380

SWITZERLAND—FRANCE.

XVII.

THE SPLUGEN PASS, SWITZERLAND.

Sail to Colico—*Chiavenna*—*Splugen Pass*—Campo Dolcino—Madesimo Fall—Summit of Pass—Descent to Splugen—*Switzerland*—*Splugen*—Via Mala—Thusis—*Ragatz*—Pfäffers Gorge—*Lucerne*—*Interlachen*—Run Home—*Chateau d'Œx*—Sepey—Aigle—*Montreux*—Geneva, ... 401

XVIII.

BIARRITZ.

Lyons—*Cette*—*Toulouse*—Lourdes—Pau—Bayonne—*Biarritz*—Railway Station—Hotels—Cold Winds—Recent Origin of Town—Description—The Season—Natural Attractions—Storms—Breakwater—Boating—Rocks—Tide—Drains—Bathing Establishments—Bathing—The Bathers—Dresses—The Scene—Aquatics—Walks—Lighthouse—Villa Eugenie—Drive to *Bayonne*—Its Fortifications—Bridges—*St. Jean de Luz*—Excursion to *S. Sebastian*, Spain—Season ends, ... 415

XIX.

PAU.

Imposing Appearance—Pension Colbert—The Season—Climate—Writers on—Rise of Pau—Town—View of Pyrenees—Chateau—Public Park—Environs—Excursions—The Cemetery—French General Election, 439

XX.

SECOND WINTER IN THE RIVIERA.

Pau to Toulouse—*Montpellier*—Climate—Town—Train to Marseilles—*Toulon*—*Hyères*—Hotels—Climate—Garden—La Plage—Hyères to Cannes—Mentone—Cold Weather—Improvements—More Building—Political Position in France—Eastern Question—English Position causes Anxiety—Death of Victor Emmanuel and Pope—Services in Cathedral—Carnival—Gaieties—Mentone to S. Remo—S. Remo to Alassio—*Alassio*—Hotels—Town—Situation—Walks and Views—Dr. Schneer on Climate—*Genoa*—Via Orifici—Galleria, etc.—*Turin*—View of Alps from Monastery—The Town—Monuments—Waldensian Church—Mont Cenis Tunnel—*Aix les Bains*—Return Home, ... 450

ILLUSTRATIONS.

		PAGE
1. Frontispiece—View from Footbridge up the Carrei to North Mountain Range, Mentone.		
2. The Estrelles from St. Honorat, Cannes,	Facing	147
3. Oil Mills, Carrei Valley, Mentone,	,,	191
4. Promenade du Midi, Mentone,	,,	205
5. Corsica as occasionally seen before Sunrise, Mentone,	,,	235
6. A City set upon a Hill on Road to Lucca,	,,	271
7. Sorrento from the West,	,,	337
8. Ponte Vecchio, Florence,	,,	345
9. Tomb of Juliet, Verona,	,,	379
10. Bellaggio, Lake Como,	,,	393
11. Port Vieux Bathing Establishment, Biarritz,	,,	421
12. Biarritz Bathers,	,,	429

PREFACE.

THE health of my wife having rendered it advisable to spend a winter in the South of France, I made arrangements to accompany her, and we left home in October 1876. After a short stay at Cannes and three months in Mentone, with marked improvement, we made a tour of four months in Italy, and then passing the remainder of the summer of 1877 in Switzerland, and the autumn chiefly in Biarritz and Pau, we spent a second winter in the Riviera, principally in Mentone, returning to England *viâ* Turin in May 1878.

We had visited so many places, and seen so much while thus travelling during our first year, that it occurred to me, during our second sojourn at Mentone, to write out some notes of what had come within our knowledge which might prove both useful and interesting to others, and particularly to those who desired to winter in the Riviera. The field, however, was large, and to bring observation into reasonable compass I could only present general views—indications merely—of what we had seen; and, indeed, more than this I could scarcely have ventured upon, because I had not travelled with any idea of writing on the subject, and the notes I had kept were therefore scanty, although sufficient, with a vivid recollection of so much calculated to impress, to enable me to describe, as far as description is perhaps desirable. We saw much, and might have seen more within the time, but it was necessary to avoid fatigue.

The descriptions contained in the following pages are therefore to be regarded not as finished pictures, but rather as the scenes of a moving panorama, exhibiting in succession views of the more salient points in the various places to which the reader will be taken, and depicted according to the fashion of such scenes, too roughly to bear close inspection or minute criticism.

When people were compelled to travel slowly, they could take with them, and had time to read and digest full narratives of all they were about to see. It was by no means impossible to carry in the lumbering carriage, or to read during the leisurely journey, a whole library of such voluminous and now forgotten books as the *Modern Traveller.* But the rapidity of railway travelling has changed even the character of the guide-book, which, with more copious and complete information, has been so clipped and condensed, been made so concisely and methodically useful,—such a veritable *multum in parvo,*—that every other virtue is forgotten, and to take up a volume of Bædeker in order to beguile an hour, or even to obtain a general notion of a place, would be one of those freaks of which wise men are not readily guilty.

People are therefore more than ever thrown upon reading of a different description; and notwithstanding the various books which have been published upon the Riviera, and the still larger list of those upon Italy, I think none of them, so far as I have seen, are exactly on the same lines as the present. It is, indeed, not a little noticeable that so many, in writing upon Italy, should have chosen to wrap their descriptions in some strange, weird story. In *Corinne ou L'Italie*, Madame de Staël depicts an exotic Scotch nobleman wildly drawn about from one part of Italy to another by a most extraordinary platonic love for an Italian improvisatrice, in order that the different localities may obtain description. The *Improvisatore* of Hans Christian Andersen, with a difference of mode, is much upon the same model for the same purpose, the machinery by which the hero is blown hither and thither being much more prominent than the places upon which he alights. The *Transformation* of Hawthorne, in order to describe Rome, forces us into strange scenes and into company with a mysterious 'faun' and a beautiful murderess; while *Romola*, by George Eliot, in describing Florence, drags us after a smooth-faced, smooth-tongued, heartless villain, who attains to power with an odd facility, and after blasting a lovely life, is, to every reader's relief, tragically removed from the world. Even Ruffini's *Dr. Antonio*, commencing amidst placid scenes with all the softness of a *pastorale*, terminates by breaking hearts, and in the din of a revolution, with guns crashing and roll of death-dealing musketry on the streets of Naples.

Amongst its many deficiencies, the present volume is undoubtedly wanting in this sensational element of popularity.

Neither, on the other hand, can it lay claim to the merit of filling the place either of the guide-book or of the medical adviser. Its chief utility may be in giving in a general way to those designing to go abroad for a period of time, some knowledge which may perhaps aid them where to go and what to see; while there is furnished for the benefit of novices, in the preliminary chapters, some practical information, which the experienced traveller, who knows it all and could state it much better, will be graciously pleased, if so inclined, to skip.

In revising at home what was written abroad, I have studied to ensure accuracy of statement, and have been rather surprised, on comparing authorities, to find how widely they frequently differ regarding matters involving figures, so much so that occasionally I have withheld any statement on the subject. Some of these discrepancies I have noticed.

Accurate ideas of places can be best formed with the aid of the pictorial art. A book of this nature is susceptible of endless illustration, and but for adding to the bulk and the expense, there could have been no difficulty in illustrating every page of the travels. I have preferred selecting a few subjects, nearly all from my own sketches, which have been lithographed by Waterston of Edinburgh. That of the Estrelles is from a sketch in colours by a lady friend.

Of these illustrations, Mentone has carried off the lion's share, and perhaps rightly, because of all the places of health resort visited by us, we conceived it to be the most charming, and it was in the winter-time our headquarters. There are those who prefer Cannes, Hyères, Bordighera, or San Remo. Even Alassio may become a favourite residence. But it was our opinion that Mentone unites to a well-sheltered, dry, sunny, winter climate (which is, however, not suitable for all invalids), the most beautiful and picturesque scenery, the most delightful walks and excursions, with a fascinating rurality which, I fear, the natives, looking at the matter from a French point of view, are bent on destroying, by way of raising it up as a sort of rival in gaiety to such places as Nice. There is one drawback, in its proximity to the Monte Carlo gambling tables. But to those who can resist temptation, a trip to Monte Carlo—a bright, beautiful, sunny spot, clean and tidy, with its tropical gardens, its broad terraces, flanked by elegant white stone balustrades—is only an additional attraction; while the adjoining unique peninsula of Monaco, running out into the sea from the mountains of the *Tête de Chien*, and crowned by its palace, its fortifications, its dwellings, its trees, is one of the many attractive points which, combined with the beautiful blue of the Mediterranean, lend such a charm to this part of the Riviera.

This book would probably never have been written had it not been begun and all but completed abroad, while in the sunshine of gladness and hope. Looking to the cause of our travels, it was unavoidable that I should mention at its close how sadly all hopes were crushed. But I have striven as far as possible to eschew the introduction of all merely personal allusions. I feel, however, I must take this opportunity of thanking the members of the legal body to which I belong, and of which I had, at the time it became advisable to leave home, the honour of being chief office-bearer, for their courtesy to me then, and for the heartfelt sympathy which so many of them have since expressed. I would only say to them as to others, that we have had of late not a few examples of valued friends who, long after it became really necessary, have toiled, and fagged, and wearied their brains out in the pursuit of an anxious and laborious profession till they have spent their last days or years in utter prostration. Better far, when they can, to obtain thorough relaxation in the enjoyment of a year, or even two years, of Continental travel over such interesting ground as in this book I have attempted in some small measure to describe.

W. M.

GEORGE SQUARE,
EDINBURGH, *July* 1879.

ERRATA.

Page 27, 19th line, instead of *for* read *from*.
,, 38, 9th line from bottom, for *any* read *every*.
,, 60, 5th line, for *visible* read *visibile*.
,, 91-3-4, for *manu* read *mano*.
,, 272, 7th line from bottom, for *tombs* read *tomes*.
,, ,, 5th ,, for *his* read *this*.
,, 305, for *Clementi* read *Clemente*.
,, 320, 11th line, for *have* read *leave*.
,, 369, 1st line, for *et* read *e*.

I.

CONTINENTAL TRAVELLING.

I HAVE sometimes thought that if it were possible for a person of mature years now living to return to the world, with memory unimpaired, after a period of five hundred or even of one hundred years hence, how strangely new to him everything would appear! Events succeed each other in these times with such startling rapidity, that he would be a bold man who would venture to predict what even a generation will bring forth. We may speculate on the effects likely to result from agencies now in operation,—as to what, for example, may be the future of Great Britain, looking to the gigantic scale on which hazardous enterprise is carried on; to the contests of labour with capital in which natural laws are set at defiance; to the growth of Ritualism in the English Church; to the penchant which our rulers seem to have for annexing or conquering remote provinces, stern and wild or insalubrious; to a thousand other things which are with more or less force influencing or disquieting our country commercially, socially, or politically,—but none of us can possibly foresee the actual consequences and the condition of things to which they will lead. In the future there is so much dependent on occurrences which appear to us to be fortuitous (though truly under the guidance of Supreme Wisdom), that we can only feel that over all there hangs an impenetrable veil of mysterious darkness. A single unexpected event may turn aside the policy of an age, or even alter the divisions of the world. A single man by a foolish blunder may plunge nations into protracted war. A single happy discovery, a single clever invention, may affect the fortunes or alter the habits of a whole people. A single convulsion of nature may change the aspect of a state. But when we turn from the future to the past, the case is different, and we can pretty well realize what the feelings of one who has lived, say, sixty years ago would be if he could now return to earth. It would, indeed, be some time ere he would begin to grasp the extent of the wonderful changes which, since he formerly lived, have been effected. But of all the changes flowing from the inventions and discoveries which the long peace succeeding Waterloo was instrumental in producing, he would probably be most struck by the revolution accomplished in the matter of travelling.

We have only to go back half a century to the time when a tour upon the Continent of Europe was attended by great expense, inconvenience, and even danger. It consumed much time, and no Englishman upon whom business did not lay a necessity to travel, could undertake any very extensive pilgrimage in these foreign countries unless possessed of ample means united to ample leisure. It was thus generally reserved for young noblemen and gentlemen of wealth, as the completion of their education, to take, with a tutor, a courier, and a sufficient retinue, the grand tour of Europe, the limit of which was usually, though not always, Constantinople. I suppose this circumstance has given rise to the Continental idea, which at least formerly prevailed, that every Englishman was a *milord Anglais*, and to its practical consequence, from which present travellers continue to suffer—the custom, gradually disappearing, of charging English persons upon a different scale from that applied to natives. No doubt many of those men of former days scattered money profusely, and to a certain extent their successors continue to do so, and are even exceeded by some of the American travellers who, accustomed to pay in dollars where shillings with us often suffice, contrive by their extravagance to spoil for others the places they frequent.

Times are now changed since the days of our grandfathers. The treacherous sailing vessel (the smack, which would take at one time three days, and at another, because of adverse winds, three weeks to go from Leith to London) is supplanted by the steady, expeditious, and almost faultlessly punctual steamboat; while the lumbering diligence or almost equally lumbering post-chaise has been driven out of the field by, wherever it exists, the rapid railway train. Nevertheless, as regards Continental railway rapidity, M. Arago's expectations that Parisians might 'on the same day examine the preparations of our squadron at Toulon; may breakfast on juicy rougets at Marseilles; may bathe at mid-day their relaxed limbs in the mineral waters of Bagnères, and return in the evening by way of Bordeaux to attend a ball or the Opera House,'[1] have hardly as yet, at least, been realized; for the railway train abroad bears about the same proportion in point of speed to the English train as the clumsy diligence did of old to our high-flyers and our ten-mile-an-hour stage-coaches.[2] Sometimes, indeed, people in former times, who were able to do so, travelled on the Continent in pursuit of health; and a very interesting account of a tour of this description, made to a large extent over the same ground as that which forms the subject of description in the following pages, is contained in *The Diary of an Invalid*, by Henry

---

[1] *Life of Watt*, 1839, p. 198.

[2] A compilation recently published gives an account of the means of conveyance had in times past in Great Britain, but does not, except very incidentally, touch upon those on the Continent. See Croal's *Book about Travelling, Past and Present*, W. P. Nimmo, Edinburgh.

Matthew, A.M., made during a journey, performed in the years 1817-18-19, through Italy, Switzerland, and France, from which an idea of the difference of travelling in those days—sixty years ago—from what it is now, may to some extent be gathered. Since the introduction of railways, which now form a complete network all over the Continent of Europe, reaching some of its wildest parts, and not hesitating even to penetrate some of its loftiest mountains, and often by means of costly tunnels connecting long stretches of country, travelling has been made so easy, and the facilities for availing themselves of the means of locomotion have been rendered so great, that there are comparatively few persons of the better classes who have not at some time or other, and in a greater or lesser measure, visited Continental lands. Our very mechanics have, especially by means of excursion trains, sometimes in connection with such great occasions as foreign Exhibitions, been enabled to see a little of other lands; and even the seeing a little of another land is calculated to remove prejudices, to enlarge the ideas, and to extend the amount of one's information.[1]

[1] The following table, taken from Croal's *Book about Travelling*, p. 575, shows the extent of the railway system in 1875 on the European Continent:—

	Miles of Railway.	Square Miles of Territory to each Mile of Line.
Belgium,	2,174	5
Switzerland,	1,300	11
German Empire,	14,472	12
France,	12,376	14
Denmark,	561	18
Netherlands,	1,016	20
Austria and Hungary,	10,154	20
Italy,	4,817	23
Spain,	3,822	50
Roumania,	770	59
Portugal,	596	61
Sweden,	2,237	63
Turkey in Europe,	965	138
Russia in Europe,	11,591	157
Norway,	339	387
Greece,	7	2,658

People in the present day travel sometimes for pleasure and to obtain acquaintance with what cannot be seen at home, and sometimes for the sake of health; and it is astonishing to what an extent this latter reason has operated on the people of Great Britain, who rush from the rigours of their northern climate—its clouds, its fogs, and its rains—to enjoy the sunshine of warmer places, avoiding and exchanging wet, foggy, and chilly winter quarters at home for pleasant sunny places abroad. So much is this the case, that whole colonies of English people, many of them owning houses, built or bought for their residence, are found scattered over the Continent, particularly on the shores of the Mediterranean Sea. They go to winter there, and the places they frequent become remarkably English in their habits and in their language—the force of the English character, and still more of the English money, bearing down and upon the native population. Indeed, it may rather be said that towns have been built by or for the occupation of the English—as, for example, Cannes, which, if it do not altogether owe its existence, is acknowledged by the natives to owe its new creation, its growth and extent, to Lord Brougham.

We had on various previous occasions taken a summer's run abroad. The protracted visit we paid to the Continent which forms the subject of this volume was dictated by considerations of health; but we combined with it, and advantageously, even for that end, some tours of pleasure. The countries visited by us on this occasion were France, Italy, and Switzerland; and it is with special reference to them that the remarks offered in this and the succeeding introductory chapters apply. I propose in this chapter to deal shortly with some of the bugbears which frighten many from crossing the Channel, to state some of the peculiarities of foreign travel, and to note a few other matters with which those new to the subject may find it useful to be acquainted previous to setting out.

The first great stumbling-block in the way of going abroad is to many, especially elderly persons, the want of knowledge of the language of the country to which they wish to direct their steps, or the want of power to converse in it freely.

There can be no doubt that it is of great consequence to have an acquaintance with the language of the country in which one desires to travel or reside for a time. People are saved much inconvenience and often money when they can talk it with fluency, and can comprehend what the natives say—usually the more difficult operation. At the same time, in all frequented parts of France, Italy, and Switzerland, either English or French will carry any one through. French is spoken by nearly every educated person who travels on the Continent, with perhaps the exception of the Germans, who, though they may know a little French, seem to give a preference to the acquisition of the English language, in which frequently they converse with great purity and ease. At the hotels, the landlord, or one of the waiters, sometimes all of them, can speak English more or less perfectly. Nay, what is very surprising is, that the man sometimes called *portier*, who sits in a little chamber at the door, has often a better acquaintance with English than even landlord or waiter. This porter or, as he is more correctly designated, *concierge*, is attached to all large hotels, and his ostensible duty is not that of carrying luggage (for which business there are men of a different stamp under him), but consists in keeping the keys of the rooms, attending to letters, and answering inquiries. In reality he is a man of superior intelligence, and acts often as the interpreter of the house; for he is generally acquainted with many languages, and usually with at least French, English, and German, and has to reply to questions in these different languages almost in the same breath. In frontier places, his acquaintance is extended to the language of the neighbouring country—it may be, for instance, Italian or Spanish. However, among employees and others with whom the traveller has to do, the knowledge of many languages is not confined to the *gens portier*. At Mentone I was informed that a hairdresser there could speak five languages; and how else could he hope, from a hairdresser's point of view, to please his patients? At Rome, having gone to the wrong shop, I had to experience the difficulties of undergoing an operation by a gentleman of the fraternity who could speak nothing but Italian; and we should never have succeeded in coming to a mutual understanding, but for the kindly intervention of a priest who was being shaved and could speak French, and after all it did not wholly save me from that 'croppiness' in which the foreign *coiffeur* delights. This linguistic faculty does not stop at hairdressers, who may be considered to be men of an advanced race. At Mentone we used to employ a donkey girl, who also could speak a little in five languages. Philippina was a bright, intelligent girl, much liked by her employers, and no doubt she found her advantage in knowing something of their different tongues. In Switzerland, for the most part, the German language prevails, and it is occasionally uncommonly hard, if one is not acquainted with German or has but a smattering of it, to get on, say, with a coachman who knows nothing else. At Ragatz, where they speak German, I put a question to a stallkeeper selling goods on the street, and was promptly answered by a young girl of the adjoining stall in English. I asked her how she came to know English. She learnt it at school. Were they all taught English, I asked. 'Oh, no; those who desired to be taught had to pay for it.' The shopkeepers abroad, however, have in many cases acquaintance with English sufficient to enable them to effect sale of their wares. They quickly discover us to be English, and when they speak our language they like to air it, and answer questions put in their, the shopkeepers' language (made, we imagine, with all correctness of expression and of accent), in our own. In Rome we found that all the cab-drivers could speak French, which, of course, facilitates going about to those who cannot speak much Italian. In Italy generally, unless it might be in speaking to women-servants, and not even always in their case, we did not find much necessity for using Italian. Either French or English was in most places understood. Sometimes we have even had English landladies, as at the Grand Hotel in Sienna, and at the Tramontano at Sorrento; but this is a species of good fortune, telling on the English traveller's comfort in many ways, which is seldom to be enjoyed. It only suggests that other English women might find Italy a good field for similar enterprise.

In former days the passport system was a difficulty which afflicted the minds of timorous travellers. Apart from the surveillance implied, there was the trouble and expense of procuring it, and having the proper *visas* affixed by the representatives of Continental Governments; the anxiety lest in passing some corner of a foreign territory—some debateable land—it might not be *en règle*; the detentions it occasioned, and the perturbation of spirit which arose, should it by any accident have been mislaid or lost, there being no absolute certainty that if imprisoned in a cold, damp, dreary dungeon for want of the necessary safe-conduct, our Government after a suitable period of fruitless negotiation would go to war with the foreign power for the defaulter's release. On one occasion (in 1855), on entering Geneva by diligence, I missed my passport (which on arrival I found lying at my feet), and did not know what would happen, but the man in collecting passports from the passengers fortunately overlooked me. This was a species of the rarest good luck, upon which of course it was utterly impossible to reckon; and the passport system was one which was felt by people living in a land in which every one is free, without inquiry of any kind, to travel where and when he pleases, to be an intolerable annoyance. It is still maintained; but with a view, I presume, not to discourage English travelling (a source of immense profit to the natives), a British subject has only on passing a frontier to declare his nationality, and he is at once passed through, except at some places where he is asked for his carte-de-visite; and if he have not one at hand, even this is not insisted on if it be apparent that he is what he represents himself to be, *un Anglais*, or, what is the same thing to them, an American. Yet a passport is sometimes useful; it now costs little, and should always be taken. It is easily got under the directions contained in Bradshaw's *Continental Guide*, and the *visas* of the foreign consuls seem now to be unnecessary, at least for the countries in which we were to travel. It is particularly important in some towns, to facilitate the obtaining of registered letters. Even ordinary letters occasionally, as I have found (1872) at Brussels on a former trip (having unfortunately lost my passport at Strasburg), will scarcely be delivered at the Poste Restante without production of the passport or other presumable evidence of identity; and it is said in guide-books, although we have never experienced the benefit of the information, that it operates as an admission to certain places of public resort.

Although to the *mens conscia recti* it may matter little, it does not follow that, with all this relaxation of former rigour, people are altogether free from surveillance. The spy may not crop up here and there as, according to Doyle, he did, to afflict Messrs. Brown, Jones, and Robinson, yet travellers do meet with evidences of the existence of a secret and prying police. At Aix-les-Bains, which, however, may be regarded as a frontier town, we found the register of visitors kept in a book furnished by the police, and containing instructions for the entry of all names and particulars; and almost everywhere, immediately upon arrival at a hotel, a waiter comes to take down the name, address, profession, etc., which, apart from police regulations, is only proper.

Besides a passport, there are other things to be attended to in order that the way may be made smooth.

People do not always, when they resolve to travel, sit upon their boxes—I mean, of course, metaphorically; yet in travelling abroad, at least for a period of any duration, some thought must be bestowed upon the *impedimenta*, and it is very proper to take such boxes as will stand the immense fatigue to which all luggage is exposed, and to which the foreign system of registration greatly adds. Very little regard is paid by porters to the conservation of the luggage. It is tossed and dragged along over iron-bound tables; and huge heavy iron-bound and iron-cornered American chests, with their piercing little iron castors, are often thrown or deposited remorselessly on the top of smaller and weaker packages. Very small articles, indeed, should never be put in the vans. It is better, and in the long run cheaper, to have fewer packages and of a larger size. At the same time, they are very inconvenient if unwieldily large, as too often one sees them to be, requiring two men for their carriage, and needing to be left outside the bedroom—an inconvenience both to the traveller herself and her fellow-travellers; for it is the ladies who are in this respect the great transgressors. Some ladies seem to travel with their whole wardrobe, or at all events with a useless number of changes of raiment. On one occasion we met a gentleman and lady, who had with them nine huge boxes, nearly filling up the top of a large omnibus, besides smaller articles, including their maid's modest provision. This is a grievous mistake. Ladies ought to travel with the least possible quantity of changes. More than is fairly needful is inconvenient in many ways. Apart from causing detentions to others, it is a source of anxiety, and is most expensive in countries where the luggage is all weighed, and every pound or extra pound must be paid for.

Among the little things to be taken, no good traveller will, of course, omit a pocket corkscrew and a flask of cognac; nor will he neglect soap. If he have not made it a rule in all travelling to use his own soap, he is charged at foreign hotels 1 franc for *savon*. I have heard a man growling over the 'imposition,' but it served him right, while the article was just sold to him like anything else, with the usual 200 or 300 per cent. hotel profit added.

We considered it advisable, especially in view of travelling in Italy, where the water is said to be often impure, and consequently unsafe to drink, to take with us a small filter; but although we used our filter occasionally, I cannot say we were frequently conscious of drinking bad water. It is, however, a proper precaution, as water may be bad without betraying its quality by the taste. An Ashantee filter with a quart tin bottle, to be had from Atkins and Co., 62 Fleet Street, London, occupies little space, and costs 8s. Were Messrs. Atkins to devise a portable little filter for use at the table by insertion in a tumbler, so as to purify the drinking water without the fuss of a large filter, which it is inconvenient to carry, and which one cannot bring to the public room, it would be of much use. It must be borne in mind, however, that filters do not destroy organic matter suspended in the water, and for this purpose permanganite of potash may be employed. A drop or two of a solution of this substance, which may be purchased in dry grains at any chemist's (easily dissolved when wanted), effects destruction of organic matter, but gives so unpleasant a bitterness to the flavour of the water that we scarcely ever used it.

There are, however, things more important to provide, and among them are good guide-books. The rapid growth and extraordinary ramifications of the railway system have created a new branch of literature in the railway time-tables. It is curious to take up an early copy of Bradshaw, consisting only of a few pages, small pocket size, neatly got up, and to contrast it with English Bradshaw of the present time. If such a book be needful in Great Britain, people are even more helpless without it abroad. Bradshaw's *Continental Guide*, special edition, will always be found to be most useful, both as a preparatory and as an accompanying handbook. It contains a great deal of information, which, however, ought to be taken in a general way, or as the lawyers say, *cum nota*. Perfect reliance cannot always be placed upon the accuracy of its railway and other time-tables and its tariffs. On arriving in a country, it is especially necessary to secure, in addition, one of its latest official railway guides. In France there is published once a week, on the Sundays, *L'Indicateur des Chemins de fer et de la Navigation service officielle*. This costs 60 centimes (6d.), and is a long folio of inconvenient size. As nearly all French travellers purchase a copy when they start on a journey, it doubtless obtains a large sale. The *Livret Chaix Spécial pour France* (there is another edition for Europe generally) is an official guide of a more convenient size. It is published once a month, book shape duodecimo, costs 1 franc, and has no advertisements, which are scattered through the *Indicateur* in a tormenting way, though sometimes useful when desired information is thereby discovered, which it might much more readily be if, as in Bradshaw, all the advertisements were thrown systematically to the end of the book. It is, however, troublesome to follow these French guides when divergence from the main lines is desired to be made. The lines are cut up into fragments without the references contained in Bradshaw to other pages where the connecting railways occur, and the neat little well-engraved maps in the *Livret Chaix* do not bear, as in Bradshaw's map, the page references where the tables of the railways are to be found. Bradshaw is puzzling enough, but sometimes it is felt that the *Livret Chaix* is one of those mysteriously-arranged productions 'which no fella can understand.'

In Italy there is published once a month, costing 1 franc or lira, *L'Indicatore Ufficiale*. This is peculiarly arranged, and requires study; but the Italian lines are so few, compared with those of France, that there is no insuperable difficulty in discovering the time-bills of particular railways. The Italian *Indicatore* contains various preliminary directions which it is well to read. They are curious, and embrace, *inter alia*, regulations relative to the transport of cats and monkeys.

The Italians have also a long *Indicatore* similar to the French weekly one; and in both countries smaller and cheaper district guides, with more limited information, are to be had.

In Switzerland, a *Guide des Voyageurs en Suisse* is published, apparently twice a year—at least those procured in the Swiss travelling season are marked 'Saison d'été,' 1877 or 1878, as the case may be.

It is never safe to trust to a guide of a past month, although changes are generally only made in the beginning of the winter season, or about 15th or 16th October, and in the beginning of the summer or spring season. By not observing a change of this kind which had just been made, we were detained at Toulon for three or four hours waiting for the next train to Hyères.

Although it is not desirable to burden oneself with many books in travelling, Bædeker's Guide-Books, which on the whole are very accurate and useful, ought not to be dispensed with. Italy is embraced in three little volumes—Northern, Central, and Southern; and Bædeker has separate Guides to Switzerland, France, and other countries; so that if one has to travel much, quite a little library requires to be taken. Bædeker's Northern Italy, however, embraces the Riviera di Ponente, in which Cannes and Mentone are, and the journey thither from Paris, and towns on the way, such as Lyons, Avignon, Nismes, and Marseilles, while southward it extends as far as Florence. Murray's Guide-Books are very useful, and are much more full and detailed, but consequently are more bulky, and are therefore more suitable for protracted visits to a town such as Venice. Neither Bædeker nor Murray, however, are to be wholly relied upon, especially for the latest information. For example, we found in Italy that while it is said in Bædeker there are no fees to pay, in the different Academie delle Belle Arti there is now charged 1 franc per person for admission. I would add, also, that Bædeker's estimates of hotel charges can by no means be relied on as exact, although they may at one time have been so, or they may in some cases be those with which Germans are charged, Bædeker being a publication originating in Germany.

These books all require from time to time careful revision; and considering the importance to the traveller of having the latest information, and the large sale they command, they ought to be revised at short intervals.

There are certain very useful guide-books published in France, of two sorts—the *Guides Diamant*, which are little pocket volumes in small type; and the *Guides Grand Format*, which are of a larger size. Each class (published only in French) contains a series of volumes applicable to the different parts of France, as well as volumes devoted to other countries. The divisional volumes for France are exceedingly useful, as containing detailed information respecting the districts to which they apply.

I may also mention that Mr. Cook, the tourist, publishes a series of handbooks for the countries to which his tours apply; and that recently Black has also added to his list of guide-books, guides to the south of France.

To those visiting Rome, *Hare's Walks in Rome* (2 vols.) will be found extremely serviceable. Unfortunately we did not take it with us, as adding to the quantity of books with which we had to travel. It is a little heavy to carry about in the hand, but it directs attention to what is best worth seeing, and may be consulted at one's lodgings before and after visiting the attractions of Rome.

In the old coaching days, when the mail or the diligence drove through a town, and generally stopped at one of the principal inns, there was not much deliberation needed or even much choice granted as to where the passenger should sleep. But it is one of the inconveniences attendant upon the railway system,—to a certain extent obviated by the erection of station hotels,—that he has not an opportunity from ocular inspection beforehand, on arriving at a strange town, of forming an idea as to where he should go. And it is an observation on Bradshaw (more or less applicable to other guide-books), that it does not do to rely implicitly on its recommendations of hotels,—a circumstance which probably arises from the notice of given hotels having been written years previously, and means not having been used to obtain a complete revision from year to year. More reliance in this respect is to be placed on Bædeker's Guide-Books. Hotels marked by Bædeker with an * will almost always be found of a good character. In the absence of other means of intelligence, we have sometimes been driven, like many others, to ask information from chance fellow-travellers, at other times to get it at the hotel from which we started in the morning—not infrequently the less trustworthy method of the two. But as it is most desirable to have reliable information on this subject, it is, where practicable, by far the best plan, before setting out upon a tour, to settle as nearly as possible the route to be taken, and to obtain a note from friends who have travelled along it of the hotels they would recommend. In possession of this knowledge beforehand, all anxiety is removed, and one is enabled to write previously, requesting the landlord to retain rooms. Letters and telegrams with such requests are always carefully attended to, the hotelkeeper no doubt considering that application to him is made from choice and not from chance.

The great increase of travelling produced by the railways, has led bankers to contrive convenient methods in which people may take the requisite supply of money with them; and of all the methods which have been devised, the best and safest is that afforded by the system of circular notes. These notes are granted by certain banks in London and Edinburgh, and are drafts upon London for £20 each, or for the usually more convenient amount of £10 each, according to the tourist's desire. They can be cashed at any town on the Continent, hotelkeepers also accepting them in payment of their bills, but without benefit of any exchange which would be allowed by the banks. Along with the notes, the banker delivers what is called a 'Letter of Indication,' which contains a list of all the banks with which he corresponds, embracing almost every place which may be visited in Europe. This letter, for security's sake, it is advisable to keep in a different pocket or box from the circular notes, which require his signature and endorsement. The banker's correspondents ought not to cash the notes without production of this letter of indication; but sometimes they are negligent or lax in this respect, particularly if the presenter appear to be respectable or a *bona fide* traveller. At some places, however, such as at Paris, the bankers are more cautious, and not only invariably ask for the letter, but they put sundry questions and take the hotel address—the object being, quite properly, in a quiet way to make sure that the notes are presented by the right person. A friend had his notes stolen from him at a railway station in Paris on arrival from England, having unfortunately put them with other things in a small hand-bag, instead of carrying them in a secure pocket about his person. His letter of indication, however, was not with the notes, and so far, though not altogether, was he safe. The thief took them at once to a bank in Paris, and, I suppose, not having the letter of indication, and perhaps not being able to give a satisfactory account of himself, they were forwarded to London, and within fifteen hours after being stolen were presented to the banker on whom they were drawn, and they were refused because the signature attached by the thief did not correspond with the usual signature of my friend.

These circular notes are exchanged for the money of the country in which they are presented for payment; but French gold is always useful, and fetches full value abroad. In exchanging, one generally gets the benefit of the exchange, subject to a fractional deduction. The usual exchange in France for a sovereign is 25 francs 10 centimes;[1] but this is seldom got, and in some places, such as Biarritz and Mentone, the bankers only give the 25 francs nett, and in other places slightly more or slightly less according to the state of the exchange. At a bank in Cannes a friend exchanged Bank of England notes simultaneously with my exchanging a circular note for £10. While I obtained 7½d. (75 centimes) of premium, he got nothing, because the banker said there was always much more trouble about Bank of England notes, which required registration. Eighteen months later, however, I found in Paris, oddly enough, that Bank of England notes were at a premium, while circular notes were at a discount. At Cannes, in 1877, I had occasion to cash a bank draft on London received from one of the colonies, and found that nominally the allowance was greater than upon circular notes; but as the banker charged a commission, it practically reduced the exchange to about the same amount. Another notable circumstance was, that while at Mentone the bankers would give nothing beyond the 25 francs, at the neighbouring town of Nice the bankers always gave exchange varying from 75 centimes to 1 franc per £10. At Pau I found that while the correspondent of the bank only gave ½ franc per £10, another banker gave 1 franc, and upon an exchange of £50

[1] The normal value of a sovereign is 25 francs 20 centimes.

even a shade more. Again, at Montreux, in Switzerland, I obtained 1 franc 25 centimes per £10, and within little more than a week afterwards at Biarritz, in accordance with invariable practice, nothing beyond the 25 francs per £. The same difference occurred in two other places. Within a similar short space, I changed in Paris and got 25 francs per £. Within a day or two afterwards, I had to change other notes at Interlachen, and received 25 francs 10 centimes. The only explanation I ever got for these anomalies was that given at Biarritz, the banker there saying, that at Montreux they were near the Italian border (in fact, a long way off from it), and could make more money out of the notes. But this was obviously an unsatisfactory reason, and certainly could not explain the position of matters at Mentone, which is within two miles of the Italian frontier.

In Italy the exchange of gold or notes on London into Italian paper is a matter of considerable importance to the holder, for the exchange allowed, though it fluctuates, is always high.[1] The lowest we received anywhere was 27·03 at Rome, 23d March 1877, and at San Remo 1878. The highest was at Venice, in May 1877, 28·25. This last was during the Eastern War, which had been declared in April, and

[1] It may be interesting to give, as far as I have preserved note of it, the rate of exchange received at different places during part of the period we were away :—

At Cannes, Nov. 1876, per £, 25·75	At Como, 11th June 1877, per £, 27·10
,, Mentone, Dec. ,, ,, 25·25	,, Bellagio, ,, ,, ,, ,, 27·47
,, ,, thereafter, ,, 25·	,, Lucerne, 25th,, ,, ,, 25·15
,, Nice, February 1877, ,, 25·75	,, Interlachen, 13th July ,, 25·10
,, San Remo, March ,, ,, 27·20	,, Paris, Aug. ,, ,, 25·
,, Genoa, ,, ,, ,, 27·10	,, Interlachen, ,, ,, ,, 25·10
,, Rome, 23d ,, ,, ,, 27·03	,, Montreux, 8th Sept. ,, 25·12
,, ,, 19th April,, ,, 27·90	,, Biarritz, Oct. ,, ,, 25·
,, Florence, 28th ,, ,, 28·10	,, Pau, 18th ,, ,, ,, 25·05
,, ,, 7th May ,, ,, 28·15	,, ,, 21st ,, ,, ,, 25·12
,, ,, 12th ,, ,, ,, 28·10	,, Cannes, Nov. ,, ,, 25·06
,, Venice, 20th ,, ,, ,, 28·25	,, San Remo, March 1878, ,, 27·03
,, ,, 22d ,, ,, ,, 28·15	,, ,, April ,, ,, 27·45
,, Milan, 26th ,, ,, ,, 28·	,, ,, ,, ,, ,, 27·37

considerably raised the value of gold in Italy. I presume the uncertainty as to whether Italy would be involved in the war helped to depress the value of the paper. It is difficult for one who has not been engaged in commerce or in banking to understand why these fluctuations occur, or to be acquainted with the causes which influence them. The current value is said to be dependent upon the position of the commercial relations between Great Britain and the Continent; but there are obviously other circumstances, such as national credit, political disturbances, war, and the abundance or scarcity of money, which affect or bias the barometer. But whatever may be the cause, the traveller obtains the benefit of the effect when the exchange is high, as his money goes so much further. The Italian paper money is, unless otherwise specially bargained for, taken everywhere in Italy—in hotels, in shops, and even at railways. It is only necessary to be particular in seeing that paper of the right sort is given. It is always safe to receive paper of the National Bank of Italy. This circulates everywhere throughout Italy, but notes of district or provincial banks are not accepted out of the province; and there are certain notes which have been called in (with which one soon becomes familiar), which, though taken in shops, are refused at railway stations and other public places, sometimes provokingly.

One curious circumstance about the Continental banks is, that they seem to possess marvellously limited stores of money, whether of notes or of gold and silver. People have just to take what the bankers can give. I have more than once been obliged in France to take a note for 1000 francs, or £40, which is practically useless, unless where residence in a place is to be of sufficient duration to enable the holder to tender the note in payment of his hotel bill. I have often had the greatest difficulty in getting small change even for half a napoleon. For a napoleon (20 francs) one is fortunate to get, as a favour from a bank, four large 5 franc pieces, the banker saying that he has no smaller change, which perhaps only means he cannot spare his lesser money. This state of matters, I believe, arises from the scarcity of silver money in France, produced by the people hoarding up their savings, which are thus withdrawn from circulation. In Italy (where apparently the same hoarding must take place, though probably not so extensively) I have for the most part had to take, except to a very limited extent, the notes proffered by the banks; and one very useful kind of note, that for half a franc, is very difficult to procure. Even 1 franc notes are scarce; the bankers will give you a pocketful of copper instead. These ½ franc and 1 franc notes are essentially necessary for fees in going about such places as Rome; but copper is freely taken as payment of fees, carriage drives, etc. Fancy tendering a London cabman his fare in copper!

At first one feels a little repugnance to the use of these small Italian notes, which are of all values; but after getting habituated to them, a preference arises for their use over metal money, which is so much heavier. A special purse with divisions for the different values should be procured.

And now, having accomplished the preparations for the journey, the next question is as to the route. It will always be found that there are greater facilities in travelling to and from a capital city, such as London, Paris, or Edinburgh; and in going abroad towards France, the voyager has generally to select one of the routes from London to Paris. The four great leading steamboat passages across the Straits are —Southampton to Havre, advertised to take in crossing six and a half hours; but on the only occasion on which I have gone by that route, which was in 1854, the voyage occupied in a calm night eleven hours, though possibly more powerful boats are now laid on. Newhaven to Dieppe, five and a half to six hours in good weather: I have been nine hours in a storm. Folkestone to Boulogne, ordinarily two hours, although one fast boat (by which our last crossing was made) accomplishes the passage in an hour and a half. Dover to Calais, one hour forty minutes; but in a storm I have known it to have taken four hours. As an inducement to travel by the longer crossings, the fares are proportionately lower. Fares by night service trains are considerably less than those by day trains. The routes by Newhaven and Folkestone are tidal, and the hours of sailing vary according to the state of the tide, which is troublesome, and infers to most people, when the boats sail at an early hour, sleeping at the port of departure, which we repeatedly have had to do.[1] The passage by Folkestone and Boulogne is by many preferred to that from Dover to Calais, because there is less groundswell. Getting into the pier at Boulogne is sometimes, owing to the state of the tide, tedious; but from a statement in the newspapers, it would appear that the authorities are contemplating the improvement of the harbour by an outlay of £680,000. In proceeding to Paris from Calais or Boulogne, one may stop at Amiens and see the town and fine old cathedral; but the routes from Havre, and from Dieppe to Paris through Normandy, are far more interesting by the way, and pass picturesque Rouen, which is well worthy of a visit, the stoppage of at least a night to explore it amply repaying the visitor.

All the world and the railway companies are largely indebted to the enterprise of Mr. Cook, who, from small beginnings, commencing in 1851, has gradually enlarged his schemes for the public benefit, till the ramifications of his system extend over all Europe and even into the other continents. Mr. Gaze followed, apparently a good many years later, and his arrangements seem to be on an equally extensive scale. Both houses have agencies in the leading towns of Great Britain, as well as in several of the principal European cities. Their success is evidence of their utility,

---

[1] Little monthly time bills or leaflets can be got at the Company's offices in London and Paris, for which see Bradshaw. Some of them also, like Cook's and Gaze's Lists, contain through fares to most places on the Continent.

and there can be no doubt that the facilities afforded by them have greatly increased the number of Continental travellers. Their Lists furnish the routes and the cost of travel; their tickets are extremely useful, and possess the advantage of being printed in English as well as in the language of the country to which they apply; while to those who are afraid of travelling in countries where they cannot speak the language, their conducted tours are no doubt valuable.

Tickets can be got from Cook's offices to Paris *via* Dover and Newhaven; Gaze supplies tickets *via* Folkestone and Southampton; and there is a little advantage in taking these tickets, in respect of saving time and trouble at the bustling London railway stations. The tickets are made up in little books, and a leaf applicable to the portion traversed is withdrawn by the ticket collector upon accomplishment of that stage of the journey. But if the traveller be going beyond Paris, to some place to which these offices book, he receives a separate packet of tickets, which is exceedingly useful to him, as, besides saving the trouble of purchasing at the Paris railway station, he is enabled on starting from Paris to register his heavy luggage to any part of his destination for which there is a coupon, and that even at every such place. For example, going from Paris to Nice, the luggage may be registered to Nice; and taking sufficient in the carriage for the journey, in a *sac-de-nuit*, one may stop or break his journey at Dijon, Lyons, Avignon, Marseilles, Cannes, and some other towns. He can be a month on the road, and find upon arrival at Nice his luggage safe in the luggage room, with a trifle per night to pay for the accommodation. The trouble of procuring tickets at each station is also saved, although at some places they require the tickets to be stamped afresh at the ticket window; but in Italy generally a separate window for this purpose is provided, so that the trouble of obtaining the *visa* is there reduced to a minimum.

The tickets issued by the two London houses for France

seem to be charged at or about the same rates as at the French railway stations. But in Italy, or for Italy, their tickets must be paid for in English money; so that it does not seem in a pecuniary point of view to be one's interest to procure them, because the benefit of the exchange, amounting to about one-twelfth of the cost, is thus lost. No doubt it is an advantage to those who cannot speak a few words of the Italian language so as to be understood, or who cannot pick up what is said at the railway booking window, to take the English tickets, and they can afford to pay for their ignorance. But if the fee-expecting *commissionaire* of the hotel do not attend to the matter, which he often of his own accord does, or will do if asked, extremely little is necessary to be said, even French, or a mere acquaintance with the numerals, being generally sufficient. Personally I never experienced any difficulty whatever in taking out the tickets at the foreign railway stations, and indeed the only difficulty I remember to have had was, because I had Cook's tickets. Conceiving there might, on a first visit, be trouble, I had at Nice taken tickets from Genoa to Rome, bearing a right to make three intermediate stoppages. Having, in perfect accordance with the conditions, stopped at Spezzia, Pisa, and Sienna, I could hardly, on leaving Sienna, get the tickets marked for Rome. They were refused at the ticket window, and doubted by the *chef-de-gare;* and it was only upon my emphatic remonstrance, and his appealing to somebody else on the platform, that I succeeded in getting them stamped. On arriving in Rome, I told Mr. Cook's agent there what had happened, and he said that if I had been required to have purchased tickets from Sienna to Rome, he would have compelled the railway company to have refunded the money, and made a complaint about it. It was no doubt just one of those stupid things that will happen under the best arrangements, well to be mentioned, that it may not be repeated; and apart from the question of time (for the English tickets are limited in time allowed for a journey extending over several towns), there is no reason why they should not be preferred, provided always that they could be procured with Italian paper money. Probably from the fluctuating state of the exchange, it is difficult for Messrs. Cook and Gaze to arrange; but if they could, it would obviate all objection.

To those intending to travel in Italy, great advantages are held out by the railway companies in the shape of circular tour tickets (*viaggi circulari*). The *Indicatore della Strada Ferrata* contains a list,[1] with plans of a large number of such tours, the tickets for which are issued, enduring, according to the length of tour, from ten to sixty days (which cannot be extended), at the large reduction of 45 per cent. upon the price which would otherwise be exigible. One of these tours is, for example, a complete round of Italy—from Turin by the west coast, embracing Florence and Rome to Naples, and thence by the east coast by Ancona, Bologna, Venice, Milan, and back to Turin, at a cost for first class of £7, 17s., and second and third classes correspondingly low. This tour, for which sixty days are allowed, enables the traveller to stop at any important town on the lines; and all that is necessary is, at starting from each place, to get the next station at which he means to stop scored through at the railway window. To those whose time is limited, these circular tickets are valuable, and they are procurable with Italian paper, so that the benefit of exchange is got. Cook and Gaze issue tickets for the same circular tours, and probably at the same price, although I suppose they are generally in connection with tickets from London; but they have, I understand, to be paid for in English money. They possess the advantage, I believe, by no means to be undervalued, of having all directions printed in English as well as Italian.

---

[1] A quarto publication, called *Voyages circulaires viâ le Mont Cenis et la Corniche*, is issued by 'Agence de Paris, Rue Auber 1, Maison du Grand Hotel,' containing circular tours in Italy, starting from Paris, Nice, and Marseilles.

The railway companies issue their tickets at every important town on the line of route to be travelled.

In France, likewise, there are for some parts circular tours, such as from Paris to Bordeaux, Biarritz, the Pyrenees and back. Information on the subject may be got in the *Indicateur*, or in the *Guides Diamant* among the advertisements.

I would just add in connection with this subject, that it is said by Bradshaw that return tickets are 'almost universal abroad, and issued upon terms far more liberal than any granted by our English lines.' Although I have on various occasions taken day return tickets for short trips, I have never yet found them to be any cheaper than the double fare.

In the course of a journey, what are called supplementary billets can be procured through the guard, so as to enable a neighbouring place to be visited by a side line. Thus, in going from Lyons to Marseilles, we obtained supplementary tickets from Tarascon to Nismes by asking for them when stopping at Valence, about the second station before reaching Tarascon. This, especially looking to the peculiarities of foreign lines, is a great convenience.

The Italian *Indicatore* states that travellers may exchange at any place to a higher class by paying difference of fare between the place at which the transfer is effected and the terminus.

After crossing the Channel, the first thing which is new to one who has not previously ventured out of the British Islands, is the examination of luggage by the *douaniers* or custom-house officers. It is now arranged that by registration of luggage to Paris, the examination may take place there. This saves detention at the port of debarkation. In general, an Englishman, if apparently a *bona fide* pleasure traveller, is very easily dealt with by these officers. If he have but a single portmanteau, it is sometimes not so much as opened, or if opened, there is but a nominal examination.

He is asked if he have anything to declare—'Any cigars?' It is curious that in almost every country, the sole special question usually asked is, 'Have you any cigars?' and the word of an Englishman that he has none is ordinarily taken. If there be several boxes, the officer points to one of them, and desires it to be opened, sometimes merely to be closed again. At other times the man will provokingly put his hand down to the very depths, and perhaps bring up something hard or a parcel, and fancy he has made a discovery. But he is easily satisfied, and things are restored in the best way possible for a tight fit. No examination of luggage seems to be made on entering Switzerland from any frontier country, indicating that the Swiss have no custom-house duties; but on leaving Switzerland and entering France, there is a more minute examination than occurs when coming from England; and although English people get off comparatively easily, a question being sometimes asked as to where they are going, those of other countries are most unmercifully dealt with, every separate package, down even to handbags, being overhauled. Once, many years ago, travelling by diligence from Geneva to Lyons, I saw every article in a French lady's boxes turned out and minutely examined at three different places on the way. I presume they are suspicious of such travellers secreting Geneva watches or jewellery. On that occasion my own luggage was only examined once, but they made a sort of examination of the person by passing their hands over my dress. The lady, no doubt, was subjected to a more strict examination of her person.

On landing in France, it is found that there is a difference of time between Paris and London of ten minutes. All the French railways go by Paris time; all Swiss railways, by Berne time, which is twenty minutes in advance of Paris time; and all Italian railways, by Roman time, which is forty-seven minutes in advance of Paris time. This is all very right and proper, and makes it easy to know the times for travelling by railway. But although the railways adopt the time of their respective capitals, every different town has, according to its longitude, its own, or what is held to be the correct time at the place according to the sun. This proves most embarrassing, more especially as the hotels regulate their hours by the clock of their own town when that exists. If not, there is the utmost perplexity in finding out what the correct time is. At Mentone no two clocks were alike. By common consent they all differed. On going south to Avignon, the time is nearly a quarter of an hour in advance of Paris time; at Mentone it is twenty minutes. If, on the other hand, the journey be westward of Paris, at Biarritz, the time will be found as much the other way; so that one of the first inquiries to be made on reaching a hotel is, 'What is the time of the town?' and to note the difference between that and railway time.

The complex and extraordinary mode of measuring time formerly in use in Italy, by counting twenty-four hours for the varying time of vespers, seems to be now wholly abandoned.

All who have travelled on the Continent are familiar with the railway arrangements; but as they differ in some particulars from those to which we are accustomed, and as this introductory chapter is mainly intended for the benefit of those who have not previously crossed the Channel, it may be useful to mention some of them.

Although in all leading respects foreigners have copied our railway system, yet their diverging peculiarities are not always calculated to reconcile an Englishman to Continental travel. He arrives at the station, which he finds he must do in France a full half-hour before the hour of starting; in Italy, in large towns, a full hour. And in France he must always, in the first instance, procure his ticket at a little wire-latticed window, falling into a *queue* of people to take his turn. Stooping to a small hole not six inches high on the table level, he has to shout through in French to the distributor of billets within, telling him what he wants, and from whom he receives in return mention of the amount to be paid. It is always well to know beforehand how much this is, which can be at least approximately calculated from the time-tables; but the exact price of tickets may usually be obtained from a board or table of fares near the ticket window, often most inconveniently placed and arranged, and so dirty and soiled as occasionally to be illegible. Without a previous knowledge of the probable cost, it is exceedingly difficult for a stranger to make out what the man says, owing to the narrowness of the aperture and the indistinctness of French pronunciation. In many places, particularly in Italy, an official is stationed (a most commendable practice) outside the window, to prevent inconvenient crowding, to tell the fares, to see that the correct billets are supplied, and to be a check on the ticket distributor giving the right change. I have been told of cases where, in Italy,—but it was some years ago,—there had been supposed attempts to cheat on the part of the distributor; but, except on one occasion, I never got wrong change. It happened at Bologna, where I received at the ticket office 1 lira too little, and at the luggage office some pence less than the correct change. In both cases it was at once rectified on my pointing out the mistakes, and I set them down to slips. At other times, on accidentally neglecting to take up small change at the window, such as a sou, I have been called back to get it. But there is an admirable check upon any attempt to cheat, or on mistakes, in the circumstance that commonly Continental tickets have marked upon them their cost—a system which might with great advantage be introduced into Great Britain.

And now the Englishman obtains a new experience of how they manage things abroad. His luggage was, on arrival at the station, deposited on a long table under the care of the

REGISTRATION OF LUGGAGE.

conductor of the omnibus which brought him. This luggage, with the exception of such little things as he means to take with him into the carriage, has, when his turn arrives, to be carefully weighed. In France each traveller is allowed 30 kilogrammes, or about 65 lbs. weight. For every pound beyond this he is required to pay according to distance. The men engaged in weighing ask for the railway billets to show the destination, and then he goes to the luggage-ticket window, where he duly receives back his billets stamped as having been used, and gets a little scrap or morsel of thin paper, which is the receipt for his luggage, and for which he has in any case to pay 10 centimes (1d.) in addition to any charge for extra weight. This receipt bears the number of *colis* or packages and of persons, the united weight of the party's luggage, the sum payable, the place of despatch and the place of destination, and a printed number; which number is also affixed to each article so registered, and is the means by which, on arriving at the journey's end, it is identified. What is the exact method by which the officials in charge manage to secure that all the multiform boxes and bags arrive at their respective proper destinations, I do not know. I presume that, in addition to an invoice or list of some kind accompanying the train, the things for each station are separately stowed away in the waggons; but whatever may be the means adopted, they ensure the utmost regularity, although I have heard of persons losing small articles, which, as a rule, ought not to be so registered. On one occasion a rather curious circumstance happened to my luggage. I went from Interlachen to Paris, and the registration number on my portmanteau was 82. From Paris to London it was registered anew, and the number happened to be 282; but the passage across the Channel was very stormy, and I presume the Paris number had been washed off on the voyage. On presenting my receipt at London, and pointing out my portmanteau, it was found that it had not the number 282, but simply 82, and I had some difficulty in getting it; but as my key opened the lock, and nobody else appeared to claim the article, I got delivery.

In Italy, no allowance is made for luggage. Every pound which is registered must be paid for, and consequently it is not in general necessary previously to take out the railway billets. The expense is not, however, great, unless one's luggage be heavy. Our luggage, which perhaps was less than many travel with, cost me, travelling nearly all over Italy, for railway charges, less than 30s. per person; but railway fares in Italy are cheaper than with us, so that the difference is thus made up.

Although the system of registration is attended by much security, and is one with which it might not be safe to dispense in travelling abroad, I do not think that, in its integrity, it could be introduced into busy England. We should never stand the minute weighing of our luggage, and, above all, the enormous loss of time which it entails. It has, besides, its disadvantages, because it results in travellers carrying and placing beside them articles which ought properly to be in the van. The luggage registered, too, suffers injury. Moreover, at the journey's end a great detention is always occasioned. All have to wait till the vans are emptied, and the contents dragged about and arranged upon long tables in a closed room. When the entire collection is adjusted as far as possible according to the numbers affixed, the doors of this room are opened, after having had to wait wearily perhaps half an hour. It is, however, by no means necessary to attend personally, except where the luggage must be passed through the *douane*, and sometimes the hotel omnibus will take home the passengers and come back for the luggage; but personal attendance enables a more prompt recognition of it to be made, and ensures accuracy. In Italy it is reckoned safer not to leave luggage at a station. The Italians have not been credited with the greatest honesty, though probably this is a thing of the past. However, they themselves manifest the sense of insecurity by refusing to receive luggage for registration which is not properly locked or fastened, and boxes arriving in such condition are closed at the owner's expense in his presence.

In travelling by steamboat, also, a charge is made for luggage according to weight. Thus, upon a little sail of about 10 miles on Lake Como, I had to pay $2\frac{1}{2}$ francs for luggage. In diligences in Switzerland, 20 lbs. weight only is allowed. All weight beyond this is charged for—a fairly reasonable regulation.

Perhaps the most peculiar and striking of all the Continental travelling arrangements is the system of waiting-rooms. It introduces to English people a difference of method of a somewhat irritating description. The *salle-d'attente* is a species of sheep pen into which the traveller is driven after he has obtained his railway billets and had his luggage registered, and where he must remain helplessly shut up till the train by which he is to travel is about to leave. Generally a separate large room is provided for each of the three classes of travellers, and the rule is that nobody is allowed to enter without exhibition of the railway ticket appropriate to that particular class; and as this cannot be done till the luggage be registered and paid for, which seldom takes less than a quarter of an hour, if ladies be of the party, they must wait with all the patience possible, guarding the little articles to be taken into the railway carriage, in the large hall of the office, where ofttimes there is not a seat or a comfortable or clean one to be had. Once or twice, in breach of the regulations, I have got them passed into the waiting-room. In the *salle-d'attente* itself, penetrated under burden of all these little *impedimenta* (for it is rare good luck to get a porter to help), a crowd of people all similarly laden is found, and there the passengers have to wait sometimes for long periods till within four or five minutes of the starting of the train, when a man opens the door of the prison-house or menagerie and shouts out,

'*Messieurs les voyageurs, pour* (naming the places) *en voiture!*' It may happen that there are several such shouts for other trains before your own is announced, and your sudden preparations for departure are stopped by the discovery that your turn has not yet come, and you are not allowed to leave the place of confinement. When your turn does come, you gather up your things, which no porter helps you to carry, and rush pell-mell out with the crowd. There is no servant to tell you where to go, and your only security not to do wrong is to follow the multitude. When you reach the carriages, it is seldom they have any board or placard indicating their destination. If there should by any chance be an official about, he is not there for the purpose of directing people; and if you ask him, he gives about as slender information in answer as possible. It is folly, however, to stop to ask him in the first instance. The plan is, trudging on with wraps and bags and all the little things, to bundle into the first open carriage where there appears to be sufficient room, and secure seats as best you can, and then get out and make inquiries for certainty's sake. If you do not do so, and a lady, to recover breath, halts an instant with foot on step before ascending, others will coolly mount before her and take possession, and there may be the utmost possible difficulty in procuring seat-room elsewhere, foreigners being just as selfishly guilty as English people of telling lies about a carriage being full. At all events, those who have got in first have probably secured all the available spaces for their goods and chattels, as well as the best seats for themselves. To avoid the expense of registration, or to escape detention on arrival, foreigners (by whom I mean natives of the Continent) almost invariably, as already mentioned, bring portmanteaus and other big articles into the carriages; and as the spaces below the seats are perhaps purposely narrow and confined, these things become very inconvenient, often occupying the places presumably intended for light articles, or they are placed on the seats or among the feet. If smoking disagrees, or you are averse to it, and desire a non-smoking carriage, the hunt for this in the scramble is an additional embarrassment; and frequently, after getting into a carriage and having everything arranged, the non-smokers discover that the compartment is a smoking one, and they have to tumble out at the last moment and endeavour to discover empty places elsewhere. The inconveniences attendant upon this method of arranging for the departure of travellers are such as would make it intolerable in Great Britain, where one walks leisurely to the train as he arrives and selects his seat, with the aid, it may be, of a porter or a guard. Free Britons will submit quietly till a next election to the imposition of heavy burdens in support of an unnecessary war, but a petty grievance like this would raise a storm which no board of directors could resist.

The Continental railways, however, have both porters and guards, who, like policemen, never seem to be present when most wanted. On arrival at a station from an hotel, there are always railway porters to carry the luggage to the registration table, for which they expect to be paid, and sometimes in expectation of a further fee they will carry the *petits bagages* to the door of the *salle-d'attente*—occasionally, though rarely, into the *salle-d'attente* itself; but where assistance is more needed, viz. in leaving the *salle-d'attente* in the rush for the train, porters are nowhere, and on arrival of the trains at their destination, it is by the merest chance (at least in France) one can be got to carry the unregistered articles— the number of which is aggravated by the circumstance that it seems to be part of the system of registration, that if luggage be forwarded to a station in advance of that at which stoppage is to be made for the night or longer, it is not possible to register separately to the stopping station what is required for immediate use. A similar difficulty happens if the heavy luggage is to be left at the railway station, to be got upon setting out upon the further journey next day—a circumstance constantly happening, we ourselves having travelled thus for days together. All must be taken or none. But at some of the larger town stations, there would now seem to be a left luggage room similar to our own, where luggage may be deposited on payment of usually two sous per package per night.

The railway porters always expect a fee (20 centimes per box, at most, will suffice in France) for moving the heavy luggage—even the registration weighers sometimes look for a copper. In Italy, however, the porters often state there is a tariff of charge, under which generally 25 centimes each package is paid, though the amount depends somewhat on the size of each. It is, however, a comfort to know in Italy, if you can, what exactly there is to pay; but although appeal has often been made to the tariff if it happened to be high, I never was gladdened with a sight of this mysterious document. I should make one exception, for the extortion was so great that I demanded to see it, though, as I might have foreseen, it was worse than useless to do so. It occurred at Geneva, where a porter exacted $3\frac{1}{2}$ francs (3s.) from me for transporting on a barrow our luggage from the steamboat to our hotel close by, we being charged in the bill in addition $2\frac{1}{2}$ francs for conveying two of us to the hotel, or 5s. for moving baggage little more than a hundred yards.

I recollect some years ago a system very equitable both for porters and passengers was in use at Cologne; a charge, I think, of 2d. for each package was made at the railway station for porterage, and the amount dropped into a box, the contents of which fell to be divided afterwards among all the porters.

One misses at the foreign railways the fee-expecting, bustling English guard. There is such a person, but he is not the important functionary he makes himself at home, where he is seen going about as if all the carriages belonged to him. Abroad, the guard arrives not or retreats until the train is about to start, and the first and perhaps the only time he makes his appearance is probably after proceeding a long way on the journey; and when the train is in full motion, nervous passengers are suddenly alarmed by seeing a man creeping along the outside of the carriage and popping his head in at the window, or opening the door to see the billets, which are seldom examined before starting. He silently gives the tickets a clip, and disappears, perhaps to reappear after another 50 miles for another examination and another clip, the want of inspection before starting removing a safeguard which exists in England against proceeding in the wrong train. But if the guard render himself invisible, he does not expect, as in England, to be fee'd for making needless announcements, or proffering superfluous information, and so the imposition is saved.

As a general rule, the Continental railway carriages are superior in comfort to our own, although latterly improvement has been made in this direction on some of the English lines. On most of the foreign lines, the second-class carriages are, or were, equal to our first, and practically almost the only difference between first and second consists in the number of passengers which they take, the first class taking eight in each compartment, and the second ten. In the line between Cette and Bayonne, and possibly on other lines, the second-class carriages are not so good, and are more like our own, and do not possess that with which those on other lines are fitted up—a netting overhead similar to what is placed in our first-class carriages for the reception of small things; hooks are substituted. Sometimes one gets into the older class of carriage, as we did once between Arles and Marseilles, where the compartments are uncomfortably narrow.

In France, it seems quite the rule to crowd the carriages to the utmost. I never learnt the reason, but have imagined that a Government duty or tax is levied on every carriage used. If so, it is highly desirable that this tax should be removed.

In all the French trains, and I think also in other countries, there is in each class a division *pour dames seules;* and as occasionally there is only one second-class carriage in the train, and the post may, if a mail train, occupy one compartment of it, there is in such a case only one compartment left for the general travellers by second class—a circumstance which is productive of inconvenience to them. The officials peremptorily keep the *dames seules* portion for ladies only. On one occasion I had unwittingly got into one with three ladies of my party, and with our whole effects; but although all the ladies in the carriage politely expressed their willingness that I should remain, the guard compelled me to descend and find another compartment for myself.

On most lines in France, Switzerland, and Italy, there are compartments which are marked as non-smoking; but although so marked, little regard is paid to the distinction, particularly on the Italian lines. The men seem to have very little notion that it is a most selfish act to pollute the air breathed by their fellow-passengers for the sake of indulging in one of their own—to many others, disagreeable—habits which might be postponed until they get out; and so little is thought about it, that it would require Sydney Smith's 'Surgical Operation' to imbue them with the idea that it is a discomfort to others, or that when asked to stop smoking, it is their duty at once as gentlemen to comply. On one occasion in Italy, after speaking to successive passengers, some of whom complied, and some would not, I spoke to the guard; but he paid no attention to the complaint (the carriage being non-smoking), and in charity let me suppose he did not comprehend what I said. But, indeed, the cigar seems hardly ever out of the mouth of the Italian, and one wonders how the humbler classes can spare the money from their small earnings to spend upon this expensive practice.

Foreigners are very fond in the hot weather of putting down all the six windows of the compartment, thus creating draughts, from which I have several times caught a cold. They have not the slightest notion of closing a window in passing through a tunnel, and on some lines the tunnels are frequent and long. But while they put down the glass, they also draw down the blue blinds placed over each window, under pretence of the shining of the sun, but quite as often for no conceivable reason except that the glass is down, or that they don't want to be bothered looking out. It is of no manner of consequence although the scenery through which one is passing be the finest or the grandest possible, down goes the blue blind without even the politeness of asking the other passengers whether they so desire or not. As often as I could, I secured a place at the window, and showed that, although a native of a colder clime, I could stand the sunshine for the sake of the view. On one occasion, on a former tour, travelling by diligence from Geneva to Chamounix, there were some Germans smoking continually, as usual, on the seats before us. These men, though approaching the grandest scenery in Europe, insisted angrily on a leather curtain being kept down, so as to exclude all view, simply because the raising of it admitted a little sunshine. But this habit is not confined to Germans; and the conclusion to which I have come is that, to say nothing of the quality of inherent politeness in true consideration for others, the generality of foreigners have no high appreciation for scenery, or are desperately afraid of their complexion, which, to say the truth, cannot rival that of the Anglo-Saxon.

I should just add, that in Switzerland, on some of the lines, the railway carriages are constructed somewhat on the American plan, by which entrance is made from end to end of the carriage, and the guard can thus pass through from one carriage to another. At Interlachen, between the two lakes, there is an upper storey to enable people the better to see the views. Carriages similarly constructed are for the same reason run upon the little line between Bayonne and Biarritz.

The speed on Continental railways is, as compared with that on English railways, very slow. There are what are called express trains, but these express trains do not attain the celerity of our ordinary trains. For example, the express which leaves Paris at 11 A.M. reaches Mentone the following day at 3.50 P.M.—that is, 690 miles in twenty-nine hours, or at the rate of 24 miles per hour; and for long journeys like this in France, first-class tickets must be taken. Express trains are not, however, always to be had, and one is doomed frequently to long and tiresome journeys. To go from Nismes to Toulouse, our train took ten hours, stopping at thirty different stations by the way between Cette and Toulouse, with twenty minutes to dine at Narbonne, the previous part of the journey between Nismes and Cette, a short distance, having been express. The distance is only 298 kilometres, or about 186 miles for the whole journey, the rate of speed between Cette and Toulouse being thus only between 14 and 15 miles per hour. In like manner eight hours were consumed in the journey between Pau and Toulouse, which is about 130 miles, or rather more than 16 miles per hour. Not only is the speed slow, but at any station at which the trains stop, there is a detention for an apparently useless length of time. Occasionally long stoppages occur also where the lines are single only. In one short journey of 37 miles between St. Sebastian in Spain and Biarritz, two hours were lost from this cause by waiting at two stations for trains from the other end to pass. More powerful locomotives were promised upon the line between Paris and Marseilles, by which it was expected the journey of 536 miles might be accomplished in twelve hours; but they do not yet appear to have been placed upon it.

If, however, the speed be less, the security is greater. We seldom hear of accidents on the Continental lines.

There are peculiarities about the French trains which render it necessary to study the *Indicateur* very carefully, as some trains take only first-class passengers, and others have no first class; and although the first train going may be taken, it does not follow that it will be the first to arrive at the destination. A still further and annoying peculiarity is, that the railway company by first-class express trains will not always book to every station on the line at which they stop. Thus a friend left Mentone for Heidelberg. On arrival at Marseilles, he found himself compelled to book to Paris to get on. Thence he went to Strasbourg. Nor would it be possible to leave the line at Lyons, because the luggage would be registered to Paris.

The arrangements of the railways in regard to stations correspond in some degree with our own; but they have their specialties, into which I need not enter. The system of *salles-d'attente* and of registration of luggage necessitate stations being built on a much larger scale than our own. Sometimes tickets are collected before arriving at the *gare*, but more frequently are inconveniently taken at the narrow *sortie* or *uscita* from the passengers encumbered with luggage. Outside the station a host of porters and *commissionaires* of hotels is immediately encountered, and beyond this crowd, often largely swelled by mere idle onlookers, and perhaps by an occasional pickpocket, a long line of omnibuses and cabs. It is the practice in many, perhaps most places, for every hotel to keep an omnibus which goes to the station for every train. Probably there is some jealousy lest cab-drivers or general omnibus conductors might beguile or be bribed to beguile the visitors to certain hotels; but whether it be from this cause or from ostentation, the consequence is that there is waiting for employment a number of conveyances altogether out of proportion to the number of passengers requiring conveyance. I have counted at Mentone, waiting arrival of a train, twenty omnibuses, inclusive of a general one, with their respective drivers and conductors, and nearly as many cabs; while the number of passengers leaving the train would not exceed twenty in all, of whom probably not three would require conveyance. The maintenance of these omnibuses must be attended with heavy expense to the hotelkeepers; and although it can by no means pay for the expense, the charge against the visitor is heavy. The general omnibus, with a few specially-adapted cabs, would suffice in most places for all the traffic. It is melancholy to see the almost hourly procession of empty 'buses, relieved only occasionally by one of them exhibiting in triumph a solitary occupant, and perhaps bearing five or six large boxes on its top. In Paris and Toulouse, and some other places, there are little district or family omnibuses holding four or six persons, unconnected with any hotel—a far better arrangement.

The charge for a seat in the omnibus is usually, in a town or general omnibus, without luggage, either 30 or 50 centimes; with luggage, 1 franc. The hotel omnibuses never charge less than 1 franc per person; and with luggage it is usually $1\frac{1}{2}$ francs. If a party consist of four, it has thus to pay 6 francs or 5s. for the drive to the hotel, which is expensive; and it is much cheaper, if there be not heavy luggage, for which the cabs are seldom adapted, to take a cab. This cannot easily be done at leaving the hotel, as the guests are expected to employ the hotel omnibus, which is charged as matter of course in the bill.

We experienced at Rome a curious species of imposition. Not finding a carriage which would have taken our luggage, we entered the general omnibus, for which the fare for three persons was, the conductor told us, 3 francs, and drove to the house where we expected to obtain quarters. It turned out to be full, and I left the omnibus, crossed the street on foot and inquired at two hotels, at the second of which I found accommodation, and the omnibus brought across the luggage. The conductor demanded 10 francs for what he called the several courses, and I was glad, with the assistance of the landlord of the hotel, to arrange for 6 francs; but we were afterwards informed that this conductor was notorious for such practices.

It is sometimes desired to send luggage or boxes by goods trains *petite vitesse*. I had occasion to do so from Lyons to Mentone. A declaration was, by aid of the landlord of our hotel, filled up, containing, among other particulars, the general contents of the boxes which he sent to the goods office, and they were duly forwarded to their destination. The time taken in the transit varies and depends on circumstances—it may be weeks. It is therefore never safe to send off by goods train luggage which may be immediately wanted. The cost of carriage is so much per 50 kilogrammes; all below the 50 is charged the same as 50. For this weight between Lyons and Mentone, I paid $5\frac{1}{2}$ francs. Between Paris and Mentone it would have been 7 to 8 francs; between Marseilles and Mentone, 3 francs. These figures will give an approximate idea of the cost. On leaving Mentone, the second season, I sent a box (under 50 kilogrammes weight) to Glasgow, to care of Messrs. J. and P. Cameron, railway agents, to go by *petite vitesse* to Marseilles, and thence by sea to Glasgow, where Messrs. Cameron passed it through the customs and despatched it to Edinburgh. The total cost was 6s. 10d. A box I sent from Naples to the care of a mercantile friend in Liverpool, by whom it was passed and forwarded to Edinburgh, cost for carriage, Naples to Edinburgh, £1, 2s. 6d. This amount embraced shipping agents' charges, and was sent as freight. Had I sent the box simply as a parcel, it would have cost 5s. 6d. less, but the shipper would not for the lesser charge undertake responsibility beyond 40s.; and looking to the thievish character of the Neapolitans, I thought it safer to pay the additional charge. The difficulty one feels about sending off things to pass a frontier, is the examination by the *douaniers;* but I believe that some of the *expediteurs*, to be found in all towns, undertake for a small fee to get this managed. I presume they procure the passing through upon the footing of known or credited respectability of the party sending. I sent to Glasgow and Liverpool an exact list of the contents of the boxes, for exhibition, if need were, to the authorities. Some of the bankers—as, for example, Messrs. Macquay, Hooker, and Co., Florence—undertake to despatch goods and works of art to any place in Europe.

II.

CONTINENTAL HOTEL AND PENSION LIFE.

'THE inn looked so much like a gentleman's house that we could hardly believe it was an inn,' is the observation made by Miss Wordsworth in her *Recollections of a Tour in Scotland in* 1803, upon arriving at one which differed signally from others, where they could hardly obtain even sleeping room, and that of the roughest kind. Books of travels do indeed afford glimpses into the state of accommodation provided for travellers in those 'good old times,' but they are only glimpses. People, in recounting their wanderings in their own country, seldom notice such matters, unless they find them either rather better or rather worse than the prevailing condition of things to which the force of habit has reconciled them. In truth, the inns of Great Britain in the beginning of this century were what would now be reckoned of a very humble class, and were frequently planted and to be discovered in localities which would now be considered most undesirable, and which were doubtless chosen from proximity either to markets or to the stations of stage-coach departure and arrival, if they did not themselves create them, and in positions where stabling and a stable-yard might advantageously and fitly be placed.

The introduction and development of the railway system have effected such an extraordinary increase in the amount of travelling as to have, in respect of such public accommodation, produced, or rather necessitated, a revolutionary change. The old little inn, with its rubicund jovial hail-fellow-well-met landlord and its horsey adjuncts, has in the larger towns all but disappeared, or, if left for the benefit of the antiquary as a relic and specimen of a past age, receives its chief patronage on market days from the farmers, who find it convenient to stall their animals in its stables, and enjoy a homely dinner at its moderate table. Instead of it, whole streets of hotels, in the best situations, and possessed of all the comforts with which modern civilisation can furnish them, are built and occupied, and in busy times are sometimes full to overflowing. The very nomenclature indicates a superior tone. The house ceases to be an 'inn,' and becomes a 'hotel.' The Saracen Heads, the White Harts, and the Georges give way to national or big swelling names. We are become imperial in the very appellations we bestow even on houses in which we tarry only for a night.

A similar or even greater reform has been attained in the Continental towns. The discomforts of the old houses there were no doubt much greater than they were with ourselves; and, indeed, even now, if we abandon the tourists' highway, or run away from the larger towns, a primitive and perhaps far from agreeable state of matters is discovered, the fact being that much of the improvement which has taken place is due to studying the requirements of *les Anglais*. But in the leading improvements the foreigners have led the van, and we may be said to follow at a respectful distance.

The tendency abroad is, as it is at home, towards building large establishments in which the rooms are reckoned by the hundred, one of the hotels in Paris, the Grand (most new hotels abroad now have 'Grand' prefixed to some other and more distinctive designation, but this is 'The Grand' *par excellence*), advertising as many as 800 rooms; another (the Louvre),

700,—figures which are beyond anything, I suppose, in England, unless it be (though perhaps not even there) in the Midland Railway Hotel, St. Pancras. There is at all times a greater likelihood of finding accommodation, and such accommodation as may be desired, in houses of such formidable dimensions; but the visitor's importance suffers a shock: he becomes nothing but a number, and as such is termed by the *employés* of the hotel, and shouted up and down the speaking tubes.

But a more important result follows from the immense augmentation in travelling, because the intercourse thus brought about between the inhabitants of countries originally differing very widely in their manners and customs has a direct tendency to assimilate not merely their manners and customs, but their modes of living. Hence the peculiarities of each gradually, if good, are adopted—if bad, are lost. We borrow from the foreigners, they borrow from us. Odd ways and angular corners get rubbed off, and Cæsar and Pompey settle down in time 'very much 'like,' specially Pompey. Yet, when one leaves the home country, he happily discerns there are still remaining considerable differences between life abroad and life in Britain. Hotels on the Continent are conducted on somewhat different principles from those which at least formerly were customary in Great Britain; and until the dead level of uniformity be reached, it may not be uninteresting to recall some of the differences, and to mention circumstances attendant upon hotel life abroad, which, to those not very familiar with the subject, may be noteworthy.

In general construction, the more recently erected hotels at home and abroad do not materially differ. Tardily we are beginning to adopt the foreign system of numerous and spacious public rooms, and especially public drawing-rooms, to which ladies can freely resort. But in one important element of comfort to the weak or weary visitor, the foreigners are behind ourselves, inasmuch as lifts (*ascenseurs*) do not seem to be very common; and really in these many-floored hotels they are needed. The only places where we have seen them have been in the hotels of Paris and Marseilles, and they were not always in working order. In addition to the long stairs to be ascended, there are often in these large hotels lengthy corridors to traverse, so that it is a journey from the outer door to the bedroom, in some cases requiring a study of the *locale,* so as to avoid being lost in the labyrinth.

Next to comfort, the matter of charges is one of primary consideration to most travellers, and can scarcely be overlooked in treating of hotel life. Generally it may be observed, that notwithstanding there has been abroad, as there has been at home, a very considerable rise in charges from former scales, the cost of living at hotels abroad is, as it used to be, still under, or on an average considerably under, the cost for similar comforts and accommodation at home.

The cost of rooms is regulated primarily by the floor or *étage* on which they are situated; and if the visitor desire to be economical, he ought to ask for rooms upon the higher floors, say the third, or even, where it exists, the fourth *étage*. First-floor rooms are always charged high, sometimes exorbitantly so. At Milan we were shown into bedrooms on the first floor, which, had we taken, would have cost us about 20 to 25 francs per night per room. In Nice as much as 75 francs, or £3 per day, have been asked for two rooms on the first floor of a leading hotel, being equal to a rent per annum of £1095. A friend who spent the winter at Cannes told me he paid 75 francs per day for the rooms he had in one of the principal hotels, but probably he had three or four rooms. In Mentone the highest I have known paid by friends has been, for a large saloon and a bedroom, both princely rooms, 50 francs, or about £2 per day, equal to a rent per annum, were they let all the year round, of £730. These, however, are season places, and such rooms would remain vacant a considerable portion of the year, and even, a consequence of the high charge, for great part of the season, as the hotelkeepers will not lower their price even for a short period.

In Italy it is always desirable, where there is an ability to mount long stairs, to take rooms as high up as possible, so as to get as far away as may be from the odours of the street; but the same rule as regards the charges for rooms prevails. Perhaps in nothing do foreign hotel charges differ more than in the charges for rooms. They differ according to the place—that is, whether it be a large or a small town; according to the hotel, whether it be first class or inferior; and according to the rooms themselves, their position, size, and furnishing, and also according as they are single or double bedded. Abroad, nearly every bedroom large enough is so constructed as to fit it for use also as a sitting-room or *salon*, in which friends may be received. Sometimes the beds are placed in a recess or back part of the room, which may be shut off at will by drawing a curtain. The rooms abound with mirrors; but unless in houses frequented by the English, there are for the most part no carpets on the floors, saving a rug at the bedside, thus and otherwise involving an odd mixture of splendour and discomfort. However, carpets are beginning to be more frequently introduced. To those accustomed to the warmth of carpets, getting out of bed in the morning is, when they are wanting, a chilly operation, more especially when the floors are constructed, as they sometimes are, I presume for protection against vermin, of composition.

On an average, I would say that a bedroom on a third floor, with one bed for a single person, costs from 3 to 5 francs per night; a double-bedded room, from 5 to 8 francs. On the second floor the price is advanced a little; but the first floor is always high, varying according to circumstances. In some fashionable places, such as Nice and Biarritz, during the season the charge for rooms is, in first-class hotels, as what I have already said shows, extravagantly high. The season at Nice is not, like many places, for two or three months only, but lasts the whole winter—half of the year. It ought not therefore, one would think, to be so expensive.

But lights have to be paid for separately, and are usually charged at hotels at the rate of 1 franc per *bougie* or candle, although I have seen only 75 centimes charged, and in some out-of-the-way places as little as half a franc, or even, as at Chateau d'Œx, 30 centimes, upon which no doubt there was a profit. I was told of the case of a visitor at an expensive hotel in Nice who was, a good many years ago, charged 16 francs for *bougies* for a single night. But this mode of plundering is now so far abandoned, and one has only to be careful that more candles than he desires be not lighted. The charge for *bougies*, if remaining only single nights at hotels, becomes heavy; but if several nights be spent in the house, the candles remain till burned down. It is said that foreigners carry off their unburnt *bougies* with them, and use them at next stoppage, as they carry off also, it is alleged, the sugar which they have not used, but for which they consider they have paid. These, however, are petty habits, to which English people have not yet got accustomed.

The charge for service is almost invariably 1 franc per night per person. As lights are not charged in England, the united charge for *bougies* and service comes, for short periods, to be very much the same as the charge in England for service alone.

Universally, abroad, the beds are constructed only to hold one person. This may be, though it is not always, because of the summer's heat. In some rare cases the beds are found to be broad enough for two; but it does not necessarily follow that the charge is in this case as for one occupant. I have seen charge made for a broad bed as much as if the room had contained two beds. In parts where mosquitoes exist, the beds are draped with mosquito curtains.

Each room has its key and corresponding number, and the visitor is expected, upon leaving his chamber, to lock his door, and hang the key upon the key-board which is under charge of the *concierge* at the entrance to the hotel. In very large hotels, there is a key-board for each floor, in charge of an attendant. So contrary is this system of locking doors to the habits of the English, that it is often neglected by them; so much so, that in hotels exclusively frequented by natives of our isle, such a thing as locking doors and bringing down keys would be looked upon as extraordinary. At one of these hotels, I asked a servant, upon leaving my room after arrival, where the key should be put, as I had seen no key-board. 'Oh, just leave it in the door,' was her reply. Foreigners always lock their doors, whatever may be the establishment in which they are; and in many places, especially in the large hotels of Paris, where nobody knows who may be his next neighbour, it is highly proper and safe to do so. In this connection I may just observe that somehow or other there are in most places hotels which are only patronized by the English, and a foreigner is a *rara avis*. Correspondingly, there are other hotels which they never visit. There must be some species of intuitive freemasonry which underlies and conduces to this result.

All hotels have a public *salle à manger*, to which both ladies and gentlemen are expected to go, and nearly all have drawing-rooms or reading-rooms, or both (*salons* and *salons-de-lecture*). A lady travelling by herself can freely go to all these rooms, and one constantly meets such *dames seules*. No necessity is imposed upon them to engage a *salon* or sitting-room. But if desirous of taking them out of the public rooms, the meals will be sent to the bedrooms, for which luxury and extra trouble, however, there is a charge made, sometimes as high, at least for dinner, as 2 francs or 3 francs per person per meal, though usually only $\frac{1}{2}$ franc.

In addition to placing in the reading-rooms newspapers,

which generally comprise one or more of the leading London journals (received in many places within twenty-four hours of their publication), there usually and most properly is in hotels, where visitors come for lengthened periods, a small collection of books sufficient to beguile an hour or a wet day.

The three chief meals of the day are breakfast, lunch, and dinner.

In what I shall call the English hotels, almost everybody maintains the good old English custom of coming down to the *salle-à-manger* to breakfast; but foreigners, consistently with their home practice, take their meagre breakfast or cup of coffee, scarcely to be designated breakfast, in their bedroom. English people cannot get reconciled to the idea of taking meals in a room in which they sleep. It is an uncomfortable and unsocial custom, essentially bad — keeps the bedrooms long from being attended to, and imposes much additional labour on the servants, who are kept flying up and down stairs at all hours of the morning with breakfast equipage.

The usual charge at all hotels, at least as against Englishmen, for breakfast proper (tea, coffee, or chocolate, with bread and butter) is $1\frac{1}{2}$ francs. Occasionally, though very rarely, I have found it only charged 1 franc, and once, viz. at Toulouse, 2 francs. Eggs are universally charged 25 centimes ($2\frac{1}{2}$d.) each; meats and fish, according to *carte*, and generally expensive.

But foreigners make a more substantial meal a little later on, which they call *déjeuner à la fourchette*, corresponding somewhat to our lunch. This is intended to be the real breakfast, and, according to true Continental fashion, it proceeds at many places at so early an hour as half-past ten, at others at eleven or twelve o'clock. In such cases it is found to be a most substantial repast, consisting of several courses, generally three—meat courses, pudding or tart course and cheese, and fruit courses; and it is in reality an early dinner, the whole company in the hotel assembling to enjoy it, unless individually they otherwise arrange. In the English hotels they have 'lunch' usually at one o'clock; but this is of a much less substantial nature, the visitor having been credited with making *more Anglici* a good breakfast in the morning. The charge for *déjeuner* or lunch differs according to the hotel, but is usually about 3 francs.

The *table-d'hôte* dinner is a regular Continental institution, which it would be well were it made the rule at home. Meaning literally dinner at the table of the host, I presume that at one time, and before the establishment of great hotels, the host regularly presided. This, however, is now rarely seen, although I have sat down to dine at a table where he took his place. Rising as each course arrived, and putting on an apron, he would with dexterous rapidity carve what was brought in, then, putting off his apron, would sit down again and take part with the guests.

Each hotel has its fixed hour for this dinner, varying in time from six to seven o'clock. I have also seen a special *table-d'hôte* dinner at eight o'clock, to suit those arriving by late trains. In places frequented by Germans, such as Interlachen, they have two dinner hours—one at two o'clock, for the Germans chiefly; and the other in the evening, to suit those who prefer dining at a later hour. The hotel people are frequently disturbed and put about by visitors, usually English people, inexcusably coming tardily to table. The charge for *table-d'hôte* dinner varies a good deal at different places, 4 to 5 francs being about the average rate, though occasionally it is less. In Paris some of the large hotels charge 6 francs—wine, however, included, as is customary in Paris.

The dinner, which is served *à la Russe*, consists of many courses, and is not, generally speaking, of the substantial character of an English home dinner. The routine is everywhere the same, and consists of the following courses, which the waiters present at the division assigned to each quietly at sound of finger bell:—(1) Potage or soup; (2) Fish, when it can be had, otherwise a substitute; (3) Entrées; (4) Vegetables by themselves, such as cauliflower, French beans or peas; (5) Poultry or game, or otherwise roast beef or roast mutton, accompanied invariably by salad or lettuce, and water-cresses; (6) Pudding or tart; (7) Fruits; (8) Sweet biscuits. In some of the grander places there is a course of ice-cream, and in other hotels ice-creams take the place of pudding on Sundays, or sometimes on both Sundays and Thursdays.[1] Such is the invariable routine, the only variety being in the specific description of the articles in each course. The great want in these dinners is of a good supply of vegetables; bread, not so wholesome, being supplied at discretion. It would be better if some of the viands were dispensed with, and more vegetables given. Such a thing as a good dry potato, what they call *au naturel*, is hardly known. Potatoes are served up greased in every conceivable way, or, if presented dry or in their skins, they are accompanied by a separate plate of butter. One course often excites remark by English visitors. It is where the game course consists of small birds, especially thrushes. These

---

[1] The following may be given as specimens of the *menu* :—

At the Grand Hotel du Louvre, Paris.

Potage.—Consommé aux Quenelles; Hors d'œuvre; Melon. *Relevées.*—Saumon Sauce Hollandaise; Pommes de terre nature; Train de Côtes à la broche; Aubergines à la Provençale. *Entrées.*—Timbales à la Joinville; Poulardes à la Demidoff. *Rot.*—Canetons de Rouen au Cresson; Salade de Romaine. *Entremets.*—Petits Pois à l'Anglaise; Biscuits Princesse; Garnis d'Allumettes. *Desserts.*

At a Provincial Hotel in France, somewhat more meagre than usual, however (verbatim).

Potage.—Tapioca. *Relevées.*—Epigrammes d'Agneau Bretonne. *Entrées.*—Poulets Sautés Maringa. *Legumes.*—Choux de Bruxelles. *Rôtis.*—Ros bief. *Entremets.*—Charlotte de Pommes Parisien, etc. *Dessert.*

afford a miserable bite apiece, and, for a party of 40 or 50, as many birds fall to be sacrificed, the rule of the table being that every guest is, or has the opportunity of being, served alike. At Cannes, at one of the hotels (season 1876–77), a round robin was subscribed by the English of the party, protesting against such use of thrushes—I do not know with what effect. They were to be sometimes seen hanging in bunches at the poulterers' doors. It seems a cruel use of such song-birds, which are fed upon grapes to fatten them for the table; yet all the grapes they could swallow, even though in quantity enough to satisfy the grape cure, would never make them more than a miserable picking.

The quantities of eggs, fowl, and game which are needed to supply so many tables must be enormous; and as one sees very few live poultry anywhere, it has occasioned me surprise to think how they can be procured. The only feasible explanation is that the country is ransacked far and near for food to supply the luxurious tables of the hotels, and the wants of town populations. In a book published in 1857 by Dr. Frederick Johnson,[1] it is stated with regard to Paris alone—

'That the great Metropolitan maw occupies 712 bakers, and daily consumes 479,015 loaves and rolls (we abandon verbal computation in despair), and annually 6,849,449 poultry, 1,329,964 larks, 26,000 kids, 9,937,430 kilos of fish (the kilo being $2\frac{1}{4}$ lbs. English), 5,006,770 kilos of confectionery, 150,223,006 kilos of pears; that yearly each Parisian swallows 69 oysters, 165 eggs, 137 quarts of wine, and 14 quarts of beer among his other luxuries; and that among them, in their little enjoyments, they gossip over 3,000,000 kilos of coffee, 350,000 kilos of chicory, 2,000,000 lbs. of chocolate, and 40,000 kilos of tea, assisted by 109,221,086 quarts of milk. Teetotallers may be alarmed for the public sobriety when they learn that, besides the wines and brandies, our Parisian pleasure-seekers dispose of 1,267,230 quarts of liqueurs, to say nothing of 350,000 kilos of brandied bonbons, and that they cool the consequences with 500,000 quarts of ice.'

If such be the consumption of Paris, and this is more than twenty years ago, what must that be of all France, to say

[1] *A Winter's Sketches in the South of France and the Pyrenees,* p. 7.

nothing of other Continental countries? Our box of figure-counters would soon be exhausted in vain attempts at the calculation. We should have to borrow largely from the astronomers.

The guests are, of course, expected to help themselves to only a small portion of each course. We once (in 1862) saw an Englishman in Paris, unacquainted with the customs either of France or of good society, appropriate to himself at one round nearly all that was in the dish, and we never could pass that untutored savage without thinking of the plateful of coarse beef which he had doomed himself to eat. But most Germans, Dutch and Spanish people feed very largely, and make no scruple as a practice to take double supplies, and the largest and best pieces of everything which comes round, leaving those who come after them wofully scant.[1] The waiters are well acquainted with this habit, and pander to it, possibly in hope of fees. At Biarritz, where we experienced a singular practice of the waiter doling out portions to the visitors (on the footing, perhaps, that some of them could not be trusted to leave even a wreck behind), they, as matter of course, placed upon the plates of the Spaniards of the company large quantities of each course, while when they came to ourselves we received often such small portions that we would occasionally complain and get more.

At many places in France and elsewhere, wine is included in the charge for dinner. In this case it is the *vin ordinaire*

---

[1] At Naples I sat next a German who helped himself to four thick slices of roast beef, then, according to German custom, began by placing one above another, and cutting the whole into little squares by drawing his knife first lengthways and then crossways through them, and having so divided the beef, took his knife and shovelled, in quick succession, all the pieces into his mouth. Fish is often a scarce commodity, yet I have seen German ladies, after having liberally helped themselves to it, call for more as they would for more of any other course, though it is unusual for others to ask a second supply of any course.

of the place, and is generally good if fresh; but as the practice is to put down a carafe to each two persons, much of it is often left. I have sometimes found the wine sour, evidently arising from having been kept from day to day, adding only what was necessary to replenish the carafes. The *vin ordinaire* costs the hotelkeeper very little, although he would charge from 1 franc to 2 francs per bottle for it if ordered. Everybody is expected to take wine, even children; and where wine is not included and set down, the waiter goes round, not asking whether you wish wine, but, 'What wine will you take?' and you have to select from the *carte*. I have been much surprised at the great differences in the price of wine at different places. The same kind of wine is charged at one place, it may be three, even four times as much as at another; and in general the price rises, and rises far out of reason, according to the distance from which the wine is supposed to come. Many lay it down as a rule to take the wine of the district in which they for the time being are; and it can, at all events, be had good of its kind and cheap, costing, some kinds, from 1 franc to 2 francs per bottle. This, which in the locality is called *vin ordinaire*, elsewhere becomes a high-priced wine. A fair quality of wine can in general be had at about 3 francs or 2s. 6d. per bottle, although it is observable that the bottles are so made as evidently to be incapable of containing a quart. If they be not small in size, they are sure deceptively to have a large hollow lump of glass in the bottom. Wine, with the exception of the better descriptions, is never drunk pure, but is poured into a tumbler and mixed with water, about half of each.

When dinner, lasting about an hour, is over, everybody is expected to rise and leave the room. At one hotel the waiters compelled retreat by opening all the windows. They have to clear the table and wash up, and are naturally anxious to have the room to themselves. Besides, in many places, the servants' supper takes place at ring of bell immediately after dinner, and no doubt the waiters are anxious to join. Their dinner bell in like manner rings after lunch. Visitors are seldom aware of these internal arrangements, or alive to them if they be.

If one does not dine at *table d'hôte*, to dine *à la carte*, by selecting out of a list, is costly, and should if possible be avoided. When arriving too late for *table d'hôte*, we have found in some places that we could order a dinner for which the same regular charge was made as at *table d'hôte*, although perhaps this might not be done for a single visitor. At other places the better course, particularly in Italy, is to order a dinner at a given figure, leaving the hotel to supply what they choose. One is certain by doing so to be better off.

At table, various Continental practices may be noticed, and among others a very singular custom which the German gentlemen have of tucking their napkins under their chins, and spreading them over the breast like a row of babies with their bibs on. I never could look at a German so arrayed without thinking of the minister who,

> 'Being wi' the palsy tribbled,
> In liftin' spoonfu's aften dribbled;
> Sae, to prevent the draps o' broth,
> Prinn'd to his breast the tablecloth.'

Some explanation of this ludicrous practice is perhaps to be found in the painful habit which the generality of Germans have—occasionally ladies as well as men—of eating with their knives. English people cannot witness this fearful and wonderful operation without a nervous dread of the result. But there is this to be said for the Germans, that although some of their customs be peculiar, and not to be copied, they are great linguists, and enter agreeably in English into conversation; and I only mention such little foibles, that they may 'see themselves as others see them.' In many places—Switzerland particularly—there is put down upon the table here and there a case of what turns out to be toothpicks. One would think that those who choose to injure their teeth by means of such instruments and perform an odious cleansing, would prefer to keep their private pick, as much as their private tooth-brush, and use it in their private room.

We found the Dutch people ceremoniously polite. They never sat down and never rose from the table, never entered a room and never left it, without bowing to all round. It always kept us in a fidget lest they should not receive like courtesy; but it is a very pleasant trait of character in a people whom we found to be not merely externally polite, but kind and cordial at heart.

At the hotels, unless they be what I have called English hotels, one usually meets with people of all countries. In one hotel in France, I was informed we had representatives of eight different nations, counting English, Scotch, and Irish as one. It has struck me, however, that although the French language is so generally spoken, the French themselves, while found travelling in every part of their own land, are very seldom seen in other countries. I was on one occasion sitting next a bright Parisian young lady, and rather wickedly, I fear, was exalting Edinburgh so as to suggest its taking the palm from Paris. She was astonished, and having asked her when she was coming to see Edinburgh, she replied very decidedly, though in the very bewitching way in which the French girls speak, 'Jamais, ne-verre,' which honestly meant there was no probability she would, although the emphasis no doubt was intended as a delicate rebuke to the heretical presumption of my thought. *La belle France* is *tout le monde* to Frenchmen; nor do they get much encouragement to cross the English Channel, for I have noticed that they are, as a rule, most unhappy sailors.

One meets with all peoples and tongues and sorts at the dinner table. Now, much of comfort at that interesting time depends upon who sit next you. Dining at a long table with a large company is never so genial as dining round a smaller table in a party of six or eight. Intercourse is almost limited to those on the right and left, unless you and those opposite have strong voices and be both remarkably socially inclined. This, bad enough at home, is intensified abroad, not merely among strangers, but strangers who are foreigners, with whose language you may not be particularly acquainted. Everything, then, turns on the question, 'Who is my neighbour?' and in this respect one is all but entirely at the mercy of the waiters, who have not the grimmest idea of social assortment; and it may be that you are for weeks together placed next to those with whom you have no *rapport* or fellow-feeling or congeniality of tastes—nay, with whom you may be unable to exchange a word. When it is otherwise, and people are social, intelligent, well read, and without necessarily being clever are cheerful, the dinner hour becomes a pleasant episode of the day.

But it is often otherwise. It is bad enough to get placed beside a foreigner whose language, perhaps, you can read, but whose oral pronunciation is perfectly unintelligible; or beside a very stout and important lady whose ideas, if she have any, run on subjects with which you have no possible sympathy—who is too ponderous, or whose composite capital, perhaps stuck tenderly on with pins, is—it may, from the steadiness of her carriage, be supposed—considered by her too fragile to bear the shaking and jolting of a joke—or really, to confess the truth, one whom, it may possibly be, you cannot be bothered to entertain; or beside a young lady who speaks so low and so timidly, that in the din of dinner it is literally impossible to hear what she says. Nor is it less distressing to be placed beside a very deaf person who not only does not catch what you say, but, as usual with deaf people, speaks indistinctly. Few have not had such an experience as this. You are seated beside what appears to you to be a very amiable, comfortable, benign old lady. The beverage before you is in a condition which it would not be safe to swallow for a little. You are both resting on your oars, or rather on your spoons. The moment is favourable for an opening speech. The subject you select is one of personal and common interest. The observation you hazard is such as would in no event occasion a division bell to ring. Quietly you say, 'The soup is hot.' She inclines her face as if she had just heard you were talking in her direction. 'The soup is hot.' An inquiring glance is directed to you. Again you repeat rather louder, 'The soup is hot.' 'Sir,' she replies. In an alto and rather excited pitch you proclaim, 'The soup is hot.' By this time everybody has been turning a listening ear. 'Beg your pardon, sir; but I am rather deaf.' 'Madam' (in an altissimo and crescendo style), 'The soup *is* HOT.' 'Yes,' she blandly replies, 'the room is very hot.' You are for ever and for ever shut up, and retire from the struggle hot enough yourself.

But sometimes the wet blanket comes in another form. I was at one place agreeably set on several occasions beside a lively young German lady, who spoke English fluently. At our first interview I asked, 'What was their national dish? was it *Sauer-kraut?*' 'No, it was larks.' 'Oh, you barbarians,' I replied; 'do you eat canaries and parrots?' at which the fair damsel was much shocked. 'What's that?' obviously whispers the heavy German next her on her other side, and this and every other like passage of nonsense had to be translated word for word into this intensely philomathic alien, but withal kindly guide, philosopher, and friend of my young neighbour.

I was for a considerable time at another place seated next a most intelligent member of the French bar, whose bad health unfortunately added to a natural taciturnity. He could speak English, and liked to do so. We formed ourselves into a mutual instruction society—I to correct his good English, and he to correct my bad French. But as he preferred English conversation, and I was too lazy to bore him with my French, the educational advantages on my side were reduced to the *minimum visible*. However, we enjoyed to some extent rational conversation on subjects of interest, imparting information to each other, and discussing where we differed. Here was 'the feast of reason.' But, though my friend could enjoy all that creates a laugh, 'the flow of soul' would not have produced a deluge, or even turned a mill-wheel of moderate dimensions. There is nothing so difficult as to get merry with those who speak another language, into which everything has mentally and slowly to be translated, and the flashes of merriment often will neither brook translation nor abide deliberative meditation. The ball must be kept up. Any efforts in that direction were therefore of a ponderous kind. Sometimes I would, with all due and becoming gravity, put a case to him in French law. 'If,' for example, I would say to him; 'if a Frenchman were to die, leaving an estate as large as this room (a tolerably big one), and twelve children?' 'Oh, but,' he would interpose, smiling, 'we have no estates so small,' and perhaps he might have added, 'No families so large.'

From him I was shifted for a time to the agreeable society of a blooming Swedish lady, who could speak no language but her own, and who was uncommonly ready to imagine others were laughing at her, and accordingly to take offence. In this fix, to make the best of it, I returned to school to remedy the neglects of early life, and being a docile and apparently a reverent pupil, I advanced with such rapid strides to proficiency in the Swedish tongue, that in not many days I learnt that in that hitherto supposed outlandish language *chrystal* is 'chrystal' and *knife* is 'knife;' and had my studies been prolonged, I doubt not that I should in time have come to know that the honest Swedish people do call a spade a spade.

This interesting pursuit of knowledge under difficulties was, however, brought to an abrupt close by my being torn away and transferred to the company of an Irish young lady, from whom I speedily elicited that she came from the neighbourhood of Kilkenny. This *was* irresistible. 'Have you seen the tails of the two cats?' 'Oh, yes' (with a merry twinkle); 'they are in the Kilkenny Museum.' This museum may, like Aladdin's palace, have been built up in a night; but ere twenty-four hours had elapsed, it was stocked from floor to ceiling with such marvellous rarities as by no possibility had been ever either dreamt of in philosophy, or, what is more, conceived in the fertile brain of the great Barnum.

In season places, such shiftings about are few and far between; but in touring localities, during the travelling season, when you are more or less frequently changing your own quarters, and all around are changing almost daily too, one is shuffled about like a card, and more vicissitudes of association are experienced than befell the noted Gil Blas of Santillane in the course of his eventful life.

The rule of the hotels seems to be that the latest comers take the bottom of the table, and move up according as those before them leave. At the same time this rule was frequently infringed, and in some places we had always to ask where to sit. Of course all meet on a footing of equality, and it is customary for those of title—especially for foreign titled persons, unless of the highest rank—to dine with the other visitors. On one occasion, at a small party of ten or twelve, an old gentleman appeared, to whom the ladies in the *salon* had, on his entrance, bowed profoundly. We afterwards learned from one of them he was a distinguished foreign prince. An English marchioness or an English duke will occasionally appear at table, but I fancy English noblemen rarely condescend to do so. We were, however, often finding that at the table with us were foreign persons of rank of all grades, and the foreigners of title with whom we became at all acquainted were always very friendly and unassuming. But generally in travelling we could not tell who were our neighbours. It was for the most part from the lists of visitors that the names of those in the hotel could be discovered, and occasionally these have been of royal rank. In this case they were necessarily notable, and although they did not come to the public table, yet they were seen in the gardens; and sometimes they travelled with large retinues, and could not escape observation. At Interlachen, General Grant and his wife came to the Jungfrau Hotel, at which we were. He was on the night of his arrival serenaded by a brass band, which played till near midnight, the musicians no doubt regarding the sweet and melodious sounds of trombones and ophicleides atoned for any disturbance of the slumber of the visitors, or even of the probably wearied General himself.

All the Continental hotels are, with few exceptions, prepared to take visitors upon pension—that is, on board. But there are establishments which, *par excellence*, are termed pensions. The line of demarcation is very slender, and some hotels are truly pensions, while some pensions are truly hotels. The pension strict, however, is a less grand house than the hotel. It is for the most part a large private house, without, though not always without, the parade of *concierge* and other distinctive marks of an hotel. As a rule, to which there are exceptions, it is more homely, there is less style in the method of conducting, less appearance about the rooms, and smaller attention paid to service and sanitary arrangements. On the other hand, the company is smaller, and as the people come to remain for periods of time, they fraternize better, and there is a good deal more of the home feeling in a pension than ever finds its way into any hotel. The better class of pensions profess to require an introduction, but it does not necessarily follow that the company is more select; on the contrary, as they are usually rather less expensive than hotels, the company is not unfrequently of a mixed description, and consequently the name pension is, to some extent, in disfavour with those English people who can afford to pay hotel charges, and prefer more style.

At hotels, the rule, sometimes relaxed for a party, is that people are not taken on pension under a week. A similar rule prevails in pensions proper, and indeed during pension season it is usually necessary to secure quarters in pensions proper, and even in hotels, by writing for rooms some considerable time previously.

The charge for pension varies very greatly, according to the place, to the situation of the rooms, and to the season.

In former days the pension charge was extremely moderate. One old gentleman told me that in his younger days the charge in Switzerland, at least, was 3 francs per day for everything; but this was a charge as against foreigners only, and he, then a young Englishman, succeeded in getting off upon this low rate by being taken for a German, he being with a party of Germans. Even till more recent years, one would hear of 5 francs per day being a normal charge. These good old times have not wholly disappeared, for to this day, in some outlying places in Switzerland, pension at a very low rate can be procured. We spent eight days at the Hotel Berthod, Chateau d'Œx, which lies up among the mountains, a long day's journey from Interlachen, *en route* for Aigle; and the charge was only 5 francs per day, with 20 centimes for service, besides *bougies*, which were charged only 30 centimes each. This was upon the second floor, which we preferred, as less noisy, to that below at 6 francs. The charge on the third floor was, I believe, even a shade less. The hotel was a wooden house of large size, and could accommodate at least eighty guests, and in the season was generally full, while the company was so far select, being out of the beaten track of tourists. The accommodation was necessarily somewhat rough, but every attention was paid, as far as practicable, to the comfort of the visitors. Considering that its season lasts for scarcely three months in the year, one would be surprised to think it possible it could pay; but it seems that the landlord's brother had formerly kept the establishment, and had retired with a competence. Everything, however, with one exception, was cheap at Chateau d'Œx, which boasts of several establishments of the same kind, one of them (though two miles off), 'Rosinière,' the largest chalet in Switzerland, and picturesquely situated in a secluded spot, dating back to 1754.

Pension includes breakfast, lunch, dinner, bedroom, and service, sometimes also lights. Occasionally service is made a separate charge, and is stated at from $\frac{1}{2}$ franc to 1 franc per day, according to place.

In many good hotels in Switzerland and elsewhere, pension can be had at 8 francs per day. At Lugano the charge, I noticed, during summer (1st April to 31st October), is 8 to 11 francs; during winter, 6 francs to 7 francs 50 centimes. Both at Interlachen and Montreux, we paid at the rate of 8 francs, and had excellent quarters in first-class hotels. With other rooms supposed to be better, the charge would have been 10 francs per day. But in the height of the Interlachen season, the hotels will not readily begin to take people *en pension*. At Chamounix we were told, on a former tour in the month of August, that the hotels there would not take *en pension* after 15th July. By that time English tourists begin to arrive in great shoals, and often find much difficulty in getting quarters. When this takes place, the applications are either refused, or the visitors are accommodated in dependencies, which are either houses or chalets attached to the hotel, or in some cases simply houses in the villages in which the natives can spare a room, and therefore not always desirable. Pension in Italy and France is charged at a little higher rate than in Switzerland. We found that, upon an average, 10 or 12 francs a day was the charge in these countries; but according to the accommodation, it would either rise above or fall below this rate, varying from 8 to 15 or 16 francs per day. As the charge of 8 francs, which seldom secures any but a north room, covers everything pension includes, there must be a profit out of it, and all above that amount ought to be clear extra gain. Eight francs per day amounts to £116 per annum, 15 francs per day to £219—a good rate of board.

In season places great contrast often exists between the charges for pension during the season and after it is over. Thus at Biarritz, during the winter months, pension might have been had at 7 francs per diem, but during the two months of summer season (August and September, on to 15th October) the charges at the principal hotels are high. For rooms alone the charge may be from 20 to 25 francs on the second floor, and from 12 to 14 francs per day on the third floor, the first floor being much more costly. However, we found at the Hotel de Paris, on 18th September, towards the close of the season, which may have made a difference, fairly comfortable rooms on the first floor, in a good situation, at a moderate rate. Sometimes with first-floor rooms the usual charges for living are made separately or in addition to the charge for rooms.

Fire in the private rooms is always an extra. Nowhere is coal burnt, at least that we have seen, unless in the northern parts of France. The visitor, when he wishes fire, is supplied with a basket of wood, the size and the quality of which vary very much, as do the prices. It consists of logs sawn into pieces about 12 to 18 inches long, and split up, and the kind of wood necessarily varies with the locality. In the olive-growing countries it is olive wood, which burns slowly. At Pau it is the short oak grown in the woods in the vicinity. In other places it is pine wood, which burns rapidly. At Lyons we paid 2 francs for a small pannier of soft wood, which lasted two nights. At Mentone a large pannier of olive wood, probably mixed with pine, cost 2 francs 20 centimes, and lasted much longer. If we had no fire during the day, and we found day fires very rarely necessary in Mentone, a pannier would last us nearly a week for one fire per evening, lit after dinner. At Spezzia, where the wood burnt very fast, the pannier was charged 3·50 francs. At Pisa the charge was 3 francs; and at Rome, had we found it needful, we should have been charged at the hotel, for each room, 5 francs for a pannier which would not have lasted more than two nights. Indeed, at Rome the expense of wood is so serious an extra charge, that I have heard of a gentleman with a large and perhaps extravagant family feeling obliged to curtail his visit on that account.

The wood is laid across two iron dogs, and emits, especially in the case of olive wood, good heat. The ashes of former fires are always left lying between the dogs, and greatly help to keep the fire in. The ashes smoulder away for a long time, and bellows, always hung by the fireside, will bring them to a glow long after they are apparently dead.

The dogs are hardly suitable for coals, but might not a good trade in coals with the Continent be brought about? I suppose the abundance of wood renders it unnecessary. But a great deal may result from the force of habit, or, not improbably, there may be a prohibitory duty preventing the people from using coal.

One very annoying item of extra expense consists in the fees with which servants expect to be tipped at leaving. Many persons refuse to give anything, on the strictly theoretically-correct ground that they have already paid for service in the bills. Such persons, at least if English people, seem to be looked upon as shabby. On the other hand, there are those, principally English, who are very lavish with their largess, and really do their successors much harm, leading the servants to be on the outlook for handsome fees. In Italy the evil is, I think, most felt. In France, however, it is bad enough. If one be but a single night at a hotel, chamber-maid, waiters, *concierge*, porters, conductors, and even drivers of omnibuses—all expect donations, and stand hovering about (perhaps perform useless little services), that they may not be lost sight of. Nor is the evil less at pensions, where I have had more than once to fee no less than seven attendants, being the whole menial establishment. It becomes a very heavy tax, amounting to no small sum at the end of a long tour, as one does not like to be shabby, or thought so. At pensions and hotels at Christmas time, every servant with whom the visitor has had to do expects his or her five-franc piece at the least; and this really one does not at that festive season so much grudge, if dwelling in the house for the winter, although the feeing process has to be repeated at leaving, and intermediately for any supposed extra services. I must say, however, that the only suggestion of a donation at Christmas came from the *portier* of our hotel at Mentone, who addressed a lithographed card to each visitor on the 1st of January: 'Le portier de l'Hôtel vous souhait une bonne et heureuse année.' And no doubt a similar lithographed card was used with effect by all the porters of the place, and made the ignorant or unthinking aware of what they were expected to do.

The only person outside the establishment who suggested a benefaction by the enclosure of a card was the postman, who, no doubt, was cheerfully boxed by every visitor.

I suppose that complaints of this practice of tipping or expecting fees reached the ears of the landlords, who, honest men, no doubt had found their advantage in it; for, in the summer of 1877, nine of the principal hotels in Switzerland announced to the public that, with a view to putting a stop to it, they should thenceforth make a charge which would cover everything, so that visitors should not be annoyed longer in this way. But the system which they did adopt was an erroneous one, and was only calculated to place an additional burden on their guests—in other words, they made an extra charge for their rooms; so that the occupants had to pay nightly, in some cases, perhaps as much as they would have paid once for all as gratuity, while in many cases gratuities would continue to be given. We came upon one of these hotels, the Schweizerhoff in Lucerne. Here, in conformity with the new rule, one charge was made for rooms per night, inclusive of attendance and lights, and a bill was stuck up in the rooms containing a notice in the following terms :—

'*Avis. Messieurs les étrangers sont priés de ne plus donner de pour boires aux employés de l'Hotel. Toute le service dans l'intérieur de l'Hotel ainsi que l'éclairage est compris dans le prix de l'appartement.*'

Such a notice was only valuable if it had borne that the servants were *expressly prohibited*, upon pain of dismissal, from taking any gratuity; but while it contained nothing but what was always previously implied in the charge for service, and left the charge for porterage of luggage as performed *extérieur* (a service which has always been recompensed by a gratuity, and which the porter here duly accepted), the very form of the notice, 'Pray, don't,' rather suggests the idea that you ought to give. The evil is really so great that a more efficient and beneficial method ought to be taken by the hotels.

In Italy I have sometimes been asked for a gratuity by a messenger from a shop on delivering a purchase made.

Hotel bills are usually rendered and paid once a week. At Bellagio an admirable system was in use. Bills were rendered every day, although payment was not expected oftener than once a week. In this way any mistake could at once be rectified; and we did find occasionally—as every one must, especially in the touring season, when the sojourners are daily shifting—rectification to be necessary. It would be much in the interest of the landlords to make the practice universal, because where any entry has been charged to the wrong person, the person to whom it ought to have been charged may have left before discovery has been made. The waiters write, sign, and deliver to the clerk a slip containing every order, as the means of making up the books, and sometimes, perhaps, from not wishing to give offence by asking, put by mistake the wrong name to the order. In London a better system is, where the guest is requested to write the order himself, heading the memorandum with his name and number. In some—I am bound to say, only a few —cases in France, the landlord regularly charges his guests with the penny Government receipt stamp on discharging the bill. Honestly, this ought to be borne by himself.

Messrs. Cook and Gaze both issue hotel coupons. These are made up as books of three per day. One portion covers bedroom, lights, and service for one person; but it bears that porterage is not included, and a charge for conveying luggage to and from the bedroom to the door is then (I think erroneously) occasionally made in the bill, though the doing so does not exempt from the customary fee expected by the porters. Another portion covers plain tea or breakfast; and a third, dinner at *table d'hôte*, with or without wine, according to the usual practice of the hotel. Cook's tickets cost 8s., Gaze's cost 8s. 6d., but the latter entitle the holder to eggs or meat at breakfast. The hotels of both firms are for the most part unobjectionable, but the question is whether the coupons are or are not of any real advantage. As to this, people who have not used them are generally much puzzled. I had never, in travelling abroad, tried them before, but thought, upon entering Italy, where it is reputed (contrary to my subsequent experience) that one requires to be upon his guard against hotel imposition, I might make experiment to a limited extent, and accordingly purchased enough at Nice to last us about fourteen days.

On an average, I believe it will be found that, taking bedroom accommodation at the lower rates, or as for the upper *étages*, the price of the coupons is very much the same as the hotel charges would come to. In some hotels, in the smaller places, the charges may occasionally come to a trifle less, especially if there be a party; in others, in the larger towns, the hotel charges will certainly exceed it. In a pecuniary point of view, therefore, and supposing people are constantly on the wing, they will find that upon the whole the saving is not large, but that, in any view, there is a clear advantage in using them in large and expensive towns such as Marseilles and Nice.

However, if it be intended to stay long enough in a hotel to warrant going upon pension, it can frequently be arranged to obtain pension at the same rate as is payable for the coupons, the effect of which is that lunch is thrown into the bargain, saving 3 francs per day.

In Italy also the advantage of exchange is lost, the coupons being only purchasable with English money.

The coupons save a little trouble and shorten the bills. To those unable to speak a foreign tongue, they are additionally valuable. On the other hand, I fear the traveller is a good deal at the mercy of the landlord in regard to rooms. It is quite in his power to say he has no better. But if the house be not full, there is a possibility of being assigned the best rooms, and so obtaining accommodation for which, without coupons, a high charge would be made.

My limited experience gave me rather a dislike for them, and led me to feel I was more independent, and had a chance of being better served, by paying my way in the usual manner. At a town in Italy, I mentioned on arrival, as is required, that I had Cook's coupons and intended to use them. When the bill at leaving was rendered, I pointed out that it had not been stated as on this footing. It turned out that for the two nights we stayed at the house, the hotel charges (we were most comfortable in every respect) came to 6 francs 75 centimes less for our party than the cost of the coupons. Yet the landlady looked black when I pointed out the mistake, and seemed, while I was actually paying more, as if she thought me imposing on her. I felt so annoyed that I would never use them again in Italy. Months afterwards, when in a town in Switzerland, I resolved to employ what remained, and in driving up to the hotel on Cook's list, told the landlord so. I noticed he did not seem to relish the intimation, and when we visited the rooms allotted to us, we found them dismal chambers looking into the courtyard. I rebelled, and we got cheerful and better rooms on the floor above. This showed that we could not always quite rely upon getting the best accommodation possible, notwithstanding the coupons in this instance came to more than we could have pensioned for at the hotel, according to its own printed tariff. I afterwards learnt that the reason of dislike is, that the London house has a small commission (which is quite reasonable, and perhaps is not much objected to), and that settlements with the hotelkeepers do not take place for, it may be, some months after the bills are incurred, which may produce considerable inconvenience to some hotelkeepers. Were it possible to arrange for more frequent, say monthly settlements, perhaps all cause of dissatisfaction would be obviated, for otherwise the system must be most advantageous to the hotels which are on the London lists.

I must, however, put against these two instances, which may be very exceptional, the fact that I had used the coupons previously at two other hotels in Italy, and subsequently at another in Switzerland, and another in France, and met with every civility and attention, while they at once gave us excellent accommodation. Friends also who have frequently taken advantage of them, have told me that they preferred them, and would always in travelling avail themselves of the system.

To vary the monotony of the pension life, or from the inherent idea that gaiety is essential to existence, the hotel and pension keepers get up, from time to time, little entertainments in the *salons*. Of these, a dance is the most frequent; but in place of a quiet dance in the drawing-room to music on the piano by one of the guests, it seems to be considered essential to hire a band of musicians. Perhaps this practice is more in accordance with the French love of noise and display; but it both occasions unnecessary expense, and has less of the social about it. At other times we have had a conjurer introduced to exhibit tricks of magic. Manifestly he has not the same facilities as in a room fitted up for the purpose, but the tricks were sometimes novel, and interest people, particularly the young. On other occasions we have had special musical evenings, and at Interlachen a band of Tyrolese singers every now and then, I think almost weekly, gave an entertainment at the hotel; and as visitors at Interlachen are always changing, the audience would for the most part be different. We have also had little plays by strolling actors, and even on one occasion a small attempt at operatic performance. Perhaps, of all the entertainments by professionals, the most novel to us and beautiful was what we witnessed at Sorrento. We were then lodging at the Tramontano Hotel, and one evening were informed that we should witness the Tarantala Dance. Round one of the larger rooms chairs were placed for the guests (numbering probably over sixty). When all were assembled, of a sudden two dancers bounded lightly into the room, quickly followed by other pairs—the men dressed in white, with Roman sashes round the waist; women in gay bodices and white skirts, all looking clean and tidy, and very specially got up for the occasion. These young people, to the number of eight, executed a most lively dance to the music performed by others on mandolins, all the dancers being armed with castanets, with which they maintained an incessant click-clack, keeping time to the music. The dance, perhaps invented and practised by Terpsichore herself, and which it would require a master of the art to describe, in general outline somewhat resembled a Scotch reel, but with what I would call Italian variations. It was sprightly and graceful, and the bright dresses added much to the effect. There were several different varieties of the dance, and between the dances we were favoured with some national melodies. One most comical exhibition consisted in the leader, who was a barber of the village, fastening a loose piece of paper behind him, and with this tail floating in the air, he danced or capered about, keeping time to the music, all the others, girls as well as men, running after him with lighted tapers, endeavouring to set this novel tail on fire; but so rapid or rather jerky were his movements, that the paper would not catch fire from the lights, and after a long chase, exciting the constant mirth of the onlookers, he escaped triumphant, and burnt his tail to show it was inflammable. After this, and as a wind up, one of the musicians—an Italian, of course—honoured us, flavoured by some peculiar linguistic embellishments, calculated to evoke an occasional smile, with first 'Yankee Doodle,' and afterwards with a still more uncommon version of 'God save the Queen,' upon which all the company, with the exception (hardly commendable) of a few Americans present, rose to their feet, and a choking feeling of home and of loyalty thrilled through us to hear our national anthem, so sung by foreigners, and so far, it seemed, after our wanderings, from our native land. With this the performance terminated, and the collection began, and was evidently good. For it is by means of a voluntary collection that these professional exertions are usually recompensed. On one occasion, a conjurer having made his collection in the middle of his performance, brought round the plate a second time, which was rather too much.

A more objectionable course to obtain remuneration has sometimes been taken at Mentone, of asking the visitors to buy tickets for a raffle. Of course, each visitor is expected to take at least one ticket (costing usually, I think, 2 francs), and some take a good many, especially when the tickets unsold are set up to a sort of absurd auction, and people in a spirit of fun keep bidding by small amounts against each other. Looking to the proximity of Mentone to Monaco, the origin of the practice may be divined, and it is rather calculated to foster the spirit of gambling which prevails, especially among foreigners, although the things raffled for are necessarily worthless trifles, offering a purely nominal value in exchange for the tickets of the fortunate prizeholders. I presume it is done because it fetches more money to the performers, although ostensibly to give the aspect of not stooping to a collection. But as collections for themselves are, twice a week at least, made abroad by clergymen of the English Church by sending round the plate during service, one can little see why a conjurer should be ashamed or consider it *infra dig.* to receive payment in the same way.

The *entrée*, however, is not always *libre*. On one occasion, at least, bills were sent round to different other hotels that a *matinée musicale* would be held in one of the Mentone Hotels—'*Entrée*, 6 francs *par personne*.' In these cases visitors from other houses are expected.

The guests themselves at the hotels and pensions frequently devise amusement for the company. Sometimes it consists in charades, more or less elaborately conducted, according to circumstances. They are diverting, and create great excitement among the performers in anticipation, realization, and retrospect. In some hotels, there is at one end of a large room a little permanent stage expressly fitted up to enable charades or plays to be performed.

At other times we have had Shakespeare readings, the different members of the party having assigned to each, one or more of the characters of the play; but the difficulty always was, by begging and borrowing, I won't say stealing, to procure a sufficient number of copies of the play, so that each reader might have one. A handy copy of Shakespeare is one of the books which those who go abroad for the winter may with advantage take with them.

On another occasion, at Florence, we had a remarkably nice series of miscellaneous readings by a gentleman of the company. But the most elaborate performance, at least at a hotel, was one at Chateau d'Œx. Here some Americans of the party arranged with showy dresses a very successful performance of the play called 'Popping the Question.' It was capitally acted, and we felt only sorry that the spectators were so comparatively few, although, to increase the number, the performers had invited their friends living in neighbouring pensions.

As I mention this last affair, it is impossible to omit in this connection two grand entertainments we had at Mentone, in the beginning of 1877, of a more public nature. These were two dramatic performances by amateurs, drawn from among the hotel visitors, the leading spirit being Captain Hartley, who was himself a highly-finished actor. They were held in the large room of the *cercle*, or club-house, which has a regular small stage at the one end, and is capable of accommodating between 200 and 300 people, and was hired for the occasion. The performers invited their friends, and so unexpectedly well did they turn out, that the room on the first occasion was more than filled—many, indeed, could not get within either sight or hearing. The performance consisted of two pieces,—the first, 'A Touch of Nature makes the Whole World kin,' and 'Box and Cox.' The plays were executed to admiration. Nothing could have been better than the acting, although it was painful to think that some of the actors were invalids, and were evidently straining their powers too much, and I fear hurt themselves by doing so, and by the labour of getting up their parts and attending rehearsals. But so successful was the performance, that on 3d February the amateurs held another *matinée*, on which occasion the 'Porter's Knot' was acted, which gave an equal amount of satisfaction to all who could witness it. These entertainments were exclusively at the expense of the amateurs. In the following season their success induced the having two more, which met with equal applause.

On occasion of the first performance of all, the *Avenir* (newspaper) of Mentone congratulated the fair little town on its waking up from its torpor in a leading article, in the course of which it said :

'Nos sincères félicitations aux organisateurs de cette charmante fête. Est-ce que Menton songerait enfin à s'amuser ? Bravo, Messieurs ! . . . reveillez un peu cette ville que les autres se donnent tant de peine à endormir. Egayez un peu cette riche colonie étrangère, veritable fortune pour notre beau pays, il faut bien la choyer, l'amuser, et surtout faire de sérieux sacrifices, pour la retenir éternellement sur les bords de cette splendide Méditerranée sous les rayons de ce bienfaisant soleil, sous nos citronniers en fleurs, sous notre beau ciel bleu—la nature a tout fait pour eux . . . à vous de compléter l'œuvre, à vous de les distraire : concerts, bals, spectacles. Voilà l'œuvre que vous devez accomplir. La matinée de lundi est un bien jolis commencement, continuez !'

Attached to nearly all season places, as well as to others frequented by visitors, there is a band of music, which during the season plays in public so many times a day, or so many times a week. In some places it plays twice or even three times a day. In Switzerland, which is a great resort of the Germans, the music seems designed to promote out-of-doors tippling, as the ground about the sheltering pavilion in which the musicians play is dotted over with chairs and little tables, at which these foreigners sit and imbibe and listen, or are supposed to listen, to the strains of the music. Nay, I have been told that the Germans also order beef-steaks and other solids, although long time cannot have elapsed since the last meal at the hotels, or it will not be long till the next meal-time arrives. If one should sit down on a chair, a waiter or waitress immediately comes forward expecting an order. I do not recollect having seen this custom prevailing anywhere in France except at the Gardens in the Champs Elysée in Paris, where professedly the music is given in connection with and to promote the drink. In Switzerland one has sometimes to pay for the music in the shape of a regular daily or weekly tax, which is stated in the hotel bill is authorized to be levied, and which the visitor is bound to pay, although he may have been deaf from his birth. We were required to make such a payment at Ragatz at the Quellenhof Hotel, where the band played morning and evening. At Interlachen, where we spent nine weeks, I found it more advisable to pay for the season, and it cost me 20 francs, which was practically a payment by me towards the support of a German drinking establishment, as I do not think during all the time I was there I looked into the *Kursaal* more than four or five times, and that merely to see if any friend were there. It is unpleasant to those who cannot drink in season and out of season, or who are not used to public potation, to go to such places.

Not having had personal experience of life abroad in villas or furnished rooms, I cannot say much upon this subject. At all season places furnished villas abound, and apartments are to be had, the cost of which necessarily depends upon the locality and the accommodation. I see from the *Avenir de Menton* of 12th December 1877, that one house-agent advertised to have had then to let sixty-five villas in Mentone, varying from four apartments, or *pièces*, as the French term them, up to twenty-four, and ranging in price from 900 francs to 18,000 francs for the season. This list was published after previous demands had been satisfied. How far those on the list may subsequently have been taken up, I do not know; but the season was considered to be a bad one, owing to the general dulness of trade, the continuance of the Eastern War, and the uncertainty as to the state of matters in France arising out of the position held by the governing Powers among themselves. Perhaps something also was due to the fact that a good many new houses had since last season been built, so that there was an extra supply. The villas and apartments are all let for the season; the owners will not let them for a shorter period, because if they were to do so they would run a great risk of not letting them for the remainder of the winter. However, in a dull season somewhat less than what is asked may be taken, and after a house has stood empty for a time it may be had at a reduction. The season at Mentone for so letting, I believe, is nominally eight months, but in reality few people occupy the houses more than five, or at most six months during the winter. During summer months (from about the end of April) Mentone is deserted.

The cost per room seems to range from 200 francs to nearly 800 francs, or about (taking five months' occupation) from 10 to 40 francs per week for each room. A small family house may be had for about from 4000 or 5000 francs, or from £150 to £200, the tenant obtaining nothing but the rooms and furnishing. It is necessary for him to engage servants; and I believe it is indispensable to have French servants in addition to those the family taking the house may bring with them, as English servants, not knowing the language, could not be a means of communication with the natives. These French servants are a source frequently of great annoyance to their employers. They demand a high wage, and as they are not employed during the whole year, perhaps there is some reason for it. A lady at Hyères considered herself particularly fortunate, as no doubt she was, in getting a French servant at 45 francs per month, or at the rate of nearly £24 per year. The amount asked, however, is, I believe, usually very much more. But this is a small matter as compared with other evils; for these servants expect to be employed to make the purchases for the house, and are, it seems, greatly chagrined if they learn that this duty will not fall within their province. The lady of the house may resolve to make her own purchases: she cannot, however, always do so, and finds that she has generally to devolve the work on one of the domestics; and hence, from what I have heard, she often finds that the expense of housekeeping becomes enormously heavy. This may probably arise from the shopkeepers charging in excess in order to afford a commission to the servants. One lady in Mentone, with a family of three young children, who had two English and two French servants, told me it cost her £16 for a single week of housekeeping, though it is possible this may have been an extraordinary week. But this is not all, for the family are exposed, unless they have very reliable servants, to pillage by pilfering and otherwise. The same lady had no doubt there were large quantities of bread and other eatables given away by the servants to their friends, or disposed of, as she could not possibly account otherwise for the quantities which were said to be consumed. These pilferings, however, were not confined to eatables. In *six weeks*, on the house-agent going over the inventory, he made out a bill for 98 francs for breakages. This included 30 plates, 3 teapots, and I know not what else beside. Of course, it was incredible that such an amount of breakage could have taken place even had Caleb Balderstone been in the house, and in frequent fry. There were no traces of it; there had been no report of it; the English servants had never seen it. It was clear that the articles had been appropriated or given away to friends. Such pilfering (of which another friend also complained) may not be the rule —possibly even is the exception; and one friend told me they had most honest native servants. It is well, however, to know that it is a possibility to be guarded against. One of the best safeguards is, besides being very particular as to the character of those engaged, to require them to sleep in the house. If they do not sleep in the house, for which there may not be sufficient room, they ought not to be allowed to bring baskets with them when they come in the morning, to take away when they leave at night.

One curious expense attendant upon the taking of a villa, is a charge which was made by a house-agent at Mentone

(I do not know if it be universal) for making out the inventory of furniture. He charged the tenant 2½ per cent. upon the rent; say, if the rent were £200, £5 for doing so was charged against the tenant. This ought to be a proper charge against the landlord exclusively, but no doubt the landlord suffered a similar charge.

For two or three persons, it is upon calculation of the cost much less expensive, and in every respect more desirable, to take quarters in a hotel, where, if a servant be brought, the usual charge for pension for her or him is 5 francs, or at most 6 francs, and occasionally, though rarely, 4 francs per day. But in the case of a large family, a villa is less expensive and more convenient, especially if the children be young, though it may require the family to be vigilant in looking sharply after their foreign domestics.

While these foreign servants are not always trustworthy, I must add this, that we have found no occasion whatever in France or Switzerland to complain of dishonesty among any of the domestics in any of the numerous hotels in which we have been. We have had our things lying openly about, and have never missed a single article, nor have we heard of any other person suffering loss in this way.

The observation may not perhaps apply so thoroughly to Italy. So much is heard of the petty thievery which prevails in that country, especially in the southern portions of it, that it is by no means proper to expose oneself more than can be helped to lose in this manner; and we were more than usually careful, while in Italy, not to throw temptation in the way. At one house we missed two articles, viz. two pairs of scissors, and could not but suspect that they had been appropriated. It is, however, I suppose, rather the railway men and the professed thieves whom people have most to fear in Italy. One hears every now and then of boxes being opened during railway transit and contents taken, although this may be only in the case of luggage sent by goods train, which in Italy should never be done. The thievery is so open in Naples and surrounding places, that we dared not leave anything exposed in a carriage. Nay, a lady told me that a thief had even the audacity, before her very eyes, to lift a bag out of the carriage in which she was sitting.

III.

LOCAL MEANS OF CONVEYANCE.

I HAPPEN to have kept the billet of a Parisian cabman, on which I find the number is 8973. I believe I have seen *voitures* in Paris bearing a number higher than 10,000. In all probability, however, there is not a licensed carriage to represent each unit of this apparent grand total. When, after many adventures and a long struggle, old age overtakes the *voiture*, and a sudden jolt sends it to smash, a pious regard may preserve the number to its shade; while the new vehicle, its successor, may just be added on to the tail of the list. But be this as it may, there is no lack of carriages of all sorts in all Continental towns.

Elegant private equipages are to be seen in Paris and other parts of France. These are often jobbed by English people. At Nice the charge for a carriage, horses, and man is £30 per month. But Nice is a notoriously expensive place, and I doubt not that in other towns of France the charge is greatly less. Dr. Johnson (p. 67) states that carriages in Pau were to be had, with pair of horses and driver, at £10 to £12 per month. His book, however, was written in 1857, and possibly the charge since that time has been raised.

But it is among the Italians, I think, that the desire

appears more manifested for a good turn-out. In such large towns as Genoa, Rome, or Naples, one sees hundreds of beautiful carriages and fine horses. In fact, it would appear that in Italy every woman aspiring to be considered a lady must, at whatever sacrifice of other comforts, drive her carriage and pair with liveried coachman and man-servant. The Italians seem to consider that it is not *comme il faut* for a lady to be seen walking,—for which, indeed, the climate is not much suited,—and they are rather surprised at observing English ladies going so much about on their own feet. The public vehicles are also of so inferior a description, that one can scarcely wonder at a resident lady being ashamed to be seen in them. I fancy, too, that the expense is not so great as with ourselves. Men-servants' wages must certainly be considerably less, and crops of hay are so abundant, while agricultural labour is so miserably recompensed that the expense of feeding is, no doubt, also much less than at home. Moreover, horse flesh would appear to be greatly cheaper in Italy than with ourselves. At Rome I asked the driver of the carriage in which we went to Tivoli what might be the cost of such a pair of horses as he was driving. They were poor hacks, although they went well. He said about 400 francs, or about £16. I pointed to a handsome pair of horses standing in a private carriage upon one of the streets of Rome, and asked him what they would cost. He said from 1000 to 2000 francs, or from £40 to £80. If this information can be relied on, horse flesh must be cheap enough in Italy. I am not sufficiently skilled in the subject to say whether the breeds are equal to our own, though I doubt it; but they look very handsome animals, and the Italians are careful to allow their tails to grow so as often even to sweep the ground; and in this way the natural grace and beauty of the horse is preserved, while it retains the protection it has received from nature against the attacks of flies, which are a great source of torment in some places.

The cart horses in France are sometimes fine, strong-looking beasts, but are scarcely equal to the more powerful breeds of Britain, although I think they are made to draw heavier loads; and these poor horses do discharge their duty most heroically in spite of the brutal treatment they often receive.

But present observation has rather to do with cabs or carriages which ply for hire.

In France, great variety of carriage is to be had. In such places as Biarritz, Nice, or Mentone, there are many elegant landaus having nearly all the appearance of private carriages, and, no doubt, most of them have been quite recently in private occupation. They are kept in good order and freshly painted, and are the best class. From them there is a descent to various kinds of smaller and inferior *voitures*. The close kind is generally of a very shaky, antiquated construction; although in some places, such as Lyons and Cannes, there is a kind of brougham plying for hire of a better quality, narrow and confined, holding two only, and even two with a squeeze, although some of them (to be seen in Paris) have also a folding down seat for a child. Other carriages have a hood. In Paris, where people are exposed to sudden showers of rain, the one-horse open carriages have an extraordinary huge kind of hood which can be promptly raised, but when turned over, falls so low as almost to extinguish the occupant and to exclude his view; but even then, and with a leathern apron drawn up over the knees, I have found in a storm that adequate protection against rain is not secured. One of the nicest of light vehicles in use is a kind of basket carriage, seated for four, or for two with a *vis-à-vis* folding down seat for one or for two more behind the box, the box seat sometimes holding a fifth, and occasionally there is a light miniature rumble behind holding another. These are drawn for the most part by a pair of smart horses, remarkably small, akin to the active little Exmoor ponies.

The horses always go most willingly, and the drivers delight in urging them at top speed. Regardless of consequences, they dash down a hill in a way which would make an English coachy's hair stand on end, and like a cannon ball through a crowd, without halting or swerving from their course, expecting the crowd to scatter right and left to make way for them. This is all done to the noise of a horrid ear-splitting cracking of the whip. The driver cracks his whip, and considers that having done so, he is discharged of responsibility, and that it is the pedestrian's own fault if he be run over; just as a golfer considers that when he has cried 'faar' before striking his ball, it is the fault of the person struck that he has not got promptly enough out of the way. This cracking of the whip goes on incessantly while the man is with his horse, and even when without, and seems indulged in most frequently from a boyish love of making the odious noise.

There is great variety in these cracks. The crack of the heavy carter's whip differs from that of the coachman's lighter one. There is the single crack, the double or back and fore crack, and the multiple crack, this last being like the dancing noise produced by those alarming crackers placed by mischievous urchins on a Queen's Birthday night under the garments of terrified young women. There is the encouraging crack, supposed to cheer the horse on his way; the crack direct, when the driver applies the lash; the practising crack, when he practises for perfection in this ravishing art; the thoughtless crack, when done in vacancy from mere force of habit; the warning crack, when he wishes pedestrians to yield the smooth part of the road, that he may avoid the rough, or simply that he, the dominant power, may maintain majestically his straight undeviating course; the angry crack, when the supposed humble pedestrian, being an Englishman, disregards the warning crack, thinking that he has as good a right or a better to pursue his way, there being room enough to pass by making a slight deviation from the straight; the annunciating crack, particularly affected by town omnibuses to intimate their approach; and the crack jubilant, employed by the hotel omnibuses when, having bagged a man, the driver thus expends all his bottled-up rapture and announces the joyful event on nearing the door of his hotel. The crack may indicate a cracked driver or a crack one, according as it is the passers-by or the driver himself who forms the opinion, and it is an obviously enviable accomplishment which many can manage with their left hand. The poor horses are expected to disregard all cracks but the crack direct, and to appearance do so; but I can't help thinking that the horrid din is to the animal very much what the buzz of the mosquito is to man, not a *malum in se*, but a sound which proclaims the existence of a torment which at any moment may descend upon its hide. The singular thing, too, is that this noise does not seem to disturb the equanimity either of the driver's own horse or of the other passing horses. With our own high-spirited horses, the mere wag of the whip will make them frantic, and I believe there would be no holding in English horses in a Continental town. Whether it be that the foreign horses are not so high metalled, or get used to the noise, as horses do to passing trains, I do not know, but to the walkers along the streets it is an intolerable nuisance; nor is it altogether without its dangers, as on one occasion a lady of our party all but got her eye struck by a flying lash. The same sort of cracking goes on in Italy; but I noticed that in Florence and Rome, and particularly the latter city, the drivers did it very seldom. Probably to do so was against some police regulation, as from the large number of vehicles with which the streets of Rome are filled, the noise would be deafening, and might even be dangerous.

I was at first inclined to think that the Italian coachmen are kinder to their horses than the French or Swiss. It was long ere I saw an Italian behaving savagely to his horse;

but I have observed it, and been informed by others of the cruel treatment they have seen practised by Italians. I have seen men behaving most savagely to their horses in France and Switzerland. For example, I have frequently seen a carter, or man in charge of a horse or donkey, when he wished it to move on, instead of quietly speaking to it, as even an English carter would, take the butt end of his heavy whip and lay heavily on the poor animal's back, or even give it a violent kick. The carters lade their carts very heavily, and often—I might even say always—beyond the strength of the horse. I have observed a poor horse struggling with all his might to pull the improper load up a hill, the carter encouraging it by the whip all the time. Several times I could not resist speaking to the men about their conduct. On one occasion, at Cannes, I saw a horse, after having struggled to the utmost of his strength with a load twice as heavy as it ought to have been (the bystanders only looking on and giving it no aid), and remaining willing but helpless to do more, when the carter took the narrow end of his heavy whip, and came down twice with his whole force with the heavy-loaded butt end on his horse's head. Ere he could repeat the villanous stroke, I rushed forward, arrested his hand, and told him, in the best French I could muster, what a brute I thought him to be. But it is not easy to give vent to one's indignation in a foreign tongue. The fellow ought to have been prosecuted, and there does exist in France a Society for the Prevention of Cruelty to Animals; but policemen as well as others, I suspect, are as callous to such offences as our own policemen are to the destruction by boys of our meadow or park trees. Cruelty to a horse, however, often consists in little aggravating acts which a prosecution might fail to reach. I have often seen a coachman waiting at a stand, or at a door, and, having idle hands, mischievously proceed to touch up his horses for doing nothing —in short, to vent his own irritation at his idleness upon the poor dumb animals; and then, when they began to caper because of the whip, the whip was again applied because of the caper. However, I am afraid this is an evil habit which is not seldom to be witnessed in our own country. Another method abroad of torturing the horse is by the use of a bearing rein strapped up to the high and heavy saddle or collar borne by the cart horses, which from its weight is also of itself an infliction. But so long as Liverpool dray horses are so tortured, we cannot reasonably complain of bearing reins as a foreign peculiarity. A more extraordinary and hardly credible kind of torture a lady told me she had witnessed was in the passing of a strap or rope through the skin of the horse, compelling him to move on to avoid or lessen the pain so produced. I would fain believe she had been mistaken, but she was one on whose relation I could rely, and whose capacity for observing could scarcely be questioned.

The Italian carriages for hire are very inferior to the French. At Naples they are of the roughest possible kind —open little phaetons made of coarse wood, at some remote period having enjoyed a coat of paint, and exhibiting a barely decent seat for two, and a little folding seat for a third. The Roman carriages are similarly constructed, but a shade better. The drivers in Naples and its vicinity are, as regards person and clothes, the dirtiest-looking ragamuffins. One shrinks to come in contact with them. In Rome, on the other hand, the drivers are generally a respectable-looking class, and they wear a black glazed hat and red cloth waistcoat. The most stylish of coachmen we have seen are those at Biarritz, where they frequently mount a grand blue broidered jacket with scarlet facings; but this grandeur has to be paid for.

At Castellamare and the district round about in the Bay of Naples, and elsewhere in the south of Italy, the horses' heads are decorated with long pheasant feathers, which give them a jaunty look; while in most places the generality of horses have fastened to their collars a string of small bells which keep a continual lively jingle,—genial, doubtless, to the animals,—and are as pleasant as the cracking of whips is odious. About Sorrento, the carriages are often drawn by three horses abreast, three being charged the same as for two. It seems a waste of power, the only explanation given for which was that the horses are not strong. Whatever may be the case in this respect, the horses in Italy always go with the greatest spirit, never seeming to require the lash. I fancy that the jingle of the bells operates as a stimulant. It was very cheery, sitting in our parlour at Sorrento, to hear every now and then the jingle of the bells announcing an arrival or a departure.

Carriage fares for drives about town are moderate almost everywhere. They are more in France than in Italy. Bædeker generally states in his guide-books what the fares are at each town. Although on the whole correct, they are not always to be relied on, probably because of alterations on the tariffs. Sometimes a board or bill of the tariffs is hung up in the carriage, and in some places, such as Paris, the driver is obliged to give the hirer his number on a ticket which specifies the fares. In Paris a one-horse carriage is charged 1·85 per course and 2·50 per hour during the day, and 2·50 and 3 francs respectively during *nuit*, or the hours of darkness. A little more is charged if the *voiture* be taken from the *remise*, that is, the stables. There do not appear to be two-horse carriages plying for hire upon the streets of Paris. When one is wanted, it must be sent for to the stables, and I believe that the charge is heavy. Fares in Paris, however, are higher than in the provinces. At Lyons the fare per course is 1·25; if taken by the hour, it is only $1\frac{1}{2}$ francs per hour in the city, and the same at Pau, but at Mentone and elsewhere fares are rather more. A large carriage with two horses is at Mentone 1·75 per course and 3·50 per hour during the day, and 2 francs and 3·75 respectively during *nuit*. A one-horse carriage is 1·25 per course and 2·50 per hour during the day, and 25 centimes more after dark. If, however, one has to ascend a height in a town, he is sure to have to pay extra. For example, we were charged extra for ascending Fourvières at Lyons, and the Chateau at Nice, although driving per hour. If there be more than a single place to go to, it is always cheaper to take the carriage by the hour. If when driving by the course a stoppage be made by the way, it is not unusual to charge as for two courses. At the same time, Continental drivers are quite up to the trick of English coachmen, when put upon hour-driving, of crawling along. We were somewhat amused at Sorrento (where the horses are invariably put upon full speed), upon taking a carriage by the hour to Massa, a few miles off, to see how the man leisurely walked his horse the whole way. Nor, in this instance, did we grudge it; because the scenery was so lovely that we had full time to enjoy it, and the rapid whisking through it, which otherwise would have taken place, would have given us but a passing glimpse.

In Italy the cab fares are exceedingly moderate. For instance, at Genoa, Florence, and Rome, the drive per course is only 80 centessimi (8d.). At Rome, for every person beyond two, 20 centimes (2d.) additional is payable. The charge per hour is 1·50. At Naples, fares are even more moderate. The course, according to Bædeker, is 60 centimes per hour, 1·40 the first hour and 50 centimes every half-hour after; but we found the actual tariff was slightly more.

One requires to be careful, especially in Italy, about driving per hour in a town, not to go unnecessarily beyond its bounds, as when this is done the tariff is no longer binding, and the fare may be completely at the mercy of the driver. Thus, at Florence, we had on one occasion taken a carriage by the hour, and after driving about for some time, went to

Fiesole, which lies beyond the bounds. When we came to settle with our driver, he charged us three or four francs additional on this account. At Naples, where one may very easily exceed the bounds, I was amused at the pertinacity of a driver in suggesting to go to places just beyond the city; but as I had made myself acquainted with its limits, and had no wish at that time to go to the places he named, I declined. The way to adopt when designing to go beyond the bounds is, as we arranged always at Rome, to make an express bargain that the charge by time should cover wherever we went.

It is a custom on the part of the drivers, notwithstanding their fares are fixed or agreed upon, to expect over and above what they call in France and Switzerland a *pour boire*, and in Italy *buono manu*. This is a provoking addition to a regulated fare. No doubt it is left in the discretion of the traveller, and he may give as much as he pleases, although it is said that in Italy the giving of too much is often regarded as symptomatic that the giver is soft and may fairly be asked for more. But the giving of too little will at once meet with a remonstrance. It is frequently a difficulty to know exactly what it should be. It is expected as a matter of right by the French coachman; it is begged for by the Italians. The best course is always to arrange, in the case of a special drive, that the charge bargained for shall include everything, as the French express it *tout compris;* and if you are pleased with the man's attention, any gratuity over and above will be unexpected. But in Italy, even although you have arranged upon the footing of *tutti compressi*, the driver will sometimes beg for a *buono manu*. So accustomed are they to this description of beggary, that I have seen a coachman, before he even knew what I had put into his hand (which was a half franc more than his fare upon a short ride upon the footing of *tutti compressi*), beg for a *buono manu*.

The fares which are charged for going to given places beyond a town, are often out of all proportion to the fares within town—*i.e.*, if charged according to the time occupied, they would be greatly in excess of a time charge. It is difficult to understand a good reason for this, as in town they might be standing long idle for chance fares; while going to a given place, occupying so many hours, is just so much constant employment. Nor is it constant driving, because nobody goes to see a place without stopping at it for some time, and perhaps even making other stoppages by the way. It is just a custom to expect a 'fat job' out of such a drive. One owes it no less to oneself than to those who come after, not to give too much, and really sometimes the fares asked are exorbitant. For instance, when we wanted a carriage to go from Interlachen to Chateau d'Œx (which we accomplished in twelve hours, stopping by the way from two to three hours for dinner, and with several other stoppages of same duration, and going at a rate seldom exceeding five miles per hour), one man wanted 150 francs, or £6; others, 100 francs. I ultimately arranged with a man for 90 francs, with a *pour boire*, which came to 5 francs more. So little fatigued were his horses, that they were driven back to Interlachen next morning, and in all probability a return fare was obtained for at all events part of the way. The sum charged for these journeys includes the feeding of man and horses, and all hotel charges in connection with the vehicle, which are borne by the owner of the carriage, and cost him little, although, were they paid by the traveller, a large addition would be made to the expense—a method of arrangement which ought to be universal. The fares are computed by distance on some odd and unequal principle. I was told afterwards that if we had taken the boat on Lake Thun to Spiez, or about an hour's distance from Interlachen, I could have had a carriage from Spiez to Chateau d'Œx for about one-half what I paid from Interlachen.

It is principally at the Swiss Passes, however, that the

exorbitant fares are demanded. For example, at Bellagio, the hotel charge for a carriage and pair from Colico to Coire, where there is a railway to Zürich, is 200 francs; 300 francs for three horses, without which it is hardly possible to ascend the mountains; and 380 francs for four horses. The journey involves—the first day, about three hours' travelling by coach from Colico to Chiavenna, where we slept; ten hours the second day, ascending by zig-zags to the top of the mountain, and then down to Splugen, and halting two or three hours out of the ten at Campo Dolcino for rest and lunch; and the third day, starting from Splugen at 8 A.M., getting by a gentle descent through the Via Mala, and stopping two or three hours at Thusis for lunch, we reached Coire about 4 o'clock, or eight hours altogether. As I knew that the fares asked were excessive, I went by steamboat to Colico a day previous to our leaving, and readily arranged, after some bargaining, for an excellent carriage and good pair of horses, with a third for the mountains (we actually had four part of the way) for 150 francs, with the inevitable *buono manu*. When we reached Splugen, finding that a gentleman who accompanied us was going to Ragatz, I proposed we should go there too, instead of proceeding from Coire to Zürich by railway. Our friend unfortunately spoke about it to the landlord, who immediately impressed on our coachman, who was also the proprietor of the carriage, that the proper fare for the additional distance was 35 francs, a distance which I afterwards found took us less than two hours to accomplish (it was down hill most of the way). I refused to give such a figure for the addition to our drive, as we could have gone by rail for a few francs; but on nearing Coire, I spoke to the driver and arranged to give him 30 francs additional, inclusive of the *buono manu*, for the whole journey, which we thought would require to be from 12 to 15 francs. It was too much, but it saved stopping an hour at Coire for a train and shifting our luggage. So confirmed, however, is the habit of asking a *buono manu*, that, in the face of my express arrangement after paying the man his 180 francs, he had the assurance to ask me for it.

It is always best, on going a long drive, to make a very express and explicit arrangement, and in Italy to make it in writing, so that there may be no room for mistake or dispute; and it is also well to see the carriage and horses you are to have, and to make sure the horses are properly shod. Generally, it is better to arrange for a carriage oneself. For instance, the landlord of our hotel at Castellamare said the charge for a carriage to Pompeii would be 12 or 15 francs. I arranged for one for 8 francs. At the same place, his charge was 10 francs to Sorrento, exclusive of *buono manu*, which would be 2 francs more. As I knew I could easily get a carriage for less, I told him I would not give more than 8 francs, with *buono manu*, and the carriage was at once sent for; but even this was more than the fare mentioned in Bædeker (6 francs). On return from Sorrento, we paid only 8 francs altogether, the regular charge, the landlady of the Tramontano, a clever and attentive Irishwoman, telling us that she made it an express arrangement with the coachman, adding, 'What was the sense of paying more, when we had arranged for a given sum?' In going any distance, it is always well to make inquiry of those who may know something on the subject as to what the fares ought to be, and as to the route.

Sometimes hotelkeepers make such excessive demands as practically to be prohibitive. Thus at Baveno we found the charge for a carriage and pair for a simple drive to be 8 francs the first hour and 5 francs for each hour thereafter. At Chateau d'Œx, in other respects one of the cheapest places we have visited, we were told by some of the young people at the hotel, that, wishing to go one evening to have a dance at a neighbouring pension in the village, not an eighth of a mile distant, but on an acclivity, the hotelkeeper asked for the double drive no less than 20 francs. They therefore gave up the idea of going. The only possible excuse for this exorbitant demand might be, that the road was rough for night driving, but carrying a couple of lamps would have put that all right.

Fares everywhere have, however, been increased of late years. Speaking from recollection, I think that at Interlachen, for a drive which is now charged 25 francs, we were charged fifteen years previously only 15 to 18 francs, and other charges in proportion.

It used to be considered that for four persons it was at least as cheap to take a carriage as to pay for four places in a diligence. If this was so formerly, it is no longer so, as it is less expensive to go by diligence. I imagine that the fares by diligence either have not been increased, or have been only slightly raised. We paid for the journey from Lucerne to Interlachen, inclusive of steamboats on the lakes of Lucerne and Brienz, 13 francs 90 centimes each for inside places and cabin, the journey taking 10 hours; from Chateau d'Œx to Aigle, occupying about $4\frac{1}{2}$ hours of mountain travelling, 8 francs 25 centimes. In either case it would have cost us considerably more to have hired. Bædeker mentions the diligence fares from Coire to Colico to be for *coupé* 27 francs 90 centimes, and for *intérieur* 24·50; so that for four passengers travelling by diligence, the fare would not exceed 112 francs; for six passengers, 168 francs, instead of the 300 or 380 francs demanded by the hotels, which no doubt affords them a heavy profit. Travelling by diligence is, however, not always desirable, as often part of the journey may have to be performed during night, or at uncomfortable hours. Diligences are now nearly driven off the field by the railways, except in such countries as Switzerland. The Swiss *Indicateur* contains a long list of the diligence routes and their time bills, and *Continental Bradshaw* furnishes a still longer list under the head, 'Diligences, Post and Mail Coaches, Germany, Switzerland, and North Italy,' with, in most cases, the fare payable.

I do not think that steamboat travelling is cheap—*e.g.*, we paid 7 francs each on the Lake of Geneva from Montreux to Geneva, taking three hours. On Lake Como the fare from Bellagio to Como, about two hours, was 2 francs 80 centimes, or about 5s. there and back. From Sorrento to Capri and back was 5 francs. I received a curious answer from the captain of the steamboat to Capri to my question what would be the fare to go from Sorrento to Naples; he replied, 'Whatever you please.' We were informed at Sorrento that if one of the two rival boats which usually go from Naples to Capri do not sail, the passengers are in the power of the boat which does sail, and may be asked for what the captain pleases, which is sure to be something different from what pleases the passenger.

The sailings of the steamboats are to be found in the *Indicateurs*. On Lake Como a convenient little flyleaf guide for the lake sailings is sold on board at the price of 5 centessimi (one halfpenny).

Most towns have their town omnibuses. In Paris there is a system of 'correspondence,' by which the passenger leaves his omnibus at certain stations and gets (with the same ticket) into another to prosecute his route. But this correspondence is puzzling to a stranger, who will always find it better to take a cab and drive direct to his destination.

Tramways are beginning to be introduced, with carriages similar to our own, but are generally placed in streets where they will as little as possible interfere with other traffic.

In some towns of Italy, such as Milan, there are laid stone-ways, being two parallel courses of flat stones, each course perhaps about a foot broad, embedded in the causeway and on the same level, on which the wheels of carts and carriages run smoothly. It has sometimes struck me that such a system of stone tramways without grooves, on which all carriages could run, and which would not catch their wheels, would be preferable for the streets of hilly cities at home, for which tram rails, especially in its busy thoroughfares, are entirely unsuitable. All the smoothness of the tramway would be obtained without its danger to life, its injury to carriages, and its interference with ordinary traffic; while the huge, clumsy, box-looking, road-filling cars would give place to a set of light omnibuses of sufficient number. The luxury of travelling a mile in a larger car could not be placed in the balance.

There are other means of conveyance, such as donkeys and gondolas, which will be more appropriately referred to when I come to speak of the places where they are used.

IV.

POSTAL ARRANGEMENTS.

By treaty agreement, the postage rates for the Continent are now very much reduced from what they used to be, and are comparatively moderate, although to those who write much the expense becomes in the aggregate a considerable item of travelling expenditure. Single postage from England to France, Switzerland, and Italy, and I think to most Continental countries, is $2\frac{1}{2}$d., and to this rate the Continental countries on letters to England conform as nearly as their coinage permits. But in France and Italy, taking advantage of the fact that a franc is between $9\frac{1}{2}$d. and 10d., they charge 30 centimes, or about 3d.;[1] so that the price of four stamps in these countries is close upon 1s., instead of being 10d., as with ourselves. Single postage on letters for the Continent covers one-half ounce in England; abroad it covers 15 grammes, which seems to be the precise equivalent. Little pocket letter-weighers are sold in France at 1 franc and $1\frac{1}{2}$ francs, containing a scale marked in grammes by which letters can be conveniently weighed, and for prolonged

---

[1] Since this chapter was written, alterations have been made on the French postal rates, and, *inter alia*, the postage to England is reduced to 25 centimes, and for the interior to 15 centimes; but I have allowed the text to stand as referring to the time we were away. There may be other changes of which I am not aware.

residence are all but indispensable. If a letter posted in England be insufficiently stamped, the post office abroad charges the recipient with double the postage the letter ought to have borne according to the foreign rate, deducting the amount of the stamps which it carries. Thus, if a person in England put by mistake a penny stamp upon a single letter, the French Government charge double the 30 centimes and deduct the penny paid, so that the recipient has to pay 5d. upon the letter. If the letter have been stamped with $2\frac{1}{2}$d. postage, but exceeds the half ounce, the recipient pays 1s., less the $2\frac{1}{2}$d., or $9\frac{1}{2}$d. altogether (more correctly, 95 centimes). It is astonishing how many blunders friends at home make in this respect. Over and over again have we had to pay for them. If people are not acquainted with the foreign postage, they ought to study the postal guides, and in event of any difficulty to make inquiry at a post office. One lady told me she had summed up what these mistakes had cost her in one winter, and found they came to 11 francs.

Newspapers posted in England require a penny stamp, but abroad are reckoned by weight. The small Continental papers go for 5 centimes, or one halfpenny; but in France, at least, English newspapers always cost one penny or 10 centimes.

The rate in France for registering a letter to England is 5d. (50 centimes), while it was 4d. in England, being another instance of the way in which the French take advantage of the small difference between our monetary values. The reduction in England of fee to 2d. applies to foreign as well as inland letters.

Letters for the interior are always less than for abroad. In France, where postage is high, the rate was 25 centimes (now 15 centimes) to any part of France except the district in which the letter was posted, when it was 15 centimes, possibly now less. For book delivery in town, the French have a 2 centimes rate, and in Italy there is a similar rate for newspapers for the interior.

Post cards are usually one-half of letter rates. Thus a French post card to England is 15 centimes ($1\frac{1}{2}$d.), as against our $1\frac{1}{4}$d. But in Switzerland, where postage is cheap,—there being half rates for letters,—and in Italy, post cards for England are only 1d. (10 centimes). English people always familiarly call a 10 centime piece a penny, which in size as well as in value it resembles.

Letters are, I think, delivered with great accuracy. I have only known of two letters which have not reached us during the whole time we were away, and one of these was misaddressed. Newspapers, on the contrary, have not, in France, reached us with the same regularity as letters. This has been attributed to the French Government being jealous of newspapers from Great Britain containing animadversions upon its policy, and during the French crisis of the autumn of 1877, we regularly missed a *Scotsman*, once a week, sometimes of a Tuesday, but more commonly of a Thursday, when, if there were no leading article touching upon the French Government, we fancied it might contain some gleanings from *Punch*. As *Punch* carries a free lance and hesitates not to strike whatever is vulnerable, it is, I suppose, fully more exposed to be stopped than any ordinary newspaper; but in spite of precaution, it finds its way abroad even when stopped.

The stoppage of newspapers, while it can do no manner of good, produces a good deal of irritation and ill-will on the part of the English. I believe that the attention of the French Parliament has been called to it, and latterly we found greater regularity. Of course, in many cases newspapers may miscarry from addresses being insufficient or getting torn off. It is always safer to write on the newspaper itself; and if a cover be used, the newspaper stamp must not connect the cover with the paper, otherwise it is liable to be charged as a letter.

When the hotel at which to stop has been decided upon, it is best to direct letters to be delivered at it. If not so fixed upon, it is usual to address letters to the *Poste Restante*, where they are got upon exhibition of a visiting card; but in some places the post is very particular, and perhaps rightly so. Thus, in San Remo, I was desired to give my card to the *facteur* (postman) in whose beat our quarters were, and the letters would be delivered at the house. In Paris, I was refused letters for my wife without a written authority from her. In other large towns, the rule is to ask for passport; and if the inquirer have no passport, he must prove his identity in a manner satisfactory to the post clerk, as by exhibition of envelopes of letters received elsewhere, or otherwise—regulations most reasonable for the security of the recipients.

Registered letters are treated with peculiar care. In France, the postman declines to give up such a letter except into the hand of the person to whom it is addressed, who signs his name in a book kept for the purpose, with date of reception, etc. If he do not happen to be in the house at the time, the postman takes away the letter, marks 'absent' upon it, and brings it back at succeeding deliveries till he find him. In Italy, they are even more particular. At Milan, I received at the hotel an intimation from the post office that a registered letter was lying there for me. In order to procure this letter, I was under the necessity of going personally to the post office, a good way off, and of taking with me a certificate by a resident in Milan of my identity. I knew nobody residing in Milan, but the landlord of the hotel was kind enough to sign the document. Delivering this document, I was also required to exhibit my passport to the post office, and then to sign my name in a book kept there for the purpose. These precautions, although troublesome to the traveller, make registered letters very secure; and all letters transmitting money orders ought to be registered and put in firm, tough envelopes, for I believe that letters are sometimes lost in consequence of the thinness of the foreign letter envelopes in which, for the sake of lightness, they are generally enclosed.

On leaving a town, the new address should be given to the post office or to the *concierge* of the hotel, and letters will then be readdressed and forwarded free of charge. Occasionally, we have found them forwarded to three or four successive addresses before receipt by us, and that without any extra payment, which would not be the case in England. Nay, I have discovered, though only after many postages had unfortunately been paid on the readdress in England, that letters arriving in England from a colony, say New Zealand, may be readdressed to the address abroad without charge,—a fact, therefore, well worthy of being noted. After a lapse of time, whether done by the post office at request of the landlord or *concierge* of the hotel or not, we could not tell, letters have been opened and returned to the writers, from whom we have received them reinclosed and restamped about a month after we had left the place to which they were originally addressed.

Tradesmen, on seeing arrivals announced in the lists, send in their business cards; and a circular of this kind, posted to our hotel at Cannes, stamped with 15 centimes district postage, was forwarded to us at Mentone. On this, 25 centimes ($2\frac{1}{2}$d.) had to be paid, showing a difference in the treatment of interior letters, which may be explained in this way, that the letter was not originally insufficiently stamped, and there was not, therefore, excuse for charging it double.

The French have a good system in regard to letter pillars which might with advantage be adopted by ourselves. When the postman has made his collection from the pillar box, he turns a dial, which indicates that that particular collection has been made; *e.g.*, suppose he has taken the first collection upon a Wednesday, the dial bears: 'Mercredi, la première levée est faite.' And this is particularly necessary in France, because the postmen are by no means particular in adhering to the time fixed for making the collection. Day after day have I seen the notice up half an hour before the collection was due, obliging one either to post early, or to go to the general post. The French letter pillars are small wooden boxes stuck upon a wall, pretty well out of reach of mischievous urchins; but their slits are very narrow, and will not admit of an ordinary English newspaper.

French postmen, for protection and security, carry their letters for delivery in a box suspended by a strap round the neck like a pedlar's tray, and registered letters are kept in a separate pocket or portion of the box. The newspapers and book packets (often immense bundles) are simply carried bound together by a strap.

It is astonishing with what rapidity letters and newspapers are received from home. London newspapers are received at Biarritz on the afternoon of the day following publication. At Venice it takes a day longer, and some places not so distant are, in consequence of the arrival of the post late in the evening, just as long. Thus, while the London newspapers are delivered at Nice the evening of the day after publication, they are not delivered at Mentone till the following morning, because they arrive after the last postal delivery at Mentone. When the mail is accelerated, as no doubt it will be in time, this delay will be remedied; but the practical effect is that letters and newspapers posted in Edinburgh upon a Monday before five o'clock are delivered in Nice upon Wednesday evening, but are not delivered in Mentone until Thursday morning. At Venice or Rome they are delivered on the Thursday. Letters posted on a Saturday are always one day longer, in consequence of there being no despatch from London on the Sunday; so that, leaving Edinburgh on Saturday, they are not delivered in Mentone till Wednesday morning. Newspapers are often a post later, and not delivered till the second or evening delivery; for in Mentone, as in many other places, there are only two deliveries in the day.

V.

SUNDAY ABROAD.

SUNDAY is kept abroad with various degrees of propriety. As a rule, it is a gala day—a fete day, and to certain classes of servants it only brings additional toil. There is no distinction, as with ourselves, unless in rare and exceptional cases, between railway trains on Sunday and trains on week-days; and, in point of fact, I believe there is more travelling on Sundays than on other days of the week. Work and business are not wholly suspended, but there are fewer carts upon the streets. In many places, workmen may be seen engaged in their employments, at all events till dinner-time, just as usual. Shops are nowhere wholly closed, at least during the earlier part of the day. But the generality of the natives attend a morning service, and afterwards walk about in their Sunday clothes; so that in large towns the streets are crowded by lounging saunterers, or scarcely less idle sight-seers. It is gratifying to observe that wherever English people form a large admixture of the population, as at Cannes, Mentone, and Pau, a greater external reverence is paid to the day than elsewhere, and particularly in the matter of closing shops. Possibly in some cases this may result from finding it is not worth while to open them, as the principal customers would not enter and transact, but let us hope that it springs from a growing influence for good. In Paris, during and after the reign of the Commune, I believe all shops were open; but they are now, year by year, getting to be more and more closed.

In Mentone the washerwomen appear to suspend operations on Sundays. It is probable that they strive to get all the linen committed to their care sent home by the end of the week to the ladies, who require their things by that time to be ready. But I have occasionally seen one or two washing away as usual, even in heavy rain; and I fancy, from appearances, they were then purifying their own garments.

To what extent theatres are open, I have no means of stating. I believe that in Paris and other large French towns, if not elsewhere, the theatres are in full operation.

In places where musical bands play, as at Interlachen, the music proceeds just as on ordinary days—once, twice, or three times a day, according to the custom of the place; but it gathers to it all the idlers, and is therefore generally listened to by far greater crowds than during the week. Nor is the music different in character from what is usually performed. There is no attempt to compromise matters by playing sacred tunes. Not improbably, in some places, there may be a better selection of secular music than usual; 'classical music' may be attempted. At Cannes, although it is a thoroughly English settlement, the band plays on Sunday near the Mairie. At Mentone the playing took place outside the *cirque*, near to some of the churches, so that the worshippers had to pass by it to reach them.

Where there are Galleries or Museums, Sunday is usually an open or free day, no payment being exacted. At Naples the Museum, and at Florence the Picture Galleries and the grounds of the Royal Pitti Palace, are open to the public, the only other day in the week on which the Museum and Galleries are free being Thursdays. Ascension Day, however, seems to be regarded as more holy than Sunday, for it happened at Florence, while we were there, and falling upon a Thursday, the Galleries were closed. The Louvre in Paris is open on Sunday, but is closed on Monday, to be cleaned. The Capitoline Museum in Rome (belonging to Government) is open on Sundays gratis, but as a rule galleries as well as shops are closed on Sundays in Rome.

The Casino at Monte Carlo is always open on Sundays, and was a source of attraction to many of the foreign visitors at Mentone, and sometimes, though more rarely, even to such English people as were not very strict in their views.

The Carnival proceeded at Nice the same as on the other day or days on which it was held. It was probably then a grander affair, and I believe drew to it much greater crowds—many, though not many English, going to see it from Mentone, and, no doubt, from all the surrounding parts.

Sunday, indeed, is regarded as a fete day. In the times of the Empire I found it, on occasion of my first visit to Paris, to be the day of the great Fête Napoleon. It was also the day for illuminations, and for playing the Grandes-Eaux at Versailles. The same practice prevails elsewhere. At Rome there was on one Sunday during our visit an illumination of the Piazza del Popolo, and a balloon was sent up in the course of the evening. At Pau also our attention was called one Sunday afternoon to an immense balloon descending, with a man suspended from it by ropes—a most perilous-looking adventure, and by no means an agreeable spectacle, though we were not near enough to see the man distinctly. Throughout France the elections take place on the Sunday, and possibly it is the same elsewhere. In Italy and in Paris, as well as in other places, people expend a portion of their earnings in driving about in cabs and other vehicles plying for hire. One summer, a few years ago, we spent a fortnight in the Champs Elysées, and found that on Sunday evening they were, if possible, more brilliantly lighted up, and more gay and noisy, than on other nights; but I think the great spectacle then to be seen was derived from the multiplicity of *voitures* driving up and down, two rows one way and two rows another, in continuous line. As each carries either one or two lights (I am not sure which, but I think two), and as nothing at a little distance but the lights is seen, the effect is curious. The broad roadway seems from the Place de la Concorde to the Triumphal Arch to be filled with an incessant stream of Will-o'-the-wisp-like lights noiselessly flitting up and down the course.

Letters are delivered by the post either as usual on the rest of the week, or at all events on the Sunday morning, but my impression is that there is no difference in the deliveries. When there were any letters to annoy us, they were sure to come on a Sunday morning, so that often we wished there had been no delivery.

In hotels at home, with a laudable view to lessen the work of servants and give opportunity to them to go to church, visitors who have private rooms are often requested to dine on Sundays at the public table, and I have heard of no less than thirteen newly-married couples at one of the English lake hotels having thus one Sunday complied. As people abroad are little in the habit of dining in private rooms, there is not scope for this observance. But Sunday is always regarded as a day for a somewhat better dinner than usual. Sometimes, if not on the ordinary programme, it is in the shape of a course of ices, or it may be some other rarity.

The employment of the evening depends upon the company. The English, as a rule, observe Sunday abroad much as they do at home, except, of course, that being in a hotel, they are thrown more into living in public. Many retire to their rooms and read. But often before they do so, in hotels frequented by them,—particularly if exclusively so,—the young people, led by some one at the piano, will join in singing hymns. Even in hotels where foreigners are the principal visitors, English people present will sometimes strike up a hymn. This takes place usually to the apparent enjoyment of the foreigners, who seem not to know what to do with themselves on Sunday. They do not read, at least to the extent to which the English do. It is not unusual for them to have recourse to cards, or drafts, or chess, while their children romp about in a way at which we should be scandalized at home. Occasionally a visitor will play and sing at the piano secular tunes and songs, though when our countrywomen go to the piano they rarely select anything but sacred pieces.

One Sunday evening I recollect its being announced that there would be a concert by professional musicians in the *salon*, from which, before the concert began, nearly all the English quietly withdrew. It was not repeated in the same house while we were there.

In travelling, those who desire to have a book for Sunday reading, ought to take one or more such books with them. They are not procurable in shops or in circulating libraries. Possibly they may be, though probably not of a high class, at Tract Dépôts; but where these depots are to be found, may not always be easy to learn. However, in season places the churches have generally small libraries attached to them, which are useful to those who are there for the season. A passing traveller of course cannot avail himself of them. It is not a bad plan to have the monthly magazines sent by book post to one's foreign address, and when read they may prove very acceptable gifts to others.

It was not often that we were induced by curiosity to go into a Roman Catholic Church on a Sunday. The proceedings are unintelligible to the uninitiated, and the service seems to be all performed for the people by the priests, who are 'the Church.' Where there is singing or vocal music, it is done by the priests alone, aided by boys, and sometimes, though very rarely, by women. I recollect, when in Antwerp many years ago, on occasion of some great festival the choir was augmented by a number of (concealed) female singers with the sweetest voices. But the congregation never joins in the singing. They listen, just as congregations do at home to anthems performed by choirs, which it would require a knowledge of music, acquaintance with the piece, a music book, and a good voice to enable them to take part in. The service is conducted by the priests, with their backs to the people, these backs being generally covered with an ornamented dress, sometimes exhibiting an inserted cross in colours, sometimes white satin with rich gold embroidery, but varying according to the rank held by the priest, and according to the place, and doubtless according, in some churches, to the importance of the day. The chief priest appears to be reading a large book before him on the altar, and mumbling something to himself; and every now and then he and they (when more than one) perform a genuflexion or change position, and sometimes he turns round to the audience and says something inaudibly, while a boy tinkles a bell as a signal to the people at certain stages of the service. The ceremony is familiar to all who have been abroad. This priest service is no doubt intended, with other things, to exalt the priesthood and to swell its power, the grasp and severity of which the world has unfortunately too often felt. It is only right, however, to say that the people listen devoutly, and seem to know something at least of what is going on, and can follow it and understand when to rise up and when to kneel down. Many of them hold in their hands the book containing the service, which is printed both in Latin and in their own tongue; and were this book (after which the Prayer Book of the Church of England is modelled) purged of some erroneous matters, such as the prayers to the Virgin Mary and Saints, it contains a service to the words of which Protestants probably could not object. Mass sometimes begins very early in the morning; and after it has been said by the priest (I think it does not take much longer than half an hour), the congregation clears out and is succeeded by another, which pours in, before whom the service is repeated. People who have so heard mass apparently consider they have done their duty for the day so far as church worship is concerned.

When a priest preaches, which seems to be only rarely, and possibly only when he has the faculty, he mounts the pulpit, by his side in which a large crucifix is stuck, and addresses the people shortly but with great animation, his eloquence increasing like the Welsh preachers as he proceeds, till he reaches his climax in such a fervent heat that the perspiration will burst from his brow. No doubt he succeeds in stirring his auditors, but I never could make out sufficiently what was said to know exactly the purport of discourse. But the blessed Virgin is frequently invoked.

Roman Catholicism, however, must be losing ground fast, as the people increase in knowledge and desire to be free from clerical yoke; and it is astonishing to what an extent Protestantism, everywhere tolerated now, prevails in countries formerly so pope and priest ridden. A book, called *A Guide to Evangelical Work on the Continent of*

Europe, and on the Southern and Eastern Shores of the Mediterranean, published by the Committee of the Foreign Evangelical Society (London: James Nisbet & Co., 21 Berners Street; Paris: 4 Place du Théâtre Français, Rue de Rivoli), gives an idea of the extent of this work.[1] I have tried to make up some statistics from it, but have not found my results to agree in numbers with the prefatory notes prefixed to some of the sections. I observe, however, that in France the Reformed Church, under the control of the State, is by far the largest of the Protestant denominations, and it is stated in the guide to consist of 483 parishes and 573 pastors. But on reckoning up the churches named in the book, it seems only to mention 124 Reformed Churches. Probably the explanation is that all parishes are not given. Of the Church of the Augsburg Confession, or Lutheran Church, there seem to be 63; of the Methodists, 7; of the Société Evangélique de France, 25; of the Société Centrale, 70; of the Wesleyan Church, 39; of the Free Church, 63; Independents, 6; Baptists, 6; Société Evangélique de Genève, 14; Society of Friends, 1; other denominations, 11 churches or stations. In all these the service is in the native French, and intended for the natives, and there is not a town of any importance in which there is not one or more of the different denominations represented by a church, so that it will be seen that Protestantism must be spreading and taking a deeper hold on the people. In Paris alone there are, *inter alia*, the following French Protestant churches:— Reformed Church, 19; Lutheran, 16; Evangélique de France, 7; Baptist, 1; French Wesleyan, 6. The native population, besides, throughout France, is reached by a

---

[1] The *Guide*, arranged alphabetically, contains information regarding the following countries and places:—Austria, Belgium, Denmark, France, Germany, Greece, Holland, Italy, Norway, Portugal, Russia, Spain, Sweden, Switzerland, Turkey in Europe, and the Mediterranean. In Denmark and Greece the number of Protestant churches is very limited. The Mediterranean embraces fifty-four towns, including towns in Egypt and Palestine.

multitude of Protestant or Evangelical associations and institutions and schools, such as Young Men's Christian Associations, mission homes, orphanages, etc., and there are not less than 85 Bible or Tract Dépôts. I state all these figures *salvo justo calculo*, and with the impression that they only represent a portion of the work, and they are at least short of the figures given in the prefatory 'note' on the Protestant Churches of France.

In some cases, as at Biarritz, French service is conducted in the English Church; in others, as at Lucerne and Chateau d'Œx, the English service is held in the native Protestant Church.

At Mentone, the French Protestant Church, under the pastoral care of a most worthy man, M. Delapierre, is largely attended by English-speaking people. Indeed, I would say that English, Scotch, and Americans of all denominations form during the season by far the principal part of the congregation. We used almost regularly to attend this church during one of the Sunday services, going to one of the other churches for the other service. A layman commenced by reading a short liturgy or formulary of devotion, then a portion of Scripture, and, having given out a hymn or canticle, as it is termed, left the pulpit, and the minister taking his place, after extempore prayer, preached a sermon. M. Delapierre spoke slowly and distinctly, and it was easy, comparatively, to follow him. His thoughts were always good and striking, though simple, often rising to an elevated and earnest eloquence, calculated to make a deep impression. He was much respected and esteemed by all, but unfortunately was, or rather is, a man of delicate health; so that he only took one of the Sunday services, and had for a short time to leave Mentone for relaxation and change of air. His assistants (young men) we never could follow so well. Hymn-books, with the canticles set to music, were placed in all the pews; and generally at the close of the service a doxology was sung, being a verse commencing, 'Gloire soit au Saint Esprit,' to the tune called Hursley, the old German melody to which the hymn 'Sun of my Soul' has been wedded. There is a striking and puzzling peculiarity in the French singing, for the words are not sung as spoken. Thus *père* is pronounced *peray*. The singing also is in slow time. The Communion was dispensed on the first Sunday of the month, all who desired being, without distinction of sect, invited to attend, and was conducted very much in the same way as in Congregational churches at home.

We once witnessed in this church the baptism of an infant. The father and mother, nurse and baby, and another man and woman—all stood up in front of the reading-desk below the pulpit, to which M. Delapierre descended, and took the baby, which had been squalling, over his left arm. Holding up his hand, and looking down upon it, its great eyes looked up into his either in terror or in wonder, and all was still, not even the water sprinkling disturbing its equanimity. The preliminary service or address seemed to be somewhat long.

No gown or vestment of any kind was used in the church beyond the wearing of black clothes and a white tie, although I believe a gown is worn in many other French churches. Everything was conducted with the reverent simplicity so consistent with true worship. The singing was assisted by a harmonium, amply sufficient for the size of the church, which I suppose might not be seated for many more than two hundred.

In Italy the Waldensian is the largest of the native churches. The *Guide* (p. 159) says:—

'Their missionaries are now found in all parts of Italy. There are 40 churches, some of them small, perhaps, but of living Christians; and there are also 10 missionary stations, with 30 ordained pastors and 20 lay preachers, who visit every month 50 other small towns where there are those friendly to the gospel. There are at present upwards of 2000 converts. This Church, which has 15 parishes in the Waldensian valleys, has a College or Lyceum at Torre Pellice, the capital, and a Theological College at Florence, with three able professors.'

Next to the Waldensian is the Free Christian Church, which 'has taken a position between Presbyterianism and Congregationalism. It has 37 stations and 24 preachers.' After it the Wesleyan Church comes, with 28 stations and as many Italian ministers. There are in Italy 14 Bible or Tract Dépôts.

In Switzerland, Protestant service is conducted in most of the towns by, *inter alia*, the National Reformed Church, the Free Church, the Société Evangélique de Genève. There are 16 Bible or Tract Dépôts throughout the country.

We attended a French service in the church at Chateau d'Œx, and found a peculiarity existing there which perhaps may be characteristic of the native Swiss churches, for all the women were seated on one side, and all the men on the other, as, I believe, is the case with the Society of Friends in Great Britain. Not till it was too late did I discover I was a black sheep among the women. This congregation sat at singing and rose at prayer. The church, a tolerably large one, was quite full, and no doubt many came from a considerable distance.

Having said so much with regard to the native churches, I shall now state a few facts regarding those conducted in English for the benefit of strangers.

There are of American churches in France, 3; in Italy, 3; in Switzerland, 1; of Wesleyan or Methodist, 5 in France, 2 in Italy (not including American Methodist, which are probably Italian churches), and none in Switzerland.¹ Apparently there is but one Congregational church in these three countries, viz. in Paris, where nearly all the above churches stated to be in France likewise are. The remaining English churches are either Scotch Presbyterian or English Episcopalian.

Taking the Scotch Presbyterian first, I ascertain from the *Guide* (by summation), in France 6, in Italy 6, in Switzerland 5—17 churches altogether, but there may possibly be other Scotch services not noted—as, for example, we found a room occupied in Venice which is not a station noted. Of these 17, I find from the *Guide* (comparing it, too, with a card obtained abroad), there are 11 in connection with the Free Church of Scotland; there is only one in connection with the United Presbyterian body; the remaining five are either in connection with the Established Church of Scotland, or are, as in Rome, and as they undoubtedly should be, 'occupied by a minister of the Established, Free, or United Presbyterian Church of Scotland.' It would be much better if all the churches were in connection with all these bodies; and, indeed, there is no reason why they might not take in Independents and Baptists and other denominations, and call it everywhere the 'Scotch Church.' It would strengthen their hands very much, and avoid, at least, the appearance of unnecessary schism. I believe, however, there is an understanding, so far commendable, that where one of the three Presbyterian bodies above named already has a station in a foreign town, neither of the others shall introduce one of their own.

In some places the Presbyterian Churches have a chapel or building devoted to worship, as at Cannes. In others a room is engaged, as at Mentone; and I may here mention that the same thing is found with regard to the Episcopal Churches or stations: frequently a room in one of the

¹ The figures in this chapter are all given subject to correction.

hotels is used, and sometimes, as at Sorrento, is devoted to this use. Where a church has been built by an Episcopalian body, a great deal of space seems often lost, as at Hyères, in the chancel; and in such cases, when the minister retires to its extreme end to read the communion service, his voice is sometimes lost to the congregation.

In Florence, Leghorn, Pau, and perhaps elsewhere, there is a permanent settled minister attached to the Presbyterian Church. At other stations the pulpit is supplied either by ministers sent out for the season, or more generally by ministers requiring to go abroad for health, to whom the chaplaincy is pecuniarily an advantage; but it can scarcely be an advantage in regard of their own health, and it does not tend to secure for the station the best men. However, if this were not done, probably stations might become vacant. At Rome, where there is a large nice church outside the Porto del Popolo, alongside of other Protestant churches, care is taken to send for a short period a man, or rather two men, of recognised ability—a very proper step in such a city, and one which, were it possible, it would be well to take elsewhere. While we were in Rome, we were so fortunate as to have, among others, Mr. Mitchell of Leith, who spoke with great power and eloquence. It was strange and gladdening to think that in the very citadel of Old Giant Pope there was now such perfect freedom of speech.

The English Episcopal Church is necessarily far more largely represented abroad. In fact, there is no town of any importance in which there is not a service conducted according to the forms of this Church. In France, as appearing from the *Guide*, there are 54 stations; in Italy, 23; in Switzerland, 43; in all, 120. Of course in other countries it is similarly, though perhaps not so largely represented, because the three above-named are the principal countries frequented by English travellers, and it is to them the present observations have had exclusive reference.

I do not profess to know much about the operations of the Episcopal Church of England, but I believe that it has two societies in connection with the Continent—the Colonial and Continental Society, and the Society for the Propagation of the Gospel. This last belongs to the High Church or Ritualistic party.

Ritualism is not, according to my limited opportunities of observing, very rampant abroad, although, looking at it as a dangerous and insidious Jesuitical attempt to subvert the Protestant Church of England to Rome, or to its errors, and to swell the power of the clergy, the least beginnings deserve to be carefully watched and reprobated by all who desire to preserve the purity of Christian worship. Even were it carried to the most extravagant lengths to which it sometimes is in England, it would pale its ineffectual fire before the full blaze of the Roman Catholic Churches around in their richly-adorned cathedrals, their great altars heaped with all manner of valuables and decorations, their innumerable candles of all sizes, their multiplicity of priests with gorgeous vestments, their full-voiced sonorous chanting, their theatrical ceremonial.

But in some places there is a tendency, apparently held under a certain check, towards Ritualistic practices.

Of course one sees everywhere in Episcopal congregations a good deal of genuflexion among the women.[1] But I imagine this is not regarded by many good people as

---

[1] Bowing the head or bowing the knee at the mention of the name of Jesus, is one of those literal renderings sometimes put upon words of Scripture, of which in reading through, long ago, as a student, the *Corpus Juris Canonici*, I found examples. The subject is disposed of in Mr. Thomas Spalding's *Scripture Difficulties*, p. 269.

Ritualistic, although it has a considerable resemblance to the observance in Roman Catholic churches of bending the knee before every crucifix which is passed.

The church is open in some places every morning of the week for reading of prayers.

Intoning the prayers is occasionally attempted; but in a small church, and essayed by one whose voice is not naturally musical, the unaccustomed performance assumes all the appearance of a timidity conscious of deviation from the simplicity of genuine worship.

Not infrequently the altar is gaily ornamented, and a large cross is placed on it, and sometimes there is in a compartment of the window over it a representation of the Saviour on the cross in stained glass. At one little town where we spent a Sunday, the minister was a young man with Ritualistic tendencies. We attended the little chapel, the congregation (one-half probably Episcopalians) being about a dozen or fifteen persons, nearly filling it. The altar was plain, just a table covered with a red cloth, but a large cross stood on it. Shortly after having read the commandment, 'Thou shalt not make to thyself any graven image, nor the likeness of any thing that is in heaven above, or in the earth beneath, or in the waters under the earth; thou shalt not bow down to them nor worship them,' etc., the young man knelt down on his knees before the cross with his back to the congregation, as if in silent adoration. Upon this an English gentleman immediately rose up, and with his family walked out, and I felt much inclined to follow his example.

The single attempt at robing I have witnessed was in the use of stoles, where the wearer, having a black one and a red one, pleased himself by crossing them on his back like a St. Andrew's cross.

The only other practice I am aware of, savouring of Ritualism, is where three or four stalwart young men, robed in white, have marched in swinging procession from the vestry up the aisle to the chancel to 'perform' the duty, not requiring great physical and still less mental exertion, of reading prayers, upon which (the watchful choir leading by rising up) great part of the congregation stood to do them reverence in the house of their Master. One almost expected the men, horrified, to turn round and call out to the people in the words of the angel, 'See thou do it not, for I am thy fellow-servant. Worship God.'

'I believe, were it not that in all the Episcopalian congregations abroad there is a large proportion who either do not belong to the body, or belonging to it, thoroughly disapprove of the practices of the Ritualists (spoken of by the Roman Catholics as 'our first cousins'), there might be more latitude taken. But this reason should go a good deal further and put an end to it altogether, because it has a direct tendency to prevent those who cannot reconcile their conscience to giving even the semblance of approval by attending service, from coming to the chapel in which they prevail, and which may be the only one in the place.

All these and any further observations, though made tenderly, must be taken as by one who does not belong to the Episcopalian communion, and as indicating perhaps the impressions formed by strangers or by those belonging to other denominations.

The practice now so common, but I believe originally not either intended or observed, of reading the Litany and Communion Service in addition to the ordinary Morning Service, is very general abroad, and, conveniently for lazy or careless clergymen, shoves the sermon into a corner, so that, losing importance, it becomes short and is commonplace, being seldom striking or impressive, although this orthodox flatness is occasionally transgressed, sometimes singularly. We once heard a sermon on Saint Michael almost leading up to the worship of angels, and at Mentone a stranger one afternoon occupying the pulpit spoke in eulogy of war at a time when war or peace were trembling in the balance, and there was little need to inflame some minds.

In the Episcopal churches there is usually a printed notice in every pew to the effect that the income of the chaplaincy is dependent on the offertory, and at every service (even, I believe, on week-days) a collection is made by sending up the collecting plate through every pew. While this is done, the congregation, or the major part, stands, although perhaps not one in a hundred could assign any feasible reason for doing so, and the minister for whose benefit the collection is made reads out at intervals certain verses of Scripture. The collecting plates with their contents are taken to him, and by him are deposited on the altar, and afterwards carried by him to the vestry. To say that this practice produces more, is only to act on the Roman Catholic doctrine that the end justifies the means. In other places, such as in Paris, the custom, in better taste, is to hold out a plate at the door as the congregation retires.

The hours of service on Sunday are generally at 11 A.M. and 3 P.M. If the second service be taken in the evening, it is not always so arranged as to avoid trenching on the hotel dinner hour. In the Riviera it is invariably in the afternoon, and it is kept short so as to allow invalids to get home some time before sunset of the winter months. The morning service is always well attended; but the afternoon service (except in such places as Cannes and Mentone, and even there, too, to a certain extent) is, in Episcopal churches, deserted, and there is only a sprinkling of people in the pews. I have at one place seen only a single person besides ourselves and those officiating; at others, only a few, and probably none of them belonging to the Episcopal Church. In these cases, sometimes only the Evening Service is read.

Out of Paris and Rome, there is hardly a 'Dissenting' Church represented; and as the worship of the other churches does not fundamentally differ, it may be convenient, in what I am about to say, to design and classify them all as Presbyterian. Putting out of view such places as Paris, Florence, and Rome, those attending the Presbyterian services are comparatively few in number; and this is partly attributable to the congregations being drawn from a smaller community, and from a nation in which, among the better classes, from whose ranks to a large extent travellers are drawn, Episcopalianism is, to a considerable extent, considered fashionable. Assuming the population of England to be seven times that of Scotland, the seventeen Scotch Church stations form just about the fair proportion as compared with the 120 English Church stations; while upon the same calculation, the numbers of those who should attend Scotch services ought to be only one-seventh, or, say, 10 for every 70. In this view of it, the Scotch churches are fairly enough represented. But, of course, this is not a practical view, and it is obvious that there must be great difficulty in maintaining, with so few supporters, stations in not very populous towns.

In Fielding's time, Thwackum's definition of religion might very well represent general opinion in England, at least among Episcopalians. By religion, he said, 'I mean the Christian religion, and not only the Christian religion, but the Protestant religion; and not only the Protestant religion, but the Church of England.' The idea dictating this expression finds utterance more recently in Dean Hook saying, with reference to an interview with Dr. Chalmers, 'It would be contrary to my principles to hear him preach.'

Many still would shrink from entering a Presbyterian or Dissenting church, though they are themselves Dissenters when across the Scottish border, where all sects are on the same level, no sect affecting a religious superiority over another, or being conscious of any social separation from others. But when bishops have quietly gone to hear popular Scotch ministers like Dr. Guthrie, and when men like Dean Stanley have even conducted Presbyterian service in Scotland, it shows that this narrow and unchristian illiberality of feeling is passing away. Presbyterians and Dissenters in general take a large and liberal view, and do not hesitate to go, at least occasionally, to an English Episcopal chapel; and where it is conducted with simplicity and reverence, they even enjoy a casual attendance, and hearing the fine old service of the English Church, although after having had to go repeatedly they are glad to get back to the less formal worship to which they have been accustomed.

Now, does not all this suggest for consideration whether it would not be possible, in the smaller places at least, to combine the Scotch and English services in such a way as would enable all to meet in common. There are marked peculiarities in both, distinguishing them, no doubt—peculiarities which at home will take long, by mutual reconcilement, to efface; but when people are from home, there is a tendency to meet more on common ground and feel members of the same great community. Thus it is not uncommon, at least in Scotland, in large hydropathic establishments, very much to the satisfaction of all, to have the whole company assembled on a Sunday evening for a simple worship by reading of Scripture, singing of hymns, extempore prayer, and a sermon or address by a Presbyterian minister.

Apart from the objection which Presbyterians have to a service which is wholly read, and is therefore apt to degenerate into ceremonious worship, there is not a great deal in what is usually read to which they would take exception. The absolution would be better out, as having a tendency to mislead,[1] and it grates upon unaccustomed ears to hear the words of the prosaic version of the Psalms contained in the Prayer Book substituted for the far grander and more poetical words of the Authorized Version. But the Prayer Book, till reformed or revised, would need to be taken as it stands. There would be, however, no need for adding to the morning or evening service the communion service — that might be reserved for those who desired to remain one Sunday in the month for the Episcopal communion, the Presbyterians taking another Sunday in the month for their communion. Nor need the Litany be always used. Then, with regard to the remainder of the service, why not have a Presbyterian minister, when he could be got (and sometimes there are even men of eminence going about), to take it alternately, or otherwise, with the Episcopalian, by giving a short suitable extempore prayer before sermon, and then preaching a sermon according to his own usage—in other words, adopting the mode of service practised in the Rev. Newman Hall's church, London.

Besides other and higher good, this alternate preaching might benefit even the ministers themselves of both communions. The great fault among Episcopalian clergymen is that, in the generality of cases, what they read has no pretence or aim at preaching, but consists rather of a string

---

[1] In Mr. Birrel's interesting *Life of Dr. Brock*, a man of great power and, I believe, of much liberality of mind, the following passage (p. 241) occurs in reference to a Sunday in crossing the Atlantic:—'Next day was all that a Sunday at home could be. We had service, Mr. Nolan again officiating—the captain, however, this time reading the prayers himself. One thing struck me painfully: when the absolution came to be read, the captain gave way to the priest, who alone stood and alone spoke; he alone had authority in the great matter of remission. The captain had none. Of what is this the germ?'

of meagre platitudes, of sentiments which nobody would controvert, a dry homily read without feeling or animation, and having no intention of reaching the soul or heart of the hearers. The ministers of the other communions have, as a rule, a higher estimate of the duty of the preacher; but they do not always have the power or the perception of the means of carrying it out successfully. Among men of mediocrity, the idea seems to be to occupy a long statutory three-quarters of an hour in a stiff, formal, methodical fashion of dividing and exhausting the subject, and an equally formal and unskilful, and therefore ineffective, application and address. While added to ignorance of the arts of arresting and maintaining attention and of persuading an audience, Presbyterian divines too often do not choose the most suitable subjects of discourse. Might not even the spirit of emulation evoke better things?

It is too much the custom in churches in Scotland, after sermon, to close with a hymn, a prayer, and an anthem. After an impressive sermon, it seems only calculated to drive out the impression to have, immediately after, the same subject and the same thoughts droned out by the congregation in a melancholy paraphrase to a doleful tune, followed up by the blare and fanfare of an elaborate high-sounding anthem performed by the choir according to book. The English method, where all this would be more appropriate, is to close quietly. But sometimes the minister stops suddenly short, and with startling rapidity utters, 'Now to God the Father,' etc. However, the rule is, whether with or without this invocation, to close with either benediction, or a short prayer and benediction. We did not often go to the west church at Mentone, though near to us, because the flavour of the service inclined to be 'high'; but the closing there was always pleasing. After the minister had pronounced the benediction, and before the congregation rose from their knees, the choir (composed principally of young ladies with good and trained voices), to the accompaniment of the organ, in subdued tones, so suitable to parting with reverent step and slow, sung to a soft sweet tune the following simple, perhaps child-like verse :—

> 'Lord, keep us safe this night,
>   Secure from all we fear ;
> May angels guard us while we sleep,
>   Till morning light appear.'

FIRST WINTER IN THE RIVIERA.

VI.

LONDON TO SOUTH OF FRANCE.

SELECTING the route to Paris by Folkestone, we left London on the afternoon of 1st November 1876, and slept at Folkestone. The steamboat was to sail the following morning at 9.15, and to have proceeded direct would have involved leaving London at the inconveniently early hour of 7.10 A.M. The train by Dover and Calais departs fixedly at 7.40 A.M., so that one is not much better off by taking that route. But on proceeding by Boulogne, there is a chance that the state of the tide may throw the time of sailing to a later hour; only when this is the case, it involves arriving at the journey's end late in the evening. The train in connection with the boat by which we were to sail, was due in Paris at 4.40 afternoon—a nice time at which to arrive.

One does not get a chance of observing whether there be any attractions about Folkestone by just sleeping a night there. It may be a very Paradise upon earth; and, from its facilities for popping over to France, to its residents it probably is. One cannot say, but it does not look like it. Possibly the quarter to which summer visitors resort may be more inviting than the portion disclosed at the harbour. Anyhow, it seems a less dreary, out-of-the-world place than

Newhaven. But Britannia rebels a little at her children quitting their native land to get enamoured with strange countries, and frowns upon their departure; for these nights before crossing are by no means pleasurable. One is brought into rather close proximity to the dreaded passage; and if the wind should howl or be even but moderately fresh, or if the sea, unwitting of its gigantean power, be only sporting in joyous freedom, the prospect for the morrow is far from assuring. Then it is a busy, bustling, uncomfortable scene at the hotel. Piles of luggage strew the hall. Apprehensive passengers are arriving by successive trains, and others in a woe-begone condition, and in all sorts and manners of wraps and disguises, by the boats. They are dining, teaing, suppering in a confused disagreeable way in the coffee-room. Anxious waiters and active chambermaids are hurrying about. Porters meet you in narrow corners laden with luggage. There is nothing to invite you to remain in the public room. There is nothing to induce you to venture long out of doors. People depart early to bed. But the search for petty utilities by the feeble light of candle, the cramped bedroom, the cheerless difference from home, produce a feeling of discomfort which, combined with the early retirement, the noise and tramping about the corridors, the creaking of ships' gearing dimly heard, and the thoughts arising,—which have little in them of the land of promise and more of the morn,—all keep the pilgrim long restless upon bed; and, after an unrefreshing night of broken sleep, he is glad to get up betimes for an early breakfast, call, with twenty others simultaneously, for the bill, settle it up quick if correct, and, after an impatient waiting for his goods, which seem never likely to make their appearance, and seeing that every little thing is brought along, to be off to the steamboat; for nobody stays, unless in exceptional circumstances, such as pending a storm, more than a night. After a little, the train arrives, and an endless procession of unassorted passengers moves slowly on board; the luggage and merchandise brought by it tediously follow. At last the gangway is dragged ashore, the vessel is released, and, after the usual backings and easings and tender movements, it tardily steams out of harbour, increases its speed, and we sit looking on the land, the return to which may be in the far future; and, thinking much of dear friends from whom we have parted, we gradually, as the distance widens, lose sight of Old England, and passing here and there a gallant ship, with its snowy sails catching, fortunately for us, but a gentle balmy breeze, we near the other—once hostile, now friendly—shore, and landing find ourselves among a foreign race, and gazing upon foreign habitations, and soon encountering foreign customs and institutions.

We made the mistake of registering our luggage at London when we left London, instead of taking it on with us to Folkestone and registering it there for Paris. The consequence was that, on arrival of the train at Paris, we were compelled to wait nearly an hour at the station, which was cold, dark, and drafty, until all the luggage which had come by the train by which we had arrived had been arranged, examined by the *douaniers*, and delivered to their owners. We disconsolately saw our luggage standing within a barred enclosure, but the men would on no account touch it till then, and no doubt where thieves abound some precaution of this kind is needful.

We had repeatedly visited Paris before, but in one respect it was new to us—to see it in its wintry aspect. On former occasions, we had visited it in the sunshine of summer. But how changed did it look now! The trees were yellow with the tints of autumn, and were nearly stripped of their foliage. The air was cold and frosty, and Paris looked bleak and miserable. We spent one or two days in it; and one of the places to which we paid a visit was beyond the range of ordinary sight-seeing. The daughters of some Edinburgh friends were at a large boarding-school in Paris, in the Faubourg d'Auteuil. We drove there to see them, and after some search discovered the establishment, the name of which, 'Une Institution des Demoiselles,' was painted up in letters a yard high. It had quite a conventual aspect. The house was entered through a narrow little door, hinged on a panel of a large one (just like what one sees in the large door of a prison), which, upon ringing the bell, was opened by a pull from the opposite side of the court-yard, around which the buildings of the school were placed. Crossing to the dwelling-house, we were shown into a parlour, where our young friends shortly came to us. They were all habited in black, with a red leather belt, being the uniform compulsory on all the pupils while in school. They informed us there were 150 boarders, of whom only 17 were English. Having introduced us to one of the governesses, this lady very kindly showed us all over the place. Ranges of large rooms were occupied as bedrooms, containing a separate bed for each of the young ladies—all kept in the highest order, and in white, spotless purity. Separate adjoining rooms were fitted up as lavatories. Other rooms were schoolrooms; others, dining-rooms, or *salles à manger*, where the young people were then at lunch or early dinner, and evidently enjoying a hearty meal. A separate building was kept as an infirmary for the sick—a very prudent arrangement, where so many young persons were brought together. For those who were in good health, there was a large garden and playground attached to the house.

On Monday, 6th November, having taken Gaze's tickets from London to Nice, we left Paris by the Lyons Railway, registering our heavy luggage for Cannes; and we were free to travel to any station on the line to Cannes, at which our tickets permitted us to stop, only taking with us what we would require for a week by the way. Some people prefer making the journey from Paris to Cannes, Nice, or Mentone without break, and say there is less fatigue in doing so; but it is a long journey, occupying from Paris to Mentone—journeying by the express leaving at 11.20 A.M.—twenty-eight hours, arriving at Mentone at 3.24 next day. For invalids in a feeble condition, it is in some respects preferable. It is only one fatigue to be overcome, and it avoids the risk of exposure to damp or rain. In cold, winter weather at Paris, the one journey is certainly preferable, and at the end of it people arrive in what is by contrast a genial summer. So proceeding, passengers have, besides other shorter stoppages, an interval of half an hour at Dijon, at 5.45 P.M., to dine; 25 minutes at Lyons, at 10.18 P.M.; and the following morning, at 6.30 A.M., 1 hour 25 minutes at Marseilles to wash and breakfast.

We desired to take the journey leisurely, and to see a little by the way. After the usual difficulty on French railways of getting accommodation in the train, we proceeded as far as Dijon. There is little to interest one by the route. Fontainebleau, at which the express trains do not stop, is passed soon after leaving Paris, but is nearly two miles from the station. Its palace with its gardens is really the only thing worth seeing, but to see them involves spending a day at the town. If not pushed for time, they are, however, well worthy of a visit. We stopped a night on our way home to see them. The palace is extensive, consisting of four distinct but united chateaux, erected at different times, with splendid suites of rooms full of historical interest. The forest, which covers 25,000 acres, is disappointing. The charges at the hotel to which we went, were as high as those of any in Paris.

We rested the first night at Dijon, a convenient halting-place. The Hotel du Jura is near to the railway station, and is most comfortable. The landlord of it is attentive, and his charges moderate. Dijon was the former residence of the Dukes of Burgundy, and is a curious old place, well worthy of a visit for a day or two days. People often break their journey at Dijon merely to sleep there, but, arriving at night and departing next morning, do not always visit the town. A forenoon may be very profitably spent in walking about its promenades and its streets, with houses adorned by quaint carvings and architecture, and seeing its large, massively-built churches, particularly St. Michael and St. Benigne, and its interesting old public buildings. On the card of the hotel there is a little plan of the town, in which the Place Grande is shown about its centre. Here there is a large edifice which was formerly the palace of the Dukes of Burgundy, now the Hotel de Ville, one part of which has been converted into a museum and picture gallery, the most interesting portion being the old banqueting hall of the dukes, with its colossal chimney-piece and its monuments, carrying one away back to the times of boisterous mirth and probably lawless deeds.

Dijon stands high, and the weather being cold on our journey south, we were glad of fires. We considered we had made a mistake in travelling so late in the season. Had we started about the middle of October, it would have been better. The fact is, the larger part of the people going for health to the Riviera make the grievous mistake of delaying their departure till winter has commenced. Many, indeed, do not come to the Riviera till the month of January, in order to enjoy the gratification—dearly purchased, in some cases—of a Christmas at home. By doing so, they are obliged to travel through France during a season when the weather is often piercingly chill, while they are exposed in crossing the Channel to the risk of encountering winter storms.

We proceeded next day to Lyons, passing through a rich wine country, in the midst of which Macon lies, where, at the station, on high days and holidays, the women may be seen wearing a witch-like hat of peculiar build. The cycle of fashion will no doubt in due course make the whole world acquainted with it, till which time the world may wait and wonder. It may require some fortitude to don this sweet marvel of a bonnet for the first time. But what observation will not the ladies brave to follow their leader in fashion!

At Lyons it was keenly cold. There is not much to be seen at the ancient city, situated on the banks of the Rhone and Saone, which effect their junction just below it. The railway journey from Dijon occupies five or six hours, according to the trains. We arrived in the dark, and drove to the Hotel Collet, one of the best in the place. It is situated in the main street, which may be said to be the only good street of shops, formerly called the Rue Napoleon, and now since the Republic, which changes even the names of streets, the Rue Nationale. On entering the large hall, round which were distributed palm trees and other tropical plants in tubs and pots, we had the first suggestion of approaching a southern clime.

Lyons is populous without being lively, and stately without being imposing. We took a close carriage next morning, and drove about for nearly four hours to see what could be seen—almost the whole of which time was occupied in visiting the junction of the rivers and ascending Fourvières, a steep hill on the right bank of the Saone, from which an extensive panoramic view is in clear weather obtained, and Mont Blanc, about 130 miles distant, is sometimes seen—its visibility being a circumstance symptomatic of approaching wet weather, as we found did happen on a subsequent occasion, when the white mountain was seen as we were nearing Lyons from Geneva. Lyons at this season was looking very dreary, and the cold necessitated our burning fires in the bedrooms. On a former visit, in summer, the heat had been almost unendurable. In the evening of the second day, we found the large central hall of the hotel—which was lighted from the roof, and afforded access by encircling corridors and concealed stairs to the different floors—was covered in by an awning, and the *salle à manger* was laid for a magnificent dinner. It turned out that the principal rooms were engaged for a wedding party (*noces*), the ordinary guests being conducted to other rooms. It was, however, a very quiet, solemn-looking affair; although the number assembled was large, they made no noisy demonstrations. At breakfast-time next morning the waiters seemed but half aroused.

We left Lyons by train at 11 o'clock forenoon. Our through tickets required to be *visé'd* at the booking-office before they would admit us to the *salle-d'attente*. The route from Lyons southward is very interesting. The railway skirts the Rhone nearly the whole way. The river has been said to vary in width from a quarter of a mile to two miles, although from the railway it does not appear to be so wide. In the sunshine everything looked beautiful. The farther south we got, the foliage became fresher, and it was very charming to see the river rolling softly on, fringed by trees, and through valleys, from which rise the vine-clad hills. We passed the Côtes d'Or, and other regions, where the famous Burgundy wines are grown. Some of the mountain ranges are lofty. We thought how much more beautiful would the river appear during summer months, and our wish as regards time was actually fulfilled the following September; but, alas! it was then obscured by clouds and rain.

The railway to Marseilles passes several interesting places, and among others, the towns of Orange, Avignon, and Arles, which all contain relics of Roman occupation. On occasion of our going south in September 1877, we stopped at Avignon, which is 230 kilometres, or about 140 miles, from Lyons,[1] the train taking about six hours. When one can manage it, Avignon is a place well worth stopping to see. Leaving the station, we drove through some narrow dirty streets till we reached the Hotel de l'Europe, the situation of which is not at first inviting; but it is considered the best hotel, and our rooms were very comfortable. It was kept by a young landlady, who spoke English, and was very attentive. On the following morning we took a cab to drive about and see the town, and, *inter alia*, saw the Calvi Museum, which contains many paintings, some of which are good, and a large collection of coins and books. Then we went to the cathedral, which is well worth a visit. Here are the tombs of several popes. The construction of the gallery of the church is peculiar. I desired to have a photograph of the interior at a shop, but they had it not. Photographs, however, were sold outside the cathedral, and possibly I might have procured it there; but we had so often found photographs sold at the show places themselves so dear, that I had not asked for them at the cathedral door. It does, however, sometimes happen, as probably it did here, that they can only be had at the place itself; and when time is limited, it is better to secure what may be wanted, especially interiors, at once. The pope's old palace adjoins the cathedral. This is a large building with very massive walls 100 feet high. It is now occupied as a caserne or barrack for French soldiers. The lofty rooms, for greater accommodation, have had a floor interposed. The rooms, fitted up

---

[1] A French kilometre is equal to 1093·633 yards; an English mile is 1760 yards. Two miles are therefore more than three kilometres, and two kilometres are equal to about one mile and a quarter (1¼). But all the foreign measures differ, and it is puzzling therefore to know from the railway guides and others what are the distances in English miles. A uniform mileage system would be exceedingly useful. In fact, the statesman who could effect uniformity in measures, weights, and coinage throughout Europe, would do more real good than is obtained by more glittering acts.

with beds and filled with the soldiery, are in a very different condition from what they must at one time have been when this was the papal residence. One of the rooms into which we were shown, was the upper interposed half of what had formerly been the chamber of torture of the Inquisition. There was nothing very special now to be seen in this dismal unoccupied apartment, which at one time echoed with the groans and cries of the tortured.

In the Place de l'Hotel de Ville, in the centre of the town, are a handsome-looking theatre and other public buildings; but one of the most interesting objects in Avignon is the old Roman bridge across the river. Avignon was a fortified city, and is still surrounded by walls having many gates, and in our drive we passed outside the walls till we reached the Roman bridge. Only part of it is now standing, the remainder having, I presume, been swept away by floods. The river is now crossed by a good modern bridge, not far from the site of the old one, and conducts to a town upon the other bank of the river which forms a suburb to Avignon.

We did not, in November 1876, stop at Avignon; but being then desirous of seeing the old Roman city of Nismes, we procured through the guard, when stopping at the station of Valence, supplementary tickets enabling us to change at Tarascon, which we reached in the dusk about five o'clock. Here we had to change carriages, and cross the platform, and enter a dingy station or *salle-d'attente*, and to wait wearily for nearly an hour till the train proceeded to Nismes. It was cold, and we had, as usual, no assistance from porters with our *petits bagages*. Nismes is about an hour's journey by rail from Tarascon. The mistral was blowing, and it was bitterly cold. The coldness of this wind is, I believe, greatly produced by the cutting down of the trees on the mountains in the south of France; and if so, the sooner they are replanted the better. It is piercingly felt all over the south of France, even Mentone, at its extreme east point, not being wholly sheltered from its influence. I fancy that in the Roman times, when such places as Nismes, Avignon, and Arles were selected for habitation, the mistral was not felt, at least to the extent it is now. It prevented our invalid from leaving the house while at Nismes on this occasion.

Nismes, as a capital city of a department of France, is a town of importance. It is the seat of the departmental courts, and it possesses various educational establishments as well as a variety of manufactures. It is beautifully situated in a fertile district. The town itself is attractive. The principal streets are wide and clean, and the Boulevards are pleasant; but it is as an ancient city, full of vestiges of old Roman occupation, that it possesses charms to attract the stranger.

The most famous of these Roman remains is the Arena, and attention is naturally drawn to it from being situated fronting a large open space in the heart of the town, called the Esplanade. It was the first of the Roman amphitheatres we had at that time seen. Exposed to the mistral, it was then intensely cold; and one could hardly suppose that it would have been built on that site if it had not been at the time a place to which the people could go without fear of colds (for, odd though it may sound, I fancy the grand old Roman nose did suffer occasionally from colds). However, an arena seems to have been then as necessary an appendage to a Roman town as a church is to an English village. The building is oval in shape, and is 412 feet long by 306 feet in breadth, and rises in upwards of 30 massive tiers from the centre to the circumference, resting on strong stone arches, and containing perfect means of ingress and egress—every separate external arch having been, no doubt, a separate vomitory. The building is computed to have accommodated 32,000 persons. The arena, though in part ruinous, is still in a very fair state of preservation, but is undergoing a process of restoration by the insertion of new stones in place of the old ones, to strengthen the structure, which, as the old stone is grey with age and the new stone is a beautiful pearly white, looks most incongruous. One could almost wish that the building were let alone, although it is to be hoped that in the course of years the new stone will assume a colour in keeping with the rest. Perhaps it might be stained to bring it into harmony. Of this same kind of stone, two beautiful churches have recently been built: one of them, St. Perpetué, is completed and in use; the other, a very large one,—I presume to be occupied as a cathedral, with a double spire far in advance when we saw it first,—was in the following year not yet finished. The designs of these churches, particularly in their spires, are remarkably graceful. There is another very elegant modern building adjoining the Arena, the Courts of Justice, which also fronts the Esplanade, in the centre of which open space has been erected a very handsome modern marble fountain at a cost of £10,000.

Leaving the Arena and passing up the Boulevard St. Antoine, we arrive at the *Maison Carrée*, or the Square House —a small but beautiful temple, with a peristyle of the Corinthian order, in admirable preservation. It is situated in a space enclosed by railings, and is occupied as a museum and picture gallery, for which it affords but limited room. From the Maison Carrée the visitor proceeds through public gardens to the Roman Baths, which are in wonderful condition, although the marble statues have nearly all lost their noses, the common fate of all marble statues long exposed to the weather. These baths are very elegant enclosures of water, now looking very stagnant and green. Upon the west side are the ruins of what has been termed a temple of Diana, in which are preserved many of the antiquities found in the vicinity of it. To the south issues, through an elegant iron rail and gateway, a very long wide avenue or boulevard called *Cours Neuf*, on a straight line, flanked by trees which, when completed, will extend, I think, a full mile in length. The north extremity is terminated by a hill, reached by magnificent stairs, and commanding a fine view of the Baths or fountains, of the long wide avenue beyond and the surrounding country. This hill is surmounted by the *Tour Magne*, the ruin of a building the object of which has not been definitely ascertained.

Nismes in summer in fine weather is very hot, but is a charming residence for a few days. We stayed two nights on this occasion at the Hotel Luxembourg, which is recommended to English travellers. The men-servants here, who are also the *femmes-de-chambres*, had quite an Italian look and cut, and were in their morning attire very comically dressed in a short jacket, somewhat like those schoolboys used to wear.

We returned *en route* for Marseilles by Tarascon, passing by the way several stone quarries and fields in which olive trees had been planted by way of experiment. These were the first olive trees we had seen. They were young and short, and were disappointing, as in fact are all olive trees, however large or old they be, to those who, like ourselves, having read of sitting under the olive tree as a species of luxurious enjoyment, found them very different from our expectations, being in leaf like the willow. But their existence indicated approach to a warmer climate.

The old Roman town of Arles lies between Tarascon and Marseilles, and is said to be, though I doubt it, as much worth seeing as Nismes; but, owing to the difficulty of finding trains to fit in to meet our time, we have not in passing visited it.

It rained heavily all the way from Tarascon to Marseilles,

when it fortunately cleared up. Part of the way is flanked by what appears to be barren desert land, possibly occasioned by the ground being high and level, so that it is not watered by rivers.

At Marseilles, we found the *commissionaire* of the Hotel du Louvre et de la Paix, to which we had written for rooms, waiting. Owing to some odd arrangement then prevailing, all carriages were kept out of sight till the luggage was sorted, so that we were fortunate to get him to send for one. The hotel we found to be a large many-storeyed one, but it had a lift. There is another large hotel at Marseilles, to which we went on the next occasion. It is hard to say which is the better. The Noailles has a large and beautiful *salle à manger*, and a good-sized drawing-room. Both are expensive. We found at Marseilles, as at Dijon, Lyons, Avignon, Nismes, and afterwards at Hyères, that the charge for *table-d'hôte* dinner included *vin ordinaire*. We had an agreeable surprise at dinner in meeting two families—old friends—from Bristol.

Marseilles is seldom visited, except as a place of halt for further travel. After staying one or two nights, those arriving depart either landward by railway or seaward by steamboat to other parts. But it is well worth at least one day's visit to see it thoroughly. It is a very ancient city, being upwards of 2500 years old, and the population is above 300,000. In contrast to Lyons, it has all the appearance of a busy place. The principal streets are always crowded, the port is the largest in the Mediterranean, and may be considered the Liverpool of France, though the docks are not so extensive. On occasion of our first visit, the weather was cold and wet, and we had only a Sunday there, so that we did not see much; but when we paid it a second visit in October 1877, we had a little more time, and drove round the town and docks. The ancient port is a large natural harbour filled with good-sized vessels, while additional docks of large extent stretch away to the westward. Outside them, a breakwater has been built, which extends about two miles in length. Bædeker says that, on an average, nearly 20,000 vessels, of an aggregate burden of 2,000,000 tons, enter and quit Marseilles annually. Our driver pointed out as we passed, in one of the docks (the Basin de la Joillette), a P. & O. steamer; and it would have been interesting to have visited it, but we were afraid we should not have had time. A large cathedral was being built facing the docks, and will be a very prominent object to those arriving at Marseilles by sea. Another very prominent and striking object, and from which a fine view of the town, harbour, and district is to be had, is an eminence to the south-east, crowned by the Church of Notre Dame de la Garde. Leaving the docks, we proceeded round the town to the Palais de Longchamps, which stands on a height. It is a large, elegant columnar structure, with spacious staircases leading up to and through it to the gardens beyond. The palace contains two museums. A fine view is obtained from the top.

Marseilles is a busy commercial and manufacturing place. The central streets are always bustling—teeming with life. An interesting part of it is the flower market, where the women are to be seen perched up on tables or platforms tying up their pretty bouquets of flowers and selling them to purchasers. The heights to the north of the town are bare, but, together with the islands which stud the sea outside the harbour, give picturesqueness to the view. But although it stands as far south as Mentone and San Remo, or rather farther south, it wants the shelter of the health resorts on the Riviera, and suffers severely from exposure to the mistral.

On leaving Marseilles for Cannes, we had not gone far by railway before we obtained a complete change of temperature. It was like passing from winter into summer, and from dreary stony mountain ranges to verdant slopes covered with mature olive trees, and with orange and lemon trees—all indicative of a warmer climate. We did not on this first occasion stop at any place between Marseilles and Cannes, but on the following year visited Hyères, and it will therefore be adverted to in the sequel.

On this first occasion, we left by an early train on the Monday morning with our friends. We had much difficulty in getting seat-room, with no assistance from guards. The carriages were filled with people who had travelled all night from Paris. In the compartment which fell to our lot, the remainder of the seats were all filled by French gentlemen who were or had been smoking, and were begrimed with dust, and looked like very ogres. The morning was splendid, the sun, pouring out his beams in rich effulgence, gave gladness to the bright scene, which we especially felt after the cold weather to which we had, ever since our arrival in France, been exposed. After leaving Toulon, the railway goes inland and does not again touch the coast till it reaches Frejus, 91 kilometres, or above 50 miles on; but the country is very beautiful. This route, between Marseilles and Genoa, and on to Pisa, passes through constantly-occurring tunnels. It is said that between Marseilles and Genoa alone there are no less than 200, and it certainly looks like it. The train is for ever rushing into and darting out of tunnels; and as French people never think of closing windows in tunnels, and always put and keep down the glass, the transit through them is very cold and trying, particularly to invalids or to those who may be afflicted with a cold in the head. After leaving Frejus, the railway skirts the coast, and as the train emerges from a tunnel, the passengers have the opportunity of seeing the most lovely bays formed by the jutting promontories and the blue Mediterranean. In saying they have the opportunity, however, this is a chance depending upon whether there are no foreigners at the windows. If there be, most mercilessly, and without leave asked, much less obtained, down go the blue blinds on both sides of the carriage. Fortunately, on this first occasion (I was not so lucky on the second), I got seated near the south or sea window, and managed to get one of the three curtains kept up; but just as we approached within sight of Cannes, where the view was becoming exquisitely beautiful, a little of the bright sun darted in: the intruder was expelled in double haste, and the blind most uncourteously and ruthlessly pulled down. It saved some sunburnt ogre from being, if possible, a little more browned or reddened, and it signified not that his fellow-passengers were deprived of an enjoyment into which he could not enter.

VII.

CANNES.

WHEN we arrived at Cannes, we could see by an occasional glimpse through a chink in the obstructive blinds, that everything was bright and beautiful and gay in the sunshine. It was quite a new scene to us, and gave a charming idea of Riviera life.

Waiting the arrival of the Paris train at Cannes, there are often, besides the usual very long row of omnibuses, many private carriages and always carriages for hire. Relatives had preceded us by about eight or ten days, and we desired, if possible, to join them. Just outside the station, looking for one of them, I was at once besieged by porters wanting to take our *petits bagages*. I asked one by whom I was importuned, how much he demanded to carry them to our friends' quarters, little more than half a mile off. 'Five francs.' I doubt if I thanked him sufficiently; and we drove off in one of the little carriages which were there waiting employment, the fare for which was 1 franc 50 centimes. The house in which our friends were was full, and we found accommodation in the neighbouring Hotel du Pavillon. This is a large, good, first-class hotel, frequented by English people, and is situated on the west bay, with a garden, such as most of the hotels at Cannes have, in which were palm and orange trees, the latter bearing their golden fruit. They sent for our heavy luggage, which had been lying for a week at the station, suffering no loss save that of a new rope which had been tied round one of the boxes, and which was feloniously stolen and theftuously away taken, as in Scotland Her Majesty's advocate for Her Majesty's interest would have charged the culprits if he had only known who they were.

Cannes is very picturesquely situated. The old town, which is not savoury, fortunately rests out of sight upon an elevation or ridge which is crowned by the cathedral church and two old towers, which give a distinctive mark to the place, and are seen in most representations of Cannes. From this height, and still better from greater heights behind the town, an admirable view is obtained all round. But taking our position on the ridge, we find the hill slopes down from it away to the south, and reaching the road below, extends seaward by a short projection, partly natural and partly artificial, forming a breakwater on one side, and pier on the other, terminated by a lighthouse. The ridge and this projection divide the waters into two distinct portions, constituting the east and west bays. About two to three miles to the southward, Les Isles de Lerins, two long strips of islands—Ste. Marguerite, with its fortifications fronting the town, and St. Honorat—lie stretched along, giving a natural shelter on the south to the little port of Cannes, and, except in the neighbourhood of the fort, both covered with tall pine trees. The harbour or port, surrounded on two sides by lofty houses, warehouses, and public buildings or hotels, is right under us, on the east side of the ridge, and does not aspire to receiving more than a few sloops or vessels of small burden and a large number of boats, apparently intended principally for pleasure sailing—although, if this be their purpose, the number seemed out of all proportion to the slender demand. On the north side of this bay, the new town—the business part of Cannes—has been built. The main street, long, and lined with numerous shops, runs through the centre of it, with streets branching off right and left. It is the highway to Nice, and forms part of the famous Corniche road, which proceeds from Marseilles to Genoa along the coast. Immediately behind the town, the ground rises, and at one part becomes a low hill crowned by a few straggling houses and solitary trees. A handsome promenade has been constructed along the beach, upon which a few of the best hotels and some magnificent villas, with their large interposing gardens full of exotic trees and plants, are situated, imparting a bright and gay look to the walk. About a mile and a half or two miles to the eastward of our point of view, we see a range of hills, the shoulder of which is called California. This range, covered with pine trees, affords shelter to Cannes from the east wind; and from its extremity at California, the hill slopes sharply down, and then the ground runs far out into the water, forming a projecting arm. The last portion, of level ground, called the Croisette, reaches to a point not far from the island of St. Marguerite, and constitutes a natural breakwater to the bay and harbour on the east side. Some miles farther to the eastward, the long, low, hilly, narrow, projecting promontory called the Antibes protrudes still more into the sea, and affords additional protection, while it creates another fine bay, greater in extent, in which a fleet of French men-of-war is often seen lying at anchor or at exercise.

On the west side of the old ridge, the sea retreats in a large, beautiful bay, called the Gulf of Napoule,—or more commonly, the west bay,—the west boundary of which, several miles distant across the sea, is formed by the glorious range of mountains called the Estérels or Estrelles. These stretch out a long way seaward, and are always a picturesque feature in views of Cannes. They are covered principally with a rich dark green, which, I suppose, is due to the existence of pine forests; but in some parts, especially

THE ESTRELLES FROM ST HONORAT,
CANNES.

towards the ocean, they are bare, steep, and rocky. Irregular, and in some places even ragged-looking in outline, and varying in height, some of them are said to be as high as 4000 feet. Though much less extensive, they are to Cannes very much what the mountains of Mull are to Oban. Only they have not the constantly-changing aspect which confers so great a charm upon the Scottish hills. This is partly owing to the greater serenity of the atmosphere, three-fourths of the days being clear and sunny, without a cloud; but chiefly because the sun gets so soon round upon the mountains that they are early in the forenoon thrown into shade, giving no doubt a murkier and grander aspect, but making the separate markings less distinctly visible. The Estrelles have been photographed as in moonlight, in which they are very beautiful, but the moonlight effect so shown is a mere trick of the photographer.

To the north of Cannes, and about three or four miles inland, the village of Cannet lies upon rising ground; and, I presume, from being away from the sea, it is preferred by some invalids to Cannes. Farther off, and distant about nine or ten miles from Cannes, the town of Grasse, famous for its manufacture of perfumes, is built among gardens devoted to the culture, for their essences, of roses, orange trees, heliotropes, and other odoriferous plants. Indeed, Cannes itself manufactures perfumes, and around are some gardens filled with a short or stunted species of acacia, growing to about the size of a large gooseberry bush, and bearing globular yellow flowers from which perfume is extracted. Beyond Grasse, the landward panorama is bounded on the north by distant mountain chains.

It is at all times difficult to realize a place from description, even with the aid of the pictorial art; but perhaps from this short delineation it may be perceived that there is a marked character about the site, locality, and features of Cannes. But when to the natural formation the glorious colouring is added which it derives from the brilliant blue of the ocean and the scarcely less brilliant blue of the sky in the bright sunny days which usually mark the weather; the rich varied greens of the abounding foliage; the tropical character of the gardens; and the enlivening effect produced by the often fanciful forms of the houses, painted in luminous whites and yellows picked out upon their jalousies with green and other contrasting tints, and glowing in their red-tiled roofs, it will at once be seen that there must be a signal beauty and picturesqueness about the landscape which cannot fail to arrest the eyes of those to whom this phase of scenery is new.

But Cannes was never a town of any importance until Lord Brougham took up his residence there. It happened in the year 1831 that his lordship was detained at Cannes by the prevalence somewhere of a pestilence. He was so much struck with the natural features of the landscape and the suitability of the place for winter residence, and so impressed, that he soon thereafter acquired ground on the west bay, where he built a house, to which he used regularly every winter to resort, and where, on 7th May 1868, he died. His example brought many English people to the locality, and Cannes is now in the winter season such a place of fashionable resort for English and Scotch families, that it may be regarded as completely an English colony, there being but a sprinkling of other nationalities. It is accordingly in both bays studded with villas, and filled with numerous large hotels, the latter said to number upwards of fifty. There are no less than three English (Episcopal) churches, and in the west bay, near the town (the handsome gift of Sir John M'Neill, who has a residence in the suburbs), a Scotch Presbyterian church. There are also both French and German churches. The population of Cannes has increased wonderfully since Lord Brougham led the fashion to it, and it is now, I believe, considerably over

10,000. A monument has been erected to his lordship in the cemetery where he is buried, and a marble bust of him has, on a long square pillar pedestal, been placed in the public gardens of the west bay. When we were last at Cannes (November 1877), it was proposed by the municipal authorities to hold a centenary celebration of the birth of Lord Brougham as the virtual founder of the town; and this festival has since (April 1879) been held, lasting four days. Nor is it any wonder that the Cannais should feel themselves under a debt of gratitude to the great English, or rather Scottish, lord. The following paragraph from an account of the fête, contained in the *Scotsman* of 4th April 1879, speaks for itself:—

'It is a matter of unquestionable fact, that, since the days of Lord Brougham's example to his countrymen, prosperity has flowed steadily in upon the fortunate people of Cannes. Those of them who were lucky enough to possess land, have had golden opportunities, and must have made ample fortunes out of the weak-chested but strong-pursed stranger to whom this winter climate is simply a necessity of life. The price of ground here, fit to build upon, is almost fabulous. Eight to ten thousand pounds an acre is a common rate for small lots near the town, and a site was quite recently sold, in the principal boulevard, at the enormous rate of £19,200 per acre. Even in the remotest suburbs, outside the cab radius, nothing available for building can be had under 10 francs a metre, or £1600 an acre.'

The Corniche road runs westward through, for upwards of two miles, a nearly continuous line of charming villas, and thence on to Napoule, upon the west of the bay of that name. Upon the right or east side of this road, about half a mile from the old town ridge, which may be said to bound on the west the town proper, the villa of Lord Brougham may be seen standing at the top of a gentle slope, where it commands a beautiful view of the bay and the Estrelles, though exposed to the west winds. It is of good size, but nothing remarkable. We did not, however, see the interior, nor does it seem to be shown to strangers. In being enclosed by an iron railing towards the road, it offers an exemplary exception to the rule, as nearly all the villas in that direction are enclosed by high walls which shut out the sight of the grounds within, and make the road for a long stretch dull walking. Nor is there a footpath except for a short way, although one was, when we were last there, in progress of formation, and very needful too, as after rain the road is particularly muddy, so that walking in that direction is not always inviting. But generally on an afternoon, when the occupants of the villas are out driving, their gateways are left open, and passers-by get glimpses into fascinating gardens exuberant with palm and other tropical trees, which, freed from their unsightly enclosing walls, would so enliven the way without the privacy of the inhabitants being really disturbed.

One of the most delightful residences in this neighbourhood is the chateau of the Duke of Vallombrosa. This Italian nobleman asked, as the sole recompense of services rendered to the King of Italy, the title which he now bears. His villa is in the castellated style, and stands upon an eminence—a very picturesque object in the landscape, and seen from all parts round. The grounds attached to the house—extending, I suppose, to at least eight or ten acres, and the oldest about Cannes—are, in the duke's absence, open to visitors. To those who have not previously seen any gardens of the kind, it appears a sort of fairyland, if such a term can be applied to a place where much of the timber is gigantic. The vegetation is rich, luxuriant, tropical, and the place looks delicious on a sunny day, under the cool shelter afforded by the trees from the rays of the sun, while here and there a fountain sends up its refreshing stream of water. Below the battlemented castle terrace, a shady grotto has been built—a cool retreat in hot weather, perhaps too cool to be safe. This garden contains many lofty specimens of a tree recently introduced into the Riviera, and everywhere to be seen there, called the Eucalyptus. A relic of the Eocene period,[1] when everything was on a huge

[1] *Vide* Figuier's *World before the Deluge*, p. 317.

scale, it shoots up with amazing rapidity, apparently something like ten feet in a year, and I believe ultimately reaches sometimes a height of nearly 500 feet. I have seen it stated in a colonial paper that the largest known, grown in (I think, speaking from recollection) New Zealand, has reached the height of 480 feet, and is claimed to be the highest tree in the world. Probably it is not of great age, as the growth of the Eucalyptus is much more rapid than that of the Californian trees. As it matures, it changes the form of its leaf from what it was when young, and sheds its bark. It possesses some very health-bringing properties, or is an antidote to what is insalubrious, and bears a beautiful white flower. In the duke's gardens some of these trees are very lofty. They were, I presume, planted about twelve or fifteen years previous to our visit, and appeared to be then considerably over 100 feet.

A hill called the Croix de Garde slopes up behind the Villa Vallombrosa, or rather to the northward. It is several hundred feet high, and its summit, crowned with pine trees, commands an extensive prospect, and forms a delightful walk to those who are able to make the ascent. The view comprises the bays and all that I have already described. A little iron cross, inserted in a stone upon the top, to which no doubt some legend attaches, gives its name to the height.

The Corniche road below, running between the lines of villas, conducts to a little village called Verviers, about three miles from town. Here there is a large forest of umbrella pines bordering the coast, furnishing opportunities of study to the artist and to the photographer, and where one can enjoy a forenoon's rambling about. The railway cuts the forest off from the shore, and flanks the beach all the way till it arrives close upon Cannes, and must therefore operate injuriously to the amenity. So far as the villas are concerned, they have, by means of bridges or otherwise, communication with the sea. Fortunately, however, for Cannes, the railway leaves the coast about half a mile from town, and passing through a tunnel proceeds by the back of the town, where the station is.

From near the point where the railway diverges from the shore, the public promenade on the west bay commences. This is lined by palm trees, but the dust and the sea air together seem inimical to their development. The main promenade is that which, commencing with the harbour, runs eastward to the point of Croisette, a distance of from two to three miles. It is a great resort of visitors both on foot and in carriages. A band of music plays alternate days on the east and west bays. In each of these bays there are bathing establishments of a construction peculiar to the Riviera, being somewhat of the nature of the Lacustrian dwellings. They are simply wooden sheds for undressing and dressing in, resting upon poles stuck firmly into the beach, with depending ladders to enable the bathers to descend to the water. As the beach shelves very rapidly down, I presume that bathers who cannot swim must always be in charge of an attendant or be tied by a rope; but whether it was that the bathing may have taken place at an early hour, I have hardly ever seen any person indulging in a bath at Cannes during our brief visits, although the temperature is seldom such throughout the winter as to forbid the exercise to persons in good health either at this or at other parts of the province. I have seen at Nice (a colder place than Cannes) people bathing towards the end of November. By a strange fatality, for one can hardly suppose it to be the result of deliberate arrangement, we observed that close by each of the bathing establishments a drain has been run into the sea, the same practice occurring also at Biarritz. These drains are so odoriferously disagreeable as to make it unpleasant to walk along the promenade, while one would think that some parts of Cannes ought in consequence to be unhealthy.

At all events, they must to a certain extent nullify the good got from residence at this otherwise agreeable and fashionable watering-place.

Near the point of Croisette, there is a large orange garden which has been dignified with the name of the garden of the Hesperides. The oranges are cultivated for sale, and the trees are covered with the yellow fruit. In all the private gardens orange trees grow, and sometimes, though rarely, lemons, which I understand do not flourish at Cannes so well as elsewhere in the Riviera—a symptomatic sign indicative of a colder climate; for the lemon is a very delicate tree, requiring warmth and shelter, and being injured or killed by frost. There are also many arbutus trees in the gardens, bearing rich red soft berries nearly an inch in diameter, which are edible, and become ripe about November or December, and are sometimes, I have been informed, put down as dessert at hotel tables. The oranges do not ripen till February, although the fruit is on the trees all the year round.

At Croisette there is a depôt for the sale of the earthenware, tinted with a peculiar blue or with a livid green, of which many fancy articles are made in the neighbouring town of Vallauris; but the stuff is brittle, and it is not advisable to purchase for bringing home any articles with slender handles—they break so easily off, while they can be bought at home in china shops.

One of the favourite drives is to California, upon the slope of which some new large hotels have been built, from which the views must be fine; but the situation, though healthy, is rather inconveniently distant from the town, and involves a pull up hill, which perhaps puts walking up beyond the power of invalids. We drove there on the 18th November. The sun had risen gloriously in the morning. There was not a speck of cloud on the sky. The day was broiling hot, and it was difficult to realize that we were no longer in July, but in a time of year when at home we should have had cold wintry weather. So warm, indeed, had we felt it at Cannes, that we were under the necessity of throwing off the extra clothing we had donned at Paris and Lyons. The road is steep, and the ascent fatiguing to horse and man, to the point where the reservoir, which supplies Cannes with water, is placed. Here we left the carriage and climbed to the top of the hill over above, the view from which amply repaid the exertion. Had we gone to a farther height, we should have seen the Alpes Maritimes; but from the height at which we arrived, the view was magnificent, the Estrelles lying straight out to the west, Antibes to the east, and the Lerins lying, to appearance, almost below us to the south. In a glowing sunshine such as we then had, the Mediterranean is always of a brilliant deep blue, while the sky is also of a rich blue of a lighter shade. One can hardly realize the beauty of the scenery beheld on such a day without having previously witnessed another like it. Such days would live in our recollection even more than they do, were they not, during several months' residence in the Riviera, of so frequent occurrence.

During the winter season, there is, for the accommodation of visitors, a tiny steamer, perhaps about the magnitude of Fulton's first steamboat, mayhap the identical one, which, for a fare of 2 francs (return ticket), crosses to the islands of Ste. Marguerite and St. Honorat. We resolved to spend a forenoon on Ste. Marguerite, and, with about twenty or thirty passengers on board, crossed, leaving at eleven o'clock and returning at four. The boat stopped at a little quay below the high walls of Fort Monterey. Here we got out, and the whole party landing, went up to see the fort, which is doubly famous as the place where Bazaine was confined and from which he escaped, and where 'the man in the iron mask' was so long imprisoned. Like some other French forts, it is not at present occupied by soldiers, though a regular fortification in masonry, and capable of affording protection against vessels seeking to attack Cannes. A man placed as resident in the fort accompanied us to the rooms which had been occupied by Bazaine. The suite of apartments was extensive, and bore anything but the appearance of a prison-house. Except for the involuntary confinement, one might regard it as a charming residence; and in its recent occupation was a public remonstrance against the barbarity of laws which imprison convicted persons who have hitherto enjoyed a good social position in the same cells as ordinary criminals, to whom such cells are in truth more comfortable than their own miserable dirty homes. We were then taken to the spot where it is said that Bazaine escaped by descending the wall and rock. The height is not great, and a descent in the daylight would be no great achievement. It would no doubt be more difficult and perhaps dangerous in the dark, and it is even alleged that the Marshal was allowed to walk out by the gate. There is no great improbability in this story, seeing that the French had gained all they wanted by a condemnation of this officer as a scapegoat for their want of success. The room in which the 'man in the iron mask' was confined, was much more like a prison—a cell with massive thick walls. We saw the hole through which he is said to have dropped the billet which was picked up by a fisherman.

There has been placed in this fort one of those semaphores which are studded along the coast of France, by which signals are or used to be made, and which, before the introduction of the electric telegraph, were no doubt useful. From the battlements we had a clear view of the magnificent landscape before us, which embraced on the extreme right distance the snowy peaks of the Maritime Alps. We left the fort, and wandered over the island and through the trees, with which the greater part of it is covered, lunched *al fresco*, and enjoyed our forenoon very much. It is an island we could have wished transported, with all its surroundings and its sunshine, to our own shores.

We spent fifteen days on this occasion at Cannes. It is a nice place for winter residence for those who are in good health; but I doubt whether, notwithstanding the records of the thermometer, it be sufficiently warm—at least, whether it affords sufficient shelter—for delicate invalids, being apparently a good deal more open to north and west winds than some other places in the Riviera. Before we arrived, there had been not a little rain, and the roads were very dirty. While we remained, we had still more; but the usual weather all along the Riviera is dry and fair, and it is of dust one has most to complain. There is no river meriting the name debouching within the limits of the town, although their insignificant beds are speedily filled when heavy rain falls.

Like most places on the Riviera, there is abundance of marble used in the houses and hotels. It is not altogether without its drawbacks and its dangers. Stair steps are of marble, and it is requisite to be careful in descending. On one occasion I slipped upon a marble step and fell on my back, and might, had the fall been more direct, have received permanent injury; but in the winter time carpets are usually laid on the stairs.

It is said that there are snakes and venomous green lizards. We never saw any snakes, and though there are plenty of lizards running nimbly about and up the walls, diving out of sight into hiding holes, yet sometimes leaving a little of their long tails sticking out, I cannot vouch for these being either venomous or innocuous. They look pretty gentle creatures, and one is rather savage to see men and boys throwing stones at them.

MOSQUITOES.

A real pest, however, to which all are exposed at Cannes and kindred places, is the plague of the mosquitoes, which abound in hot weather. We were told they were off by the 1st of November, but we found upon arrival at Cannes, and throughout our stay there, that this insect plague was in full force. It is a small gnat, with long legs and yellowish-brown wing. The first thing that we did was to kill as many as we could see resting on ceiling, walls, or bed, and this is best effected by coming quickly down upon them with a damp towel; but they are very agile, and unless the arm be vigorous and prompt, they escape the swish. They are also remarkably knowing and cunning, and soon discover when an enemy is bent on their destruction, when they manage unaccountably to disappear. Nay, even without attack made, they will hide themselves during the day, conscious that they will get a good feed during the night. Every now and then they came buzzing about you with a peculiar hum, which becomes more loud just when the insect is about to strike. This it does by driving its proboscis like a lancet into the skin, extracting a drop of blood, and leaving behind, I fancy, a minute drop of poison or other cause of irritation, producing a small red mark. Most people do not suffer inconvenience from the bite itself beyond the mark it leaves, and with which the brow, a favourite point of attack, soon gets dotted over. One lady at Cannes was so severely bitten that she could hardly see, her eyes being nearly closed by the effects of the bites, so much so as to prevent her coming to the table. Another lady was so affected by the bites that the parts bitten rose in large swellings, requiring her to consult a doctor, by whom they were lanced; and the cure was tedious, leaving long after marks on the skin. But the great annoyance which they occasion is their tormenting vicious hum, revealing their presence, and showing that at any moment they may be down upon you. If you wake through the night and hear this hum, it is impossible to get any further sleep. If there be anything worse than a mosquito humming about you, it is to have two of them; but one is enough to keep you lively, and furnish you with incessant employment; and where one is, there are generally plenty more. Apparently the mosquito, like the king, never dies, for as fast as one is slain another reigns in his stead. All sorts of remedies for the bite are prescribed, but we found that prevention is better than cure; and the most effectual prevention, besides taking care to close windows early and not to light a candle before closing, was to burn a pastille, specially prepared for the purpose, by placing it on an iron shovel, and just before bed-time carrying it burning round the room and holding it within the bed curtains. The smoke of it appears to stupefy the insect, although it does not kill it; and in the morning the mosquitoes, evidently wanting to get out to breathe the fresh air and take their revenge at night, fly in a sickly condition to the windows, where, or elsewhere about the room, they are easily killed. When killed, a bloody streak is left, indicating they have been fed somewhere. One extraordinary circumstance is that, although the fecundity of this creature is enormous,[1] yet those which find their way into rooms are comparatively few, and it puzzles one to know where the rest go to. I believe the insect's existence is not so much due to great heat as to bad drainage. We found Cannes to be worse than Mentone, and Hyères worse than Cannes; but by Christmas-time, when cold weather has set in, they nearly vanish, although, when a fire is lighted, sometimes they are either attracted or revived, but are then in a weakly condition.

[1] I have seen the numbers produced by a single insect in the course of a year stated in a newspaper, but unfortunately did not preserve a note of the information, which is not given in the usual books about insects.

VIII.

NICE.

WE were due at Mentone on Wednesday the 29th November, and intended to have spent two nights at Nice by the way; but the Monday was so very wet at Cannes that we delayed leaving till the Tuesday morning, and by so doing obtained a brilliant day for the short but delightful railway ride. Passing the Croisette, we first skirted the Bay of Antibes, where the French squadron was then lying at anchor, and in which is the spot, denoted by a commemorative monument, where Napoleon Bonaparte landed from Elba. A little farther, the distant snowy Maritime Alps came into view. Here, as elsewhere in the Riviera, curious villages, looking very dead-alive under their rotten brown roofs, are seen upon the tops of hills. These villages were so built in the olden times, with the view of securing some protection from the Moors, who, crossing the Mediterranean from Algeria to capture the inhabitants for slaves, kept them in terror when they landed. We passed over the wide course of the Var, and in about an hour from departure arrived in the gay town of Nice.

Nice is a large town in the province of Nice, formerly part of the Sardinian kingdom, when the boundary line between France and Italy lay about four miles to the westward of the town. Ceded to France, it is now the capital of the French department of the Alpes Maritimes. The population, which forty years ago was 34,000, is now stated by Bædeker to be 50,000; but as the town has been from year to year rapidly extending under the influence of the railway facilities, and now covers a large area, it is probable that this estimate is much under the mark, and that it numbers greatly more. Arriving by the railway, the station is left, and the town entered by a wide handsome street or boulevard called the Avenue de Longchamps. This leads straight down to the Place Massena and the Pont Neuf, where are the public gardens, the Promenade des Anglais, the Boulevard du Midi, and other noted parts. The river Paillon passes through Nice, and is crossed near its mouth by the Pont Neuf.

Nice is a very lively place, and in some respects is attractive. The town is well laid out, and it has many good shops, though none of them large. It is a commercial town, but does not possess many notable public buildings. The cathedral lies in a quarter I never visited; but a handsome Roman Catholic church, externally large, but internally contracted, has been recently built of a fine white stone, and forms a feature in the avenue. The streets, houses, and hotels are imposing. The Promenade des Anglais is a long wide roadway along the beach, extending westward between one and two miles; and upon its landward side, many of the largest and best hotels, a theatre, and other buildings have been erected. This promenade is the great resort, particularly on a Sunday, of the inhabitants and visitors, and it has certainly a magnificent aspect. A handsome iron bridge of three arches over the Paillon connects it with the Boulevard du Midi, which forms a continuation eastward towards the harbour.

Nice was, and I suppose still is, a free port, and therefore possesses some advantages. Its harbour affords accommodation for many large ships. Before reaching it, however, and to the south-east of the town, a hill interposes, rising abruptly above 300 feet high, popularly called the Chateau, of which castle, however, nothing is now left but its ruins. The slopes of the hill are covered with trees, many of them exotics, through which the road winds gently to the top. We drove up this winding road to the harsh music of innumerable French drummers and trumpeters (one would have thought the tyros of all France were here assembled) practising upon their respective instruments all sorts of disagreeable rat-tats and military signals of contradictory import in dinning, hoarse, distracting, discordant, ear-cracking immaturity—a very Babel of uncertain sounds, tending to realize, perhaps faintly, the Highlander's dream of heaven,—that delectable thought of 'four and twenty bagpipers all in one room, and all pleyin' different chunes.' Nevertheless, every visitor desirous of obtaining the best view of Nice and its environs should make the ascent, previously bribing the concierge to ascertain if possible at what hour the unhappy musicians dine or otherwise disappear. On the top of the hill there is a platform, from which is obtained a most striking panoramic view. Below, on one side, lie the harbour, and the hills beyond to the eastward, over which the Corniche road proceeds to Mentone and Genoa; then on the south, the beautiful Mediterranean Sea, hemmed in by promontories, and basking and glittering in the sun; westward, the promenades; and thence northwards and eastwards, the city, bounded in the distance by mountains. But what arrested our attention most was the extraordinary torrent bed of the river Paillon. Crossing the Var, we had seen a similar bed, and much wider. In a railway train, however, one has little opportunity of catching more than a passing glimpse of things, especially when the railway line is nearly on the same level. But from the platform of the chateau we were looking down upon the bed of the Paillon from a considerable elevation, which enabled us to see up the course of the river for some miles away to the mountains, where it became lost to view. As the torrent beds are a remarkably characteristic feature of the Riviera, I may just describe their appearance. The bed or channel of the river consists of a broad stony course, through which usually a streamlet trickles; the bed being out of all proportion to the size of the stream as usually seen. It is, however, stony, and no grass grows in it; and sometimes, after heavy rains or from snowy meltings, the water comes down from the mountains in torrents, and more or less covers the channel from side to side, even occasionally, when the rains are more than ordinarily protracted, flooding it considerably—a fact which I believe the contractors in forming the railway found to their cost. But although we have seen heavy rains lasting for days together, I do not think that, with one exception, we ever witnessed such a flow of water in any of the river beds as completely to cover it. The strange aspect of the river course, however, is produced by men continually digging into it when and where dry, and riddling out the fine limy earth which has been borne down from the uplands, and carting it away for building and other purposes; by doing whereof they leave behind them all over it large holes and little heaps of riddled-out stones, imparting a very mottled and singular appearance to the channel. The river Paillon, therefore, extending for miles in this condition, had a most novel and extraordinary aspect from the chateau. Although there had been heavy rain the day before, the stream was very diminutive.

We stayed but one night at Nice, although we went several times afterwards from Mentone to spend the day there. I do not therefore pretend to know it well. It is the most expensive town in the Riviera, but is alluring to those who go in good health for pure enjoyment. For promotion of enjoyment and gaiety, it is, I presume, everything that can be desired; but although the climate is better than that of some other places, being, it is said, equal or similar to the climate of Florence, it wants the shelter which is so necessary to invalids. The mountains are not near enough to afford protection, and cold winds, keen and piercing, blow down the streets, very trying to delicate constitutions, especially to those suffering from pulmonary complaints. In fact, it would seem to be the battle-ground of all the villanous winds which afflict the south. The *bise*, the *marin*, the *tramontane*, the *mistral*, the *sirocco*, are in continual conflict for the ascendency; and sometimes the one and sometimes the other has it, and enjoys its triumph for a few days in dealing misery on the inhabitants. To many the sea-breeze is most trying. I met on one occasion, on the railway, a gentleman in bad health returning from Nice to Rome because he could not stand its sea-breeze. But given good strong health and a relish for the kind of life, and Nice is charming.

The hotels and pensions are legion in number; but those considered good by English people, it is well to know, are costly.

Theatres, skating rinks, bathing, exhibitions of paintings and sculpture, each in turn claims patronage, while delightful excursions by carriage can be made to places of interest in the neighbourhood. There is a constant stir of life in Nice, aided not a little by military promenades and military music, a band playing each afternoon in the public gardens.

But we were impatient to be off to Mentone, which, from all we could learn before leaving home, was thought to be the most desirable of all the health resorts in the Riviera for winter residence. Our friends had preceded us from Cannes, and secured quarters for us in the same hotel with themselves.

The carriage road from Nice to Mentone, about 24

miles, is one of the most charming parts of the Corniche drive, and, if weather be not cold and expense be no obstacle, it ought, unless the traveller be an invalid, to be preferred to the railway, which, although it skirts the Mediterranean just at a sufficient elevation to give a charm to the view of its lovely waters, suffers the great drawback of passing through numerous tunnels, some of them long. On the other hand, the drive by road, for which 40 and even 50 francs are asked (though less will be taken), rises at one part to a great height, overlooking the ocean, and being there on the top of the hills, is without protection from the cutting north wind.

It was not warm enough to warrant our venturing to drive, and we decided to go by rail. Soon after leaving the station at Nice, we crossed the torrent bed of the river Paillon, but were still in the town or suburbs of Nice, and in the midst of orange gardens, the fruit shining, like everything else, in the brilliant sun. At the other end of a long tunnel we reached Villefranche, where the gulf of that name presents a large natural harbour, in which one or more men-of-war are sometimes to be seen. From this point the railway hugs the coast, passing under or through the hills by tunnels, whereby many fine points of view are missed, and particularly the sight of Eza, a curious town perched on a precipitous rock, formerly a Saracen freebooter's stronghold. The Corniche road is more inland, and commands the whole prospect uninterruptedly. As the train emerged from these tunnels successively, bay after bay, filled with the beautiful blue Mediterranean water, hemmed in by rocky promontories, upon which lonely trees sometimes grow, met our sight, but, most tantalizingly, immediately after disappeared from view, eclipsed by the next tunnel. At last, after rather more than half way to Mentone, the bold, peculiar rocky promontory of Monaco, for which we had been watching, appeared, stretching out like a tongue of land, or rather a long steep rock, into the ocean. The view of Monaco either from west or from east is very striking. The rock is from 200 to 300 feet high, and dips perpendicularly into the ocean, crowned by the town, the handsome palace of the Prince of Monaco, and by fortifications. It is inaccessible on three sides, and can only be reached by a fortified road upon the east side sloping up the side of the rock. Upon the north end, which is also steep and inaccessible, it is connected at the bottom by a low narrow belt of land. I shall, however, recur to Monaco in describing a visit to Monte Carlo, which lies about half a mile to the eastward. After leaving Monaco station, the passenger, looking down, sees on the ground below, and leading up to Monte Carlo, a number of villas, pure and bright in their colouring, looking so clean and tidy in the sunshine with which on this occasion we were again favoured. Monte Carlo is not well seen from the railway, as the line and station lie below and even in part under it. All trains stop both at Monaco and Monte Carlo, and at the latter place they generally set down and take up a considerable number of people, who resort either to the gaming tables, or to the delightful gardens which surround them, or to the music room of the Casino. Leaving Monte Carlo, we came in sight of another long projecting though not precipitous point of land, or rising hill ground, covered with trees, principally dark pines. This, the promontory of Cape Martin, is the west boundary and termination of the western protecting arm of Mentone. It necessitates another long tunnel, escaping from which, and passing extensive terraces or forests of old olive trees, and crossing two river courses, we at last arrived at our long anticipated destination, the subject of many thoughts during past months—Mentone.

IX.

MENTONE.

THE union of bold grandeur with soft loveliness in the Mentone landscape, arrest and powerfully strike the eye upon arrival. Familiarity with its scenery, after a residence of months, scarcely dims the first impression. We had heard much in a general way regarding it even before leaving home, but every expectation was at once far exceeded by the reality. We had just left Cannes and Nice, and witnessed them both in their brightest aspects; but Mentone in its natural features, and seeing it, as we did, for the first time, in glorious sunshine, threw them both into the shade. It was an agreeable surprise, and made us instantly feel that a more beautiful spot for winter residence could not have been chosen.

Originally the town of Mentone consisted simply of a collection of high old houses, rising ridge upon ridge like so many terraces resting upon the steep slope of a hill, the crest of which was at one time crowned by a castle or palace of the old feudal lords, now converted into a picturesquely-situated cemetery. This hill or ridge, with its curious old houses,—among or above which the cathedral and other churches stand, from which there rise two elegant minaret-like spires, one taller than the other, conspicuous from every quarter round,—forms a very striking object, especially when seen from the east, and from that side may be said in miniature to resemble a little, though of a different character, the old town of Edinburgh, which, however, is far more lofty and extends at least ten times farther. The harbour or port of Mentone lies at the bottom of the seaward end of this ridge. Curious old high houses, resting upon odd long-shaped water-worn rocks, the terminals of the hill, abut and hem in the harbour on the north or land side; while on the south side, a long breakwater is in course of formation for protection from the ocean waves, which, coursing over the whole width of the Mediterranean Sea without interruption, occasionally, under the pressure of a southwest wind, dash up and over with great vigour. An old building, at one time a small castle, standing at the end of the original pier, makes an object in the landscape, and perhaps could tell some tales. The water in the port is extremely shallow, so that the anchorage is only adapted for vessels of a small size, of which there are always a few moored to the quays. The hill ridge, with the projecting pier, form, similarly to Cannes, the dividing line between what are termed the east and west bays.

The books which have been recently written on Mentone, particularly those of Dr. Bennett and of Mr. William Chambers, but more than any book, the good reports of visitors, have induced such an influx of winter dwellers from distant lands as to have created a new town in both bays. Rather, it may be said that the hotels extend in both directions, for in reality the newer parts of Mentone are made up chiefly of lines of large hotels, the street or shop part of the town being only a necessary sequence. From the ridge eastward to the gaping gorge of St. Louis, which is now the boundary line between France and Italy, the distance by road is about two miles. Hotels line upon one side nearly the first mile, the other side being open to the sea, and villas dot the remainder of the way. From the gorge, south or seaward, a mountain called Belinda (1702 feet) springs up, and from its shoulder a promontory juts out to the sea and forms the termination of the east projecting arm of the bays. From the north side of the gorge a mountain range rises more loftily into the majestic Berceau and Grande Montagne, and, stretching away to the north and northwest, form the great shield to Mentone from the east and north-east winds. These mountains attain an elevation of about (more or less) 4000 feet,—the Grande Montagne being stated by one authority to be 4525 feet,—and show themselves boldly and almost perpendicularly in some parts like enormous colossal walls of bare rock. Due north from Mentone, and from two to three miles distant from it, another chain of mountains lies almost at right angles right across from east to west—St. Agnes in the centre, and behind it the high and sharply-pointed Aigle (4232 feet high)—affording shelter from the north winds; while the Agel (3730 feet high), and some other lesser mountains, terminated by the long promontory of Cape Martin, all lying from north to south, afford shelter from the west and north-west winds, and particularly the cold mistral. Within these greater mountain chains, a series of high ridges or hills standing in front, or issuing out of them like huge tumuli, all covered with olives in terraces, afford additional shelter; so that were it possible for the wind to blow down the outer rampart, it would be withstood by this inner wall or circle of lesser heights, some of which are 1000 feet high. In the distance on the other side of the great mountains, but invisible from Mentone, the Maritime Alps rise to a height of from 5000 to 9000 feet. It will thus be seen that the configuration of the mountains is that of a great semicircle, and that on every side save the south or sunny side, open to the sea, Mentone has protection from the cold winds which in reality blow over the tops of these great walls and strike at some distance away,—

the north or prevailing winter wind reaching the sea some miles out. It cannot be said that the cold of the winds is not felt, but it is so greatly averted or modified that Mentone is practically sheltered; and hence it is that, coupled with the long continuance during the winter of dry open sunny weather and the absorption and radiation of the sun's heat in and from the limestone rocks, it becomes so admirable a place for the invalid.

Our quarters were in the west bay, considered to be more bracing and less relaxing than the other, which is said to be three degrees warmer, and, from being so, and more enclosed and protected, better suited to the extremely delicate. The hotels and houses in the west bay—in which is also situated the new or shop portion of the town—extend, though not continuously, about a mile; and there has been formed in front, by the border of the sea, a roadway called the Promenade du Midi,—a good and fairly-wide pleasant road for foot-passengers and carriages,—which is, in the early part of the forenoon, the great resort of invalids and other strangers, who here meet their friends, and can view the sea uninterruptedly in their walks, or enjoy a book or a newspaper on one of the many seats provided for the weary or lazy. A low stone-built bulwark protects the promenade from being washed away by the sea, which sometimes, though very rarely, sweeps up forcibly in heavy waves, and even occasionally in a storm, so as to dash over the road. But when the wind is from the north, the sea retires under its pressure 60 to 100 feet from the bulwark, and there is scarcely a ripple upon the water, which then looks like one sheet of blue glass. And this is its predominating or normal condition during the winter. When the waves come, they trundle over monotonously, without gaining or losing a step. It is the great drawback of the Mediterranean that it has no tide, or a tide that is all but imperceptible. The difference between high and low water at Mentone is only from two to three feet. The consequence is, that the sea does not carry away sufficiently the impurities which are conveyed to it; and there is wanting that interesting feature of a tidal beach, the change from hour to hour of the appearance of the shore. It is only right, however, to add, that Mentone enjoys comparative immunity from the noisome influence of exposed drainage. Small drains only empty into the west bay; and they are not particularly offensive, though they might be improved by carrying pipes down into the water,—only the likelihood is, that the first storm would sweep them away. Another empties in the east bay, at the corner formed by the junction of the old town at its north end with the shore. This is at all times disagreeable to passers-by, and must be insalubrious to those residing in its neighbourhood. But it seems difficult to understand how Mentone is drained, unless the east pipe conveys the great bulk of the sewerage to the sea; although, so far as the old town is concerned, it has been explained that the natives collect all manure to carry it off to the country, thus combining thrift with cleanliness. That the town is not as yet so disagreeable as Cannes, may arise from the population being greatly smaller. When Mentone increases much, as it is threatening to do, it may be quite as discernible.

I have never seen any place so strikingly enclosed as Mentone is by its semicircle of mountains and the minor hill ridges. The higher parts of the mountains are steep, rocky, and bare; but all over the ridges, and far up away into the mountains, the olive tree is cultivated in terraces built for their reception. The orange and lemon trees mingle with the olives at a lower elevation, and in some, especially the higher parts, pine trees furnish a deep green covering. But all combined add a rich beauty to the imposing grandeur of the scene. Some of the buildings also contribute materially to the effect. On the summit of a lofty ridge, between the Carrei and Boirigo valleys, a monastery conspicuously rears its head. On the other heights there are houses of peculiar construction, curiously painted; and the whole place is dotted over with bright-coloured villas, of all tints and shades of white and yellow, relieved by the almost invariable roofing of red tiles, and the usual gay greens of the outside venetian jalousies. But next to the mountain heights, the most marked lineaments of the Mentone scenery are its valley depths or ravines between the various ridges, and in which rivers find their beds, although in the dry weather which generally prevails they are but trickling streams, and in some cases usually almost dry. The greater valleys are three—or rather, it may be said, four—in number, consisting of two larger, with their torrent beds, the Carrei and Boirigo; a third, containing a smaller river course, the Gorbio; and a fourth, the Mentone valley and streamlet, the smallest of all, but obtaining its name from, or giving it to, the old town, at the bottom of which, or underneath the streets, the rivulet passes. The valleys, three of them of considerable width, in which these rivers run, form beautiful adjuncts to the town; and the torrent beds, which are not so long or so wide as those at Nice, are striking without being distasteful to the eye.

Such are the general outlines of the landscape. I shall have to recur to some of them hereafter. To those who can appreciate scenery, the *tout ensemble* cannot fail to produce a feeling of intense admiration; but added to all, there is that which lends its peculiar charm to Mentone. This is its rurality. While it contains many large hotels, which do not contribute much to the adornment of the scene,—though year by year becoming more essential to meet the demands for accommodation,—none of the buildings in Mentone possess the palatial appearance of those at Nice, neither in the large hotels nor in the street buildings. Indeed, with regard to the latter, there is only one street proper in Mentone, not half a mile long. On issuing from the railway station, which stands on high ground, the town is, or was, hid from view by a curtain of trees, which afford a beautiful fringe to the ocean, seen lying placidly beyond. The road to town is along an avenue of tall plane trees by the bank of the Carrei, one of the torrent beds. The road on the other side of the Carrei is also flanked by trees, as yet young. On arriving at the main road, which crosses the river bed by a wooden suspension bridge, there is a piece of ground, not large, on either side, laid out as a public garden. From this point, the road each way, east and west, continues to be lined with plane trees. The villas passed on the way are built in gardens, wherein orange, lemon, pepper, and palm trees grow; and so it is everywhere, except in the heart of the town. I fear much that, from year to year, as people continue to flock to Mentone, and more lodging-room becomes requisite (for in sixteen or eighteen years Mentone has risen from being, so far as strangers are concerned, a mere wayside stopping-place to its present ample dimensions, embracing a native population of above 5000, besides a stranger population of probably 3000 more), and as land becomes in consequence more valuable, this peculiar charm of rurality will disappear; and though, mainly from the impossibility of its becoming a great seaport, it will never be a large commercial town like Nice; and although it will always continue to possess natural features which no buildings can obliterate, and which neither Nice nor any other town wanting them can secure, yet it may in time rival in towny aspect such a place as Cannes, which is at present very considerably larger.

As the first duty of the visitor is to see to his quarters, it is only right here to make some observations relative to the hotels such as they were during our stay. They were then reckoned, in 1877, to amount to forty-four in number; but the number is year by year increasing, and at least one large hotel (the National) has been built since we left, although the advertisements do not disclose its whereabouts. The hotels are found either fronting the sea or back from it, and either in the west or the east bay; and as the question of locale is not unimportant, invalids should endeavour in this respect to suit their particular case, noting, too, that, like every other place, some hotels are more expensive than others.

It is not unusual for those who have not been previously in Mentone, or who have not secured apartments before arriving, to take rooms for a night in the Hotel Mediterranée or the Hotel Royal, or some other hotel in the town (of which there are several), and then look about. At the beginning of the season there is abundance of choice; but if the visit be delayed, as so often is the case, till after Christmas, it is not unlikely to be discovered that the best rooms have, for the most part, been taken; and it is much more difficult to secure what is suitable, and especially good south or sun-visited rooms. When such delay is unavoidable, the better course is, if possible, to write to a friend in Mentone previously to make inquiries and engage rooms. In the spring, many migrate from Cannes and Nice on to Mentone, *en route* a little later for Italy. As proximity to the sea air, or to be within hearing of the monotonous noise of the waves, does not suit some persons, while the proximity may benefit others, and as the temperature of the east and west bays differs considerably, it is not inadvisable for those in delicate health to consult a medical man, who should decide which part of Mentone is best suited to the particular case. There are about twenty doctors practising in Mentone. Of these, the English doctors are, I believe, the following:—In the west bay, Drs. Siordet, Marriott, Gent, and Sparks; and in the east bay, Dr. Bennett. It is also well to know that the fees of the resident English medical men are high, and are paid at each visit. If the visit be to two persons of the same party, two fees, I have been told, are charged or expected. The fees of the French medical men are greatly less. It would seem, on some points, the doctors of the two countries differ,—as, for example, English doctors advocate sitting in the sun, and foreign doctors, sitting in the shade; and knowing how foreigners abhor their friend the sun, I can well believe they do.

In viewing the hotels in order to make a selection, it will be observed that some are more sheltered than others, and a certain preference may be given to those which seem to be the better protected from the north wind, which in winter months, especially during December and January, prevails and blows sometimes with a piercing cold during night and in the morning. I am afraid this is a circumstance but seldom studied by the builders of the hotels, for I suspect there are few houses—particularly on the Promenade du Midi—which are not exposed to cold in consequence of having doors opening to the north side. This of itself is not desirable, and perhaps in most cases is unavoidable; but the evil is increased when such door is in direct communication with the staircase without outer porch and lobby, or if a corridor connect it with an entrance on the other or south side. Considering, also, how important it is for invalids that the temperature in-doors should be maintained throughout the house at a proper degree, I have been surprised to find that means are not universally taken to heat the staircases and lobbies, delicate people being very apt to suffer great harm by passing out of heated rooms into cold corridors. So far as I am aware, there is but one hotel in Mentone which fully attends to this important particular — the Hotel des Îles Britanniques. Possibly, however, there may be others. If not, this may be taken as a valuable hint.[1]

---

[1] It would be hardly possible for me to give from recollection a complete list of all the hotels and pensions in Mentone, but I may note some at least of the most prominent. Having had friends in many of them, we had occasional opportunities of seeing them, and learning a little regarding them; but only residence in each could enable anybody to speak authoritatively, and therefore observations now made must be taken in a very general way, and subject to all allowances, and as perhaps mistaken.

HOTELS—FURNISHED VILLAS.

The rate of pension varies according to the hotel and to the floor, and runs from 8 to 16 francs per day, exclusive of wine, candles, and firewood.

To those who prefer taking either a furnished house or rooms in a lodging-house, choice of villas or rooms can be had in abundance at very varying rates, but generally, like the hotels, high. The number of villas is constantly on the increase. When last in Mentone, there were no fewer than about 250. During a bad season, many remain unlet. Lists of houses can be had from the house-agents, of whom

At the extreme west, the Pavillon is, I believe, a well-appointed hotel; but it is fully half a mile outside the town, to some a recommendation. Between it and a small house, now called the Hotel Anglo-Americaine, near to the Boirigo Bridge, there are several elegant villas, some of them to let furnished. East of this bridge, facing the promenade, are the Pension Condamine (small and moderate) and some other minor houses and pensions; then the Hotel de Russie (one on Gaze's list); and crossing the Carrei, the first house beyond, and overlooking the public gardens, is called the Pension Americaine, in reality an hotel, with good cuisine, kept by an active, clever, and attentive landlady; near to it, the Pension Camous, a tall, overtopping, narrow building, at which the town street may be said to commence; adjoining it, the Pension or Hotel de Londres; and a little farther east, and more in town, the Hotels Westminster, Victoria, and Menton—all large, and, I believe, expensive; and, last of all, the Hotel du Midi. Beyond the Promenade, close to the market-place, and not far from the harbour, the Hotel Bristol. With the exception of the two last, all have gardens of more or less size between them and the promenade, and all have access on the other side to the public street.

Back from or on the other side of the main street, there are many other hotels and pensions, among which may be mentioned, west of the Carrei, the Splendide (on Gaze's list), a comfortable hotel within a garden; the Hotel du Parc, on the avenue leading to the railway station, with good rooms, although the entrance or site is not promising. On the east side of the Carrei and some way up beyond the railway, which it dominates, the Hotel du Louvre, a large, well-appointed hotel, apparently frequented by Germans and Dutch; behind it, and rather higher, there is the great Hotel des Îles Britanniques, commanding good views, in every respect first class, patronized by the English (though not exclusively so, one long table being set for the English and another long one for the foreigners). The landlord claims it to be the most expensive hotel in Mentone. Both these last-mentioned hotels are near to the railway station, but carriages have to make a circuit to reach them. Both are under shelter of an olive-covered hill rising high and steep immediately behind, which also affords similar shelter to the Hotels the principal apparently was M. Amarante, Avenue Victor Emanuele.

An institution maintained by subscription, and called Helvetia, provides at a small rate of board (£1 per week), a home for, I believe, fifteen invalid ladies, who are not in circumstances to incur the much heavier expense of boarding at a hotel.

Six Roman Catholic churches supply the wants of the Roman worshippers in Mentone.

There are two English Episcopal churches. One, in the

des Princes, Venise, D'Orient, Turin, and others, lying nearly in a line to the eastward. The D'Orient and Turin have both gardens in front,—that of the former is large, and in the garden of the latter a bed of roses flourishes in full flower all the winter through. Both are good houses, but the views from the windows and grounds are confined, and street houses shut them out almost entirely from the view of the sea. If, however, view be not considered important, the position is comparatively sheltered. There are also about this part several pensions, such as the 'Des Alpes,'—a small house, and moderate charges.

In the east bay, after passing the old town, which in the afternoon always casts a dank shadow on the part of the road which underlies it, called the Quai Bonaparte, requiring the invalid to take special precautions, and passing the drain pipe, the first hotel met is the Grande Bretagne, one of the oldest houses. It is that upon Cook's list for Mentone, and consequently seems to be always well filled. Up on the height behind, a little to the eastward, are the Hotels d'Italie and Belle Vue, both comfortable; but the ascent to them is steep, the fatigue being, however, rewarded by the fine view from the terraces and windows. Returning to the road below, which is a part of the Corniche, we observe the East English Church, and next to it the Hotel de la Paix close to the street, but having a garden to the back. Facing it across the road is the only bathing establishment of Mentone. Adjoining its east side, but back from the road within a garden, the Hotel des Anglais where Dr. Bennett obtains his quarters. A little beyond, a small piece of ground, probably an acre in extent, has recently been acquired and laid out as a public garden, in which the band occasionally plays; and amidst a cluster of other hotels and pensions farther east, the Grand Hotel, a comfortable, large house, charging moderately. If the visitor prefer or is recommended to reside in the east bay, he will find the extreme east (called the Quartier Garavent, though so much farther from town, and though hot and dusty) is the choicer situation. There is, however, an omnibus to town every hour from the far east to about the Hotel du Pavillon, at the extreme west end.

west bay, succeeds in obtaining good music and good congregations. The chaplain of this church was till recently the Rev. W. Barber, who, after officiating for many years, died on 24th February 1878, and was succeeded by his assistant, the Rev. Henry Sidebottom. One of Mr. Barber's sons was the able organist and choirmaster. The other and earlier church in the east bay, built in 1863, is more simple in its services, and, I fear, was therefore not so much in favour as the more fashionable chapel in the west bay, to which, notwithstanding the distance, many of the east bay visitors resorted. The regular minister was Mr. Morant Brock. But last winter (1877–78) his place was supplied by Mr. Boudillon, the author of some books, and a good old man.

The Free Church of Scotland has Presbyterian service in a room of a villa in the east bay; but, whether owing to the distant and elevated situation, or to not having a church building, or to the paucity of Scotch people, it was generally attended by only a few, though the small room was filled when the preacher was popular.

There were also a German church and a French Protestant church, the latter being under the pastoral care of M. Delapierre. The Scotch church had no afternoon service, while that held in the French church in the afternoon was usually poorly attended. A good arrangement might be, were the Scotch to give up their room, for which they pay £30 per annum, and to have the use of the French church for one service in the afternoon; and the second French service might, with advantage in that case, be held in the evening.

Having had occasion to make inquiry for a good school, we found most highly recommended an excellent French school kept by M. and Mme. Arnulf in a house adjoining the Hotel Bristol, and which was attended by young ladies from several of the principal hotels. The teachers are

Roman Catholics; but many of their pupils being Protestants, they made a point of avoiding any allusion to religion in their classes. The school was mainly intended for girls, but M. Arnulf had a class for boys. French, music, and the ordinary elementary branches of education, including a little English, were taught, the pupils receiving tuition also in drawing from M. Bouché, who paints pretty little pictures of Mentone, which are occasionally seen in book-shop windows for sale, and which are valuable to purchasers as agreeable reminiscences of their visit. The charge for all branches, music included, for the hours from 9 till 12 (lunch hour), six days per week, was 90 francs per month; if lunch and additional hour's tuition were taken, then so much more. Mme. Arnulf, a most pleasing French lady, had an excellent mode of retaining the interest of the pupils by giving a donkey excursion party (which all the young people could attend) about once a month. This was looked forward to by all the scholars with great glee, and sad was the disappointment if any unexpected sickness seemed likely to disable one of them from being of the cavalcade. In their daily walks, the young people were freely allowed to play after getting out of town, showing a great amount of good sense in the management of children, of which in other parts of France, I have seen it stated, teachers are in this respect innocent.

Young ladies and others can likewise obtain lessons in Italian, music, and other branches from resident masters and governesses. Young men who are not invalids are scarce in Mentone, and I doubt whether, in the midst of so much else to attract, their ardour for study is intense.

A botany class was successfully formed during the winter of 1877-78 by Mr. Henry Robertson, a visitor. The study of botany is very suitable for the Riviera.

Pianofortes can be hired for the season, though not by

the month; but the charge made is usually high—from 150 to 300 francs.

There is, besides a public library, a small museum of natural history, etc., in the Hotel de Ville, consisting principally of flint implements found in the caves of the Rochers Rouges, and of specimens of snakes, fishes, and other animals caught in the neighbourhood.

A theatre exists, but the performances seem to be rare. I never was in it.

In an open place or square, there is what is called the Cercle Philharmonique, or Club, admission to which is by ballot and subscription (annual, monthly, or by the season). Here are held concerts, dances, and occasional dramatic entertainments, while newspapers lie in the reading-room.

Two newspapers are published in Mentone—the *Avenir* and *Le Mentonnais;* but newspapers from Marseilles, Nice, and other places are brought by train daily, and are procurable at the railway station, shops, and a kiosk, or covered round stall in the middle of the Place Nationale.

Having given this general description of Mentone, and noted some of the institutions which are of the nature of essentials to the visitor's comfort, and being now settled down in the place for the winter, the natural wish is to know what is to be seen which will help to make residence agreeable.

There are various guide-books[1] which may be bought

---

[1] A recently-published guide-book to the south of France says, with regard to Mentone:—'A kind of gloom pervades Menton. The strip of ground on which it stands is narrow, and so are the streets.' 'The valleys are narrow and sombre. The roads up the mountains are steep, badly paved, and are generally traversed on donkeys, which go slowly and require so much chastisement that an ordinary walker will find it less fatiguing to dispense with them.' It also sets down the population at 12,000, and that of Cannes, by far the larger town, at 7000. These are statements which require revision, as they do not accord with the facts.

and consulted for this purpose, and it is no part of my plan in these pages to take their place or to describe after their manner. One of them, titled, *The Splendide Hotel Handbook to Mentone and its Environs*, would be more useful were it less of a puff of the Splendide Hotel, which really does not require any puffing. This book, in tagging and dragging the unhappy hotel into almost every paragraph, reminds one of De Foe's puff of *Drelincourt on Death*, which he brought or endeavoured to bring into notice by repeated mention of it in his remarkable *Vision of Mrs. Veal*. The author of the guide—(who doubtless laughs in his own sleeve and not that of De Foe)—mentions that there are fifty-nine excursions from Mentone, all of which he describes shortly, and I would refer to the book for its recital. Fifty-nine is a tolerably large number, and will, in any view, afford constant employment to those who are of an exploring disposition. However, people cannot always be on the trot, more especially if they be not in strong, good health. Much less will suffice for ordinary existence, and if all be accomplished in three or four winters, these winters will not have witnessed inactive lives. The number, however, is an odd one; and to make it even, I must add one which the writer fails to describe. It fell to my lot the very first night.

I was impatient to look about me, and on the evening of my first day took, with a young Scotch gentleman residing in the hotel, a walk as far as the gorge of St. Louis. It is the evening aspect of Mentone which I regard as my first and the additional excursion, and it is one of, if it be not, the most lovely. The moon was full and shining brightly. Now, the moonlight at Mentone is so clear and strong that everything comes out sharply, and all objects on which it rests are seen with almost the same distinctness as in daylight. Even quarter moon illuminates surprisingly The great orb of night sheds her effulgence upon the grand, steep, abrupt mountains, upon the rugged rocks, upon the glittering trees, upon the hill-tops, upon the white houses, upon all I have already attempted to depict as contributing to the magnificence of the landscape. Bold and varied as everything looks, as usually seen when the sun is in the heavens, the soft, wondrous silvering on the parts which are moonlit, set in contrast against the deep, sombre, unrelieved blackness of the parts which are cast into shade, developes the features of the panorama, with an impressive *chiaro oscuro* effect which can never be observed or attained in the broad light of day; while, turning round and looking upon the ocean below, we see the waves roll softly ashore in lambent lines of dazzling light, and the yielding water is dancing and glancing with the restrained restlessness of girlish glee, and tossing up little flickering tongues of fire, which cover the sea in the moonlight gleam as with thousands of short-lived electric sparks, darting up to snatch a kiss from their pale but glorious mother, and expiring in the vain and feeble effort. We had not far to go for this lovely tableau, which, when beheld for the first time, produces the sensation of being in the presence of a scene of enchantment.

But the scene is scarcely less beautiful, though different, when, the sky being clear, and especially on those evenings which are slightly touched by frost, the moon averts her face; for then the stars assemble with a twofold brilliancy, sparkling with a lustre which is unknown in our dull and foggy northern clime. Venus first of all appears like a great lamp in the west. We have had simultaneously other planets shining brightly, and particularly Jupiter, Saturn, and Mars, the last two having been in the winter of 1877-78 in close conjunction, but ruddy Mars not being so full as we had at Interlachen seen it some months before, when it was nearer the earth. The sky glows with constellations, chief among which stands prominently out Orion, which rises from the sea in the south-east, and passes slowly and majestically over the firmament to the north-west, every star in it, with generous but governed emulation, stinting not its oil and burning with redoubled energy. Then, almost right below Orion's belt, Sirius, the largest and most beautiful star visible from earth, radiates in full intensity, shining and scintillating with a luminous green splendour which has emanated from that grand orb twenty-two years previously—a light so strong that it casts a streak or tail across the Mediterranean like that of the moon, though fainter and less. Then overhead are galaxies of glory, in the midst of which the Milky Way, the nearest of the nebulæ (for it is that to which we ourselves belong), stretches over the great expanse its belt of pearly sheen, the dwelling-place of countless myriads of starry habitants whose light as now seen dates back to a period anterior to the creation of man—all of them far too distant to be discernible by the unassisted eye. Cold though the evenings sometimes were, I was often tempted to turn out and see the matchless sight. The promenade was close by, and there all was open to the view.

Visitors, however, are no sooner settled in a place than, according to immemorial usage, it seems to be their paramount duty to escape out of it and see its environs, and perhaps I shall best illustrate the locality by describing some of our excursions.

Besides the main road which leads in one direction to Monaco and Nice, and in the other to San Remo and Genoa, and another road up the Carrei valley to Turin, and roads which go a short way up the Boirigo and Gorbio valleys, there is not much opportunity for varied driving; but the mountains which connect themselves by their ridgy tentacula with the very coast, afford innumerable excursions on foot and on donkeys, and parties, often large in number, are daily in good weather to be seen starting on such expeditions. The donkeys are patient, sure-footed, know every inch of the way, and require little encouragement by means of the whip. There are many roads or paths constructed expressly for them up and over the ridges, although rather intended for the rural traffic than for excursionizing. The animals are let out for hire at 5 francs per day, or $2\frac{1}{2}$ francs for the half day, the day being considered divided by the lunch or dinner hour of twelve, and detention of half an hour beyond twelve reckoned as a whole day. Girls or boys, sometimes women or even men, attend the donkeys and act as guides, expecting a trifle of a fee to themselves— generally half a franc per donkey per day, and half that for half a day. There are plenty of carriages of all kinds, but principally light basket-carriages with one or more horses. The only other mode of conveyance is the railway. Steamboats do not touch at the port, and boating is not much indulged in, the open sea not being particularly safe, although near shore usually placid, and offering imposing views towards the land.

A few days after our arrival, we joined a party of friends for Castellar, which is about three miles distant. We started after lunch, about half-past one, having six donkeys for those who rode. It was the 2d of December, and the day was overpoweringly hot. The ascent commences at once from the town, and the mounting was almost continuous, diversified, however, by stretches of level path. For protection of the road, which would otherwise be soon worn away, it is, like most other donkey paths, in its steeper parts paved sometimes with the small round stones commonly called petrified kidneys, which are very trying to the feet of the walkers, at least till they get accustomed to them. After we had gone up a short way, we obtained the shelter of trees, which lessened the fatigue. It was a lovely walk the whole way, the views at every turn being so fine; the sky overhead, bright, clear, blue, against which the bold outlines of the adjacent mountains broke in most picturesque lines ;

while, whether we looked down the thickly-covered slopes below or across the ravines to the wooded slopes of the Berceau above, or to the hill ridges fringed with trees or capped by picturesque buildings, it was a scene of grandeur and beauty blended; while the silver-lined blue-green of the olive leaf, mingling with the dark green of the pines, and the grass and the wild shrubbery, combined with the bright glitter of the sun through the branches to make it fairyland. Notwithstanding the shade afforded by the trees, I felt the ascent very hot work, and perspired at every pore. At last, in about an hour and a half, we reached Castellar, perched upon the summit of the rock or acclivity, which is 1200 feet above the level of the sea. We found it a very curious old Italian village—a type, however, of others which we subsequently saw. It consists of two long narrow streets, and of three ranges of miserable old houses, offering wretched uncomfortable holes for the inhabitants, the wretchedness being probably to some extent redeemed by the natural purity of the air. On the outside walls, the windows, where they exist, stand high, and are small (in many places merely loopholes for guns), the town being so built as to afford some protection against the roving expeditions of the Moors. Poor and miserable as the place looks, it has, like all such villages, a grand church—that is, grand in comparison with the dwellings and with the apparent poverty of the people. The church is adorned by the usual spire, which forms a feature of the little town or village, which, though picturesque at a short distance, does not afford as much scope for the pencil of the artist as some other similar villages. From the platform on which the town stands, we obtained a splendid view of the mountains of Mentone and of the bay below. After halting a very brief time, the party descended, to be back before sunset—a precaution essentially needful to be attended to by those who are subject to any weakness in the chest, and by no means to be neglected even by those in robust health, as just before sunset, and for an hour afterwards, a cold clammy air descends or envelopes these regions. Going and returning occupied altogether about three hours. We returned highly satisfied with this our first expedition. On the way down, the graceful towers of the churches at several points came prominently into view.

After this hot day, we had two continuously wet days. The rain poured heavily, the wind blew violently from the south-west, and the torrent beds of the rivers were filled to an extent I never saw subsequently. The rain was no doubt very beneficial to a country which gets so little, while the flood must have proved useful in clearing out the bed of the river, with all its accumulations of dirt, soapy washings, and olive refuse. As the stream in flood brings down with it soil from the mountains, on this and on other similar occasions, the rivers, by carrying out what they hold in solution to the sea, discolour the water, and the sea was a deeply-marked brown for a considerable distance on and along the coast. The waves were high, and dashed grandly on the shore, and broke beautifully over the pier. Only on one occasion during this winter were they so violent as to dash over the promenade. We were informed it was a good sign that the winter should commence, as it had done, with heavy rain, as it generally ensured a long continuance of fine weather further on in the season. There were a few wet days in November and December, and all January and February we had it, nearly continuously, fine, dry, and open. The clearness of the atmosphere of Mentone is one of its great recommendations. There are no fogs such as we have at home, though what seemed to be the mistral produces an approach to them; but there are occasional cloudy days, and when the sun gets behind a cloud, the air is cold, sometimes keenly so. Wet days, however, are exceedingly useful to the visitor for keeping up correspondence, which the attractions out of doors tempt him to neglect in fine weather.

During one of the days of the week upon which it did not rain, I took a walk with a friend to the gorge of St. Louis. The road was very muddy, in consequence of the rain which had fallen; indeed, it is very seldom this road is in an agreeable condition. It is laid with soft limestone, which is ground down by heavy carts laden with enormous stones which are being conveyed from the rocks from which they are blasted to the breakwater. The dust so formed lies about three inches deep upon the road. Every horse, carriage, and cart which passes raises a cloud; but when the wind blows, it becomes insufferable, and there is hardly any possibility of brushing the dust out of one's clothes. Rain converts the dust into mud, and when the mud has obtained a consistency by being baked in the sun, it forms into hard ruts trying to the pedestrian.

The gorge was fully two miles distant from our hotel, and was a frequent point to which we subsequently walked or drove. To reach it from the west end we may pass through the Avenue Victor Emanuele, where the shops are, and its continuation, the Rue St. Michael. The road then skirts the water by the Quai Bonaparte (so called after Napoleon I., who constructed the Corniche road, of which this is a part), and looking up, we saw the old town with its ridge upon ridge of high old dingy houses, like so many terraces one over the other—a very hanging garden (though garden is anything but the suitable word) of old roofs and chimney-tops; while, looking over the parapet wall, the water lying 15 or 20 feet below, a fine view of the bay and little harbour is had. But this part of the road is always under shade after twelve o'clock, and is exceedingly trying to invalids. I have often thought that the municipal authorities might effect a vast improvement if they would construct a diagonal road across from its commencement at the well to the Hotel de la Paix. The water is very shallow, apparently only a few feet deep; and though it would be a work of time and would require much material, it would really be of vast importance to Mentone, as then the invalid could walk or drive either to or from the east bay at any time of day without danger. The space intervening between the embankment so to be formed and the Quai Bonaparte, might afterwards be filled up and converted into a large public garden. The operation, however, would be costly, although the stone for forming it is at hand. But taking things as they are, the road continues in front of the various hotels I have already mentioned. Whether it was that the air here is more confined than in the west bay, I know not, but we never could walk along this long dusty stretch without a feeling of languor such as was not experienced in other and much longer walks, so that we were always ready to take rest on one of the seats placed by the roadside. After proceeding a good way, the road at the east bend of the bay divides, and one fork winds up to the gorge and on to Italy. The other fork turns aside into a promenade (now in course of formation), as yet short, by the margin of the sea and along the rocks of the coast, which will, when completed, become, as even now to some extent it is, a very agreeable accession to the amenity of the east bay, where there are not so many nice walks as are in the neighbourhood of the west bay. Reaching the gorge, which forms a dividing ravine between the mountains of the Berceau and Belinda, and is crossed by a bridge, conspicuous from most parts of Mentone, standing about 200 feet above the stream below, and a good deal more below the rocks towering above, we can at the north end of the bridge place one foot in France and the other in Italy. The Italian *douaniers* have a station-house a little beyond, perched prominently on the summit of the rock. The French *douaniers* have theirs on the road near to the junction of the above-mentioned two roads, the two houses being stationed considerably apart, as if to prevent the possibility of quarrel.

The view from the bridge is remarkably fine, and should be seen in the morning, as when the sun gets round to the west or south-west, it throws much of the scene into the shade, and is, besides, too dazzling to behold. The harbour lies under us, a good mile off, with its few ships and boats, and the picturesque old town; beyond it, the west bay, Cape Martin, and all the panorama of mountains which stretch to the north and north-west of Mentone, the aspect of whose outlines and rugged tops, being so near, changes at every different point of view.

In the afternoon of the same day, we took a walk up one of the valleys. These valleys are all favourite walks to those residing in the west bay. The views from the bridges which span them at the mouths of the river or rivers, supposed to run below them, are each different from the other, and are exceedingly picturesque. The one next to us was the Carrei or Turin valley. The torrent bed of this river course is confined from its mouth, where it is narrowed (speaking from recollection) to about 60 or 80 feet, and for a considerable way up and beyond the railway viaduct, by sloping bulwarks of masonry. After this the bed, no longer so confined, widens very considerably, and about a mile from the mouth gets broad and bare; farther up still, it narrows again, and becomes the rocky bed of what sometimes may be called a river, but usually is nothing but a small stream. Within Mentone the bed is crossed by two wooden foot bridges, one wooden suspension bridge for carriages and foot passengers, and a railway viaduct. Looking up and northward from the wooden foot bridge which spans the river course at its mouth, and placed for the purpose of connecting two portions of the promenade, one of the grandest views in Mentone is had.[1] On either side of the spectator the Eucalyptus and Spanish fig trees, the flowering aloes and other trees of the public gardens,

[1] See Frontispiece.

offer a leafy inclosure; and carrying the eye along upon the left side up the right bank of the Carrei to the railway viaduct, and beyond it, we observe the tall plane trees of the avenue leading to the railway station casting their shadows over the road, and in the afternoon over the river course, giving the aspect of agreeable shelter from the sun. On the right side, like theatrical side scenes run in one behind the other, bright-looking villas with their coloured jalousies and red-tiled roofs, diversified by an occasional one in blue lead and French roof, project out of gardens,—the Hotel du Louvre and the Hotel des Îles Britanniques, in the rear of all, being by a bend of the river scarcely visible from this bridge. Then a mountain ridge within half a mile from the bridge crosses the view above 1000 feet high, and crowned by a monastery (St. Annunciata), and with slopes here concealed by olive, lemon, and orange trees, in regular terraces, and there broken and exposed by rock and steep earthy-looking sides, as if washed away, and dotted elsewhere by coloured houses, and with straggling pine trees bristling up from the immediate background; while behind all this, as a grand back scene, rising boldly out of rounded, verdant, or stony slopes, mingled and varying in aspect each hour with the course of the sun, which throws the shadows in the morning westward and the afternoon eastward, and sometimes bathes them in light, and sometimes veils them in shade, the rocky, rugged heights of the mountains (seen here in part only), some of them only two to three miles distant, tower up, thrown, in lines clear and strong, upon the limpid blue sky lying cloudless and serene above. The subject is one which frequently engages the pencil or the brush of the amateur; but the situation is public, and one cannot attempt a sketch without inviting inquisitive looks by crowds of those who are too polite to stop and hang over one's head in heaps, like the wondering and intently watchful, concerned, and admiring *gamins* of the street, but who are rude enough sometimes to pass repeatedly back and forward, shaking the bridge with every footfall, and jostling each other and the artist for a look over the shoulder as they pass. The scene is one which I never could tire of beholding. It has been photographed, but photographs never give a mountain view with the clearness and effect of a good drawing.

But leaving the bridge and proceeding to the Avenue de la Gare, we find on inquiry that this is the commencement of the road to Turin, which is nearly 100 miles off, although about half way it is met by a railway from Cuneo to Turin, and is now all but superseded for traffic by the coast railway towards Genoa, the direct line to Turin branching off at Savona, making a distance by rail of about, according to my calculation, 183 miles. This road is the only one up the valleys which can be traversed for any distance. A strong current of air frequently blows down the valley and renders it occasionally in its shady parts a cold walk for the invalid, who must in winter months carry wraps for use when either he gets out of sunshine or the sun retires behind a cloud. This current is, I presume, the cause of the west bay being cooler than the east. It is, however, a charming walk up the road, level for nearly two miles, and the greater part of the way—indeed, almost the whole of it—being fringed with trees. For a little distance after passing under the railway viaduct, pretty houses, in gardens full of orange and lemon trees covered with fruit, are seen on both sides of the river; and in spring, women are constantly met bearing on their heads to town immense basketfuls of lemons and oranges. Farther on, and on emerging from the shade of the monastery hill, a curious range of oil-mills has been placed like steps one over the other on the slope of the hill, driven each by a separate water wheel of large diameter—the same water, apparently, by an economical arrangement, driving the wheels successively as it falls. Some way beyond these mills, the

OIL MILLS CARREI VALLEY,
MENTONE.

road begins to ascend and to wind, and, as the valley closes in, thickly planted with trees on both sides, seems to become more and more inviting; while peeps are had of Castellar, high overhead, on the right, embosomed among olive groves. Rocky mountains, bold and bluff, oppose themselves nearer and nearer to the spectator; the small village of Monti and its white church and long spire is attained, and after some miles by a zig-zag road, the summit, upwards of 2000 feet high, and three miles from the sea, is won. An excellent excursion by carriage along this road is to the picturesque village of Sospello, 22 kilometres, or about 14 miles distant from Mentone, passing and visiting by the way the curious old town of Castiglione, which lies perched up among the mountains (inaccessible by carriage) at a height, it is said, of over 2500 feet above the sea.[1]

The valley of Carrei, partly from its proximity to our hotel, was with us a favourite walk, and could be visited also by a more sunny road for a short way on the east bank of the river course. Here, as elsewhere, the municipality have placed wooden seats, which are very acceptable to pedestrians. Sometimes a whiff of cold air blowing down the valley proves too trying to allow of sitting long; but one scarcely tires of the bright glad sun, or the view of the hill slopes and verdure with which they are covered all the year through, or of the bold mountains, on the foremost central one of which may be discovered— particularly with the aid of a glass, for it is at first hardly distinguishable by the eye from the rocks on which it rests—the ruined castle of Ste. Agnese, elevated like an eagle's eyrie high up on the apparently inaccessible summit.

A trip to Ste. Agnese is generally taken by all who are

---

[1] It is impossible to place reliance on the exactness of such figures. They must throughout be taken as obtained from different sources, and possibly in no one case correct. I should, for example, here doubt whether Castiglione stands as high as the castle of Ste. Agnese.

not infirm. Though not so arduous as the ascent of the Berceau, of the Grand Mont, or of Mont Agel, which all command extensive views, but can only be undertaken by the able-bodied, it is a somewhat fatiguing excursion, and most people perform the ascent on donkey back. On the 13th December, the morning and day being fine, we started, a party of twelve, with eight donkeys and two donkey-drivers. To reach the point from which the ascent begins, we proceeded along the Nice road westward to the Boirigo valley. The view from the bridge across this valley was then (even still is, notwithstanding the erection of buildings on each side, some of them lofty and uninteresting, has somewhat contracted the view) much more open and extensive than that from the Carrei bridge. It took in west, north, and east, the whole panorama of mountain, twenty-eight peaks and pinnacles, enumerated in Giordan's little *Mentone Guide* (1877), being counted from the bridge. A road runs up each side of the river course, which is hemmed in like the Carrei by bulwarks of masonry. The road upon the left bank does not proceed above a mile, when —at a picturesquely-situated olive-oil mill, embosomed among olive and lemon trees, and bordered by a pretty stretch of the channel of the river, lying at the bottom of a dell closed in by wooded hills on both sides—it is shut in and becomes a donkey path buried among the trees of the valley, the river in the ravine below meantime narrowing correspondingly. The walk by this delightful path through the woods arrives at an old stone bridge leading to the village of Cabriole, whence by a steep ascent Ste. Agnese may be taken. The road upon the right bank terminates more speedily, entering at a large pottery upon 'the primrose valley,' the river course of which, delightfully shut in by high banks, is usually all but dry. Up both valleys we have had many pleasant strolls. On the present occasion, proceeding only a short way beyond the railway viaduct, we left the last-mentioned road, and, ascending by a steep donkey path, gradually gained the top of a ridge, along which, at a gradient gently inclining upward, a walk lies, protected, like that to Castellar, by trees, and looking down on the Gorbio valley — on the one side, its great plain thickly planted with olive trees, and terminated at its north end by the town of Gorbio, as if resting on an island peak; and on the other, on the Boirigo valley and the monastery heights. It took us some time to reach the base of the mountains, when the path became rough with loose stones, and steep and toilsome. Nearly three hours elapsed from the time of our leaving the hotel till we reached one of the mountain roadside chapels, with which the country abounds, constructed not only to point religious feelings, but as covered places of refuge from a storm. As usual, a cross stood by it, bent to the north-east, indicating that south-west were the violent and prevailing winds. This chapel, which could easily have held all our party and more in a storm, was a short way below the town of Ste. Agnese, and afforded a convenient resting-place ere proceeding farther. We had from it a good view of Ste. Agnese, which, being placed back on the north side of the mountain, is not visible from Mentone. It stands about 2100 or 2200 feet above the level of the sea. The castle, now in ruins, on the summit, is above 300 feet higher. As a stronghold it was no doubt almost unassailable; for on one side the rock may be said to be perpendicular, and the other sides are, as I learnt from the ascent, very steep. The town of Ste. Agnese, which we had yet a good pull to arrive at, is another of those curious villages which are seen in the Riviera. From a little distance it has a deserted, ruinous look, and the place does not improve upon nearer acquaintance. Of course, notwithstanding the apparent poverty of the inhabitants, it has a grand church with a spire to it, and we had chanced to light upon a fête day; for, as we were sitting on the rocks beyond it at lunch (brought with us as usual on such excursions, and forming no unacceptable part of their enjoyment),[1] we cast our eyes down upon the steep hillside below, and there we saw winding up, quite a number of priests and people with images, banners, and other insignia. On reaching the plateau on which we were, they halted to rest, and then formed into procession, one priest bearing in front a large crucifix with a figure of our Saviour on it, life-size; and all chanting, proceeded to the church.

Resting some time, a few of us ventured to climb to the castle. An interesting legend (fully narrated in Pemberton's *Monaco*, p. 351) attaches to it. During the latter half of the tenth century, Haroun, a bold African chief, in command of a formidable fleet, was cruelly ravaging the coast and carrying off captives, among whom was a maiden of Provence called Anna, of illustrious birth and marvellous beauty. The vessel bearing her to Spain had been taken after a bloody battle, in which her father and two brothers were killed. Haroun had first pitied and protected her, and then fell violently in love with her. His jealous wife, divining the fact from his altered demeanour, gave orders to bind her and have her by night cast into the sea. Discovering this in time, he saved Anna's life, and in his rage caused his wife to be strangled. Arriving opposite Ste. Agnese, and struck by the advantage of the position, he landed with 100 men and his captives, the natives flying before him, ascended the mountain, and built the fort. Here he importuned the disconsolate maid to renounce Christianity and marry him, but in vain; till, finding her one day praying for him, he was overcome, embraced Christianity himself, and fled with her and all his treasure to Marseilles, where they were joyfully received and were married.

The return took rather shorter time than the ascent; but the expedition occupied nearly the whole day from breakfast-time till dark. We might have descended by two or three

---

[1] It is the custom in the Riviera, and probably elsewhere in France, to give free of charge, to those who are on pension, their lunch to take with them on such excursions, which they would otherwise have had at the hotel.

different routes, but chose the way by which we had come. One of the other routes would have been by going round the mountain and descending upon the east side; but I believe it is very steep, and not much approved by the guides or donkey people. Another route would have been by diverging from the road by which we had ascended and coming down another ridge, called the Arbutus Walk (from the circumstance that it is filled with arbutus trees, with their brilliant scarlet and gold flower and fruit, so tempting and attractive to young people), and terminating in the Madonna Hill, a very favourite walk from Mentone. All in the hotel who had not taken part were eager to hear about our expedition, and we became for the nonce heroes, as famous as if we had made the ascent of Mont Blanc.

If one were to ascend simply to obtain a view, that from Ste. Agnese, or even from the castle on the top, would scarcely repay the fatigue of the ascent. It is dominated by a chain of rocky mountains, which surround it on every side except that to the sea; and the view towards the sea —that is, towards Mentone—is not more extensive than what may be obtained from many lower points upon which we there look down, and among others the monastery of Annunciata, which seems a long way immediately below, although it stands high, and is a prominent object from Mentone.

To this monastery we paid several visits. It stands on the ridge between the Carrei and Boirigo valleys, and is said at one time—by no means, looking to its position, unlikely—to have been the former site of Mentone and of a castle. The plateau on which now the chapel and monastery are built is above 1000 feet high, and is attained by another of those donkey paths of which there are so many on the hills. In fact, various such paths, more or less steep, conduct up to it from different parts. The main ascent from the Carrei valley is sharp and steep enough, and has the usual allowance of twelve or fifteen chapels or stations by the way—little places like sentry-boxes, in which sometimes objects of worship are placed. A small church or chapel forms an adjunct to the monastery. Its walls are covered over with votive pictures in commemoration of miraculous escapes from great dangers, but of the rudest description. They depict the danger escaped, and the Virgin opportunely appearing in the clouds to interpose and save, and are very singular specimens of art, drawn by the merest tyros—or rather babes—in art. It is surprising how those in charge of the church could allow it to be desecrated by such trashy attempts at the pictorial. The thing, however, is to be seen in many other such churches. Our first visit to this spot was at Christmas-time (29th Dec.), when the monks dress up a little crypt below the chapel in a very curious way, so as to represent the Nativity of our Lord. On a raised platform a country-side is seen, with rocks, and plains, and rustic bridges, studded over by little puppet figures or dolls about a foot high, others in the distance smaller, personating different characters — kings, Roman soldiers, shepherds with some woolly sheep, and Joseph and Mary standing in the midst of all. Near them a little babe lies on the ground, and kneeling before and adoring it a figure, I suppose, representing one of the Magi. Nor are angels wanting to complete the representation; while in a recess in the distant vista a toy Noah's Ark is set, supposed to be resting on Ararat, satisfactorily proving by ocular demonstration that Noah's Ark was, at the time of the Nativity, visible. The figures are evidently carved by the hands of the monks, as the faces differ entirely from those of ordinary dolls, and from each other. It must cost the monks a good deal of labour to make the arrangements; but they have, I presume, little else to do, and it no doubt furnishes an agreeable occupation, which doubtless they grievously want. At stated hours of the day they may be heard with sepulchral voices chanting service; and as they seem to have nothing else to do, I suppose it may literally be said their vocation is, ' *Vox et prcterea nihil.*'

The most westerly of the valleys is that of Gorbio, which in some respects is the most beautiful, as it is the most secluded of all the three. It has no broad torrent bed like those of the Carrei and Boirigo, and in fact the river can scarcely be seen between its entrance to the sea and a long way up the valley, the road between these points lying at some distance from the river, in a ravine below, winding its course over rocks and among trees which hide it from sight. The valley, everywhere wooded, and river derive their name from the town of Gorbio, which crests a lofty conical-shaped rock or height 1400 feet high, about three miles distant from Mentone. The olive-covered ridges rise also on either side the valley pretty steeply, and hem it in.

On 14th February a party was made up from our hotel to go to Gorbio, sixteen in number, with nine donkeys and three donkey attendants. We left at half-past nine in the morning and got back at five o'clock. There is now a good carriage road for a considerable distance up the valley; but at that time it was only in course of formation, and was very rough. Where the road ceases, the ascent, hitherto gentle, becomes more perceptible; and on arriving at a point below the height on which Gorbio stands, we had to look up to it far above on the summit of its bold abrupt rock. It looked magnificent, and the sketchers of the party longed exceedingly to take it from that point; but the donkeys, or their drivers or riders, had no compassion, and, as it was not desirable to separate on such excursions, the chance on this occasion was lost, though, by starting a little earlier than the party, I got it on a subsequent visit.

The ascent to the top was steep by a donkey path, but the town was very curious. It has been, I believe, the scene of many battles. After inspecting it amidst the gazing of a crowd of idle inhabitants, we adjourned to a grassy bank a little outside, where we enjoyed our lunch, and the four sketchers were recompensed by obtaining a view of the town from an excellent point. As Gorbio is an excursion frequently made, we were surrounded by children, who kept us in a state of siege for coppers, which they are led by the injudiciousness of visitors to expect, and it was no easy matter to shake them off. We had still a great deal before us to do; so, as soon as possible, the donkeys were remounted, and we proceeded along a mountain path, gradually reaching an elevation several hundred feet above Gorbio, on which we then looked down. All along this path we had splendid views, including one of the village of Ste. Agnese and the mountain on which it stands, which, from that point presenting its edge to us, appeared like a sharp Swiss aiguille. After a long circuit, we reached a point, at which the party dismounted and walked to the top of a hill commanding the valley; and then began the descent by a rough, stony, mountainous path to Rochebrune, about two miles off. Some of our party, keeping too high up, had to descend the mountain so perpendicularly that they could only liken the declivity to the side or face of a house.

Rochebrune rests upon the slope of a hill looking westward, down upon the Corniche road, on Monaco and the sea, between 600 and 800 feet below. The ruins of a castle stand upon a rock, which is said to have slipped down from a cliff 200 or 300 feet above. This, if true, would be a remarkable and unique circumstance. The town itself, which is about three or four miles from Mentone, from which it is a favourite excursion, is very picturesque, and affords many choice bits for the artist, I think more so than any similar town in the neighbourhood. One of our party jocularly proposed to come and spend a fortnight there, and take sketches; but to any civilised person it would be just as agreeable to spend the time, if that were possible, in a rabbit warren, to which another compared it. The view towards Monaco and the hills beyond it is very fine, but requires to be seen before the afternoon sun comes round. There are two ways of reaching Mentone from Rochebrune— one, by going down to the Corniche road a little below; and the other, by descending through terraces of fine old olive trees, one of which, in the pathway leading out of the village, is of immense girth, and must be of great age. It is said that some of the olive trees in this neighbourhood are considered to be nearly two thousand years old. The trunks of these olives are often very curious, from the mode in which they divide or split up and twist about. By either way to Mentone, splendid views are obtained, and the usual course on an excursion to Rochebrune is to go by one route and return by the other. In going by the road, we skirt the tongue of land called Cape Martin.

One of the most interesting and most usual walks or drives from Mentone is to this Cape Martin—to the point it is above two miles distant; and it is at present, or was while we were there, reached either by the rough, stony beach, disagreeable for the feet, but the shorter way, and pleasant, as passing by the ocean and having the view open to the scenes around. In time, it is expected that the promenade will be extended all along the coast to the cape, which will make approach to it by the shore a most agreeable walk. The other access, much longer, is by proceeding along the dusty high road leading to Monaco to some distance beyond the Hotel du Pavillon, and passing under a railway viaduct which crosses the road to a rough side road or avenue which diverges to the left and winds through a delicious plantation of fine old olive trees, with knotted, and gnarled, and divided trunks, and long, vigorous branches which stretch fantastically overhead and interlace; while the sun glinting through them here casts alternate lights and shadows on the white limestone road, and there shoots in streaks through the openings, speckling the forest with glancing radiance, shifting and changing as the olive boughs wave, and their tender leaves turning now their silver breasts and now their green backs to the breeze, shimmer in the light; while the carpet of grass is spread underneath, dotted over with violet and anemone; and the distance is dark, shut out by the thicket of trees, and the background of shrubs, and banks, and hill. As the road proceeds, it again passes under another railway bridge, the trains over which whistle and whirl on, scaring the passers-by, and breaking incongruously on the quiet of the scene, as if winged demons had escaped and in a state of fright rushed in hot and fiery to disturb the tranquillity of the land and break its peace. Then walled gardens are passed, closely planted with orange trees, laden in bunches with their tempting fruit. Still keeping on this rustic road amidst more olive trees, we at last arrive upon an open part, and behold a church of curious design on the one hand, and the blue Mediterranean on the other, and before u· the avenue along the margin of the promontory. Here it had unhappily been intended to have built a town, and as a commencement three villas have been erected; but the situation is not only too distant from Mentone, but is on the wrong side of the hill, seeing the sun leaves it in cold shade soon after noon; and thus, though commanding a splendid view all along the coast eastward, they have not found favour, and stand silent and all but deserted. Beyond these villas, and at the entrance to the wooded hill, the carcass of an unfinished Roman arch, intended no doubt as a grand portal to the projected new town, spans the road, which, proceeding by the border of the promontory, and overhanging it, looks down through the trees and rocks to the lovely sea sporting about in little pools, or surging and breaking on its natural bulwarks, while the slopes of the hill above on the right hand side are densely overspread with wood. At the end of the avenue, where the shelter of the hill terminates, the strength and usual lie of the wind are manifested in the bent and twisted forms of the trees, most of which are inclined, curved, or in some cases doubled down, as if bowing in lowly obeisance towards Mentone in the north-east, the south-west winds blowing fiercely across the ocean when they come. The walks through the forest and up to the semaphore on the top are charming, and make Cape Martin one of the most enjoyable of the easy excursions from Mentone, so that the visitors have great cause to congratulate themselves that the building speculation came to nought. If building be ever resumed, it is to be hoped the forest will be spared to the public, and that any houses will be placed on the west or sunny side; although it would be a mistake there too, as it is wholly without shelter from the west. It is not unusual for large parties to come to picnic in the woods and enjoy the scene, bringing their lunch with them. Some houses were commenced on a level plateau at the point, one of them suspiciously like an incipient restaurant, but, no doubt, being found to be too much exposed, were abandoned, and what little was put up is now going to wreck and ruin. It is to be hoped that Cape Martin will never be desecrated by any such concern in the future. Here, at and round the point, the land is surrounded by a belting of rocks and sharp pinnacles, worn so by the breaking of the waves, and upon these pinnacles the sea is continually breaking. In stormy weather, it is beautiful to observe the waves rolling in and striking the rocks with great violence, and dashing high into the air, shivering into millions of shining particles, forming spray, which spreads and scatters in brilliant showers all round. Nor is it less beautiful, when the breeze is gentle, to watch the waves rolling majestically in, the hot sun shining through the long well-dressed line as if it were through purest glass of the brightest sea-green, and then to observe the rearing crests tumbling grandly over as they charge to the death and deliver themselves one after another on the rocky beach, which with a calm steadiness receives the shock.

From Cape Martin fine views are had of Monte Carlo,

Monaco, with the more distant Antibes, and even the Estrelles; while north-eastward, as if in long white robes, the young Mentone lies nestling or cradled in at the foot of the high range of mountains which, like gigantic Titans, in mute serenity hang over, and watch and guard with placid pride the smiling, sleepy little town to which they have given birth. With scenery so romantic, the point of the cape has become a very favourite haunt of the artist. It is seldom a visit is paid to it in which, if the weather be fine (for in cold weather one cannot sit long), persons are not to be seen taking sketches or elaborating more finished pictures, for which a capital foreground is furnished by the bent and distorted trees.

But it would be endless to describe or even to enumerate all the many walks and excursions which are possible from Mentone. These are principally from the western side; but we had occasionally walks in the other direction. I have already mentioned the walk to the gorge of St. Louis. There is another walk which we sometimes had to the rocks below and beyond the gorge, called 'Les Rochers rouges' from their red colour. These derive a peculiar interest from their containing certain caves or fissures in the rock, disclosed or opened up by the formation of the railway, out of one of which was exhumed the skeleton, or what is called the fossil skeleton, of a man. This, of course, is held up as evidencing the existence of man anterior to the creation of Adam, by those who believe in the existence of Pre-adamites. The skeleton is in Paris, and I have seen neither it nor the *brochure* of Dr. Rivière describing the discovery; but I noticed that the sides of the cave—as it at present stands, after the excavations for the railway—are not more than 20 feet apart at the bottom, the cave extending probably 40 feet inward, and about 50 or 60 feet high; but these eye measurements are sometimes deceptive. It is of very soft limestone, and in other parts of the rocks there are huge stalactites depending. It may therefore be very safely said that stalactite would at an early period form with great rapidity, and speedily cover up what the cave contained. I was informed, however, that the skeleton was found about 9 feet below the surface, in the midst of debris. In these caves, and elsewhere round about, many flint implements have been found, and some of them are collected in the Natural History Museum in the Hotel de Ville at Mentone. The workmen finding them sell them to strangers for a few pence.

Dr. Bennet's and Mr. Hanbury's gardens both lie in this direction—Dr. Bennet's, on the rocks above the Italian *douane* station; Mr. Hanbury's, about a mile and a half farther on the road to Ventimiglia. They may properly be called hanging gardens, and are not laid out as gardens are with ourselves. Many tropical plants are growing in them in the open air.

Our best excursion in this direction was that to the top of Belinda. We started on 31st January 1877, a party of eleven, with six donkeys. The walkers drove to Pont St. Louis, where they were overtaken by those on donkeys. All then proceeded a little beyond the bridge and the station of the Italian *douane*, and ascended by very steep paths to the village of Grimaldi, about 700 feet above the sea, on the slope or shoulder of Belinda, and seen from Mentone picturesquely buried among the olive trees. This is another of those curious old towns with the usual appendage of a church and spire. The slope on which it is built is all but perpendicular, so that house rises over house, and the back base of a house is greatly higher than the front. Clovelly in North Devon is nothing to it. Roads are impossibilities. There are no streets, only narrow paths, or at best donkey tracks, through it. By one of these paths, winding upward, we were led to a point right above the gorge of St. Louis. From this dizzy height, the party, halting, looked down upon the precipitous yawning gulf below, and then across the bay towards Mentone, and upward towards the mountains, which this new position threw into shapes different from any observable from other points. Having taken in this striking view, we are urged to proceed by a very rough path, some parts of which are so uncommonly steep that those riding were compelled to dismount from their donkeys, and manage the ascent, like the others, as best they could; and so, alternately scrambling up pretty nearly perpendicular parts, and alternately winding up and jogging on by gentle ascents, where the donkeys were remounted, and through a forest of young trees, we, in about two hours and a half from the time of leaving the hotel, inclusive of a halt of half an hour at Grimaldi, attained the top of Belinda.

This mountain is, as already stated, 1702 feet high, and the view from the top of it is very extensive. We fancied we saw westward along the French coast, beyond the Estrelles, as far as the Îles d'Or off Hyères. If so, this would be a distance of fully ninety miles. On the east side, we could not see along the Italian coast beyond Bordighera, as the mountains rise and shut out further view in that direction. The huge rocky Berceau towered up in close proximity, to the north; and behind it, away to the eastward, we saw the tops of the snowy Maritime Alps peering up in magnificent white drapery; while between them and the coast lay a peculiar species of high, barren, bleak, desolate-looking mountains, intersected by wild and bare river courses; and more immediately below us, portions of the ramparts of Ventimiglia; and beyond, the long arm of Bordighera, appearing, from this point of view, stunted and different from its aspect at Mentone. The wind was blowing piercingly cold from the north-east at the top, so that we could not gaze at the scene in this direction above a few minutes; but just below the top, on the western slope, we found shelter and sun warmth, and enjoyed our lunch

PROMENADE DU MIDI, MENTONE.

and the splendid prospect. On returning, we descended by a different path, which in many parts might well be termed a *mauvais pas*. It was often so bad and so precipitous that the riders, in dread of their necks, were soon obliged to leave their saddles and walk. At last we reached the Corniche road, near to Mr. Hanbury's garden, and by this road returned home. From the heights we had seen a cloud of dust hanging over the road to Mentone, in consequence of the wind having risen to a gale. We now were under the necessity of encountering this dust, and, barring the chill blast on the hill-top, it formed the only obstacle to a thorough enjoyment of this most delightful excursion, which occupied altogether between seven and eight hours.

Although Mentone thus possesses so many walks and excursions in its neighbourhood, of which only a few have been touched upon, there are some people who, going there, fancy that it is an unattractive place. The fact is, that these people do nothing but walk up and down the promenade, perhaps also proceeding a short way up one or two of the valleys, and in all likelihood never even so much as venturing through the obstructions to the pier or the breakwater wall in course of formation, and now extending some length, from which one of the best views of the mountain range is to be had. It may be imagined, therefore, that a monotonous perambulation up and down the same road, however attractive in itself, may in time become tiresome, even if we put out of consideration those numerous dullards upon whom fine scenery or the charms of nature are altogether lost. In reality, however, it is one of the most captivating promenades to be found anywhere; and I always felt it to be in itself a very cheerful scene, whether when gay with its moving crowds in a morning, or when in the quiet repose of still life. But although preferring a quieter time, it is when thronged and all 'the world' of

Mentone is there that seemingly to most people it is most inviting; and between the hours of 10 A.M. and 12, the Promenade du Midi is alive with promenaders, for the earlier part of the day is considered to be the best period for so walking. Twelve o'clock is the general lunch or early dinner hour, and after that, or even before, the wind sometimes rises; but before 12, it is usually warm—nay, hot; and many men as well as women walk out with white parasols (lined with green), and many with blue goggle spectacles, to protect their precious eyes from the white glitter of the road. Although the glistering blaze of the sun upon the water, if caught direct, is too dazzling to abide, I never personally found either the heat or the general glare so oppressive as to require these protections, and it rather appeared to me that it was beneficial to accustom the eyes to the light. On certain days a band of music plays in the gardens in the afternoon (at other times playing at the *cirque*, or at the new gardens at the East End), but we seldom heard it, except by accident, as we devoted the afternoon to more distant walks. To some people, however, the music was evidently an unfailing attraction, although, so far as I could judge, the audiences were mainly confined to French and Germans, and other continentals, who, with some excellent exceptions, never seem to have any enjoyment beyond occasionally a little light reading, a good deal of idle smoking, or an endless elaborate thrumming on pianos, and on whom, therefore, time hangs heavily. English people, women especially, have generally an occupation of some kind. In reading, writing, sketching, and other occupations, I was never myself without employment, and sometimes was pressed enough for time.

On the promenade one sees a good deal of the peculiarities of the different countries represented in Mentone, especially in the matter of dress; and on this account, if for no other reason, it affords opportunities for observation not without their interest. Let us take a walk. It is, we shall suppose, the 21st December, the shortest day, cold and shivery in the north, and verging to eleven o'clock of the forenoon. The fishing operations of the morning are over, and the boats engaged in it have been drawn up upon the beach. The water carts, small wooden boxes drawn by men, have performed their rounds, and the roadway is moist, but is rapidly drying up under the burning beams of the hot sun; but the dust is laid. The sea is tranquil—not a ripple disturbs it, except at the very edge, where it lazily turns over in the tiniest of waves, as if the exertion implied far too much fatigue for this melting day. A ship has ventured out of the harbour, spreading its white sails in vain attempt to catch a breeze. A flock of gulls are resting, in quiet happiness and contemplation, their snowy bosoms on the glassy water. In the distance, bright Bordighera is stretching its long green sleeve far into the blue sea, its fair hand lighted by the sun; while its cathedral window, like a jewel on the finger, catches and glistens with a blazing ray. Nearer, the fortifications of Ventimiglia are peering round from behind a jutting hill. Belinda, high and verdant; the gorge of St. Louis, deep in the shade; and the lofty Berceau, just emerging into the solar beams, fill up the near background, against which is cast the pier, terminated by its old castle, and half concealing the little sheaf of masts which it girdles, and bounded landward by a line of tall picturesque old buildings, out of and above which the minarets of the town churches gracefully rise. Then down along the promenade, on the one side, rests the irregular and diversified line of hotels and houses and gardens, partly filled with low trees, refreshing to the sight; while a low, scrubby, ill-kept belt of evergreens, dusty and withered, strives at some parts to guard the frontier on the other side against a careless tumble down the bulwarks bordering the beach; and all along this level road, common to man and to beast (for there is no footway), a crowd of people is streaming. In the view of so much that is grand in nature, we are at first hardly conscious of the concourse. We begin to move down the promenade,—'cric-crac,'—turn the shoulder suddenly, and find a *voiture* has almost run us down. Neither man nor horse apologizes. They pass on unheeding our well-merited indignation; and, as we cast a fierce look and waste an English word, down comes another at full speed with angry 'crack, crack.' Glad, like others, to jump unscathed away, we are about to sit down upon one of the many wooden seats or forms which the providence of Mentone has placed here and there to lessen the lassitude of the human frame. In the very nick of time we luckily discover a warning label, and are thankful we have not become for the day men of mark; for the bright green seat, so delightfully clean and pretty and enticing, has just been repainted. We look out for another, for the sun is hot, and our limbs are getting jaded, and fortunately detect one to which the attention of the municipal adorners of Mentone has not as yet been directed.

And now pass in review before us all the inhabitants— no, not all the inhabitants, but a considerable section of the visitors, intermingled with a few of the residents of this remarkable place. Here comes a short Cockney, broiling in a long Noah's Ark Ulster—the young man has no other upper coat, and, besides, it adds a span to his stature. Then follow him in a row, three or four tall, lanky young Dutchmen in their dapper little coatees. Then a party of German ladies, plump in figure and peculiar in their body-gear and head-dress, their good looks set off by a most comfortable-looking ruff or frill about the neck. They are accompanied by a fair German gentleman in gold spectacles. As they pass, their 'Yahs' and their 'Achs' betray their origin. Close after saunters along a pleasant-looking clergyman, who, far from official cares, wisely doffs official costume, and is accompanied by two blooming English daughters. Near to him follows meditatively a priest without daughters, whose bluish-black cheeks and chin disclose it to be three days off from last shaving night. Now we must feel nervous and think and shake about our misdeeds, for who should follow in the full dignity of office but an imposing gendarme with fierce moustache, and in cocked hat and hot blue cloth clothing, adorned by yards of twisted cord, and swinging a murderous sword by his side. The little boys could see him a mile off. We breathe more freely when he is past—this terrible man of office. But nothing afraid, three women of Mentone are close upon his heels, perhaps in gaping admiration. Two of them bear on their heads each a large basket of dirty clothes they are taking to some dirty pool to wash. The third leads a child, and wears a broad Mentone flat hat, 16 inches wide at the very least. All are sturdy, and their carriage is erect. The little child wears a red hood, which tightly fits the round bullet head, and descends upon the neck and shoulders. The women wear short woollen jackets reaching to the waist, their lower drapery decently short. Another woman is behind, dressed similarly, except that, instead of hat, she, in common with most other native women, ties a coloured handkerchief round her head, and thus with a presumable thickness of bone beneath becomes proof against solar heat. Then succeed rows or groups of unmistakeable English in all varieties of home costume, suitable or unsuitable, though occasionally a damsel will glory in French attire, possibly a little Anglified. Then other groups of equally unmistakeable French. Here and there a solitary Frenchman steps out in full Parisian costume, with trig kid gloves, high chimney-pot hat, and smart cane or white parasol. And now and then a pale-looking young man, tended by an anxious sister or still more anxious mother, walks slowly past. He has come too late to obtain good. Had he come a year sooner, he might ere this, had it been the Divine will, have regained his strength. All health resorts abound with clergymen, particularly English and Scotch clergy—men of all denominations, whose ministerial exertions seem to necessitate occasional 'retreats.' Mentone is a favourite gathering-place for them. Here comes one, with a broad, low-crowned wide-awake (clerical undress), with white choker and lengthy surtout, his round face red and jovial, and beaming with laughing jollity; and alongside of him stalks a younger man of a sad and sallow countenance, whose greater length of coat proves more veritable descent from the apostles. He has just arrived from London, and is on his route to the great city of the Italian king—perhaps hopes to have a secret meeting with the Pope. 'I can't linger here,' he says; 'I am on my way to Rome.' 'Ay,' replies the older one, 'so I see. I am content to remain here; half way, you know—ha! ha!' They stop a moment, shake hands, and as the younger one turns carelessly to go, he nearly upsets an old fisherman with a coil of ropes in his hand, a pending striped cowl on his head, and clothed in a short wrought woollen coat and indescribable trousers, patched, like the famous Delphian Boat, till no trace of the original remains. One trouser leg is down, the other is drawn to the top, and discloses a long, bare, dirty-looking, unwashed, hairy leg. The feet are shoeless, the body spare, and the face pinched, as if he saw more work than victuals, and browned, as if he handled more fish than *savon*—in all likelihood the very personification of the fisherman of Cæsar's time. And now a nursery-maid with three lively little English children toddle along, the young ones attired in Mentone hats of narrow diameter, prettily decorated in worsted, but rather difficult articles to attach to the head. Fortunately the wind does not blow. And now jauntily trot up two riders—a young Englishman on a milk-white steed and lady on a chestnut. They are off for a canter along the road to Cape Martin. And then, as if in mockery, immediately follow an ass with panniers, in each of which will be found planted a fat, chubby, small child, looking dreamily contented or ignorantly happy, attended by donkey-driver, pleased attentive nurse, proud mother, and a big little brother with toy whip in hand astride another donkey. But here walks up an old friend, a divinity professor, presumably of the Broad Church; for is not the brim of his wide-awake broad enough to drive a coach and four round it? We must rise and shake hands, the more especially as we see stealthily approaching the lean painter, casting hungry looks at the seat, as much as to say, 'By your leave;' and feeling really desirous of being regarded blacker than we might be painted, we quit, join our friend, and move on. All this time we have been revolving the peculiarities of French female attire; for, generally speaking, we could tell a French woman by her long sack-like cloak. According to the fashion then prevailing, which may most likely be now changed, this sack hung down from the shoulders, tapering outwards as it descended to the bottom without any waist; for it seems to be the practice of the French for the men all to dress so as to give them the appearance of a wasp-like waist, and for the women all to dress as if waist they had none. Nor can I say, having had no opportunities of knowing, unless in observing the specimens of Mentone women walking about, whose conformation, unaltered by dress, is striking, and apt to convey this idea, being broad at the shoulders, broader still at the waist, and broadest at the haunches. Then all the French ladies, in defiance of surgical laws, wear high heels upon their shoes—sometimes no less than three inches high; and perhaps I am not far wrong in saying that, with few exceptions, every one of them in consequence walks badly, with a short hobbling step. To crown all, there is often stuck upon the head a bonnet like the hat of a typical Irishman, resembling an inverted flowerpot, with a brim, if brim it be, no broader than that of the article from which it is copied. Often, too, one sees a long gown tail flourishing in the dust, which next morning is shaken vehemently by the owner outside her room, and is brushed assiduously by the maid on the staircase; so that out of the deposits from this stupid fashion, the wearers do not positively kill their neighbours, but thoughtlessly compel them to bite the dust. The picture of French women, therefore, is not particularly inviting, though there is often a spicy jauntiness about the mode and ornamentation of their costume which is peculiarly taking. Upon a Sunday or fête day, young French children are habited in the gayest of attire, sometimes smart and pretty, but at all times to our eyes Frenchy, and frequently with alarmingly short, expanded petticoats, and long, lanky, bare legs. In every case, these children must be dressed out of all proportion to their position in life. Occasionally a child dressed entirely in white, denoting its dedication to the Virgin, will be seen. English young ladies may be at once distinguished from French, inasmuch as they usually exhibit a most disquieting tightening of the waist. Real wasps, however, in nothing but the waist, it is truth to say they carry the palm in appearance and good looks over the representatives of every other land.

One of those customs which Sterne could hardly have said were better ordered in France, is the French mode of passing people when walking. Instead of doing so upon the right hand, they pass upon the left, which certainly does not appear to British people to be nearly so natural as their own mode; and till the English stranger becomes habituated to the foreign custom, it is not inapt to produce a startling, if not a striking, method of seeing eye to eye. Similarly, a contrary rule exists as regards horses and vehicles. It would be well if there were one general system observed all over the world for walking and driving. In sailing, I think there is already a universal rule. In saluting, foreigners always lift the hat, be it to man or woman of their acquaintance, making a very ceremonious swing of the chapeau, but little inclination of the body, and no movement whatever of the countenance, thus imparting the impression of a very superficial, heartless politeness. Perhaps there may be more kindliness in the practice, at Mentone and elsewhere, of every man or woman met in the mornings in the hotel saluting you and expecting you to salute them with a 'Bon jour.' At home in some rural districts a similar usage is occasionally encountered.

I have not observed many beggars in France, but in Mentone, so close upon Italy, there are some professional or regular mendicants always hunting the promenade and other parts; while all the native children have been taught a very evil custom, which many men and women also practise, of coming up to visitors, holding out the hand and saying, 'Donnez moi un sou,' or simply, 'Un sou' (Give me a halfpenny); and some visitors, unconscious of doing harm, give them sous. An American gentleman told me he had given away 8 sous in a single forenoon, being all that he had about him. The children do not require them, and it teaches them a very bad lesson, sapping their independence. Sometimes the method is varied by presenting bunches of wild-flowers, or by lying in wait and tossing the bouquet into passing carriages; for which, of course, they expect, if accepted, to be recompensed.

An excursion to Monte Carlo and Monaco is one which even the most inveterate promenade walkers will at times take; and it is, indeed, a very favourite one with most Mentone visitors, many going weekly, and even oftener. The distance to Monte Carlo is about six or eight miles, and young people occasionally walk it. Driving by carriage is undoubtedly a most enjoyable mode of going. The road, after passing some elegant villas, including the palace of the Carnoles family, the former residence at Mentone of the princes of Monaco, for great part of the way is bordered by olive and other trees, embosomed in the midst of which, here and there, are brightly-painted houses and large villas with a grand background of lofty mountains. Glorious views are had by the way not merely of the mountain scenery, but of the bays, of Cape Martin, of Rochebrune, of white-terraced Monte Carlo, and of the singular projecting rock of Monaco with its castellated walls and buildings, and overtopping it, rising with great abruptness, the mountain called Tête de Chien, resembling very much in shape Salisbury Crags at home, only three times as high, the height being stated to be 1810 feet. Just below Rochebrune, the road, keeping by the coast to Monte Carlo, diverges from the Corniche road, which slowly ascends and surmounts the Tête de Chien.

The railway is a more rapid means of conveyance, but its hours do not always fit in with the visitor's time.

The famous gambling tables at Monte Carlo, established in 1856, are, I believe, the only thing of the kind now left in Central Europe. The French Government, it is thought, would fain acquire the principality, so as to put down this pernicious institution; but I presume it would be too costly, at least in present circumstances, to arrange. To attract visitors to the place, the grounds have been laid out in beautiful terraces flanked by elegant white balustrades, the borders being filled with palm and other exotic trees and shrubbery. The main attraction, however, is contained in the Casino, which is a long handsome building, in which are a spacious concert room, a reading room with newspapers, and the gambling rooms. A first-class instrumental band, numbering between seventy and eighty performers, attached to the establishment, plays gratuitously to the visitors every afternoon and evening, and on Thursdays gives a selection from classic music. This daily concert, to which dramatic and other entertainments are sometimes added, forms an excellent excuse to many for going to Monte Carlo; and I have seen persons whom I would not have suspected of passionate fondness for music, visiting it day after day—the real moving cause being, no doubt, the hazard table. To see the mode of operation, I once entered the room where the gambling is carried on. For this purpose, application must be made, in a room off the hall, for a ticket of admission, which specifies the length of time, say a month or two months, during which the holder desires to use it. Upon presenting a visiting card, and stating residence and country to which the applicant belongs, the admission card is at once filled up and handed over; but it is refused to natives of Monaco, nor are young people allowed to enter the room. The roulette tables are divided into squares, and corresponding numbers from 0 to 36. The gamesters place their money stakes upon the squares, or, if they desire to spread their chances, upon the lines which divide them. A revolving wheel and a small ball are then simultaneously set in motion, and both circulate many times before they stop. According to the divisional number of the wheel into which the ball eventually falls, the fate of the stakers is determined. The table has the advantage of 1 in 36 in its favour, so that in the long run it always gains. If the gambler stake upon a number into which the ball rolls, he gets thirty-five times the amount of his stake; if upon the line between two numbers, and the ball fall upon one of them, he gets only half; if staked at the junction of four lines, correspondingly less. If 0 (zero) turn up, nobody gets anything, unless zero have been staked on, and the player then gets thirty-six times his stake. I do not profess either to describe the rules or even to know them, and state these facts, possibly inaccurate, merely upon casual information. The roulette stakes are not less than 5-franc pieces, and are often gold; but the highest amount which can be staked at one adventure is 6000 francs, £240. It is astonishing with what rapidity the game is renewed and carried on. The sums are laid down by the eager onlookers, and as soon as the table is formed, which it takes a very short time to do, round goes the wheel; and when the ball falls into one of the spaces marked on the wheel, one of the men stationed at the table calls out the number, rapidly pulls in the losing money, and shovels out with equal rapidity the sums which are gained. Not a moment is lost; the table is again formed, and the ball again decides the fate of those who peril their money on its uncertain movements. There are three such tables in the rooms, at each of which there are three or four men in charge; and each table is always surrounded by a crowd of onlookers and players, many of whom are persons who evidently cannot afford to lose money. There is a fourth table, at which the lottery is decided by a foolish game at cards, called '*trente et quarante*.' The stakes here are always in gold, and the play is for much higher sums than at roulette, the lowest stakes being 20 francs, and the highest 12,000 francs (£480). I believe that most people not withheld by principle, upon visiting the rooms, try their luck; and some visit the neighbourhood with a given sum, which they risk from time to time till all be lost, —a species of 'limited liability' which is better than total want of restraint. Whether a first loss always is the least, or often withholds from further play, I do not know; but I fear that, in general, a spirit of infatuation seizes upon people, tempting them either by failure to retrieve loss, or by success to go on further and lose all. Most of the habitual players watch the turning of the wheel, and form their own ideas or calculations as to what numbers or combinations of numbers are fortunate, and act accordingly. It is a sad temptation to silly young men, who are often led on from bad to worse, till they lose all they possess. The consequences are sometimes distressing. At Mentone we heard that in one week, while we were there, two young men, visitors, had committed suicide; but such occurrences do not reach the newspapers.

It was pleasant to leave this gay though sad scene of a vicious institution to stroll into the tasteful little shops

MONACO. 217

permitted outside, in which enticing fine-art wares in choice variety are displayed, or wander about the gardens and terraces, sitting in the sunshine under shelter of the trees from the air, which is often cold at Monte Carlo when mild at Mentone, and looking at the lovely scenes around. But there is, out of doors, one object suggestive of any feeling but that of admiration; it is the pigeon palace, upon and around which, unconscious of their fate, the poor pigeons are seen in crowds, bred to become marks for the would-be sportsmen. The shooting of these gentle birds is one of the most barbarous descriptions of pastime; it has not even the recommendation of sport. The shooters might as well fire at barn-door fowls.

The drive from Monte Carlo to Monaco is down a decline of little more than half a mile. The Palace of Monaco is visible upon Saturdays, and to see it specially, we devoted a forenoon. After ascending by a long fortified or walled road within the castle, the flat summit of the rock was reached; and here we found a large open space, or esplanade, or *place d'armes*, facing the palace and between it and the town. The palace, however, was not open to the public till one o'clock; so that we first visited the town, which of course is a small one, limited to the size of the rock, but possessing a population of about 1500. It is intersected by narrow streets, outside of which there are shady walks upon the south and west margins or edges of the rocks, among which we rambled, and at parts could look down to the water, more than 200 feet below. As the rock projects so far into the ocean, it is withdrawn from the shelter of the mountains, and is exposed to the mistral as well as to the north wind; so that the town itself, inhabited solely by the native population, is no doubt often a cold residence during winter. The principality, whose independence was recognised by the Treaty of Paris of 1815, used to extend on the mainland fifteen miles in greatest length by six in greatest breadth.

In 1860, the Mentone portion was ceded to the Emperor of the French for £12,000. Monaco is now, therefore, greatly shorn; but the revenues are said to be 350,000 francs, or £14,000 yearly. The palace, a large one for a prince whose territory is now so circumscribed, is square, with a courtyard in the centre, round which the buildings are placed, and on one side of which a handsome outside marble staircase leads to a splendid suite of state rooms. We were shown through these rooms, each of which is hung and decorated in a uniform tint or hanging, but each room differing from the others. It was interesting, a sort of Versailles in miniature. We were also conducted through the adjoining gardens at the extreme north and more sheltered end of the rock, which, though small, are filled with palm and other trees and plants growing luxuriantly, forming a pleasant retreat to the inhabitants of the palace.

Monaco is a place of great antiquity, its origin having been traced back as far as 1700 years B.C. Its history has been most eventful, and is set forth in full detail in Pemberton's *History of Monaco*, where the oppression suffered by the people at the hands of its princes, and the spirited resistance made, especially by the Mentonnais, who ultimately succeeded, without violence, in throwing off the yoke, will be found narrated.

The villas about Mentone are, as already mentioned, like the generality in the Riviera, painted in lively colours, and surmounted by tidy-looking red-tiled roofs. Slate is unknown, though sometimes roofs are covered with what appears to be lead or zinc, imparting a little variety. The windows of all the houses have outside jalousies, generally painted green. These Riviera houses resemble somewhat in colouring the houses in a German box of toys, or one of those vividly-coloured dolls' houses sold in toyshops. They give a remarkable brightness to the landscape, more especially where the hills are covered extensively and monotonously with the sombre olive tree. All houses are painted, and sometimes very fantastically, in imitation of shaped stones, carvings, projections, and other architectural features, and even of roofs, and they are so cleverly executed that a stranger has often to approach close to them to detect the illusion. So far is this sometimes carried, that I have seen a good substantial house painted to represent it in a state of decay—an odd freak; at other times, painted as if vegetation were, under neglect or abandonment, springing out of chinks between the painted layers of stones. The houses are built—with a certain amount of substantiality, though with wonderful rapidity—of a species of rubble, which is plastered over and sometimes neatly ornamented with stucco mouldings. Internally, they are in general nicely finished with abundance of decoration, particularly at the painter's hands; though one is sometimes annoyed to find that the plaster work is of such inferior quality as to be full of cracks, and even to give way and tumble down. The paintings on the ceilings are certainly wonderful specimens of art. Accustomed as people so often are at home to paper ornamentation, they are apt to suppose at first that these ceilings must simply be stained paper pieces pasted on; but on examination, it is found that they are, with some occasional imitations, all hand-painted. And although there are many coarse specimens of this style of decoration, they are frequently finished with great delicacy. The rooms we ourselves had in Mentone were in this respect, as well as in others, finished with good taste and skill; and although the ceilings were prettily painted, they were light and suitable. Sometimes the decoration of houses is carried the length of painting cleverly outside garden walls with scenic views, imitation staircases and theatrical trees, fountains, grottoes, etc. Marble is used in abundance in the houses, in chimney-pieces, staircases (outside sometimes as well as inside), and other portions of the buildings. Proximity to Italy renders cheap the carriage of the rough marble, which is wrought up according to requirement at local marble workshops. Windows are all constructed on the French fashion of opening up the centre—a method which is suitable to the climate, although, not being so close-fitting as our window-sashes, it would not answer in our own sterner climate. They are fastened by a bolt, the working of which the inhabitant requires to understand, as, if not properly fastened, a window may blow open, as it once did to us in a gale at Marseilles during the night; and in ignorance of the way of turning the bolt, much trouble will be occasioned in the dark. Nearly all rooms open into those adjoining, on both sides, by a door, sometimes two-leaved. The consequence is, especially when the partition walls are thin, that all that goes on in your neighbour's apartment is overheard. To remedy this inconvenience, in part, as well as to add to the warmth of the chambers, the doors are in first-class houses double, for which a certain degree of thickness of walls is necessary. Terraces and balconies are common adjuncts, and enable the inhabitants in many cases to enjoy the air and the views without leaving their houses, or scarcely their rooms.

The gardens attached to villas are usually planted with orange, lemon, and red pepper trees, with aloes, and the ever-green, and health-producing, rapid-growing Eucalyptus, besides other trees and plants, natives of a warm climate.

At Cannes we were taken by a French gentleman through a large villa he had just built for his own occupation. Upon the first floor (what we would term the street floor), above the ground floor, or that occupied by the offices and servants' accommodation, and opening out of a large hall, there was a suite of public rooms, consisting of dining-room and drawing-room, with intermediate ante-drawing-room—all looking to the sun, and of a library and another room upon the north or non-sunny side of the house. On the floor above, there were six bed-rooms, separate sleeping chambers being devoted to the husband and wife. The south windows opened out on each floor to a broad terrace, looking down upon a large garden, beyond which fine views were had of the sea and Estrelles. Every room was finished in the best style.

As I have already said, there is only in reality one street in Mentone occupied with shops. This is in the heart of the town, and the shops are few in number, some of them evidently having a struggle to exist; but coupled with a vegetable and fruit market, they are abundantly sufficient, if not more than sufficient, for the wants of the inhabitants and visitors. None of the shops can be said to be of any size—except, perhaps, one of the bazaars, of which there are several, and in which almost every description of ware except eatables is sold. And at Christmas-time they are packed with purchasers in quest of nicknacks for presents—toys, photographs, woodwork, and ornaments of divers descriptions, many of which are marked with the letters 'Mentone;' for it is curious that the old Italian name is thus preserved in preference to the French Menton, which is not so euphonious. Things are generally dear in the shops; in fact, nearly every description of article is dearer than at home, unless, perhaps, it may be French writing-paper, which is sold at a moderate price. All articles of household consumption are dear; sugar, for instance, is 8d. or 10d. per lb., showing the French people themselves do not benefit by their system of bounty on sugar enjoyed by their refiners. Many things, however, have to be brought from a great distance,—butter, I believe, comes from Milan, and is good; fish, from Bordeaux and other distant ports; books, from Paris and London,—and a large percentage is added to the price. I have been told, but cannot say from experience, that shop-keepers follow the Italian custom of asking more than they will take or than the goods are worth, and that the disagreeable custom of bargaining is necessary. But the things we have bought have generally been such that there could be little room for difference of price. However, it is extremely likely that, in the market, bargaining is absolutely needful, and possibly also in some shops. A lady said to me that at Nice they had to bargain about dress.

The booksellers have circulating libraries, in which are many English books, including a quantity of Tauchnitz editions; but the collections are principally of works of fiction and light reading, and for our second winter at Mentone I thought it advisable to have a box of selected books from home.

If asked to say what is the great industrial occupation of the inhabitants of Mentone, I think I could not be far wrong in naming that for women as consisting in the washing of clothes. In fact, all along the Riviera, as well as in other parts of France, washing of clothes seems to the women portion of the working population the sole vocation of life; although it is difficult to comprehend from whom all the clothes to fill their hands and baskets come, unless France be the washing field of the world. At Mentone, go where one might, women were washing clothes, and that in a manner most disgusting and repulsive to English notions. Instead of washing them in some rural part with pure hot water and soap, wringing out the water and bleaching on the grass, these women will walk to any spot where a drop of water can be had, no matter how foul, or whence it comes, or what are its surroundings. Thus at Mentone they haunt the rivulets, which are full of olive juice sent down from the olive mills, the water passing over, as it trickles down, beds thick with the deposited accumulations of months of olive refuse, mud, and other dirt; and then, ensconcing themselves in the baskets in which the clothes are brought, and on their knees, they stoop down, put the clothes into the filthy water, and with a wooden roller-pin beat the unfortunate articles till one might suppose they were beat into a jelly, or at least into a thousand holes.[1] The clothes are thereupon hung up or spread on stones to dry, all in the view of the population, and along the beach and elsewhere. There was, indeed—for it is now disused, in consequence of the remonstrance made as after mentioned—one public washing-place, constructed for the purpose of washing in; but this was nothing but one long continuous stone trough, for the use of which, I presume, a small charge was made. Here I have counted fifty-two women washing at one time, as close as they could be packed, upon both sides of this trough, which seemed about sixty feet long and three or four feet wide. All the garments were washed in one water, which, I presume, could scarcely be said to have been changed oftener than once a day at best, although a trickle of new water might ooze through it. The washing in this trough, however, was purity itself compared with what took place elsewhere. I have seen women washing at one pool of dirty water for weeks together, any fresh water which could possibly percolate through it being utterly unable to carry off the soap and dirt of the washings which stuck to the sides and bottom. Nor was this the worst. At one narrow aqueduct, full of the blackest dirt, and with the veriest drop of water struggling through it, little more than an inch deep, and only secured by damming it up, and only changed when a flood unexpectedly came, women were to be seen constantly engaged, it is to be hoped only on their own clothes.

So offensive has this custom been considered by the English, that a representation was made to the civic authorities, and some change for the better was promised; but whether it has been or will be such as will adequately meet and remove all the evil complained of, or whether it

---

[1] At Biarritz a different practice prevails. Instead of beating the linen, the linen is employed to beat the stone. We have seen a lady's fancy petticoat thus thrashed against the stones without mercy.

will simply remove them out of sight, I cannot say. It is most uncomfortable to think, were there no other objection, that one's clothes may be washed in the same water as that in which, it may be, the clothes of those who have been suffering from disease are being soaked. Towels and sheets have, when fresh, a most disagreeable soapy smell. Linen articles of wearing apparel, however, seem to come home remarkably pure, and it is to be hoped that they are, after the first bleaching, put through clean water. Buttons, however, soon get loose after the violent treatment to which linens are subjected.[1]

Another grand pursuit of the Mentonnais is that of fishing. Two or more fishing boats are engaged almost every morning in this occupation. A boat takes out the net a long distance, when it is dropped in the water. By two long lines the nets are then laboriously drawn in upon the shore by from twelve to twenty men or women. A great deal of this labour might easily be saved by the use of windlasses. When the net comes near the shore, a crowd of visitors and other idle persons surround the fishermen to witness the result. Often I have seen the net pulled up without a single fish in it; at other times, a small basketful of little fish which they call sardines. Sometimes a few larger fish, a dozen or half a dozen mackerel, may be taken; but at other times I have seen little more brought up after all this waste of exertion and time than a quantity of minute fry about an inch or so long, the young of fish which might otherwise have attained maturity. The result is miserable, and one could wish not merely that the men were better employed, but that there might be some stoppage put to a mode of catching which must prove so injurious to the fishings. Is it not likely that a deep-sea line, baited with so many hooks (such as our fishermen use), would take

[1] The expense of washing at Mentone, though not moderate, is less than in Paris.

large fish and leave the young to develop? But the fishermen have no doubt fished for two thousand years or more in the same way, and could not possibly take in the thought of any novelty; and, patient as they are, one would wish to see this patience change to enterprising and inventive vigour. It is, however, to be kept in view that the sardines for which they lay their snares may apparently be caught only on the surface, as when there is a surf falling on the shore I have seen the nets dragged into the boats upon the sea, and many sardines thereby caught. In stormy weather, a rare occurrence, the fishing is altogether stopped. Judging from what I have seen, I should say it was unlikely that the fishermen earn more than the merest pittance (a few pence a day) by their calling, in pursuing which they dress in their worst clothes; and it is well they do so. I have seen an active young man knocked over and sucked in by the surf, disappear for a moment, and come out dripping.

But wretched as this occupation is, there is a still more pitiable phase of the fishing life, consisting in grown men—not one alone, but many—angling the whole day with a long reed rod and a hook baited with chewed bread. After enduring hours of waiting, during which their hearts may have been rejoiced by glorious nibbles, they will entrap some unfortunate little fish—generally a small sardine, only fit to be tossed back into its element; while around the noble fisher, various idle spectators are congregated, watching his float and deeply interested in his success.

Another pursuit, curious in its mode, is that of the shepherd. Hardly a morning passed but we saw an Italian shepherd standing about, singularly attired in shaggy coat and rough knee-breeches, and a species of stocking leggings, with a short, tawny-coloured Italian cloak on his shoulder, and a long, conical, Italian wide-awake on his head, the whole suit bearing traits of the wear of a lifetime. Sometimes he was accompanied by a boy, a representation or copy in miniature of the same; the copper-brown complexion and bright dark eyes of both revealing them to be children of the sun. Near to them on the hard stony beach, a flock of thin small sheep as gaunt-looking as their herds were hobbling about on the stones and picking up dried leaves and anything that once was green which they could find in this, to them, barren land. He moves, and they follow. No dog scares them, or collects or pursues them. They hear his voice and, as if affectionately attached, obey. When they have traversed the beach, he produces a sack and spreads upon the ground what looks like sawdust, but is probably bran, which they eagerly devour. It would seem as if the sheep never had a chance of browsing on the hillside, for I do not recollect ever seeing a sheep upon the grass. Whence they come I know not, but their food by the road is just the fallen leaves.

A better occupation than the fishing, although it is dependent on the weather, is that of letting out donkeys. What we would regard as great fortunes cannot, of course, be made out of the small remuneration which the donkey people receive, but it seems enough to enable them to appear respectable.

Some employment is also had in the making of wooden inlaid articles for sale in the shops, generally with the word 'Mentone' on them. The articles sell well; but it is said that many of them come from Sorrento, which is the headquarters of this description of work, and where it is carried to the highest perfection, or at least to its largest extent. The prices asked at Mentone are sometimes double what are asked for similar work at Sorrento; while the same variety and beauty of work cannot, I think, be procured, although a Mentone workman laboured to make me believe his *modus operandi* was superior.

The great mass of the Mentone men, however, seem to be occupied in the various trades connected with house-building—in quarrying stones; and upon the works of the town, such as metalling and watering the roads forming the promenades, etc.; and I must say that the men appear to be industrious and steady in their application to their appointed tasks, as well as sober, for during all the time we were in Mentone, I never witnessed but once a case of drunkenness, and it was that of two men who apparently were not of the town, but from the rural parts. Not that they do not drink, for even the women carry to their work a huge litre bottle, but their drinking must be in great moderation and of a weak quality of wine. It is, however, very desirable to have some saving of human fatigue effected. For example, instead of lifting large stones by means of cranes, three or four men may be seen tediously and laboriously moving them by means of levers, keeping time to an unearthly sound ejaculated by the foreman or leader of the group. Labour is no doubt cheap. I suppose that wages do not exceed 2 francs per day, but the employment of so many men unnecessarily must add to the expense of public improvements. I suspect, however, that in this also, as in other things, there is a conservative clinging to old habits and customs, and fear of innovations, which it is very difficult to eradicate, and that men follow in their fathers' ways just because their fathers had always done so before them.

Necessarily the visitors bring with them employment to the inhabitants, such as in dressmaking and the various other requirements of life; and if one be passing along the main street of Mentone after the sun has reached the meridian, for no public clock strikes or bell sounds, he will find it crowded with girls and men leaving work and going to dinner.

The rural population is mainly occupied with the cultivation of the olive and the gathering of the olive berries, which are beaten off the trees by long rods, and picked off the ground by women and girls; and also, but to a much more limited extent, with the cultivation of the lemon and orange trees, and the gathering of their fruit, which is borne off by the women in large baskets on their heads. There appear to be few vines about Mentone, although there are a good many kitchen gardens to supply the needful vegetables for the population. Connected with the olive cultivation, is the employment of building terraces on the sides of the hills for the planting of trees. These are very neatly executed with a smooth facing of stone. The crushing of the olives in the olive mills also affords employment to a small class of men; while the building of water reservoirs or tanks in connection with the terraces, in order to secure supplies of water for the trees, gives further occupation. These reservoirs, and the conduits which are found running all over the hill-slopes to supply them, or to turn the mill wheels, are scattered everywhere: the tanks look ugly places to tumble into.

The wages of agricultural labourers, I believe, do not exceed from 1 to 2 francs per day.

Assisting the operations of labourers of different kinds, there are horses, mules, and asses. Frequently a cart will be drawn by a combination of all the three, a small ass leading the van, followed by the larger mule, the rear being brought up by a horse yoked within the shafts of the cart. The carts are, as a rule, laden far beyond the strength of the animals drawing them, and it would be well that the police could sometimes interfere. The horses are willing, though it is sad to see them occasionally brutally beaten, to urge them to efforts under which every muscle is strained to the utmost. But the mountaineers depend mainly on the ass. On this animal they throw the burden of carrying up and down the steep and rough hill paths, stones, barrels, bags, wood, and agricultural produce, etc., and patiently and intelligently do they perform their work.

One sees here and there poultry, but few comparatively to the number which are requisite to meet the daily consumption at the hotels.

Small wild birds are scarcely ever seen. I have counted up six sparrows fluttering about or chirping in the trees; but a sparrow, like every other small bird, is in France a *rara avis*. Three broad-shouldered men, dressed in blouses like labourers, go out daily with guns to shoot them. One could almost wish a visitation upon France of the Colorado beetle, or if birds do not feed on it, of some other insect plague, to open the eyes of the French to the impolicy of allowing these small birds to be shot. One of the most pleasing diversions in Mentone is to sit and watch the flock (perhaps now only two or three hundred in number) of sea-gulls which frequent its shores. While you are witnessing the joyful flights of these beautiful birds, suddenly you hear a shot fired, and the whole flight rises and skims away, leaving perhaps a distressed comrade, who has probably had its wing broken by a bullet. It is making frantic attempts to rise or to get out to sea. With right good-will could one pitch into the fellow who had done this wanton, cruel harm. I believe that the consequence of the shooting is that the poor birds find their muster roll greatly reduced, and they may in time disappear or migrate to some safer locality.

There is one animal which everybody could more readily wish to disappear, and that is the mosquito. I have previously mentioned that we did not find this plague so great at Mentone as at Cannes and Hyères. This may partly have arisen from our having visited these other places earlier in the winter; but I think a good deal also is due to Mentone being better drained, or at least to the drains not being so offensive.

At Cannes we were also more plagued than at Mentone with flies. These little animals are very impudent. They walk over your face and hands, nibbling as they go, and play at hide-and-seek in your hair. They are not to be deterred by the most stringent prohibitions; and while one has no mercy on mosquitoes, you hesitate to inflict the extreme penalty of the law upon a fly—nay, rather help your tormentors out of their scrapes when they tumble into water, milk, treacle, or the like.

It is commonly thought that it must be a disagreeable feature of Mentone that visitors encounter in their walks so many invalids there. No doubt there are a good many invalids at Mentone, and some of them have all the appearance of being so, but they do not predominate by any means. Many of them keep their rooms, and those who go out seldom go beyond the promenade, except for a drive. It is indeed painful sometimes to see some delicate invalids who are hopelessly beyond recovery, and particularly young men, thin, gaunt, and white, well wrapped up, even on sunny days; but they are never so numerous as to make Mentone a painful residence. The English people, as a rule, are wiser than the Continental. They come at an early stage of their complaint, and get rapidly cured; while it is said, on the other hand, that people of other nations come when they are incurable. Of course, some of these invalids succumb, and from time to time a death occurs; but a funeral is seldom or never seen. When a death happens, the hotel people keep it as long quiet as possible. The authorities take charge of the burial, and the body, which must lie unburied twenty-four hours after death, is removed in a coffin after dark to the mortuary adjoining the cemetery, where the relations assemble usually on the following day, and it is buried. The expense of burial is said to be moderate, the charges varying according to circumstances. But there is one repellent fact connected with this subject which I have heard exists. It is, that some of the hotels put up a notice in the printed bills of charges, which are hung in the bedrooms, that a death occurring in the house will be charged so much. This is no doubt done to prevent disputes, and there is fairly reason for a charge, seeing that the bedding on which the dead person lay is burnt or otherwise destroyed, the room is unoccupied for a short time, and it is against the hotel; but the making of this prominent notification shocks one's feelings, and may sometimes be injurious to the invalid. I have not personally seen it.

The cemetery of Mentone, surmounting the hill, on the ridge and slopes of which the old town is built, has a picturesque look from below. As usual abroad, the Protestant ground is separated from the Roman Catholic; the Catholics, by the narrow feeling of religious exclusiveness, refusing Protestants burial in the same ground with themselves. But it collects the strangers the more together, and it is painful to walk round and think of the many who are buried so far away from their homes and friends. We have seen at different places one or two funerals, when the English service was performed, but at Cannes had the opportunity of witnessing a funeral service conducted by the French Protestant clergyman. He was a remarkably fine-looking old gentleman, and in place of a formal service, or perhaps in addition to it, for we had not arrived at the commencement, he made a very touching address to the relations and others present, and offered a simple earnest prayer. We could not help thinking that it was so very much more appropriate than the formal service of the Church of England, however stately and beautiful, which so often is rattled over without much appearance of feeling, and is uniformly the same to all.

We were three months in Mentone during our first winter there, and, as may be gathered from what I have previously said, we had ample means of spending the days pleasantly. Perhaps the evenings, though pleasant, had too much of the public life about them, living so much in family with others. We occasionally longed for the quietness of home life, which could not be said to be had by simply retreating to our rooms. Sometimes the evening was varied, as I have elsewhere mentioned, by little entertainments, such as conjurors with their tricks. But we had, even amidst all the pleasant days we spent there, some peculiarly red letter days, embracing our more extensive excursions, and days to be noted.

Of these, the first was Christmas day. Among the English people this was maintained in the usual manner; but we had heard that there would be a grand service according to the Roman Catholic form in the cathedral or parish church, and we went thither. The Church of St. Michael, a large one, dating back, it is said, to the thirteenth century, was draped with crimson cloth, and a profusion of gold or gilt articles was displayed at the altar, which was lighted up with an immense quantity of candles. The place was crammed with people, the crowd even extending a good way outside the door. After the usual service and chanting, the great event of the day took place. Several priests, preceded by a tall janitor in cocked hat and uniform and halberd, in humble imitation of the grand man of the Madeleine, commenced parading through the church, one of them bearing in his arms a wax doll, baby size, as if new born, which he held out to be kissed; and every one, even respectable-looking people, pressed forward as they slowly progressed to kiss the doll's foot. When he came our length, the priest, a jolly fat man, who, whatever he may have felt at the absurdity of the scene, contrived to keep his countenance, quietly, seeing at a glance we were Protestants, or what was the same thing, 'Anglais,' presented it to others, and did not give us a chance. A priest behind him took up the collection. Each person, besides, had to pay for the use of a chair, some paying for two, one being used to kneel on.

New Year's day is, however, the great day among the native population; and gifts among the foreigners are usually then exchanged, in place of, as with the English, on Christmas day. A very common form of such gifts is that of a large bouquet of flowers, generally more than a foot in diameter, laid out in circular symmetrical rows, the flowers on short stalks being supported by wires. They look pretty, but stiff, and do not last so long as our assorted bouquets with their long stalks. On occasion of a birthday, the heroine of the day, if popular, and the event were known, would often get three or four such sent to her.

On the 3d of February we saw bands of young men parading the streets in an uproarious manner, with flags, and preceded by drummers beating the usual rat-tat-tat. We could not imagine what this meant, until informed that it was the day upon which the young men drew lots for the selection of those who were to serve as conscripts in the French army. The noise and merriment were, like the tom-tom at a Hindoo suttee funeral pile, doubtless intended to hide the agony and to drive away thought, if they any had, from the ' chosen few.'

A week later witnessed the grandest event of the season, for on 10th February the keeping of the Carnival commenced. For some days previously, the shops were full of false faces, wire gauze masks, strange dresses, and confetti; and cars were in course of decoration for the event, which necessarily, in a small place like Mentone, could only be upon a small scale. The coming affair was the grand talk of the town, and we had even some masquerading before it came. At last the eventful morning dawned. It was a complete holiday. Every one turned into the streets, or took possession of windows, balconies, and other salient points; while the promenade was ornamented with long venetian decorated poles, such as we had planted in the streets of Edinburgh when the Queen came to unveil the Prince Consort's statue in 1876. Balconies were draped, flags were everywhere fluttering in the breeze, and the Cercle where prizes were to be distributed was gaily dressed with evergreens and coloured calico. At mid-day the procession was expected to move; but it was much too important to move off so early, and did not commence till two o'clock. Meantime the streets were filled with people in the oddest and most comical attire, with masks on their faces, rendering them unrecognisable by their friends. One of these figures was absurdly dressed in feathers as a huge cock, while another represented a still larger eagle. All this time the people were peppering each other with confetti, small round chalk pellets smaller than peas. But the grand peppering was reserved for the procession, which at last hove in sight. It was preceded by a car filled with musicians in carnival costume, who did not play, being probably afraid lest their instruments might suffer damage. Then a long row of fancy soldiers ambled forward on horseback, two and two, dressed in a uniform of blue coat and white trousers, looking very gay. Then various cars were dragged slowly or staggeringly along in odd devices, one of which was the representation of a gigantic lobster pie filled with men dressed out in red as boiled lobsters, while the horses had vast coverings as black or unboiled lobsters. Another car personified classical statuary, the men and women being chalked or painted over in white, and intended to be motionless, but as taken being well shaken, not always succeeding in preserving either rigidity or composure. Various other cars, besides walking figures, and people in carriages, all disguised, completed the procession, which, like a stage army, to make up for the want of numbers, passed round the circle and repassed repeatedly. All this time, the people in the street, or on the balconies or scaffoldings erected for the occasion, and in the carriages and cars, continued to fire away at each other a copious shower of confetti. These were discharged with a right good-will; but all, except the improvident, being protected by masks

CORSICA AS SEEN BEFORE SUNRISE.
MENTONE.

and calico garments, no damage was suffered, except when a man audaciously appeared in a good hat, which hat was battered by discharges of confetti without mercy. Young men and young ladies adopted the novel method of flirting by vigorously pelting each other, and wicked men would quietly and furtively slip a handful of confetti down a woman's open neck. This tomfoolery was begun upon the Saturday and continued upon the Monday, but was not practised upon the Sunday at Mentone. At Nice, however, where the English do not preponderate, the Carnival, which was there upon a larger scale, was kept up on the Sunday, and about twenty of the visitors (foreigners, of course) at our hotel went to Nice to see it. On the Monday night the promenade was lighted up by means of paper Chinese lanterns, and there was an exhibition of fireworks, concluding with setting in blaze a giant figure representing 'the Mentone man,' well stuffed with tar. The streets on the following day, as well as previously, were covered with the chalk pellets, and it was some time before they were swept and restored to their ordinary condition.

Of a different sort were other days regarded as eventful in so quiet a place as Mentone. A fall of snow was an event, the discovery of ice in the river, even a rainy day was to be noted. But of all days of this description, those in which Corsica was visible were the greatest, and the query when friends met on such days always was, 'Have you seen Corsica this morning?' It was only in peculiar states of the atmosphere that this distant island became visible, and it happened perhaps six times in the winter. Just before sunrise,—generally from a quarter to half an hour before, if the atmosphere was particularly clear, and especially if frosty,—the sun rising behind Corsica revealed the tops of mountains from 90 to 130 miles off, and from 6000 to 9000 feet high: the vision remained till the sun rose to the horizon, when it disappeared. I was always on the watch on likely mornings, and succeeded in taking a sketch of the view, which, by verifying at each successive appearance, I rendered exact. The engraving opposite is a little more than half that of the original sketch, which was just as seen. Only on one occasion was Corsica visible during the day. This happened in the second winter, on 26th November 1877. I had seen it in the morning, and was incredulous when informed in the forenoon that it was then visible. Seeing was believing, however; for there it was, and it remained in sight the whole day till four o'clock, the sun throughout shining brightly *on* it instead of behind it, so that this appearance was quite different from what was seen in the morning. I looked upon it as the harbinger of wet weather, and accordingly for some days afterwards we had rain.

By the end of February we began to prepare for leaving Mentone to travel in Italy. During December we had five days, during January two days, and during February three days with more or less rain—eleven days altogether out of ninety. Besides these days, which were also cold, we had as many more days which were cold or stormy without being wet. All the other days, even with the north or east winds blowing, were fine and sunny. There were very few days in which an invalid could not venture out. In fact, more than three-fourths of the weather was fine and sunny, and often as hot as a hot day in July at home. On 27th February, however, we had an eclipse of the moon, which was total. It must, I think, have had a serious effect upon the temperature, for immediately afterwards it became extremely cold; so much so that there was ice for the first time on the river, and it was needful at last to don our winter attire. We had planned to leave upon the 2d March, but the day was such as to necessitate postponing our departure till the morrow. We proceeded by carriage to San Remo.

ITALY.

X.

SAN REMO AND GENOA.

WE were now proceeding into a country with which many old associations were united, running back to schoolboy days,—a land over whose sunny skies and vine-clad fields so many raptures have been uttered; a land bearing evidence in its deeply-interesting ruins of the power of a great empire long since passed away; a land of the old classic literature, and of so much that was grand in ancient art. The pleasure of visiting it, long looked for, had come at last, and with high anticipation (a feeling, I suppose, common to most people) we entered Italy.

Our great difficulty on leaving Mentone was the weather. Friends who had just been travelling spoke of having had in Italy great severity of cold and much rain. One of these friends advised against going so soon, but another thought we might now without any hesitation set off. Perhaps impatient to leave after having formed our plans, we resolved to adventure, upon the theory of the Scotch saying, generally applied to the converse of the case, that the cold would be, as the spring advanced, 'a fault aye mending.' As it turned out, we would have been better to have waited eight or ten days longer after the 3d of March, the date of our departure; and, judging from our experience on this occasion, I should say that about the middle of March is the earliest time to commence a tour in Italy, after spending a winter in the sheltered regions of the Riviera. It is not only cold previously, but, except in favoured spots, the prospect is bleak and wintry. The vines which in the summer grow so luxuriantly and are so extensively cultivated, are leafless, the trees are bare, and the fields black.

We left old friends, and as we rattled through the street of Mentone we passed familiar places sorrowfully. Shortly afterwards we reached the Pont St. Louis, and were in Italy.

At the *douane* station beyond the bridge, we were stopped by the *douaniers*, who made a show of examining luggage; but they saw we were *bona fide* travellers, and we were not detained more than a few minutes. This brevity of detention and being spared the annoyance of having all one's luggage turned out and tossed about, are two great advantages of proceeding by carriage. Passengers going by railway to Italy from Mentone are stopped at Ventimiglia for a weary hour, and must submit to the usual inspection.

The *douane* roadside station, to which we had often walked, stands high, and commands a remarkably good view of Mentone and all its surroundings. We looked back from this point and others on our way, not knowing if we should ever see this cherished spot again.

At the time we left Mentone, and for the greater part of the way, the air was full of an odour not over agreeable, and I fancied that it might be that the olive trees were being manured,—a process to which they are subjected every second or third year, when a ditch is dug round each of them, and part of the manure placed in it consists of old rags, which the better answer their purpose the older and filthier they are.

The day was fairly bright in the morning, and while we had the sun everything looked beautiful; but a black cloud which had been looming in the south arose, and, spreading, for part of the way obscured the great luminary, so that we could not see everything in perfection, and might only imagine how much more charming some parts must have been, had they been brightened by its rays. The want of sun also, as usual, chilled the air.

We passed Belinda and Mr. Hanbury's garden, and came in sight of Ventimiglia, which lies about seven miles from Mentone. It is fortified, and commands the Corniche road and access to Italy in that direction. The town itself has rather a striking appearance, and is well worth a visit. It was an old Roman station, and in the time of Augustus a flourishing place, adorned and supplied with temples, baths, and other accessories of Roman life. Many remains of these ancient times have been found, and at present the ruins of an amphitheatre about a mile eastward have been discovered and are being exposed. Enterprise in the direction of excavation is sure to reward the authorities, who are undertaking it. A broad torrent bed intersects the town, through which the Roja, a stream larger than any at Mentone, flows. The banks of this stream, which really contains water, were lined by washer-women pursuing their occupation according to the manner of those at Mentone, already described. This river is crossed by a bridge, whence a fine view is had up the wide wide valley to the mountains.

The road onward from Ventimiglia is dotted on each side by Italian houses, and offers a pleasant drive. After proceeding four miles, we arrived at Bordighera, or, as it is sometimes spelled, Bordighiera.

The promontory on which this small town lies, stretches far out into the sea. The town itself has been built on its west slope, and from Mentone always looks clothed in sunshine. Probably its half insular position may give a certain amount of softness to the air. It is now becoming a place of resort for invalids. The stranger population apparently is about from 150 to 200, more than one-half of whom are English. It is thought more bracing than Mentone, and may suit some constitutions; but it seems to want the shelter which most invalids require, and which is obtained elsewhere. It is, however, a bright-looking place, with several hotels. The Hotel de Bordighera, newly opened, is very pleasantly situated, with large garden in front. The other hotels are 'D'Angleterre,' 'Beau Rivage,' 'Bellevue,' and 'Pension Anglaise.' There are also about twenty villas, besides other houses, in which quarters may be obtained.

The people of Bordighera obtained from the Pope the privilege of supplying Rome with palms at Easter, in the manner afterwards mentioned (p. 298). The palm tree here, therefore, is a subject of special cultivation. We found the palm garden closed, presumably in preparation for Easter. Leaving the carriage, we ascended to the church or cathedral in the old town,—always a prominent object from Mentone,—and from this point, whence an extensive view is obtained, we took our last look, for that time, of the place where we had spent the previous three months so happily. Returning reluctantly to the carriage, we drove on, and soon passed round to the other side of the promontory, which thereupon shut out of view all the places whence we had come, and after proceeding seven or eight miles, reached San Remo.

SAN REMO.

San Remo is a place much recommended by physicians, often in preference to Mentone. Its air is said to possess all the invigorating qualities of that of Nice, with the warmth of that of Mentone; to be warm, exhilarating and soothing, and conducive to sleep. The mean winter temperature is stated by some accounts to be from 54° to

59° Fahrenheit; spring, 63° to 68°; summer, 72° to 85°; and autumn, 66° to 72°.[1] The icy Tramontane wind is said to be only slightly felt, and that in the west and more exposed end of the town, while the mistral is only known as a high wind. It is also asserted that the natives are healthy and long-lived. With all these recommendations as a health resort, San Remo cannot be considered to possess the attractions of Mentone, and it was with a feeling of disappointment we first entered the place. Perhaps our disappointment was increased by the difficulty of obtaining accommodation, and by the contrast in what we did obtain with what we had enjoyed at Mentone.

Arriving at the West End, we found all the hotels there full, and were glad to secure accommodation in one within the town, possessing a garden, dreary and overlooked by houses. The place—at all events externally—was not inviting; and as the weather was, during the greater part of our sojourn on this occasion, bad, with rain, our first impressions were not favourable.

San Remo is, like Mentone, surrounded by a half circle of mountains, but of a much softer-looking character. Bignole, the highest, is 4300 feet high. They do not approach so closely to the town, nor do they rear their heads so boldly, grandly, and picturesquely, but they do so without gap. In rear of them, though not visible from the town, are other and higher mountain ranges, belonging to the Maritime Alps. What are called rivers exist,—small narrow streamlets, scarcely amounting to what in Scotland we should term 'burns,'—which trickle through the town (the Romulo after heavy rain was only three or four feet wide and a few inches deep); but they do not pass through valleys like those which give so marked a character to

[1] Mr. C. Home-Douglas (p. 177) publishes observations giving much lower mean temperatures. I suppose in these matters observers seldom agree.

Mentone. San Remo also wants the protecting arms which Cape Martin, and Belinda, and Bordighera send out west and east into the sea. Capo Nero on the west and Capo Verde on the east no doubt create a bay, but are comparatively stunted arms. Then the railway passes along the coast and cuts the inhabitants off from the sea. There is therefore no promenade or road along the coast—a stupid mistake, to which the authorities ought never to have consented, and which deprives San Remo of what otherwise would have been its main attraction as a place of residence. The new town contains only a few good shops, in which things are not cheap. The old town, with a population double that of Mentone, is much larger than that of its rival. It is situated on a similar, but larger and loftier hill; but, unlike Mentone, which rests on the east, it rests mainly on the west slope of the hill, and is no doubt very picturesque, probably one of the most picturesque towns of the kind built for protection from the Algerine pirates. But though this may give value to it in the artistic eye, it is not a quality which contributes either to health or comfort; and one may justly say, parodying a common saying, 'picturesque and nasty.' Dirt, indeed, everywhere reigns—nay, some of the drains, even in the newer portion of the town, would seem to be above ground; and we found on our first visit the smells villanous,—a remark I am bound, however, to observe was not so applicable on occasion of our visit in the following year.

The railway station occupies a prominent position in the town, and passes by or cuts off the harbour, which lies outside of it. From the battlements or breakwater of this most untidily-kept harbour, a good view is had of the town and the mountains behind it. I made the ascent of the town through long narrow dirty winding vias, like Edinburgh High Street closes, only they are narrower, steeper, and tortuous, and far more dirty and unsavoury. Sometimes the road, paved with stone throughout, lies under dismal arched vaults, while the houses on each side are irregular and dilapidated—foul, dark, and dreary dens, rather than habitations for human beings. It was some relief to reach the platform on the summit, on which the large church called the sanctuary stands. From this point an excellent view is had all around. I descended by another of those curious vias, in which the houses support each other by arched flying buttresses, intended as a security against the effects of earthquakes, of which, however, we obtained no specimen shock during either of our visits to San Remo.

The mountains and hill-slopes surrounding San Remo are densely covered with olive trees, and to some extent with lemons, and afford shelter and walks to the visitors, but of a character differing entirely from those at Mentone. On the hillsides many wild flowers grow in rich profusion—hyacinths, narcissi, anemones, tulips, mignonette, gladioli, and others. Those who have been out exploring the country in the spring, return generally laden with bouquets, or rather bundles, of bright-coloured flowers.

Various excursions which may be taken to places among the mountains by assistance of donkeys, are described in a little volume called *San Remo as a Winter Residence*, by an Invalid, 1869 (Wm. Hunt and Co., London), to which, for further information regarding the town and locality, I would refer. I believe a lady is bringing out another guide-book with information up to date. In 1869, it would appear from the 'Invalid's' little book that there were then only five hotels and twenty-three villas. Since the extension of the railway to San Remo, the number of both has largely increased. Now there are nine hotels and pensions in the east division of San Remo, and eleven in the west, some of which are said to be expensive. Of the West End hotels, one or two are situated well up on a hill-slope, the fatigue of greater ascent and the additional exposure being no doubt considered to be balanced by the expanded prospect. There are now also fully eighty villas east and west.

San Remo possesses, besides, a small public garden to the west of the old town—a very nice piece or strip of ground at the West End, laid out in walks and shrubbery, gifted by the Empress of Russia, who had honoured San Remo by her residence there some years ago. The gift is an accession to the place, and a pavilion has been erected, in which the band plays on certain days of the week. On other days it plays in the public garden or in a rondo at the East End. The West End of the town, where several of the best hotels are, has an open view to the sea,—that is to say, the sea can be seen from the road and public grounds,—and it is consequently more cheerful than the east; but it is much more exposed to the winds. The east end is more sheltered, and is thought to be more healthy. From the centre of the town eastwards, a broad pavement runs, provided here and there with wooden seats for the wearied pedestrian, and is practically terminated by the Hotel Victoria—a comfortable house, having a large garden reaching down to the sea, though the railway intersects a small portion of it at the bottom. A large hotel, called the Mediterranée, has recently been built adjoining the Victoria, having a similar piece of ground stretching to the railway and sea also, though of course more newly laid out as a garden. All along this road, till it reaches a point nearly two miles from the old town, it is cut off even from the view of the sea, to which the only access is by many narrow filthy walled lanes. Beyond the Victoria there are various nice villas, one especially, called the Villa Patrone, a choice specimen of elegant design, and of a mode of wall ornamentation in pebble peculiar to the Riviera.

I found, from a list of strangers published at San Remo on 21st January 1877, the following interesting analysis:—

STRANGERS.

Allemands,	dont 46	avec fam.,	160
Anglais,	,, 56	,,	126
Austro-Hongrois,	,, 8	,,	20
Belges,	,, 2	,,	2
Danois,	,, 0	,,	1
Espagnols,	,, 2	,,	2
Français,	,, 8	,,	17
Hollandais,	,, 1	,,	5
Italiens,	,, 16	,,	41
Roumains,	,, 1	,,	1
Russes,	,, 14	,,	30
Suedios,	,, 0	,,	1
Suisses,	,, 2	,,	5
Americains,	,, 12	,,	23
Asiatiques,	,, 0	,,	1
Total,	dont 168	avec fam.,	435

In the following year, the *Liste Générale des Étrangers*, dated 16th February 1878, gives the names of the strangers then in San Remo under their several nationalities, and winds up with the following 'recapitulation,' showing an increase on the whole. But it should be kept in view that, generally speaking, places in the Riviera are fuller in February than in previous months, the number of visitors being, in fact, then at its maximum.

RECAPITULATION.

Allemands,	dont 52	avec fam.,	171
Anglais,	,, 70	,,	167
Austro-Hongrois,	,, 10	,,	25
Belges,	,, 4	,,	6
Français,	,, 13	,,	21
Hollandais,	,, 8	,,	15
Italiens,	,, 24	,,	64
Portugais,	,, 1	,,	1
Roumains,	,, 1	,,	1
Russes,	,, 11	,,	30
Suedois,	,, 3	,,	5
Suisses,	,, 5	,,	11
Americains,	,, 13	,,	28
Total,	dont 215	avec fam.,	545

From these lists it appears that San Remo is principally frequented by the Germans and the English. A reason for the Germans flocking to San Remo, is no doubt to be found in the fact that Cannes, Nice, and Mentone are within French territory, where Germans are not particularly welcome—in truth, are sometimes, as I know in one instance, received by the French with marked rudeness; though it is to be hoped that this state of feeling, not unnatural after the late calamitous war, is now subsiding. But it may be taken as corroborative of this observation, that, judging from the lists published in the beginning of December 1877 (the very commencement of the season), out of about 850 names of strangers in Mentone (I state it roughly and without computing the number of families these names represent), only between 70 and 80 were German, principally ladies; while, so far as I can ascertain, there was only one German doctor in Mentone against six German doctors in San Remo—a fact, if I be correct, which speaks for itself.

Excluding the German element, therefore, it will be seen that the English very nearly equal all those of other nations put together. At the same time, one must observe that such lists require to be taken in a very general way. Implicit reliance upon them cannot be placed, as I have so often seen that names which ought to have appeared have been omitted for a whole season. Everything depends upon how the list is made up. If made up from persons handing in their own names to the newspapers, then it fails, because there are many who never think of doing so, while even hotelkeepers (whose interest one would think is to reveal the popularity of their houses) are very careless in furnishing complete information.

The San Remo *Liste Générale des Étrangers*, besides other intelligence, gives the names of the 'Medicins,'—viz., six German, three English, one French, one Russian, and thirteen

Italian doctors. There are both German and English Protestant churches. The English church is a commodious building: the incumbent is the Rev. Mr. Fenton. The United Presbyterians of Scotland—I think the only station possessed by that body abroad—had worship in two rooms of the Villa Marguerita, where once a day on Sundays, the Rev. James Robertson of Edinburgh (just deceased) was, during our first visit, addressing, in a homely manner, crowded audiences; while in the evening he had service in a room of the Hotel des Londres, in which he was then residing, the English visitors of the hotel turning in to listen to one much respected by them all,—all sympathizing, too, in the sad cause which brought him to a place where he was destined, like so many others, to leave a loved one behind.

The great industry of San Remo necessarily consists in the cultivation of the olive tree; but one minor occupation is derived from the olive groves in the fabrication of articles of olive wood. That of San Remo is of a lighter colour and richer grain, and takes a higher polish than the olive wood of Sorrento. In the matter of inlaying, however, it does not appear to me that San Remo comes up to the better quality of Sorrento work, while the articles made are sold at a much higher price. The shopkeepers, I was told, consider the foreigners, and I suppose especially the English, as legitimate prey, and charge them more than the natives; nor do they ask high prices, as they do in other Italian places, with the intention of after abatement, but they stick to the price demanded, and are very stiff to move.

On one of the hill-slopes about a mile and a half out of town, we found a chocolate manufactory, the material for which comes all the way from Bordeaux.

The women when young are good-looking; many have the dark Italian eye, but, like the Mentone women, soon acquire, from the drudgery to which they are exposed, a hard-looking and dried-up appearance. They are treated as very beasts of burden, and are accustomed from early years to carry enormous loads upon their heads, far more so than at Mentone, and they glory in the amount they can carry. I have beheld one carrying an enormous log of wood on her head; and barrels, and every description of heavy articles, are constantly to be seen so carried. A lady told me she had a heavy oak table carried home to her house by her gardener's wife, and it was thought nothing of. Such a thing as a rope and pulley, much less a crane to lift stones from the ground to the floors where masons are building a house, are utterly unknown. The women are employed as day-labourers, at something like a shilling a day, to carry the stones aloft on their heads. I have seen a woman, time after time, carrying a stone or a couple of uneven stones balanced, the one on the top of the other, on her head, up ladders nearly perpendicular, to a height of two storeys, to the stage where the masons were working. All they do is just to twist a handkerchief in a coil on the head, and then, with a most extraordinary power of balancing, they convey the load to where it is wanted. Men very seldom undertake the drudgery. If they do, they carry a lighter load, not, however, on their heads, but on the bent back or shoulders, protected by a sack. I have observed a woman carrying a stone on her head which it took four of them to lift. Their skulls and spines no doubt thicken and acquire some strange amount of hardy strength, but any nobler faculty must be crushed out of them; yet they never seem to feel their degradation, and would resent, I presume, the introduction of appliances by which their labour would be saved, and at the same time a means of livelihood taken from them.

Of all the instances, however, of this nature which I witnessed, the most marvellous was that of carrying a pianoforte on the head. On our second visit to San Remo, a lady informed me she had seen this sight. It seemed truly incredible, and perhaps, as she was an American, I was at first inclined to set it down to the national tendency to imaginative exaggeration. I looked anxiously for visual corroboration, seeing being in such a case believing, and I was not disappointed. The very day of leaving I had the good fortune to witness the scene, and was thus enabled to give full credit to the story. Happening to be in town, I met three women walking steadily along the street, their bodies erect, one in front and two behind, with the huge load of a heavy cabinet piano on their heads. I think each had one hand, at least, raised to steady it—a very painful exertion of itself to most people. Apparently, keeping pace together, this burden was sturdily carried as if it cost them no effort; while by their side marched a man in charge, who, I was thankful to observe (although, as I have read somewhere, it may be observed elsewhere, I think at Pompeii), carried no instrument of flagellation in his hand. Probably he would condescend to assist in raising the piano at starting, and in lowering it at its destination.

On this subject the writer of the little guide-book I have already referred to (*San Remo as a Winter Residence*), makes these observations (p. 26):—

'The inhabitants of both sexes, but more particularly the women, are very good-looking, especially those from the country. You see most lovely faces amongst the girls from fifteen to twenty-five; they have as a rule good figures also, and neat feet and legs. They walk remarkably well, with a firm easy step, holding themselves erect. This results from their always carrying burdens on their heads, with which they go along at a quick steady pace, uphill or down, on rough roads or smooth, without ever raising a hand to support them, unless very large or clumsy in form. You seldom see a woman without something on her head; if she has not her bundle or her panniken, she will place the pad there on which she carries them. But this constant bearing of weights on the head has another and less admirable result, which is that the women very soon lose their beauty and their youth. I am told that it is quite usual for a woman to carry 100 kilogrammes on her head (220 lbs.) up to the mountains, and this every day; she will also bring a heavy bundle of grass or something back again. The men walk beside them empty-handed, or oftener still ride the mules and donkeys. Almost all the carrying is done on women's heads. If a man has to transport a heavy weight, he takes his wife with him to carry it. I ordered a wooden horse for my saddle; the joiner who made it brought it home certainly, but on his pretty little wife's head, not his own. The men consider it a disgrace to carry anything, a parcel even, and a woman's highest ambition is to keep her husband in perfect idleness. A friend of mine, an English lady, was riding on a donkey one very hot day, accompanied by my servant Giovanni, a San Remese, who was, of course, trudging on foot by her side, and reflecting the heat of the day on her face. As they went along, they met a party of country people coming down from the mountains. In passing, a man, one of the party, stopped and spoke earnestly to my servant, who gave a laughing reply. When they had passed, my friend asked what the man had said. "Oh," replied Giovanni, "he was telling me I ought to make you get off the donkey, and ride myself instead." We had lectured him so often on the disgrace of the men taking their ease while the women worked so hard, that he quite entered into the facetiousness of the man's proposition, an Englishwoman being in the case.'

In the redress of these women's wrongs, might not an excellent field for the operations of the Women's Rights Association be found?

Photographs are not cheap in San Remo; but one photographer (P. Guidi), under the direction of Signor Panizzi, has produced a large collection, numbering, I think, upwards of 150 specimens, size of nature, of the botany of San Remo. These are beautifully coloured from the plants themselves, and form a valuable and interesting illustration of the flora of the district.

We remained in San Remo from Saturday till the following Wednesday. The weather having been wet and disagreeable, we were by no means sorry when, the Wednesday morning proving fine, we resolved to quit a place where we had felt far from comfortable, and to proceed to Genoa by railway. I had, on arrival, exchanged at the banker's a circular note, for which I got at the rate of 27·20 francs or lire per £ in Italian paper money. It was my first experience of this kind of money, and although it brought a premium of 22 francs per £10, the bundle of little notes was at first by no means assuring. However, I soon began to find it extremely convenient as well as profitable to exchange into paper. I paid the hotel bill and the railway fares both in paper, even although in the former case there was a notice up in the hotel requiring (although paper is a legal tender) visitors to pay in gold; and everywhere afterwards in Italy, paper was received as full value for what it represented. We had here for the first time to pay for all registered luggage according to weight. Putting railway fare and luggage cost together, however, the expense was, especially reckoning a deduction of 9 per cent. by use of paper, moderate. The fare first-class from San Remo to Genoa was 15 francs each, adding proportion of charge for luggage, nearly 3 francs[1] additional for each, say 18 francs or 15s., and deducting exchange, 13s. 4d. for a journey of about eighty-five miles, which is probably about a shade more than the average at home for second-class fare for a similar distance. However, the cost necessarily varies according to the quantity of luggage registered. To most Italians, who register none, it would be so much less; to many ladies who cannot travel without innumerable dresses, so much more.

Upon escaping from San Remo, the railway leaves the coast line and keeps a little inland—at least it nowhere cuts off any of the coast towns from the sea; nor could it well do so, as nearly all are built close upon the beach. It therefore proceeds rather behind them or through their outskirts; and, partly owing to this and partly to the numerous—vexatiously numerous—tunnels through which the railway is, from the hilly nature of the country, constrained to run, the views had, of the towns at least, cannot be equal to what is obtained by driving along the Corniche road. These Italian towns are exceedingly picturesque, both in

[1] I shall use henceforth franc for lira, the Italian name, for simplicity's sake.

appearance and in situation, and there can be no doubt that one misses much by travelling by rail, although it must be added that the route between San Remo and Genoa by no means equals that between Nice and San Remo. Clear, pleasing photographs of the towns on the line are published, and may give one some idea of them; but they are not, with one or two exceptions, the views seen from the railway. All views from railway carriage windows, however, even where no ogre sits to pull down the blinds, labour under disadvantage, and are too transient, and often too detached and interrupted, to enable passengers to catch and retain in memory general views of any place which a railway passes. On this occasion we had the carriage to ourselves, and eagerly availed ourselves of the opportunity to draw up blinds and gaze out right and left.

About three miles from San Remo, looking up a valley, one of those curious old towns which are perched on the top of a hill becomes visible. I had thought it to be Ceriana, which lies in that direction, a visit to which is one of the excursions from San Remo; but it proved, according to Bædeker, to be a similar town called Bussana. The picturesque town of Porto Maurizio is invisible from the railway, which passes under it; while a little farther on, Oneglia and its harbour are just seen in approaching, and the railway stops at the landward end of it. However, at next station, Diana Marina, the railway traveller is rewarded by a most charming landscape. A chain of mountains hems in a valley, in the centre of which a conical hill rises abruptly, and on its top Diano Castello stands, another of those curious and picturesque towns which are so common in the Riviera and in Italy. The scene is one in which an artist's pencil might luxuriate. The *tout ensemble* would make, as it no doubt has often made, a striking picture. At Alassio, nine miles farther on, we rested on our journey in the following year, and I shall return to it, therefore, further on. But leaving Alassio and passing under its west boundary the promontory of Santa Croce, looking seawards there was seen, perhaps about two miles out, the small rocky desolate-looking island of Gallenaria, on which a former proprietor had built a house for residence, but where, we were told, and could readily believe, his more sociable wife refused to live. Farther on upon the left, inland, but near the railway, the town of Albenga appears prominently. This is an old Roman town, and is an episcopal residence. Its many and thickly-planted towers give to it quite the aspect of a cathedral city. Touching shortly afterwards at Finalmarina and Noli, in about three and a half hours from the time of leaving San Remo, the large and imposing town of Savona, beautifully situated, came into view a massive-looking fort towering over and protecting the harbour below. Here many who travel by carriage leave the road and proceed to Genoa by rail, and those for Genoa going westward take carriage from Savona, the reason being, that the road and rail between Savona and Genoa run parallel to each other, while the route lacks the attractions of the remainder of the Corniche drive. From Savona, also, there is a direct line of railway to Turin. The train moves on, and eleven miles beyond Savona, reaches Cogoletto, which is said to have been the birthplace of Columbus, and is therefore a town of interest. The town, like so many others, lies on the beach, and the railway station only affords a view of backs of houses. Shortly after, the train stops at Pegli, a place about six miles from Genoa, a place of winter residence, and famous for its gardens, which attract excursions by visitors at Genoa, besides inducing others to take up their abode for more or less time at the hotels of the place. A little after six o'clock we arrived at Genoa, the train slackening speed as it passed amidst ranges of lofty buildings, which looked all the more grand that our eyes for so long had been unaccustomed to the dimensions of a town so large.

GENOA.

For many miles before arrival, we could, from the railway carriage windows, descry the 'superb' city with its tall lighthouse standing like a sentinel in advance. But one loses much in arriving by railway instead of by sea. The view had upon entering Genoa for the first time by sea is always spoken of as magnificent, and it must necessarily be very striking. The large natural basin which forms the port, protected by two long moles or breakwaters, emanating from each side like two arms, forms a semicircle nearly two miles in diameter, the east end terminated by the lighthouse, said to be 520 feet high above the level of the sea, and the west end crowned by the large and lofty Church of St. Maria de Carignano. From the harbour, filled with shipping, the ground rises all round to a height of 500 or 600 feet in steep slopes, upon which the city is built; a line of warehouses or other great white buildings, connected no doubt for the most part, if not altogether, with the trade of the port, forms the front rank, and gives an imposing facing to the whole. The buildings on the west side, however, exhibit but a slender cordon: the compact mass of the city lies upon the hill-slopes and hills of the east side, which extend outward considerably to the south of the east mole. The view, therefore, on arriving by sea, must be that of looking upon one-half of the sloping tiers of a gigantic amphitheatre; while backward from the city, which is surrounded by a double wall or line of fortification, the Apennines rise in still higher slopes, bold and stern, and probably afford some protection from the north winds.

Thus looks the famous city, once thriving by commerce,

and powerful, till a spirited foreign policy led, as its natural consequences, to expensive wars, to weakness and decay. It revived, however, in time, and manifests a scene of peaceful busy industry, conferring upon it the position of being the first commercial town of Italy.

The façade of the railway station is one of great elegance. It is built of white marble, with beautiful columns surmounted by rich sculptured entablature. In the large open space or piazza in front, in the midst of shrubbery, there has been placed a beautiful monumental statue of Christopher Columbus, on a high round pedestal which rests on a large square base. The circular part, forming the upper portion of the pedestal, adorned by prow heads of an ancient or conventional type, is surrounded by four allegorical seated figures, one at each corner, representing religion, geography, strength, and wisdom, and by bas-reliefs delineating events in the hero's life. Columbus stands pointing with his finger to a recumbent nude American-Indian lying at his feet. The whole is of white marble, and bears on the base a simple dedication.

It is a noble monument, and affords, as it were, at the very threshold of Italy, a remarkable specimen of Italian skill in sculpture, and particularly in graceful grouping of figures, and in designing a pleasing and handsome pedestal, from which those who have had charge of some recently-erected monuments at home might have done well to have taken a hint.

However, we had no opportunity then of studying either station or monument. We hastened to the omnibus of the Hotel de Gênes, and drove there with a large company of English, by whom this hotel would seem to be principally patronized. Some of the hotels in Genoa are planted in undesirable localities. This one is situated facing the open piazza, where in the morning market is held, and in the immediate neighbourhood of all the principal buildings and good streets, the principal theatre, Carlo Felice, being opposite, and the post office within a stone-throw. Like most of the buildings in Genoa, the hotel is of a somewhat palatial order, having wide lofty staircases and rooms, some of them oppressively large. A bedroom we had seemed to be about 30 feet long by about 20 feet high.

The day continued fine throughout, but heavy rain fell through the night, and the next morning was very cold. We drove about for two hours to see the town; but it became so cold, wet, and windy, that we had to give up further visiting for that day. Among other places we visited Santa Maria de Carignano, a great church, built by the munificence of a single Genoese citizen, which crests the eastern height overlooking the town; and from the terrace on the top of it there are magnificent views of the entire panorama—the harbour, the coast east and west, the city, and the mountains, which there lay, covered with a coating of snow, which no doubt had fallen through the night, and gave a very bleak appearance to the surroundings. I could gladly have remained up for a long time (the others had not ventured), but the cold was so great that I could only take a momentary glimpse. We had also from the opposite extremity of the town a different view, looking from the harbour near to the lighthouse upward to Genoa, rising in crescent form line above line from the basin of the port. The street itself, which surrounds the port, is for the most part noisy, bustling, and dirty—by no means, therefore, attractive. At some parts the passage is nearly blocked by loiterers, who may perhaps, by a stretch of charity, be supposed to be actively prosecuting some busy calling, just as may be seen on the street of a country town at home on a market day.

The following day was dry, but cold, and afforded an opportunity for going about a little on foot, and seeing some of the large churches and the streets of grand palaces for which Genoa is famous. These palaces (some of them now used for purposes other than those for which they were built) are principally situated in a line of streets, called the Vias Balbi, Nuova, and Nuovissima. Like those of many of the Italian towns, these vias are paved with large flat blocks of stone, neatly, closely, and uniformly laid. The palaces themselves are massive stone buildings of the elegant Italian style now so often adopted by our architects in designing banks and public offices, the walls generally in rustic work, and the cornices rich and heavily projecting, the large windows protected from assault by thick outside iron gratings and stanchions, imparting a very prison-like look. The palaces are lofty and handsomely built, and the entry is generally by a large gateway to an inner court, round which further buildings are placed. Wide handsome staircases, quite a marked feature, conduct to the upper floors. The streets which are lined by these palaces are so narrow that the elegance of design is greatly lost to the eye. On this the occasion of our first visit, we had only opportunity of seeing the Palazzo Brignole, which contains a fine collection of paintings by the great masters Vandyke, Guido Reni, and others. Among them we observed a particularly good St. Sebastian by Guido. In the following year we visited some additional palaces,—viz., first, the Palazzo Durazzo on the Via Balbi, a magnificent house with a much-noted staircase. Notwithstanding the family were then residing in this palace, we were shown through about a dozen rooms, in which the hangings were of superb elegance, and the walls richly adorned with pictures. Thence we went to the Palazzo Balbi, a fine mansion, but not equal to the Durazzo; and thence to the Palazzo Reale, one of those royal palaces which the King of Italy seldom visits, but which he nevertheless appears compelled to maintain. The rooms are beautiful, the queen's bedroom particularly rich and dazzling. The facilities afforded for seeing these palaces, which no one going to Genoa should, if possible, omit to visit, are very commendable. A fee of 1 franc to the attendant is all that there, as elsewhere in Italy, is expected.

The churches of Genoa are, like all Italian churches, very dark and very dirty—purposely ill-lighted, no doubt, to produce a dim religious light, and dirty because it is part of an Italian's religion in church to spit upon the floor and otherwise to consider that cleanliness is next to ungodliness. The Cathedral of San Lorenzo and the neighbouring Jesuit Church of San Ambrogio are large buildings, especially the cathedral, and possess fine altars, surmounted by show pictures, and otherwise are richly adorned. The Church of San Annunciata, on the way to the railway station, is profusely gilded.

In the afternoon we walked to the Aqua Sola, a public park, which is evidently a place of resort of the Genoese gentry. Being a winter day, there were not many going about; but we saw a number of handsome equipages with Italian horses, their long flowing tails touching the ground. A very curious kind of curricle, such as we saw nowhere else, was constructed with high wheels, and seated, like a country mail cart, for one person only. This was drawn by one horse at full speed, and between two of them a race was run round and round the park. We had seen a good many of the women walking about town, having a mantilla or veil depending from the head—a graceful Genoese fashion, although one would hardly think it could afford much protection from either cold or heat. But here, for the first time, we saw some of the grand Italian nurses, who are generally dressed in a most peculiar and magnificent attire, their hair fantastically decked with large pins, very gorgeous to behold. There were evident degrees of magnificence, dependent, I suppose, to some extent upon the condition of the family in whose service the nurses were. The children also in their charge were attired in costumes more or less brilliant and rich, everything in Genoa being, I presume, from a palace to a hair-pin, necessarily 'superb.'

Next morning we resolved to proceed to Spezia, but before going, drove out to the famous Campo Santo. It is situated about a mile and a half out of town, and the road to it is by no means choice; but the place itself is remarkable. The cemetery covers a good many acres of ground, and, judging from the inscriptions on the tombs, is little more than a quarter of a century old; but the mode in which it is laid out is peculiarly Italian. It was the first of the kind I had seen. We subsequently visited others in different parts of Italy; but there was not one which could be compared, for combined grandeur and tasteful, refined elegance, with that of Genoa. The main portion of the grounds is laid out in a large square, enclosing a piece of open ground, probably, speaking roughly and from recollection, six or eight acres in extent. This open ground apparently is used for the more common burials, and is in no way extraordinary, except for the contrast it affords to the enclosed portions. The monuments, thickly planted in it, are of the paltry, frippery kind,—little tumble-down, uneasy-looking crosses, gewgaw wirework, top-heavy miniature lanterns pending from poles agee,—mingled with tawdry remains of immortelles and withered flowers, so commonly seen in Roman Catholic grounds abroad, though, to do the Genoa burying-ground justice, it is much more tidy in this respect than is customary. A colossal statue of the Virgin stands in the centre of the open space. Round three sides of this ground (besides the fourth regarding which anon) there have been built, in white marble,—of which material there are quarries in the neighbourhood of Genoa,—two long, parallel, spacious enclosures or vaults. In the outer of these vaults, monumental tablets are ranged down the side walls row above row in great uniformity, recording the names (with usual dates) of the deceased persons who have been, or are presumed to have been, buried in cells of which these are the outer ends or sides. The tablets are all of white polished marble, and black lettered. There is nothing particularly striking about this part except its extent and, to our eyes, novelty. But the inner aisle or arcade and all the corners or prominent parts are devoted to statues and figures, and sometimes representations in *alto relievo*—all cut out of white marble, and erected in memory of the more eminent or more opulent citizens of Genoa, or members of their families, who are buried there. The monuments evidence possession not merely of the beautiful material out of which they are produced, but of great natural capability on the part of the Italian sculptors, and of a taste on the part of the public, either natural or educated, in that direction. Without according indiscriminate admiration, one may say that there was scarcely a piece of sculpture of which our best artists at home could reasonably be ashamed. On the one side of each arcade the memorials are, for the most part, mural; on the other, which opens by arches to the Campo, the principal monuments are placed one under each arch. The general character of the mural monuments is stately repose, some exceptionally being in action. But under the arches, between the supporting columns, the figures are often in startling resemblance to life. For example, one group is of a lady sitting up in bed, with an earnest fascinating or fascinated look, grasping the right hand of another in a long garment, loose from the neck to the feet, whose left arm and forefinger of the hand are pointing upward. In another, a charming female figure appears soaring with an angel upward resting on clouds, the group being pervaded, like so many more, by a marvellous grace and freedom of execution. Another is a mother with a babe in each arm. But it would be endless to describe them, the more especially as to do so effectively one would require to make each monument a special study—not to be recommended, because the vaults are cold, and it is not safe to linger in them. Only the west of the three sides of the quadrangle, and part of the south side, were then so occupied.

The fourth side of the square lies upon the slope of a hill, and advantage has been taken of this natural feature of the ground for the formation of terraces, in the centre of which, at the top of a magnificent flight of marble steps, a large circular church of white marble has been built, upon entering which we look upon a majestic row of black marble pillars, standing in a stately circle round vacancy as yet. When we saw it last, the church was not completed, and evidently would not be for a long time to come, for no expense seems to be spared to render it in every respect the grand complement of its beautiful surroundings. Upon the arcaded terraces, stretching away right and left from the church, we found some of the choicest groups of sculpture in the whole place. They are large and costly, and harmoniously graceful embellishments of the symmetrical structure. Behind these arcades, vaults have been built akin to those on the other three sides; while beyond, to the north, open ground on the hill-slope has been laid out for interments,—as yet sparsely dotted by monuments.

A burial-place such as this would at home cost such an enormous amount of money as practically to remove from our thoughts the possibility of erecting it. I presume it is only possible in Italy from the circumstance that the sculptor's occupation is more common, and is less handsomely remunerated; but much also is due to the proximity of the material, and to an appreciation on the part of the public of the forms of high art. In regarding this wonderful enclosure, a mingled feeling will in many minds arise; for its solemn impressiveness, its silent grandeur, its touching monuments and bas-reliefs, its very unadorned inscriptions, carry us away in thought and sympathy to sad scenes of death and sorrow; while the brightness and purity, and the exquisite forms and seraphic tranquillity of the sculptured white marble, point to that beatific life beyond the tomb, where all is bright and pure and exceeding lovely—where the spirits of just men made perfect, in serene, undisturbed calm, dwell for ever in the rapture of heavenly joy, and, arrayed in the beauty of holiness, are surpassing glad amidst the burning thrill of boundless love and the celestial beams of ineffable glory, and the sweet music of angel song—for, they stand in the presence of GOD.

XI.

SPEZIA, PISA, SIENNA.

We had to hurry away from the Campo Santo to get money changed, prepare for travelling, and be in time for the train at half-past one. When we reached the hotel, we found there were about forty leaving by the same train. We were therefore advised to take the first omnibus, but it involved waiting an hour in the cold *salle-d'attente* at the station. I had taken at Nice, Cook's tickets from Genoa to Rome, with a potentiality of stopping at three places by the way; so that all I had to do was to get the tickets marked for Spezia, our first stoppage, and stamped for the commencement of the journey, and to get luggage weighed and paid for. The trouble saved by taking these tickets was, I found, so insignificant that I never afterwards procured them.

The railway journey (57 miles) from Genoa to Spezia is very tantalizing. It takes three hours, including stoppages, and in that time we passed through thirty-eight tunnels. The line is close to the sea, and the views or peeps throughout of ocean, rock, and village are lovely and picturesque, the many small coast towns by the way being brightly Italian in their character. We had scarcely time, however, to enjoy any scene when the view was suddenly cut off by a long tunnel, the same thing to happen time after time provokingly. It is said that the tunnels, which must have rendered the railway a very costly undertaking, are giving way, and that the line may require to be abandoned. Be this as it may, to those who would enjoy the scenery, nothing could be more charming than to drive, in warm enough weather, by carriage along the Riviera di Levante, the scenes by road being considered to equal those of the Riviera di Ponente. Some towns, such as Nervi, in sheltered situations on the route, are used to some extent as winter resorts, although comfortable accommodation is difficult to procure. Even with all the disadvantages attendant upon travelling by railway, we were greatly delighted with our journey, the pleasure being much aided, no doubt, by the brilliant sunshine of the day. And here I may just observe, that, notwithstanding the drawback of travelling by rail and passing through so many tunnels, travellers of the present day are greatly better off than those of only a few years back, when, in consequence of the expense and insecurity of proceeding by road, most people went by sea from Marseilles to Naples, touching at Genoa and Civita Vecchia by the way. Splendid general views, doubtless, they sometimes in day-time had; but not only did the vessels keep too far out of sight of land to permit of close observation of the lovely coast, but the voyages appear generally to have been made in great part by night.

SPEZIA.

Spezia, on arrival, appeared beauteous, and, though a tolerably large town, quite rural after Genoa. We drove to a large new hotel, the Croce di Malta, the omnibus entering the hall of the hotel itself, which we found to be spacious, with long flights of stairs and lofty ceilings, and profusion of white marble,—in fact, the use of marble for some purposes might well enough have been dispensed with. However, Spezia is a summer and not a winter place, and these cool appearances must be very grateful to the summer visitors. The Genoese largely resort to it in summer months, and I suppose the sea-bathing obtained at its beach is excellent. During our visit the weather was intensely cold, and we had the utmost difficulty in heating our lofty rooms with fires of a soft wood which rapidly burnt down. But what was thus a source of discomfort, added a charming effect to the landscape. Snow had fallen, and the Carrara Mountains (some of them between 5000 and 6000 feet high), which are seen from Spezia, lying to the south, were covered with a mantle whiter, perhaps, than the white marble they contain, ranges of hills and mountains of a lower height in their own green clothing lying between. Add to this fine effect the splendid harbour to which nature has so much contributed, containing the great arsenal of Italy, and the bay filled with large men-of-war, at one time riding at anchor, at another steaming about in order to exercise their crews, the handsome many-storied ranges of buildings fronting the shore, and behind them the town with a ruined castle on a height, and rising directly in the north a huge protecting wall of high mountains, and the panoramic picture is complete. A London artist who was there at the time (Mr. Pilleau), and whom we afterwards met at almost every place which we visited in Italy, made a drawing in colours of the scene, with the Carrara Mountains in the background; and I do not think that there was among all his Italian drawings, which he subsequently kindly showed us, one which had a finer pictorial effect.

We arrived on the Saturday. English service was held in a room of the hotel on the Sunday, and was well attended in the forenoon; but, in accordance with a too common laxity of practice, few attended in the afternoon.

The Monday was a warmer day, and we enjoyed a ramble and ascended the hill lying to the back of the town, from which we had a grand view of the Gulf of Spezia, which is a tongue of sea running up northward from the Mediterranean, and studded by islands at the entrance. A delightful drive may be had to Porto Venere (more charming when leaves are out), but we did not feel it sufficiently warm to hazard the exposure.

It would undoubtedly have been a gratification to have seen the arsenal and the large 100-ton gun, but we were informed that it was necessary to obtain from Rome a permission to see them, and this difficulty put it beyond our power.

We remained three nights at Spezia, and on Tuesday morning left for Pisa, the weather having again become raw and cold.

The journey to Pisa occupied about four hours. We passed many interesting places, and among others the Carrara quarries. Immense quantities of the white marble, quarried from the hills adjoining the railway, lay at the stations ready for transport. The quarrying of this famous marble, the purer quality of which is of close grain (the fine statuary marble), is a source of employment to a vast number of workmen. When the traveller has time to spare, it is no doubt worth stopping a few hours between trains to visit the place. At last we arrived in sight of Pisa, and as we entered the town got a glimpse from the carriage windows of the buildings which have made it celebrated.

PISA.

The weather was cold, and lunch hardly helped to warm us, so we speedily set out to get a brisk walk and see the lions. We had hardly emerged from the door of the Hotel de Londres when we were waylaid by one of the loitering guides. We could not shake him off, and engaged him at 3 francs. He proved of little use beyond taking us the most direct route to the objects in view by a handsome bridge over the Arno, which is probably from 300 to 400 feet wide; but it was then in full flood, the snow melting on the mountains bringing down much water. Proceeding up a long street, we came at the end of it, on the outskirts of the town, to the Piazza del Duomo, where are congregated all that may be said to make Pisa famous in the world— its cathedral, its baptistery, its Campo Santo, and its leaning tower. Here we stood face to face with what had been familiar to me through pictures from boyhood as 'the seventh wonder of the world.' Whether it be the seventh or the seventieth wonder of the world, I don't know, but it was with a strange feeling I thus for the first time saw the reality. The day was too cold to venture the ascent to the top, from which there is an extensive view. Controversy exists as to whether the fact of the inclination is due to design or to subsidence of the ground. I think the latter is the real or more likely cause, the more especially as to all appearance the baptistery also is off the vertical. The bell tower or Campanile (178 feet high) is one of those detached belfries not uncommon in Italy, and of which few specimens occur in England. A rather uneasy feeling is produced in hearing the bells ring, and thinking of the vibration to which doubtless the motion subjects a building which seems as if ready of itself to topple over. We were glad to take refuge from the cold in the cathedral, constructed of marble, and eight hundred years old. Unfortunately, the sun being under cloud, we could not see it to the same advantage as if it had been a clear day. In length it exceeds 300 feet. The transept is over 250 feet. The interior, divided into aisles by double rows of columns, is a wonderful collection of enrichment of all kinds—

pictures, statuary, carved marble, bronzes, articles in gold and silver, and finely-ornamented pulpits and altars. We afterwards saw many cathedrals and churches in Italy, but none to compare with this cathedral in its peculiar description of magnificence. St. Peter's of Rome and St. Mark's of Venice have their own distinguishing characteristics entitling them to the first rank, but the Cathedral of Pisa is just as much worthy of honour in its own line for what it contains.

From the cathedral we stepped across the piazza to the baptistery, where we were so fortunate as to witness two new-born unhappy infants undergoing the ceremony of baptism; which, indeed, was rather a serious ordeal, as the poor little things, not a day old, were well rubbed with oil, besides being sprinkled with water and tickled with salt.[1] The priest rattled through the service with great rapidity, the women uttering the responsive amen at apparently the right places with promptitude, as if quite accustomed to it. Before the priest came in, I asked one of the women what was to be the name. 'Would you give it?' was the reply. The building, thus detached from the church like the Campanile (of which other specimens occur in Italy), is circular, 100 feet in diameter, surmounted by a dome 190 feet high. It is an exquisite piece of workmanship, the font and pulpit being peculiarly rich; the sculpture outside is also good. Within the building there was a great ring of sound or hollow echo when the priest read the service.

Leaving the baptistery, we rung the bell at the door of the Campo Santo, and were admitted. It is small in size compared with that at Genoa, and of a very different description and interest. Its age is great, about seven hundred years having passed since it was founded. In shape it is a

---

[1] The ceremony of baptism in the Greek Church is even more trying to the poor child. See *The Englishwoman in Russia*, p. 265.

parallelogram, probably about 400 feet long by about 150 feet wide. The walls are covered with curious frescoes, some of which are getting indistinct. Round the enclosure and by the walls, under cover, many fine monuments in marble, old and new, mingled together, are disposed more like objects in a museum than as forming memorials in a place of sepulture. The interior court or burial-ground is said to have been made up of earth (fifty-three ship-loads) brought from Mount Calvary or some other place near Jerusalem.

In returning to town, we saw many shops filled attractively with Italian sculpture in alabaster and in Carrara marble. Alabaster, however, is soft, and is more liable to injury than marble, the groups in which material are much dearer, but at the same time fairly moderate compared with prices at home, although in computing price the risk and expense of carriage have to be added.

The town of Pisa is situated upon both sides of the Arno; the streets, wide and lined with high houses and other buildings, look tidy and clean; but about all there is a deserted look, although the population is stated at 50,000, and the place, which is a University town, is compactly built. It has a mild humid atmosphere, said, rightly or wrongly, to have curative properties for those affected with asthma. Centuries ago it was a leading commercial city, the great rival of Genoa, with which it was long at war, and to which it ultimately succumbed. Merchants had not at that time learnt that their true power and proper glory lies not in war but in commerce.

The next day was fine, with a bright sun to warm the air; and we took advantage of it to drive to Lucca, said in guide-books to be fifteen miles distant by rail: by road it seemed little more than ten. Calculating according to Bædeker, we should only have had, by time occupied (six hours), to pay 6 francs for the carriage; but the driver asked

15 francs, and agreed to go for 12½, which we were informed was ample fare. On return he wished us to go by some other route, and if we had agreed, it would, we were told, have enabled him to make his own terms at the end of the drive. The road to Lucca is well-formed, hard, and level, and would therefore seem to have been one of the old Roman roads, the more especially as it lies between what were two ancient Roman cities. It was a most delightful drive through many picturesque valleys, and through a mountainous country, and it would have been more so two months later. At this time the trees were bare. On the way, near Ripafrata, a bold, steep rock rises like an island from the plain, crowned by a small Italian town, which our driver named Lugliano—a very striking object, especially with the snow-capped Apennines peering in the background over the nearer hills, quite an artist's study,—and of which, stopping the carriage for a few minutes, I made a rapid sketch. As a characteristic specimen of 'a city set upon a hill,' of which we afterwards saw so many in Italy, the drawing is given in illustration. Lucca is a fortified town, in regular wall and ditch formation, three miles in circuit, and there is a good deal to see in it. We visited the cathedral, and walked round a portion of the ramparts, from which views are had towards the mountains which surround Lucca.

There are two routes from Pisa to Rome—one by Leghorn and the coast, which would have obliged us either to stop the night at the uninviting town of Civita Vecchia, or to have arrived at Rome late in the evening. We chose the other route by Sienna. To go by Sienna, the traveller proceeds eastward about half-way along the railway to Florence, and changes carriages at Empoli. From Empoli the railway strikes off southward to Sienna and Rome. Sienna stands high, being 1330 feet above the level of the sea, and is considered a place of summer residence for its coolness.

A CITY SET UPON A HILL,
ON ROAD TO LUCCA.

I was therefore somewhat apprehensive, considering the cold weather we had endured, lest it might be too cold. Although, however, it stands high above the level of the sea, it does not seem to be more than 200 feet above the level of the surrounding country, or of the railway, and we did not find it very cold. But a change had taken place in the weather, and it was again a fine cloudless day. Having decided to go by Sienna, we could not resist making another excursion to the cathedral before starting by the mid-day train, and were all but tempted to ascend the Campanile. But to an invalid it looked chilly outside, and the height deterring; and I being the only one who might have gone, the custodier could not take me alone, the rule, to guard against accidents or suicide, being that not less than three must make the ascent at a time. The cathedral looked much finer in the sunshine, and we could have lingered long examining it in detail, and would gladly have had there the wearisome time, well-nigh an hour, we were, according to Italian custom, required to spend in the *salle-d'attente* of the railway. The journey from Pisa to Sienna, about seventy miles, is through a mountainous country, with some places of interest by the way, though our prospect was much contracted by reason of a passenger in the carriage who would draw down all the blinds on his side and read a book the whole way, till his wife, out of shame, seeing our disappointment, persuaded him to allow one of the three blinds on his side to be raised, there being no sun peering in even to justify an excuse, which, indeed, never was made. In four hours and twenty minutes we arrived at our destination.

SIENNA.

Sienna, resting on the top and brow of a hill, looks picturesque from below. The railway station lies in a hollow, and the road up to town is steep. We drove to the Grand Hotel, which, though not mentioned in Bædeker, unless its name has been changed, is in by far the best situation of any, its windows looking down upon the public park and across to the fort or citadel; while, to add to its attractions, it is kept by a worthy English landlady, and is consequently possessed of all English comforts. We had an hour to see the town before dinner, at which we enjoyed its famous Chiante wine presented in flasks.

The following morning, having engaged a guide from the hotel, we desired him to take us to the places of most interest. Accordingly, he led us through the long, narrow main street of Sienna, where there is scarcely room for two carriages to pass, and no footways, and all paved, according to Italian mode, with large flagstones. There are shops in this street, and, I think, nowhere else, but of a very inferior description. It terminates near the Collegio Tolomei, which we entered to see a large gallery of the old masters, including some good paintings, one especially by Perugino. From this we proceeded to the cathedral, which is built in alternate courses of black and white marble, the façade very richly ornamented. The interior, though highly adorned, is not so rich in works of art as the Cathedral of Pisa. The interior pavement, composed of marble mosaics, representing Old Testament scenes, had unfortunately been so much worn by the worshippers' feet as to require to be boarded over for protection; but a part of the boarding is removed, to allow the visitor to see a portion as a specimen. We were shown into the library, which is surrounded by huge illuminated tombs, some of which lie open for inspection. It is a great lofty hall, ornamented by sculpture and by large frescoes, executed by a fellow-pupil of Raphael, his great master having been said to have had a hand in the designs. These frescoes are very bright and perfect, and were among the best we saw anywhere in Italy. Leaving the cathedral, and just looking in at the baptistery below, we crossed over to the large open place called the Piazza Vittorio Emanuele. Here a curious sight met our eyes. A dentist, who had been driving through the town in a carriage and four, with a band of music to congregate the people, stood on the box of the carriage among a crowd of people, and was gratuitously extracting their decayed teeth as fast as the unfortunates could pass up to him. The patient was seated, a moment's inspection, the tooth (probably the right one, not impossibly occasionally the wrong one) was drawn and tossed into the air among the crowd; the person so operated on descended, relieved, on the other side, and in a twinkling another unhappy one took his place to be similarly treated. We understood that the operator was paid from some charitable source.

Several public buildings are situated in the Piazza, and among them the town or public hall, containing many frescoes and paintings, through which we were conducted. A very high, slender-looking tower or campanile rises from it, and is one of the most prominent objects in Sienna. Leaving the town-hall, we walked to the Instituto delle Belle Arti, which contains a collection of old paintings, particularly of the school of Sienna, principally interesting to the student; thence to the large Church of St. Domenico, where are various paintings, and among others, frescoes by Sodoma.

The places which we thus visited were among the principal in the town, and they showed that several days might profitably be spent by students and lovers of art at Sienna. Returning to the hotel to lunch, we afterwards crossed the esplanade or public park to the citadel, and enjoyed the views of the surrounding country from the battlements. The walls are high, with deep fosses. I think it was here for the first time we saw the Italian soldiery; and besides those stationed in the fort, there was a large force in barracks outside the walls, in front of which the soldiers were being drilled. The Italian soldier is of small stature, generally young or even boyish-looking, as if newly conscripted. The uniform—a curious mixture of hot and cold attire—is a blue cloth surtout, and white canvas trousers and gaiters, with a black-glazed, round, broad-brimmed hat, adorned with a bunch of cock's feathers, and stuck upon the one side of the head — a most unmilitary and unbecoming head-gear. The undress, a cap covered with white canvas, is an improvement.

The following morning we left for Rome. There is not much of interest by the way, unless it be that the railway runs by the river Tiber more than half the journey; but as we approached our destination, we strained our eyes in eager longings to catch the first view of the glorious old place. Rome, however, is not imposing at a distance. Almost the only object which catches the eye is the dome of St. Peter's. At length we passed slowly through the Campagna, skirted an ancient aqueduct and some other ruins, entered the walls of the fortifications, and in a modern railway station were deposited in the grand old Eternal City.

XII.

ROME.

WE had about a month previously taken rooms in Madame Tellenbach's Pension for the 15th of March, but at her suggestion, as the weather had been cold and wet, had given them up. We obtained quarters in the Hotel de Londres, on the opposite side of the Piazza di Spagna. This is a large open space, in what is considered to be the strangers' quarter, and most of the principal hotels are in it, or in its neighbourhood. It is very necessary to be cautious where one sleeps in Rome, and we heard that cases of fever had happened even in some of what are considered the best hotels. It is said that it is not desirable to have rooms immediately under the Pincian Hill; while, oddly enough also, it is believed that the most healthy localities are those in which the houses and their inhabitants are most crowded, as in the Ghetto. I cannot vouch for either of these theories. After being two nights in the Hotel de Londres, we procured rooms in Madame Tellenbach's. There are some advantages attaching to a house of this description in a place like Rome; principally because the people mingle more sociably together than in an hotel, arising, I suppose, from the lady of the house sitting at table and introducing her guests to each other. It is also less expensive than an hotel. It cost me from 4 to 5 francs per day for each of my party more at the hotel than at the pension, the difference necessarily being more or less according to circumstances, and especially according to the rooms taken in the one and in the other. But it must be admitted that there is a certain amount of additional comfort, tidiness, and appearance, which are usually obtained at an hotel, which a little judicious expenditure in a pension might secure. And for a short visit the hotel is, in any view, preferable.

Those who intend to spend the winter in Rome can, if they so desire, procure lodgings; and sometimes they can be obtained at a moderate rate. A friend had (winter 1878–79) for six months a suite of rooms (two public and three bed rooms) neatly furnished, in a good street near the Piazza di Spagna, for 320 francs per month, service included. The rooms, however, were on the fourth *piano* or storey, and on a lower floor would have been greatly more. But in Rome, as in Italian towns generally, it is an advantage to be high up; and, indeed, one may toil up a long stair, as we have done, and find an excellent private dwelling on the top floor; for many of the houses in Rome resemble the 'tenements' or 'lands' so common in Scotland, divided into 'flats,'—that is, a separate dwelling on each floor, and communicating with the street by a common stair.

The Piazza di Spagna is a very convenient central position for all parts of Rome, and it is filled with carriages for hire—both landaus with two horses, and little carriages with one horse, principally the latter. None of the horses look very strong, but they go actively about. Carriage fares are moderate, a course in a one-horse carriage being 80 centimes, with 20 centimes extra for each passenger beyond two; nor is *buono mano* (drink money) expected. Per hour, the charge is 1 franc 70 centimes for one horse, and 2 francs 20 centimes for two (scarcely 2s.). It is well that fares are so moderate, because Rome is a place where people are cautioned not to fatigue themselves by much walking.

We were fortunate enough to get into good genial weather, with the exception of an occasional shower, and remained in Rome at this time for nine or ten days, when we went to Naples, and on our return spent about a fortnight longer. Both visits combined made but a short period in which to see all that is to be seen in Rome; but we did see (in a general way) a great deal in that time, which it would be impossible for me to describe fully in small compass. My object here is not to describe in detail, or to furnish the information which may be had in guide-books, or in more important works, and particularly in such books as Hare's *Walks in Rome*, which is a most exhaustive guide to all that can be seen, or Sir George Head's *Rome, A Tour of Many Days*, which, in three volumes, furnishes very full accounts of everything; it is simply to give a mere outline of some places we saw, so as to offer a general idea of them, and be as hints to those who visit the old city. Photographs and engravings have made all the important objects familiar to the eye.

Some people set about the seeing of sights in Rome in a very methodical, systematic manner, and so as to ensure their missing nothing, planning minutely each night what is to be done next day. This exhaustive method of 'doing' Rome is calculated rather to make a toil of a pleasure; but some degree of pre-arrangement is necessary, so as to economize time and to see as much as possible without weariness. Having decided where to go, we usually after breakfast engaged a carriage by the hour, or, if desirous of seeing a gallery of paintings or a palace, which would consume an hour, drove to the place, dismissed the cab, and on leaving took the first vacant one at the door. In the city itself there is no difficulty in at once procuring one anywhere. But in the outskirts they are not so easily found. This difficulty happened once to ourselves, on occasion of visiting St. John in Lateran. Having in view to see the church, museum, baptistery, Santa Scala, and other neighbouring places, which would take at least two hours, we unluckily dismissed our carriage, and when we left had to walk some distance before obtaining another to take us back to town.

Our first day in Rome was a Sunday. We readily found the Presbyterian or Scotch church just outside the Porto del Popolo. It is a large, airy, nice place of worship. The climate of Rome, however, does not suit every one, and may produce weakness or develop what is latent. We met at Mentone, in the following winter, an esteemed Scotch clergyman, who ascribed debility to having in a previous year had three months' duty in Rome. He had never, he said, been in good health since.

Next morning we drove to St. Peter's, which is generally the first object of attraction to the visitor. The way to it leads through narrow insignificant streets till the Ponte St. Angelo be reached. This bridge across the Tiber is decorated on each side parapet with five white marble statues, looking very black with exposure to the weather. The Tiber rolls below, yellow, muddy, and unalluring, and is in breadth between 300 and 400 feet, or about one-third the width of the Thames at Blackfriars Bridge.

The Castle of St. Angelo is one of those marked features of old Rome which engravings enable us at once to recognise. It was built by Hadrian as a mausoleum for himself and succeeding emperors, and the square base of this immense monument covered an acre and a half of ground. The round tower, which rises from the base, is now 188 feet in diameter; but it is stripped of its outer case of stone and white marble, and it no longer possesses what it is believed to have had, a dome 300 feet high, together with encircling statues. When built, it was no doubt a monument of the greatest magnificence; but its massive strength caused it to be for centuries occupied as a fort, and the successive sieges to which it has been subjected have brought about the destruction of all its adornment. Its history is to a large extent, since it was built, the history of the city of Rome, and may be seen set forth in Mr. Storey's *Castle of St. Angelo.*

Passing the castle on the right, the Tiber being on the left after crossing the bridge, the way lies along one of several narrow streets terminating in the great Piazza San Pietro, so that till the Piazza be reached St. Peter's is obscured. It was not without emotion we arrived in view of this noble building, sending out from it on each side, like huge arms, imposing colonnades, consisting of no less than 284 columns each 64 feet high, which enclose so far the Piazza. The Egyptian obelisk brought to Rome by Caligula has been placed in the centre of the Piazza, attaining, with its pedestal, a height of 127 feet 6 inches, and yet dwarfed in presence of the great temple, the dome of which, however, is not well seen from the Piazza, or, indeed, from any place near. The obelisk is flanked on each side by a large and handsome fountain always playing, and in windy weather sending a shower of spray to a considerable distance leeward.

The cab stopped at the bottom of the long flight of steps which led up to the grand portico, and ascending it, we passed through, and pushing aside the heavy mat which, as usual in Italian churches, depends upon the door, looked eagerly in, and were—must I confess it?—at first disappointed. One expects a great deal, and the magnitude of the building at first sight did not strike us as so overwhelming. I suppose this was partly owing to its admirable proportions; but when we had walked round the interior, the vastness of the structure seemed to grow upon us, and with every successive visit we felt its solemn grandeur and majestic harmony impressing more and more. We contented ourselves on the present occasion with walking round, Bædeker in hand, studying the plan, and making ourselves familiar with the different parts. St. Peter's drew us to it repeatedly afterwards, and as this is not a journal of visits, I may here simply notice the result of the impressions which we formed.

This grand edifice, the largest church in Christendom, is in every respect on a colossal scale. There is nothing paltry about it, unless it be the statue of St. Peter himself. This is frightfully hideous, and why it should have been allowed to be set and to remain in a place where everything is in such good taste, is very extraordinary. The statue is a sitting one, bolt upright, and holding up two fingers of the right hand in a stiff manner. The face is ugly, and certainly has not anything of the Jewish type about it. Every minute people are seen coming up to kiss the toe of this odious image, the kissing being performed by all classes of people. I observed how inconsistent it was with the character of the apostle, who, with all his forwardness, had a profound consciousness of his own sinful humanity, and who himself, when 'Cornelius fell down at his feet and worshipped him, took him up, saying, Stand up, I myself also am a man.' A story goes that a person affected with sore eyes had gone up and rubbed them upon the toe, and immediately afterwards a gentleman, ignorant of this remedial operation, coming in, kissed it. Let us hope he was straightway informed by some charitable onlooker of what had previously been done, and that the fact opened his eyes to the grossness of such superstitious idolatry. It is strange that Peter should be forced into association with Rome, because, as those who have anxiously investigated the subject consider, there is no actual proof of the 'first' (called) of the apostles ever having been there.

And yet in the Mamertine prison, the place is shown where it is given out that Peter and Paul were imprisoned; and so far do they presume on credulity, that a hollow in the wall is actually pointed out and gravely affirmed to have been made upon it by contact with the energetic apostle's head, I suppose during animated discussions with Paul. If I am not mistaken, it was Adam Smith who left the mark of his head on the wall paper of the room in which he wrote his *Wealth of Nations;* but Peter's head must have been formed of stuff harder and rougher even than that of his statue, to have hollowed out a hole in a stone wall. A more wonderful stone, however, is shown in a little chapel outside the gates, fixed on the floor, where we were gravely informed, for the charge of, I think, 5 soldi (twopence halfpenny), that the deep impression of two feet—pretty large ones too —were the marks of Peter's feet. This marvellous petrifaction is protected by an iron grating.[1] To crown all, the dome of St. Peter's is held to cover the site of the burial-place of the apostle, and beneath lies his tomb. Over the supposed tomb and over the high altar attached, at which only a pope or a cardinal delegate can officiate on important occasions, a canopy (*baldacchino*) rises ninety-five feet high, to which, architecturally, exception has been taken. More exception might be taken to the reality of the place of sepulture. It cannot even be proved that Peter was put to death at Rome, and is it likely that his persecutors would allow him to be buried in the spot alleged, or that any succeeding emperor, supposing he was desirous of removing the martyr to a place with which he, the apostle of the Jews, had no peculiar connection, would have been able to have recovered and identified the body?

The grand central aisle of the cathedral is flanked by colossal columns, the size of which can hardly be appreciated without actual measurement or veritable comparison with

[1] I have since seen a different account given of this stone.

other known heights. On each side the aisles, of proportionate size, contain large chapels, one of which is used for the ordinary services of the Church, which are chanted by the pope's choir. Gigantic statues and monuments of popes adorn the aisles and transept. The altars, as usual, are enriched by paintings, which at our first visit, being in Lent, were, as in all the churches at that season, veiled. The altars themselves are rich, but not obtrusively so—all in quiet keeping with the august building. In the transept, wooden confessional boxes are set, each different confessing nation, England included, having one. Looking up the gigantic dome, we find the walls covered with mosaics. The four Evangelists occupy a first course, and high above them other figures.

Once a week, Thursday mornings, before ten o'clock, the public are admitted to ascend the dome, which, to the top of the lantern, is 403 feet high, the extreme height at the summit of the cross being 435 feet. The ascent, which can be made on horseback to the roof, is extremely interesting, and gives a better idea of the magnitude of the building than any perambulations below. It is effected by a special tower situated near the portico. By a gentle slope the passage rises, winding and winding round this huge tower, along the sides of which inscriptions, cut in the stone, bear the names of monarchs who have made the ascent, till, after a long and wearisome progression, the roof of the cathedral is reached, and stepping out on it we see its great extent and the gigantic size of the statues, which, having regard to view from below, are three times the size of life. Walking across the roof and mounting a few steps, we enter the dome, and get into the first gallery which encircles it within. Even from this elevation, gazing down, the people walking on the floor below looked like pigmies. At this point we were brought into proximity to the mosaics, and perceived the colossal scale upon which they are constructed. The Evangelists, who look like life-size below, are found to be of immense magnitude; and what look like small cherub boys below, are huge giants, the dimensions of which I would not venture to name, because in St. Peter's all computations by the eye are deceptive, and it is only by referring to actual measurement that sizes can be safely reckoned. Here also the width of the dome (178 feet) is observable by finding what a long walk it is round the gallery. A further ascent up narrow stairs leads to the second gallery over the first and inside the dome, and from this gallery everything below is still more dwarfed. Then, by contracted stairs between the inner and outer walls of the dome, the lantern is gained. It would be a dizzy height were it not for the platform of the roof more immediately below. From this point an admirable bird's-eye view of Rome is had. Unfortunately the day we ascended was gusty and wet with occasional showers, rendering it undesirable to stand at the embrasures, and disturbing our view. But we could catch a glimpse of the lie of the town and its extent, which appeared less than we had expected to see it. Rome is compact, and this city, once the mistress of the world, and said to have in the days of its glory possessed a population exceeding that of London, does not appear to cover one-third of the ground on which the city of Edinburgh stands. The greatest length of the inhabited part seems to be about $1\frac{3}{4}$ miles, its greatest width about the same. According to the last census, the present population is under 250,000. The town, as now occupied, dates back only to the end of the sixteenth century.

The second Sunday we were in Rome was Palm Sunday, and after an early breakfast we drove to St. Peter's. A tedious service kept us waiting about an hour, when the priests formed in procession and marched to the portal with palms in their hands. These were blanched palms, twisted into fantastic shapes, and not, as one would suppose, of the long natural green branches, which would certainly have been more suitable. The great door was opened and half the procession passed through and stood outside, the remainder standing within. Some form of blessing or other ceremony took place, and then they all marched back again. Altogether it was a very poor affair, although, when it used to be performed by the pope himself, I believe it was more imposing; but the absence of the pope (Pius IX.), who since 1871 had never appeared in public at this or other ceremonials, stripped the pageant of its wonted attractions.

The Vatican adjoins St. Peter's, and consists of immense ranges of buildings, said to contain 11,000 chambers. It is no ornament, architecturally, to the cathedral, upon which it impinges, the portion seen from the Piazza of St. Peter's having too much the appearance of a huge factory. Attached to it, and seen from some of the windows of the Vatican, the pope's garden occupies a large piece of ground, very stiffly laid out, in which His Holiness can, uncommoded by the public, who are not admitted to it, take his walks or drives. Admission to the Vatican is by means of *permessoes*, which are procurable through booksellers and others. To obtain these documents, people are put to trouble and expense, while it must cost a little to issue them, and really they seem required without adequate reason. As the *permesso* is given up at the door, a fresh one is necessary at every visit, unless the visitor express a desire to retain it for use again; when he intimates this at entering, gets it back at going out, and pays the doorkeeper 1 franc for the privilege. Whatever may be the object of employing them, it does not save fees, which are payable at every door which is opened. The doors are very numerous, but fortunately the fee expected is small—half a franc, or even, in some cases, quarter of a franc from each party suffices for each janitor. These 'proud porters' have no objection to copper. It would be really much better if all fees and *permessoes* were abolished and strictly *prohibited*, and a fee not exceeding a franc for a party of, say, four were exacted at each visit. The galleries of the Vatican are places which most people desire, when they go to Rome, to see over and over again.

The great gate of the galleries, in which the sculptures are deposited, is reached by driving or walking all round St. Peter's; and by making the circuit, although it is rather long, one obtains another idea of the vast extent and huge proportions of the cathedral.

The galleries containing the paintings are situated in other rooms, and require separate days as well as separate orders for their examination. The entrance is reached by the Scala Regia in the Colonnade, on the right side approaching St. Peter's.

We devoted two separate afternoons to each.

The sculptures are far more numerous than the paintings, and even after two inspections, we could only consider we had seen them in a very general way. To do them justice, one would almost require to bestow upon each different group of halls a distinct visit. The number of statues, busts, urns, and other sculptured objects exhibited, is very great. Most, if not all of them, have been recovered from the ruins of ancient Rome while under the government of the popes. The visitor is brought face to face with the original of the Apollo Belvedere, the Laocoon, and many other statues and groups familiar to all by copies or by engravings. But it is necessary to watch carefully, lest omission be made of some of the rooms; for we discovered, on going a second time, rooms we had previously overlooked, and which contained some of the finest statuary. Of many of the halls and of the individual statues, photographs can be purchased in the shops, which, to those who have not seen them, convey some idea of the galleries and their contents, and are exceedingly useful to those who have, in recalling them. Without this help, the multiplicity of objects tends to obscure and confuse the recollection. There is one annoying feature about the statue galleries of the Vatican, that in place of the names of the objects, there is painted upon them the name of the pope by whom they were placed where they stand. One gets quite irritated by the vanity of Pius VI. and Pius VII., leading them in so objectionable a manner to obtrude their names upon the public.

The examination of the picture galleries is much more easily accomplished. The good paintings are in reality confined to two or three rooms, and one or two more, in which are fine frescoes by Raphael and others. The great attractions of this gallery are—'The Transfiguration,' by Raphael; 'The Madonna di Foligno,' a fine work of the same great master; and 'The Communion of St. Jerome,' by Domenichino. The upper portion of 'The Transfiguration' is so exquisitely beautiful as to suggest whether it would not have been better severed from the lower half, representing the writhing boy in the midst of the perplexed disciples, which, though it may have been designed by Raphael, was painted by his pupils. Indeed, the insertion of the scene may be said to be an anachronism, because the cure was effected on 'the next day,' while its introduction detracts from the feeling of sublime elevation above the world and the things of the world which the upper portion of the picture breathes.

There are many other fine pictures in the rooms by the old masters. One in particular, which struck me for its softness and beauty of colouring, was a 'Madonna and Child,' by Sasso Ferrato, although it must be confessed both the mother and child are rather plumply fat. I asked the price of a photograph of it for sale in the rooms, taken from an engraving, and was asked 4 francs. It is so often the way in such places to demand long prices.

We had not an opportunity of seeing the library of the Vatican.

The Sistine Chapel is what nobody omits to see. The entrance to it is from the Scala Regia, just before coming to the picture galleries. We saw it once, and I must own it fell short of expectation. The chamber is dark, the frescoes are fading, and to see some of them it is necessary to lie on one's back and look up. The view, therefore, is indistinct and uncomfortable; but though they are from the hand of a great master, the eye experiences a want of repose, the effect of over-decoration.

It is usually recommended to people visiting Rome for the first time, to take a preliminary drive of some hours, to form a general idea of the city. This, after our first visit to St. Peter's, we did, and found it attended with considerable advantage. Except where it is bounded by the Tiber, Rome is surrounded by walls of defence, in which are several gates. Outside of some of these gates, the town has slightly extended; but, for the most part, the walls stretch a good way beyond the inhabited portion of the town, which is very compactly built, there being no large public gardens or parks within the city, and scarcely an open square, while the streets are narrow and the houses high. The seven hills upon which Rome has always been regarded as standing, are rather hillocks than hills, and do not, seen from the Campagna, bulk much upon the eye. They vary in height from 156 feet to 218 feet above the level of the sea; so that, deducting at least 40 feet for the general level of the city, the highest is but low. From the Porto del Popolo, outside of which the Protestant churches are, with one exception, placed, and inside of which is one of the largest piazzas, or open places, in Rome, three straight-leading streets branch out, diverging at acute angles—viz., the Via Babuino, conducting into the Piazza di Spagna; a centre street, the famous Via del Corso; and a third, the Via di Ripetta, which passes by or near to the banks of the Tiber. All these streets proceed (a wonderful circumstance in Rome) in straight lines to a considerable distance, the

Corso fully a mile in length, the vista of all being terminated at the one end in the Piazza del Popolo by the Flaminian Egyptian obelisk, the third in altitude in Rome. The Corso, the longest and central one, terminates at a point not far from the forum of Trajan and the Capitoline Hill, in the vicinity of which the principal ruins of Rome lie. Out of the Corso, however, except where it is crossed for a short way after leaving the Porto del Popolo by a few regular streets, the streets of Rome are so tortuous that I do not recollect any other city, at least similar in size, where it is so puzzling to find one's way about. I did once or twice adventure on a walk, just to try and familiarize myself with the streets, but in doing so found it necessary to take the bearings very exactly, and to keep the map in hand, to prevent my getting bewildered. These tortuous streets are irregular and narrow, sometimes with scarcely room for two little cabs to pass. They are causewayed, but have no footpath. Even the three leading streets I have named are extremely narrow. The Corso is only 40 to 50 feet wide, and the footpaths which have been placed there are proportionately contracted, leaving, I may say, no room in some places for two foot-passengers to pass each other. The streets are now, however, like other Italian towns, lighted with gas, the want of proper lighting previously having been much felt. The principal shops are in the Corso, the Piazza di Spagna, and the Via Condotti, which crosses from the Corso to the Piazza. Some of the chief booksellers are in the Piazza, but the jewellers' and photographers' shops are the kind which are most largely patronized by strangers. None of the shops, however, are capacious, and the wares they contain are in general marvellously limited in quantity.

Beyond the inhabited part of Rome, there are many good roads, principally conducting to or from the gates, and leading to the country beyond. As one passes along the streets, the eye is continually met by churches, palaces, and other public buildings; but the great attractive interest lies in what remains of the grand buildings of ancient Rome, which for the most part are found in proximity to each other.

Of these, the one which predominates, and by its imposing mass generally claims the first examination, is the Colosseum. It stands nearly free from other buildings, in all the sublimity of age and magnitude. But not far from it are the Arches of Titus and Constantine, the ruins of the Temple of Venus, of the Basilica of Constantine, of the palace of the Cæsars on the Palatine Hill, of the Forum Romanum, and of many other ancient buildings and places, familiar to all who have read about Rome, and which one could not see for the first time without being profoundly stirred. There are gentlemen—I suppose they may be called clinical lecturers—who give descriptions on the spot of these interesting old places, and the information so afforded is useful, because the results of study are imparted by the living voice in a familiar way, and special attention is called to the historical associations, which otherwise to most people might remain unknown. One of these gentlemen, Mr. Forbes (charge, 3 fr. each), makes up two parties per day, one before and one after lunch— regularity in taking which, in Rome, is always recommended as essential to health. I had an opportunity on one occasion of accompanying him, and there was certainly an advantage in hearing his explanations. There is so much, however, to see in Rome, and that of a diversified character, that this was the only time I managed to do so. Mr. Shakespeare Wood is another who occasionally goes out in this way, but I was apprised that he would not form a party during the time we were in Rome. He is said to be remarkably well informed, and is usually engaged by Mr. Cook for his special excursions. To those who would study old Rome, great assistance might be found in a series of instructive papers, evincing great literary research, and evidently of minute exactness of statement, printed in the *Transactions of the Architectural Institute of Scotland*, written by the late Mr. Alexander Thomson of Banchory. It would be well if these scholarly papers could be collected and published by themselves, for, as they stand, they are not within the reach of the general public. Some of the statements I shall hereafter make on Old Rome will be on his authority.

It would not be possible, according to the plan I have adopted of a rapid survey of what is to be seen in Rome, to give any detailed description of the various ancient buildings, which, besides, are by means of photographs and engravings so familiar even to those who never have visited Italy.

The Colosseum[1] is an immense mass of building, notwithstanding not only that it was long occupied as a fortress, and subjected to the injury resulting from attack and defence, but that it was, like so many others, used for centuries as a quarry for its stones, its marble, and even its iron. Happily this species of destruction was stopped by the French, and steps have also been taken for its preservation by building strong and lofty supports. The Colosseum is at least twice as large as the arena at Nismes, and even as it now remains it is twice as high,[2] but that at Nismes is in much better preservation. The outer walls, galleries, and arches of the Colosseum are built of massive blocks of stone, bound

---

[1] So called from its colossal size. It is sometimes spelt Coliseum, a corruption of the word.

[2] The arena of Nismes is 148 by 112 yards, height 74 feet, and accommodated 32,000 spectators; arena, 74 by 42 yards. The Colosseum, 205 by 170 yards, height 156 feet, accommodating 87,000 spectators (besides containing standing room for 23,000 more in the porticoes and surrounding passages); arena, 93 by 58 yards. But in stating these and other measurements, it is always right to keep in mind that in different books the figures do not correspond, and one well-informed and most reliable writer states the dimensions of

together with iron; but brick composed what was below. Brick, evidently of a hardy quality, cemented by a very strong, durable mortar, appears, indeed, to have been very largely used by the Romans for the carcases or substantial and concealed portions of their buildings. These brick carcases, however, were either built over with substantial stone-work, or faced with slabs of marble, sometimes both; and in a building of this magnitude, even the outer deceptive covering of stone or marble would be of immense mass. By the removal of vast quantities of the large stones forming the casing, a great deal of this brick carcase or underwork has been laid bare, so that the interior of the building has a very ruinous look. Externally, also, the removal of courses of stone, in some parts combined with the ravages of time, impart to it the aspect of a huge ruin. There is free entrance to the public to the arena or central area. We seldom passed the Colosseum without going in to take a glance at it. One could hardly, however, forget what deadly scenes had been enacted there, what agonies had been endured, what cries of pain had been uttered, what savage shouts had once filled its walls, or help feeling thankful that the barbarous and brutalizing spectacles which were then found necessary 'to make a Roman holiday,' were now happily things of a long-past age.

I was so fortunate as to be in the city on Saturday, 21st April 1877, which was held as the birthday of Rome (the 2630th, I believe), and beheld a spectacle in the Colosseum which never had greeted the eyes of the old Romans. Nearly the whole population was, in the evening of that day, drawn to the great amphitheatre and its neighbourhood. Joining a party of ladies from our house, with considerable difficulty we drove through the crowded streets, and, dis-

the Colosseum at about 40 feet more each way than the above. Mr. Storey's figures for the Colosseum also vary from the above several yards in each measurement. For a pretty full account of the Colosseum, reference may be made to Storey's *Roba di Roma*, vol. i. chap. ix.

missing the carriage, we succeeded in getting inside the Colosseum along with a large but orderly mass of people. After waiting long, we were at last rewarded. All of a sudden, the various galleries, which I suppose had been lined with soldiers, were illumined with coloured lights. On one half of the huge building red lights were burned; on the other half, green. When the powders were burned down, others were substituted, the colours being reversed. The effect was magnificent. Every figure in the place was bathed in coloured light, while the walls were one mass of a glowing hue, disclosing the colossal proportions in all their ruinous irregularity, and, where red was burned, looking as if it were a huge lump of burning lava or molten iron. This over, with some trouble we managed to edge away from the crowd to the outside, to see the further operations elsewhere. The Colosseum itself was first lighted on the exterior, which, fine as the effect was, I think could hardly be compared with the interior view. Lights were then successively burned to illuminate the Arches of Constantine and Titus and the Basilica of Constantine—the figures of the persons running about in charge appearing at a little distance, wrapped in the carmine colour, like so many incarnate demons. Last of all, the Forum, the Capitoline Hill, and the surrounding buildings and ruins, were several times similarly illuminated, while a display of fireworks from the Capitol terminated this very imposing spectacle.

The grand dimensions of the Colosseum drew us often there. It seemed at every visit more and more imposing. Leaving it, and proceeding by the Via Sacra to the Capitoline Hill, which lies about half a mile distant, one passes upon the left the Arch of Constantine, standing at the entrance to a broad wooded roadway, called the Via di Gregorio, running between the Palatine Hill (on which are the ruined palaces of the Cæsars) on the right side, and the Church of San Gregorio Magno and other buildings on the left side, and leading out towards the Appian Way. The fine sculptures upon the arch are well preserved, and give a richer appearance to it than to any other arches now standing; but have been taken from buildings of an earlier age than that of Constantine, and thought to be of the time of Trajan, whose life they illustrate.

About 200 yards farther on we pass under the Arch of Titus. The bas-relief, exhibiting the triumphal procession and captive Jews, is of itself sufficient to confer a lasting interest upon this arch. It forms a grand contemporaneous record of the siege of Jerusalem, and of the forms of some of the sacred furnishings of the temple.

Here we find and drive over a portion of the veritable paving-stones of an old Roman road, the Via Sacra. Considering how frequently our roads and streets require to be re-paved, re-laid, or re-macadamized, it seems little short of a miracle that any portion of the old Roman paving should have remained for so many centuries. But the Roman roads were constructed in a special manner, with the great object in view of ensuring their being solid, dry, level, and direct. The under foundation was of three courses of broken stones of different given sizes for each course, and altogether 3 feet deep, with a top course of closely-jointed stone, generally basalt, a foot thick. The roads were narrow, sometimes only 12 feet wide, and had a rise of 3 inches in the centre to allow the rain to run off. The making of roads was considered a matter of prime importance and a most laudable undertaking, so that enormous sums were spent on them. In Britain alone there were 2500 miles of Roman roads. The roads of Rome were the more durable, inasmuch as they were not subjected to the heavy traffic of our streets, the carriages being small and light; while, as no gas and water pipes underlay them, there was no everlasting turning of them up to get at things below, and as little were there tramway lines to shake the foundations or injure the surface.

The space of ground on which the Forum Romanum stands lies on the Colosseum side of the Capitol. It is sunk many feet below the level of the roads which now surround it, and which, no doubt, have been so raised above it by the accumulation of rubbish during centuries. Little is left entire in this open or excavated space but the Arch of Severus; the remainder, inclusive *inter alia* of the once splendid Basilica Julia, and the temples of Saturn and Vespasian, are in ruins, only a few pillars remaining to testify to what they were, and in some cases not even so much. But enough remains to show how very elegant these buildings must have been, although one would think, judging from their present appearance, they were rather too much crowded together for effect. The whole of the space, however, between the Capitoline Hill and the Colosseum was at one time a scene of great magnificence, and all glistening in white marble. Classic temples and other buildings apart from the Forum were ranged upon one side, with the Quirinal and Esquiline Hills, and Trajan's Forum and Column in the background; while the other side was bordered by the Palatine Hill (118 feet above the valley), crowned by the grand palace of the Cæsars. This is now almost a mass of ruins, but much excavation has of late years been made, rendering a visit to it exceedingly interesting. We spent some hours one day exploring the ground, admission to which is by payment of one franc each.

The Capitoline Hill, attained from the Forum by two roads, and covering an area of 16 English acres, is crowned, as seen from the direction of the Colosseum, with a building which has little but some age to recommend it, and from which a square tower rises. It turns its back on the Forum below. The hill, however, in the time of the old Romans, was undoubtedly decorated with imposing buildings worthy of its situation. The temple of Jupiter Capitolinus is now ascertained to have stood upon the highest part of the hill, on the site of the present Church of St. Maria in Ara

Cœli, reached by a very ladder of steps (124 in number) from the level plateau on the main crown of the hill, formerly the valley of the Intermontium, now called the Piazza del Campidoglio. This church dates from the tenth century, and is the oldest extant in Rome. It is large, but, though curious, cannot be said to equal many others, and, I suppose, derives its chief importance from its association with the miracle-working Bambino, which marvellous doll finds its abode there. The Capitoline Museum stands on one side of the Piazza, and the Palace of the Conservatori on the other. These are modern buildings, but they contain a large collection of sculptures found in or about Rome, and a large picture gallery comprehending many fine paintings by the old masters. One of the sculpture rooms is devoted to busts of the Roman emperors, and is considered to be the best collection of them. It is strange and deeply interesting to look at these marble representations, executed from the living person, of men who existed so long ago, and whose actions are so noted in history. Where there are more than one of the same man, they invite comparison to notice their accordances or their dissimilarities. The galleries also comprise many other objects of great attraction; for example, what is commonly called 'The Dying Gladiator,' which, thus seen in the original, far excels any copy. Indeed, it is seldom that copies approach originals. They want the delicate shades and lines, and other evidences of masterly power denoting that marked superiority which raises the great creations of genius above the works of the common herd. In another room we saw the famous Capitoline Venus.

In a side street we were shown the place which is held to have been the site of the Tarpeian Rock, from which malefactors were hurled; but if this be the true site, the ground below has been much filled up, as the height seems little enough for producing so violent a death. Near to it the spot is also pointed out where Tarpeia opened the gate of the citadel to the Sabines, and received the reward of her treachery.

In the centre of the Piazza the noble equestrian statue of Marcus Aurelius arrests the eye. There is a vigorous power about horse and rider to which no other similar statue rises. I have felt it impossible to compare with it the equestrian statue of Charles I. at Charing Cross, in London, or even that of Charles II. in the Parliament Square, Edinburgh, although this last is considered a fine work of art. A broad, handsome flight of steps conducts to the town below. Descending a little way, there may be seen two wolves, kept within an iron-barred cage in memory of the traditional story regarding Romulus and Remus.

We found not far from the Capitoline Hill the beautiful little circular Temple of Vesta, which has been made familiar to everybody by photographs and engravings, and in its neighbourhood a small part of the Cloaca Maxima. This is a portion of the great system of drains (either for sewage or for removing stagnant marsh water) with which Rome was supplied. There it stands to this day, for everything with the Romans was not only made adequate to subserve its purpose, but built to endure, if only the destructive hand of man would let it alone.

It would, however, be perfectly endless to attempt to enumerate, much less describe, all the ancient buildings of interest in Rome. There are now upwards of twenty temples, about a dozen triumphal and other arches, and many other buildings, more or less in a state of ruin. To describe all these would be beyond the scope of the present work. But I can hardly, in narrating our visit, omit to advert to one or two more of the features of Old Rome still remaining.

There are scattered over the old city various prominent

pillars and obelisks, which naturally attract attention. The most important of the monumental columns are those of Trajan and of Marcus Aurelius, and there is also in the Forum Romanum a small pillar of a different character, that of Phocas.

The pillar of Trajan is familiar to all by engravings. The *bassi-relievi* which encircle it contain no less than 2500 figures of men, besides those of animals and other objects. It was erected not merely as a monument to the man, but as a record in its height of the depth of the huge work of excavation on the Quirinal Hill, undertaken and accomplished at its site. The sculpture which adorns it is a beautiful and interesting record of events in Trajan's history. The pillar was planted in the middle of a forum, and surrounded by buildings of such wonderful beauty, and composed of materials so rich and varied, that those who beheld them found themselves utterly at a loss for words to express their admiration; but now, so far as any remains are extant, altogether in ruins, while the rest has been built over.

The column of Marcus Aurelius in the Piazza Colonna, is a similar though less perfect structure.

But the obelisks in Rome are more remarkable than the columns. When we think of the difficulty we have recently had in removing to London a single obelisk, and that not of the largest size, it seems incredible to hear, notwithstanding Rome is so much nearer Egypt, that at one time there were no less than forty-eight Egyptian obelisks standing in that city. Of these, only twelve now remain visible and erect, and most of them have been removed from other positions they formerly occupied in Rome. The remainder, excepting two (one taken to France, and the other to Florence), are, it is supposed, buried in the ruins of ancient Rome. The twelve now standing vary in height from a very short one, 8 feet 6 inches high, to the largest,

102 feet high, not reckoning the pedestals, which—in some cases inappropriate—add much to the height, nor the additions, equally inappropriate, made to some of them upon the apex. All have been hewn out of the syenite red granite quarries of Egypt, but three of them, including that in the Piazza of St. Peter, were extracted by the Romans themselves from these quarries, and have no hieroglyphics, the hieroglyphic inscriptions on the remainder attesting their true Egyptian origin. The obelisk now in London is 68 feet $5\frac{1}{2}$ inches high, being scarcely the height of the fourth in size in Rome, which is 69 feet. But the weight of the London obelisk is only 186 tons, while the weight of the largest (also the oldest, dating back to 1740 B.C.) obelisk in Rome, that placed before the Church of St. John Lateran, is 437 tons, or considerably more than double. The removal to Rome of this last-mentioned huge and weighty block of stone, and its erection on its pedestal, was an undertaking of immense labour and cost, taxing the resources and appealing to the honour of emperors for its accomplishment. The mere erection upon its present position of that now standing in the Piazza of St. Peter's (the second in size, and weighing 331 tons), in the time of Sextus V., cost £9000. It was on this memorable occasion, when under pain of death, certain to be inflicted, all were commanded to be silent, and the ropes were about to give way, the Italian sailor from Bordighera, at the peril of his life, called out, 'Wet the ropes!' and saved the obelisk from destruction. He was himself pardoned, and obtained for Bordighera as reward the privilege of supplying Rome with palm leaves at Easter.

Outside the walls of Rome, particularly on entering or leaving by railway, long lines of lofty arches are seen, more or less ruinous (having suffered dilapidation at the hand of enemies), which supported aqueducts by which ancient Rome was supplied with water. At one time there were no less than twenty-four of these aqueducts, entering Rome from various distances. The water was brought along on the gravitation principle, the inclination being believed to have been 1 foot in 400; for although it seems the Romans were acquainted with the scientific fact of which we now avail ourselves, that water in a closed pipe will find its own level, they did not to any extent act upon their knowledge of it. The water so brought in was distributed to an immense number of small reservoirs, or wells or fountains, for the use of the inhabitants, the surplus water being scrupulously employed to flush and scour the sewers. But it was also used to supply the baths of Rome. The bath was regarded by the old Romans as a necessary of life; and many luxurious men, who had not the newspaper or the last new book to wile away the time, bathed as often as seven or eight times a day—great and small, men and women, all mingling promiscuously in the water. To provide for this voluptuous habit, the baths were numerous, and constructed on an enormous scale. There were no less than sixteen establishments throughout Rome, intended not merely for the purposes of ablution, but to supply other means of recreation, and public places where the citizens might meet each other. The Thermæ of Agrippa, of Caracalla, of Constantine, of Diocletian, and of Titus, still exist in ruins, some of them exemplifying their magnitude. Those of Diocletian, close by the railway station, were the most extensive, measuring more than a mile in circumference. Our time permitted of a visit to only one of these Thermæ, the Thermæ of Caracalla, which, enormous in extent as they were, were only half as large as those of Diocletian. They lie about three-quarters of a mile from the Arch of Constantine, and usually, in a drive to the Catacombs of St. Calixtus, are taken going or returning. The extent of the rooms is something marvellous. The building itself was an oblong enclosed by walls, and is stated to be above 700 feet in length, by nearly 400 feet wide, or nearly half a mile in circuit.[1] Little remains of the structure excepting huge walls or carcases of brick, at one time covered with plates or blocks of marble, which have been removed, and either used in churches or other buildings, or, in accordance with a very vexatious custom, burnt for lime. The rooms, as indicated by the ruins left, must have been of great magnificence, not merely from their size and their marble pillars, coating, and flooring, but from the mosaics with which they were inlaid, and the splendid statues with which they were adorned. Some of the statues have been dug out of the ruins, and among them the famous large group called the Farnese Bull, which we saw in the museum of Naples, with many others now deposited in the museums of that city and of Rome. To accommodate the bathers, there were placed around the baths polished marble chairs (cool seats for the undressed), in those of Caracalla to the number of 1600, in those of Diocletian to the number of 3200. The scene during the bathing hours was no doubt very animated, for the baths were crowded.

I may here state that the supply of water to modern Rome is both abundant and of good quality, a circumstance of great importance, and not always to be reckoned upon in other Italian cities, where the water is looked upon, perhaps justly, with great suspicion.

The Catacombs of Rome are very numerous and of great extent, and it has been calculated that if all the passages

---

[1] The extent, however, is variously computed. One writer, generally very exact, says: 'According to Romani and Nibby's plan of Rome,' Caracalla's baths 'covered an area of 370 yards square, or 28 English acres.' 'Eustace makes the extent twice as great.' Gibbon states that they were a mile in circumference, which would be 193,600 square yards, or 40 acres. Hare says they covered a space of 2,625,000 square yards, which is equal to 542 acres. It is not improbable that some measurements may refer merely to the ground covered by buildings, and that others comprehend ground not so covered. But even this explanation will not account for such extraordinary discrepancies.

were placed in continuous line, they would extend to 545 miles. Those of Calixtus are what are most commonly visited.

The drive to the Catacombs of Calixtus is very interesting; the ground lies by the Appian Way some distance out of the city, and beyond the Porta St. Sebastian. On the way the tombs of the Cæsars and Scipios are passed, and in a neighbouring private garden (on entering which it is highly proper to settle the fee to be paid) there are two buildings sunk in the ground, termed Columbaria—pigeon-holes—apartments probably about 20 feet square, judging from recollection. Descending by a narrow stair, the walls are found covered over with small plates of marble, and under each plate a little niche is formed, containing a vase. The marble plates bear the names of persons deceased, and in the vases below their ashes were deposited. They are curious, carrying one back to ancient times, and becoming, too, a sort of preparative for the visit to the Catacombs, to see which a *permesso* is requisite, a fee being, however, paid at exit to the conductor for each person, varying a little in amount according to the number. As soon as a sufficient party is collected, and waiting until the party which may be below has reappeared, for only one set is taken at a time, the man in charge of the Catacombs makes up the company for the visit. Each person then lights the taper with which he or she ought to be provided (which, as tapers are not supplied at the place, must be brought from the city, a circumstance sometimes overlooked), and descent is made by a stair. The visitors are rapidly marched or whisked along the narrow intricate passages, on each side of which they see the catacombs in which the bodies of persons deceased were formerly laid—the great burial-place of the first Christians. There are many old Latin inscriptions, which the guide stops a minute to point out; but with a very large number it is difficult for all to get near him. It does not appear as if the passages lay far below ground, I should imagine not exceeding 50 feet; but though the air is warm, it is a dismal place, which the generality of people, seeing once, will not care to see again. One requires to be careful to follow the guide to avoid being lost. The examination does not occupy so much as half an hour.

On returning to the light of day we were glad to take a drive farther along the Appian Way. This famous old Roman road was constructed at enormous cost, and was 26 feet wide. At one part a mountain was cut down 120 feet, to obtain that levelness which the Romans always desired for their roads. In its original state it must have offered a very remarkable scene. For, though not unusual for the Romans to bury, or at least to erect monuments to the dead, along the side of public roads, the Appian Way was the favourite part for entombment. For many miles on each side it was lined by sculptured monuments or tombs in marble, of more or less size or magnificence. But all that is now left is, in general, nothing but portions of the brick carcases which underlay the stone or marble surface. Vast numbers of these monuments have been destroyed for the sake of the material. The only notable monument remaining to some extent in preservation is the large and massive tomb of Cecilia Metella—a circular tower 70 feet in diameter, the walls of which are 25 feet thick. Its strength caused it at one time to be used as a fortress. The Appian Way itself fell into ruin and became impassable, but has now been cleared; and one can look along it and see it proceeding as far as the eye can reach in a straight line. It terminates at Puteoli, which when we were at Naples we visited, and so had the good fortune, if it may be so called, to pass over both ends of the road, immortalized by the Scripture record as that by which the Apostle Paul went on his way to Rome.

Mr. Thomson, in an interesting paper on the *Recent*

Excavations in Rome, in which he gives, by illustrative restorations as proposed by Canina of monuments in portions of the Way, some idea of its grandeur, says (p. 28):

'Altogether the Via Appia, when in its pristine glory, must have been a wondrous scene, with its innumerable monuments extending on both sides of fifteen miles of roadway, varied by occasional villas of great extent and beauty, by temples, by exedræ or covered seats, and by fountains. These are of every age and style, from the simplest republican to the richest adornments of imperial times.

'The Via Appia was the road by which travellers from Spain, or Africa, or the East, arrived at the city.

'How striking this approach to the Mistress of the World! How heart-stirring the memories of the illustrious departed which it must have called up in every heart!

'We are not aware of any similar arrangement of equal extent and grandeur among all the remains of ancient times.'

So numerous are the churches in Rome, that I believe it may be said there is one for every day in the year. They abound everywhere, and during a short visit one can only, of course, see a few of those which may be regarded as among the chief. All of them, however, possess some distinguishing mark to attract attention. We entered a good many, the very names of which we did not know. And it is useful to notice that in general it is necessary to visit the churches before twelve o'clock; after the hour of noon they are closed, except in the case of some of the more important.

The Pantheon (built B.C. 27) is the only ancient building in Rome which is now standing entire, although bereft of its ornamentation; but such has been the accumulation of rubbish around it, that the steps leading up to it are now considerably below the level of the street. The edifice itself, also, is much hid by surrounding houses, and is not seen till one is close upon it. Passing through a grand columnar portico, we enter a vast circular expanse 140 feet wide, surmounted by a dome 140 feet high. There are large recesses or deep niches around, which were formerly used as receptacles for statues of the gods, when it became a Roman temple. The place now looks very vacant. The building has been stripped also externally of its marble covering or skin and other adornments, so that it no longer exhibits the magnificence it once possessed. But here Raphael and other great painters have been buried, and here the body of Victor Emmanuel, the gallant first King of Italy, has found its resting-place. Mr. Thomson observes:

> 'The noblest of all the remains of ancient Rome, the Pantheon was, without doubt, originally built as a portion of these (Agrippa's) baths; it is proved by the contiguity of the other fragments, and by the identity of the style of the brickwork. It was turned into a temple by Agrippa himself, on which occasion he added the portico of sixteen Corinthian columns of granite, each of one stone, 50 feet 9 inches in length and 5 feet 9 inches in diameter. Thirteen of these remain as originally placed; the three on the east side are modern restorations.'[1]

San Pietro in Vinculi is visited because it possesses Michael Angelo's grand colossal statue of Moses. Notwithstanding its masterly power, it is far from pleasing in the confined space in which it is placed.

The Jesuit Church (under which one of the lost obelisks has been unfortunately buried) is very gorgeously adorned, and the altar of St. Ignatius (the body of Ignatius Loyola lies below it) exhibits a globe of lapis lazuli, said to be the largest known. This, like every other church at Rome, is besieged by beggars at the door, who whiningly importune for coppers, and one of them always officiously pushes open the thick, heavy, greasy mat placed swinging at the doorway, to keep out the cold air and to offer a convenient asylum to the insect world, and thus, as it is never cleaned, affording a valid excuse for a demand (were reason required). But in all the churches where anything is to be seen inside, a spider is on the

---

[1] Bædeker says: 'At the back of the Pantheon are situated the ruins of the Thermæ of Agrippa, the proximity of which to the Pantheon once gave rise to the absurd conjecture that the temple originally belonged to the baths, and was afterwards converted into a temple.' In a matter of this kind, however, the authority of such a man as Mr. Thomson is much to be preferred to that of any writer in a guide-book.

watch in the shape of a guardian, who, keys in hand, proffers his services to open locked doors and exhibit the treasures of the church, or to draw curtains which conceal principal paintings. However, the fee is small; one franc or half a franc for the party generally suffices.

One of these churches, containing a veiled picture, the celebrated St. Michael of Guido Reni, is that of the Capuccini. The picture is certainly well worth seeing, and, in some respects, it may claim a preference over that of the same subject by Raphael in the Louvre. But why should such pictures—except for fees—be veiled? The veiling is very detrimental to the colour, as the exclusion of sunlight will in time make a picture black. Italian churches are dark enough as built, without shutting out the light of day from the paintings by an impervious curtain.

That for which, however, people chiefly go to the Capuccini is the extraordinary vaulting below the church. Here are arranged in all manner of devices the bones of the monks attached to the Capuccini monastery, of which this is the church. The skeletons of the more noted are exposed entire in their garments, some of them 300 years old. It is a ghastly spectacle, and was shown to us by a monk, who told us he expected his own bones, when he died, would be placed in the vaults, although we had understood the practice had been stopped.

Of a very different kind of interest was what is underground of two other churches,—San Clementi and San Cosmo in Damian. In the vaults below them we were shown the remains of the original churches, built not later than the fourth century, though the precise date cannot be ascertained. Those of San Clementi, discovered in excavating since 1858, are extensive and extremely interesting, including frescoes of the eighth and ninth centuries— one of them being the Crucifixion. It carries one back to Christianity in Rome of a very early period.

No visitor to Rome fails to visit San Giovanni in Laterano.

This is a spacious edifice with altars all round, and is one of the grand churches in Rome, dating back a long way, and historically celebrated. It is, of course, splendidly adorned. The baptistery, like that at Pisa, is an entirely separate building in the Piazza. The Lateran Museum adjoins the church, and on the ground floor contains a collection of ancient statues, the entrance to which we had some difficulty in finding. The upper floor is chiefly remarkable for its collection of inscriptions inserted in the walls, taken from the Catacombs, and of which there is an immense number; but there was nobody to give any information. The famous Santa Scala, said to be the steps of the staircase of Pontius Pilate's house, up which, it is given out, our Lord walked, is on the opposite side of the Piazza. The steps are covered with wood to prevent them being further worn. We saw a good many of the faithful painfully and laboriously ascending it upon their knees,—a very tedious operation, and sometimes, it is said, from its difficulty and unwonted novelty, a ludicrous one, the people (who are of all classes, and fine ladies as well as common men) in their contortions nearly tumbling over or knocking each other about. At every few steps there is a fixed cross to kiss, and at each step fresh paternosters are said; and when at last they attain the top (the stair consists, according to my reckoning, of twenty-eight steps), they kneel upon a small bench and look through an opening into a sacred chapel beyond, and perform further devotions. We heretics ascended more rapidly by one of the two side stairs by which the devotees descend.

A more splendid church than that of the Lateran is the Santa Maria Maggiore, so named from being the largest of eighty churches in Rome dedicated to the Virgin Mary. It is also one of the oldest churches in existence, and has a handsome façade, in front of which a lofty Corinthian column stands, surmounted by a statue of Philip IV. of Spain. The interior is profusely decorated, and is remarkably beautiful.

But perhaps the church which of all others, after St. Peter's, attracts most attention, is that of 'San Paolo fuori le mura.' This is situated about a mile and a half outside the Porta San Paolo, in a road where foot passengers had been lately robbed, and was not, therefore, considered to be very safe for them. But no apprehension was felt in proceeding by carriage, and it forms a pleasant drive from the city. In going, the English cemetery, and the Pyramid of Cestus adjoining, both outside the walls, are passed. These we had intended visiting, but by a mistake of our driver we were taken some way beyond the entrance gate, and then unluckily postponed our visit for another opportunity, which never came, and our return to the city on the occasion was by a different route. The Church of St. Paul, erected on the road to Tre Fontane, where it is said the apostle was beheaded, is a new one, the former one having been destroyed by fire in 1823. The original church was founded so far back as the fourth century, and became in time one of great magnificence. Externally there is nothing remarkable about the present building, but internally it is one mass of marble ornament on a grand scale. It was expected, when commenced, the cost would amount to £1,500,000; but it is alleged that as much as £10,000,000 sterling have already been spent upon it. This may be quite the case. £10,000,000 according to some, and £20,000,000 according to others, have in three centuries been expended on St. Peter's, and that during times when money was more valuable. But whatever has been the cost, it must necessarily have been enormous. The church consists of immense, square-shaped rooms,—huge boxes,—which are not over-pleasing architecturally. Floors and walls are covered with large plates of marble of every description, and long rows of costly granite pillars (80 in number) and of oriental alabaster pillars imposingly line the aisles. Four of the oriental yellow alabaster columns are supported on malachite pedestals presented by the Emperor of Russia. The ceilings (flat) are decorated;

and along the walls under them a very long series of portraits of all the popes has been executed in mosaic. The windows are filled with stained glass containing representations of sacred events. The decorations of the church, which comprise some saved from the fire, are not yet completed, and at present (that is, when we saw it) a feeling of emptiness was conveyed; but when, in course of time, it is filled up with fine statues, paintings, and other ornaments, like other Roman Catholic churches, as no doubt it will be, this feeling of vacancy will disappear, and although in design it may not brook comparison with other churches, it will probably be the most sumptuous building in the world. Outside the church there is a beautiful court of cloisters of the Benedictine monastery; but the site is unhealthy, and the monastery cannot be inhabited during the summer. If nobody remains in charge of this costly church during summer, I do not know how it is guarded from depredation. It seems a great risk to build it in such a situation. Perhaps the laws against sacrilege may be so severe as to deter.[1]

There are many other churches in Rome which should be visited, but cannot be described in a sketch like the present. Indeed, the fullest description of such places can only enable a stranger to realize them very imperfectly.

The palaces in Rome, or what are termed such, are as great an attraction as the churches, and to many much more so. There are about seventy of one kind or another, generally huge old buildings, some of which are open to the public on certain days of the week, or on other stated days,—a fee of 1 franc per party being given to the doorkeeper at leaving, which is always the time in Italy when fees are paid, except when admission is by ticket, paid for at entrance. Most of these palaces are visited for

---

[1] It seems that at *Tre Fontane*, above a mile westward, which we did not visit, the Eucalyptus tree has now been largely planted; and if it will grow, it is expected to render the locality healthy.

the collections of paintings and sculptures which they contain, some of which are very valuable. Generally the second storey is devoted to these collections, the first being sometimes occupied as shops or as servants' apartments, and the upper floors by the family. Leaving umbrellas and sticks at the door, visitors pass from one room to another unattended, although there are men usually going quietly about to keep watch. There are lists in each room, printed on cardboard, of the pictures in it,—one side being generally in Italian, and the other in French. It would be perfectly endless to describe these various collections. Those most worthy of notice are specified in Hare's *Walks in Rome*, which is a useful guide to them. But it would really be conferring a great boon upon visitors to Rome if some one were to publish a catalogue of all the collections in the manner of the *Academy Notes*, illustrating the noteworthy. Only by such means is it possible to retain in memory, or recall distinctly and without confusion, some recollection of their varied contents, and where given pictures are to be found.[1] Photographs of many can no doubt be procured, and are useful, and, so far as they go, better than the little rough sketches of the *Academy Notes;* but the collection of such photographs is limited (they are for the most part taken from engravings), and they can only be picked up by degrees. There is, however, a very valuable collection of engravings, published under direction of the Italian Government, of the choicest of the pictures and sculptures; and a few pounds may be well spent in purchases, which can be safely carried home rolled in tin cases which are supplied for the purpose. The shop in which they are sold is close to the Fountain of Treves, No. 6 Via Stamperia. The catalogue, extending to 33 pages, is divided into three parts, —*Pittura, Scultura,* and *Architettura,*—and in the first part

---

[1] Miss Kate Thompson's *Handbook to the Public Picture Galleries of Europe,* Macmillan, 1877, is a useful little volume in its way, but its illustration would occupy volumes.

comprises the works of 43 painters. The engravings are fairly moderate in price.

The galleries for the most part contain specimens of the great masters,—such as Titian, Guido Reni, Vandyke, and almost every other master of note,—though most frequently of the Italian masters and artists. Some of these collections are very extensive. That of the Borghese Palace occupies no less than twelve rooms. Among so many pictures there is always to be found a great amount of mediocrity, interspersed with works and gems of the highest art, over which one could gladly linger. On most of them age has bestowed its mellow tint. There is a richness and power in these old masters which one misses in modern galleries; and after visiting the principal collections in Italy, and fresh from the Louvre in Paris, I felt as if landed in a new world on entering the Royal Academy in London.

In some of the galleries persons are usually to be seen making copies of more or less merit of noted paintings, the copying of pictures being apparently, as it is in other Italian cities, a considerable branch of business in Rome. The casino of the Rospigliosi is visited principally for the celebrated Aurora of Guido Reni, with which that of Guercino cannot compare. It is a large work of art, which, like too many others, is painted on a ceiling, at all times an awkward position in which to be seen; and so awkward, too, for the artist, that to copy it always seems a very wonderful effort of execution. In this case, however, with much consideration for visitors' necks, a mirror is placed on a table below for the purpose of reflecting it at a convenient angle, and in this way it can be studied. As the masterpiece of the great painter (for Guido can hold his place alongside of Titian and Raphael), this picture is a very favourite subject of copy; and while we were in the room, there were three or four artists making copies of it varying in size. I asked the price of one good-sized copy, the execution of which was remarkably good, and the answer was, 600 francs—£24 nominally, or about £21 calculating according to the then state of the exchange (which, however, does not enter into the artist's calculations) with England. There was a good deal of work upon it, and it might possibly be fairly worth the money; but, according to the Italian mode of dealing, more may have been stated than would be taken, although it is only fair to say that in any transactions I have myself had with the Italian painters, this does not seem to be a practice which extends to them.

At the Barberini Palace, the favourite subject of copy is what is termed the head of Beatrice Cenci, by Guido Reni, although doubt has been cast upon the statement that it is the portrait of her who was executed upon being, rightly or wrongly, condemned as one of the murderers of her father. Whoever it may represent, the eyes in this lovely pale face, with a quiet, tender, inexpressible sorrow, fix themselves on the spectator; but it is a melancholy and suggestively sad picture, to which the white headgear very much adds. Why people should desire to have copies of it, it is difficult to say. Its attraction lies in its inimitable painting, which none of the copies reproduce. Indeed, some of them are simply hideous or grotesque. Yet copies, more or less bad, are seen everywhere; and not merely is the head copied on canvas, but it is transferred to china, to wood, and other material on which reproduction is necessarily coarse; as if the subject in itself were attractive.

Besides the palaces, there are regular galleries, such as the Academia di San Luca, a collection of the old masters, although not very extensive. Visitors also can obtain admittance to the studios of artists and sculptors, who are always glad to see them. We did not do much, however, in this way. We called on Mr. Glennie, an English artist settled in Rome, to whom we had an introduction, and had the pleasure of seeing several of his pictures, principally in water-colour. Mr. Lawrence MacDonald, the venerable-looking old Scotchman, since deceased, kindly with his son showed us over their studio, in which were many fine pieces of sculpture; and Signor Rosetti was also good enough to let us see his collection, which contained a large number of finely conceived and executed sculptures in white marble, at prices much below what is expected at home for similar works. A small fee (1 franc) is given at leaving to the workman who attends or opens the door.

We heard that the Royal Palace (Quirinal) could be seen, and accordingly visited it. After inscribing our names in a visitors' book, we were shown round the rooms by an attendant. The palace is on the Quirinal Hill, and is one of several which the King of Italy maintains; some of which, I doubt not, he would gladly dispense with, as adding unnecessarily to the cost of his establishment. It formerly belonged to the Popes, and the room was shown us in which the cardinals used to sit in conclave for the election of the Pope, which, when completed, was announced from a balcony to the people congregated outside. There are several spacious apartments in the building, adorned by some interesting paintings and sculptures. We were taken through the audience and other public *salons*, including the ballroom, which is decorated in a peculiar manner, especially by mirrors, on which appropriate figures have been depicted. The ceiling is painted to represent dancers in the air, and the floor is of polished wood. Some of the rooms are tapestried. A franc to the attendant, and a half-franc to the porter who had charge of our umbrellas, was all that was expected.

The grounds of some of the villas about Rome are also opened to the public; but they are not kept with the neatness and tidiness which characterize gentlemen's grounds at home. The most important or most extensive is probably the Villa Borghese. The gate of entrance to this great park, laid out in a way which is peculiarly Italian, is just outside the Porta del Popolo. The grounds are open daily, except on Mondays, and it is a favourite resort for all classes in the afternoon. After a long drive through them we reached the Casino, a building of many rooms, on two floors, devoted to a very large collection of sculptures, which well merits several visits. The Roman ladies, like other Italians, are very fond of driving about in style, with coachman and footman on the box; and a good part of their afternoon appears to be spent in these grounds and on the Pincian Hill, which adjoins, and in the gardens of which a band of music plays in the afternoons, attracting, as the only public garden—and it is of small dimensions—which the Romans seem to have, a fashionable crowd. The Pincian gardens are very prettily laid out, and there are excellent views of Rome from this height (one of the two highest of the hills of Rome), especially looking towards St. Peter's. A splendid survey of the city is also obtained from the hill on which San Pietro in Montorio stands, being to the south-west of St. Peter's, and therefore facing the Pincian Hill. From both points, as well as from others in Rome, the eye takes in the prospect of the Campagna, and of the mountains beyond; among which nestle several villages by name well known, such as Albano, Frascati, and Tivoli.

To see the last mentioned, together with a little of the Campagna, we devoted a day. For this purpose we hired a carriage, the charge for which was 35 francs. Bædeker says it is 25 francs; one of those instances which show that implicit reliance cannot always be placed on guide-book figures, although it is quite possible that a person resident in Rome, and acquainted with the ways and language, might bargain for the lesser sum.

There had been some wet weather, and the morning on which we were to start was overcast; but our coachman was confident that the day would be fine, as indeed it proved, and we left at half-past seven—a necessarily early hour, so as both to afford time for the trip and to obtain the cool of the day for the drive. Although the excursion was very enjoyable, a great part of the road lay through the flat, uninteresting Campagna, relieved by here and there a few houses, by an old robber's castle, and by other ruins. It is melancholy to observe these extensive plains now so unhealthy, formerly so salubrious and fertile; now apparently all but uninhabited, but in the days of Rome's glory so full of life. Hardly a tree is to be seen, and one could wish very much that there was an extensive planting of the Eucalyptus tree, which, if it would thrive, might probably contribute to the restoration of the land to a healthy condition, or to some extent neutralize the malaria, believed to arise from the destruction of the villas and gardens and groves with which it was formerly covered, and from the festering of the ruins below ground. It is said that the natives, who probably get to a certain extent inured to residence in a locality so unhealthy, object to plantation; and perhaps the climate might in winter be too severe for a tree which is easily blighted by the frost. Other and hardier trees may, however, be equally well adapted for the purpose, and as the whole subject has been and is under consideration of the authorities, perhaps we may soon hope to see better things. Indeed, I should imagine that the Campagna has already been improved by drainage or otherwise; at all events, if haze be a symptom of the unhealthiness, we did not observe much haze hanging over the fields. The way was enlivened by occasionally passing regiments of Italian soldiers, here as elsewhere engaged closely at drill, no doubt in preparation for the possibility of being called upon to engage on one side or the other (for the side was a matter uncertain) in the war which had then recently been commenced, or at least declared, between Russia and Turkey, and into which there seemed the lamentable possibility of the other European nations being drawn. These little Italian soldiers were clad as usual in that compound of warm and light clothing which is suitable for a climate where one part of the day is cold and another hot. In fact, it is very curious, in a country with which one associates so much of sun and heat, to see how universally the Italian men, at all events in spring-time, go about with heavy thick cloth greatcoats or cloaks, sometimes half on, dangling from the shoulder, but ready to be wrapped about them when the cold descends. We also occasionally passed one of those picturesquely-dressed mounted shepherds which are seen in pictures; more frequently we overtook some of the country carts, drawn by the strong and patient buffaloes, so common in Italy, but which strike a native of Britain as singularly primitive.

About half-way to Tivoli, which is sixteen miles from Rome, we approached the Lago di Tartari and a sulphurous stream which issues from it and flows under the road, scenting the air for some distance around. As we drew near to the mountains, which are all along in sight, the country improved; and diverging by a road to the right, we arrived at Hadrian's Villa, the admission to which is by ticket, 1 franc each. This is the ruin of an extraordinary country residence, built by the Emperor Hadrian on a most magnificent and extensive scale. It contained a theatre, a hippodrome, baths, temples, and every description of edifice in use in the time of the Romans, and that on a grand plan, and adorned with marble and sculptures, some of which have been recovered from the ruins—a walk among which gives, though imperfectly, a wonderful idea of the extraordinary splendour and opulence of the Roman emperors.

Returning to the main road, and slowly proceeding up a long, steep ascent, the town or village of Tivoli was reached. It stands high, and the ruins of two temples are situated close upon the famous waterfalls. Visitors here stop at the little Sibylla Hotel, usually bringing their lunch with them, as we did, and a table is spread under the temple of the Sibyl, on a platform which commands views towards the falls and mountains. For the accommodation so afforded we were charged 4 francs, and we enjoyed their Frascati wine. When we rose to make the usual round, we were besieged by loitering guides and idle people offering to take us to the falls. Having hired a donkey for my wife, I told the rest we had no need for them. But they would take no refusal; and although informed decidedly they were not wanted, two men with a chaise *à porteur* persistently followed us all the way down, asking to be engaged, and diminishing their demands as we descended and the prospect of employment became more and more hopeless. We were also annoyed by all sorts of begging and methods of asking money; one respectable-looking woman, who had a child suspended in a peculiar sort of go-cart, which, as a curiosity, we were looking at, was not ashamed to ask for some *soldi* in respect of the 'bambino;' in fact, nobody there, or elsewhere in Italy, seems ashamed to beg.

The falls were not so grand as we had expected to find them, although there is one thundering cascade. We had intended going to see the Villa d'Este, but a lady who had been there before dissuaded us, as not worth seeing, though I understand the grounds are; and as it would have taken time, and we were anxious to be home early, for it is not good to be out in the Campagna after dusk, we left in the afternoon in spite of the protestations of the coachman, who for some unknown reason would have detained us two hours longer, and got back to Rome about half-past six, in time for dinner, and sufficiently late at that season to be out. Outside the walls we stopped at the Church of San Lorenzo fuori le mura, and entered it. Its old pillars, pavement, and mosaics, its pulpit and its peculiar construction, make it remarkable, and well worthy of a visit. On returning to the carriage, one of the ladies missed a cloak, which in all likelihood had been adroitly abstracted by a loitering beggar, of whom there were several at the gate of the church.

In any mention of a visit to Rome, one can scarcely omit some notice of the Roman shops. I suppose that no visitor to Rome leaves without making purchases of one description or another, or of all. Apparently, the Americans go in more largely than others for purchases of all kinds, and one reason for that may possibly be the fear their visit to Italy may never be repeated. One lady, in the house in which we were, had bought so many things of divers sorts that she required to get seven boxes made to hold them. They comprised marble busts, copies of paintings, bronzes, photographs, and I know not what besides. All these can be bought at prices not only greatly less than in America, where everything is dear, but also much less than in Great Britain; if indeed they can be had out of Italy; but to the price the purchaser requires in his calculations to add the cost of carriage and import duty (where exigible), and to take into view the risk of transit.

There are many photograph shops in Rome, and at most of them one can purchase cheaply all descriptions. They are often filled with people selecting examples, chiefly of buildings and pictures. It is needful to know where to go, but this is soon learned, either by experience or by recommendation of fellow photograph-hunters. I have seen the same photographs, and equally good, sold at one shop at half the price they were sold at another. The cheaper shops are therefore crowded, while the others (in which, however, some large and good photographs claiming to be high-class are sold) enjoy their *otium cum dignitate*. Some of the photographs exhibited in the windows—as, for example, of St. Peter's and the Colosseum—are of great size, requiring to be printed on two or three large sheets.

Another description of shop, the most numerous of all, is that for the sale of Roman, mosaic, and other species of jewellery. The windows of these jewellers' shops are filled with very elegant specimens of mosaic work, in the form of brooches, bracelets, ear-drops, shawl-pins, etc., composed of minute coloured stones put together in all sorts of devices, sometimes in miniature copies of well-known pictures. The execution is marvellous.[1] The prices are moderate, but one requires to keep in mind, in some cases, the Italian method of demanding a larger price than will be taken. Even in shops professedly dealing on the principle of fixed prices, the shopkeepers are not insusceptible of a diminution, at least upon goods of a high price, although an offer of a lower price should be made only when it seems likely to be accepted. The Italians' idea of selling in general apparently is, that if they can make a profit, however small, rather to sell than lose the chance. The system of asking a long price, to be met with an equally low offer, and by gradual approximations to come to terms, is a mode of transacting extremely repugnant to British habits, but it is sometimes encountered. I have heard of the same article being offered to an English person at one price, and sold to a native at little more than half. At the same time, it is only right to say that this was not in Rome, where, I think, on the whole, prices seem to be fair and fixed.

Ladies find in the pretty silk Roman sashes and ribbons, woven, I believe, by girls on antiquated small looms in the shops where they are sold, another species of attraction.

Other shops, again, are devoted to the sale of bronze and marble copies, on a small scale, of statues, heads, and ruins, particularly columns in the Forum and elsewhere; and some have small alabaster or Roman marble copies of sculptures, though for such articles Florence is the greater mart. Other shops sell copies of celebrated paintings. The visitor, therefore, has very little difficulty, if possessed

[1] After being in several shops, we concluded that C. Roccheggiani, Via Condotti, had the largest and most varied stock.

of time, inclination, and money, in making a good collection to take home of objects of *virtu*, or, at least, of what will give a pleasing recollection of what one has seen in Old Rome.

But what one sees in Rome can only give the faintest idea of what it was when mistress of the world. In place of being confined to the comparatively circumscribed limits of the walls, a space which at present it only partially covers, the city, besides being composed of high, many-storied houses, like those in the Old Town of Edinburgh, extended for miles over the Campagna, and that perhaps very densely. Instead of a population now of scarcely a quarter of a million, the population then is thought to have greatly exceeded that of London at the present day. Indeed, some have not hesitated to state it at as high a figure as 14,000,000, while others, more moderate in their calculations, have placed it at from 4,000,000 to 6,000,000. But whatever it may have been (for this is a *questio vexata*), it was many times what it has now become. Then consider the magnificent multiplicity of its buildings and decorations. For, besides 700 temples[1] and other structures of whose number no record perhaps exists, there were in ancient Rome at one time, 31 theatres, 11 amphitheatres (and we have seen the scale upon which these erections were constructed), 48 obelisks, 66 ivory statues, 82 equestrian statues, 3785 bronze statues, 1352 fountains, 2091 prisons, 9025 baths, 17,097 palaces. Then keep in view that this was all during a period when classic taste prevailed, and everything, as the remains now left testify, was in the utmost perfection of art, and sometimes of the most wonderful magnificence. Keep also in view that thousands of Roman citizens were then of immense opulence, one

---

[1] This number is stated upon an authority which differs in the further figures here given, some of which seem almost incredibly large. How the 9025 baths can be reconciled with the statement (p. 299) of sixteen bathing establishments, I do not pretend to say.

evidence of which was that they were possessed of crowds of slaves, some of them having as many as 10,000 or even 20,000; and think what pomp and style must have been kept up in the 17,000 palaces of Rome, surging out upon its 360 spacious streets and its countless minor *vias*, and one approaches to an idea of the superb grandeur of the great city; in the presence of which it does make us feel small to think, that while we lavish millions on war, we cannot so much as, at the hundredth part of the cost of one of our little wars, build and complete a single temple in the perfection of the ancients, seeing we have the National Monument on the Calton Hill, so bravely begun, in a condition calculated merely to expose the indifference to high art with which the British nation is afflicted. But we cannot be sorry for the fall of Rome, and only should take warning from it, because its power was built up on military force, and its riches were got, not by the successful prosecution of peaceful pursuits, but by the conquest and plunder and the subjection of other nations.

Nor can we any more deplore that modern Rome is now shorn of the prestige it enjoyed while the Popes were once all-potent. Strangers can no longer be gratified by the sight of priestly pageants and papal shows. But let us be thankful that, as the Pope hides his head, the civil power has risen; and now, in place of persecution, torture, and death for those who would not bow the knee to a corrupted religion, the Inquisition — that cruel, hateful instrument of religious intolerance and priestly tyranny — is at an end, and every one can worship God within the walls of Rome as his conscience dictates, none daring to make him afraid. The only strange reflection[1] which arises is,

---

[1] I see it stated that in 1851 the number of Romish priests in Great Britain was 958; of Romish chapels, 683; of monasteries, 17; of religious houses for women, 53. In 1879 these numbers were increased to 1238, 1386, 118, and 272 respectively. The number of the laity doubtless has increased, though possibly, and as it is to be hoped, not correspondingly.

that while so many in England, where education prevails and people should know better, are allowing themselves to be drawn back again into the trammels of Rome, the people of Rome and of Italy, with all their ignorance, are shaking off a yoke which neither they nor their fathers were able to bear, and rejoicing to be free.

We had been nine days in Rome, and before seeing it further, thought it advisable to take a run to Naples, and rest in that locality, for so much sight-seeing was fatiguing. During even this short time we had done a great deal, and the break of going away operated, as it were, as a first visit, preliminary to a further investigation upon our second visit of what then became to us in a manner as familiar old friends. Even in both our visits, made out of the common motive of curiosity, and with no higher aims, we could only consider we had examined things in a most superficial way, leaving besides a great deal that was unexplored. It is often said that even a whole winter in Rome is inadequate to do justice to its sights. In a single forenoon we have been to as many as a dozen different places. We entered Rome with the idea that it would be the first and only visit of a lifetime. We left it with the feeling that we had only seen enough to make it more easy for us to comprehend the subject at home, so that some years later we might all return to investigate it together in greater detail, or with more perfect acquaintance with what we had to see, to know, and to think about. Alas! how little did we then anticipate that that future day, to one of us at least, whose hopes were bright and whose enjoyment of all was deep and thorough, would never come!

x .

XIII.

NAPLES, POMPEII, SORRENTO.

It proved a very wet morning in Rome on the day we had settled to go to Naples (for it can rain in Rome remarkably well); but we had taken our rooms at a hotel in Naples, and were packed and ready to go, and accordingly left, arriving at the station at half-past eight for the train leaving at 9.20, and were not a bit too soon. The traveller has to hang on for his turn to get his luggage weighed and to purchase his railway tickets; and after these operations were accomplished, and admission was at last accorded to the *salle-d'attente* (for none, according to the evil custom which keeps ladies hanging about on their feet, can enter previously), we had but a few minutes to wait in that apartment until the doors were opened and announcement made that passengers might now hurry to the train.

For a considerable part of the way the rain fell and heavy clouds hung upon the mountains, so that little could be seen of the scenery in the early part of the journey, which is the most interesting, as the line commands in many parts historical ground. We passed the Alban and Volscian Mountains; the town of Capua, where are interesting Roman remains; Caserta, where there is an immense royal palace; and many curious old towns resting upon the hills which the railway skirted. It would have been well worth while to have stayed at Capua and Caserta to have seen them, but it is difficult to arrange for doing so without spending a night by the way, or continuing the journey by a night train, because trains do not suit. This being the 26th of March, vegetation was in a very backward state, the trees just beginning to show symptoms of being about to throw out their buds, so that everything looked somewhat dreary. At last we arrived in Naples, after a seven hours' ride, just in time to settle down before dinner.

The following morning we took a cab to drive through and see the town, and, looking to select a good one, I was beset by a host of cabmen, all wanting to be engaged, even after I had engaged one, and told them so positively. There is very little choice among them. The vehicles are all equally shabby, and the drivers all equally dirty. Their fares are very low, which may account for the disreputable appearance of the men and cabs, which are as numerous as bees in a hive. The coachmen will take any amount of trouble to get a hire. If, upon going to a place, say the Museum, they be dismissed, they will hang about for an hour, hoping to get the return fare. But driving is really the only way by which one can see some parts of Naples. The town swarms with people to an extent which, unless seen, can hardly be either realized or credited. In England, every rood may maintain its man, but in Naples, and even all about the Bay of Naples, it would seem as if not merely every square yard, but almost every square foot maintained its man, woman, or child. But how they all live, or even where they all sleep, is a mystery. The main street, the Toledo, a mile long, is so crowded, that one wonders how the carriages can possibly penetrate; and the people are such notorious thieves and such adroit pickpockets, that it is dangerous to attempt to walk on foot. Even in driving, the passenger must be very careful, as a thief will think nothing of abstracting loose articles, even in his very sight. At the railway station the traveller should keep a sharp look-out that the very porter who is taking his portmanteau to a carriage does not quietly run off with it. Knowing these habits, we left the most of our luggage at Rome, and only took with us what was indispensable, as every additional package is in such a case an additional anxiety.

The Bay of Naples is naturally the first point of attraction. One hears so much of its transcendent beauty that expectation is highly raised. I thought the accounts of it exaggerated; but then it was not summer, and therefore we could not see it in perfection; while we had just recently come from Mentone, where we had been living for months in sight of lovely bays. The blue waters of the Mediterranean in brilliant sunshine are always charming, and here they are enclosed in a very large bay—for it is about twenty miles each way—with one long arm stretching away and terminated by the island of Ischia, and the other long arm stretching away and terminated by the island of Capri; the outlines of all being picturesque, and all sides being dotted with villages. In the centre of the landward side Vesuvius boldly rises (the eruptions from time to time causing variations in its height, which, however, averages about 4000 feet), with a stream of smoke, betokening its character, constantly ascending from the summit as if from some colossal chimney; while below, a line of houses stretches continuously from Naples, probably fifteen miles, or perhaps even more, indicating how populous is this part of Italy. In the distance, behind Naples and Vesuvius, a range of the Apennines lies.

Naples itself, the largest and most populous city in Italy, is, from a little distance, picturesque, resting, somewhat like Genoa, on a half-circle of sloping heights, with a broad margin to the shore, the houses towards which are lofty, many being five and even six storeys high. In the central and denser parts of the town they are even higher, while in these portions the streets are mere lanes, 15 to 20 feet wide, and irregular; and if they be not absolutely unsafe to visit, must form a very labyrinth of perplexity to the stranger. In the newer parts of the city the streets are spacious and elegant. Every here and there, a jutting prominence or a bold height crowned with some peculiar structure gives character to the scene. The Chiaja is a long strip of land turned into a public garden or park lying in or towards the north end of the town, and fronting the sea. A broad street, the Riviera di Chiaja, flanks it, lined by the trees of the park on the one side, and by hotels and other buildings on the other, and terminated at the north end by Posilipo, a hill perforated by the famous grotto of that name, or tunnel, I presume half natural and half excavated, which affords an access to the other side. Up from the Chiaja, on a height, the Castle of St. Elmo stands, the interior of which our limited time did not afford us opportunity of seeing. Leaving the Chiaja by a handsome drive which has been formed by the shore, we pass the Castel del Ovo, which stands out into the sea, cresting a large rock or small island connected with the land by a mole or breakwater. It is ugly and old, but can scarcely, because it is so, be called picturesque, though at least it is striking or prominent; and I suppose it does or can, with other fortifications, offer some protection to the port; but it was, and perhaps still is, used as a prison, and, in spite of sunshine, is gloomy enough for that. From this point southward, commencing with the broad Strada San Lucia, the harbour lies, in which there is a moderate amount of shipping, but small as compared with that of Genoa. Life abounds about this harbour and the adjoining quays, along which broad streets run, filled with sellers of fish and other commodities, and with crowds of pedestrians and carriages.

The road turns up from S. Lucia into the large open space called the Piazza del Plebiscito—one side occupied by a handsome semicircular colonnade, and the other by the royal palace, where the king was at the time of our visit residing, two equestrian statues in the centre of the piazza contributing to its adornment. The Toledo or High Street of Naples issues out of it. Proceeding farther along the harbour, and at its extreme south, we come to the Castel del Carmine, also forming a feature in the landscape, and from it a road leads up to the railway station, which is just outside the inhabited part of Naples. From the harbour, or any point which commands a view, the town looks bright and picturesque, and in rather striking contrast with its dirty population. Ascent of the lighthouse for the sake of the view is recommended.

The only church in Naples which we thought at all comparable to those in Rome was the cathedral, which is a large and handsome building. One of its side chapels is that of the famous St. Januarius, where the blood and other relics of the martyr are preserved.

The hotels are situated principally on the line of buildings facing the sea from the Chiaja southward to S. Lucia. But some new hotels have been opened on the high ground near the Castle of St. Elmo, thought to be a more healthy locality. This may or may not be, but one requires to be careful as to where he lives in Naples. In fact, the natural air of Naples must be extremely salubrious, to counteract, as it seems to a large extent to do, the evil influences arising from so large a population living upon so comparatively small a portion of the tideless Mediterranean. Were it otherwise, fever would be constantly raging, and Naples depopulated.

We spent the forenoon of the following day in the Museum. This is an immense collection of antiquities, principally from Pompeii, and is well worthy of several visits, without which, in fact, it cannot be properly studied. Illustrated catalogues can be procured, which are no doubt useful, but are expensive. Our time would only allow of a general examination. The Museum contains thousands of articles of great interest, and very many which show to what a state of perfection art had arrived at the time Pompeii was destroyed. The sculptures of all descriptions and pictures are very numerous, and among many others deserving of special note was the grand group called the Toro Farnese, of masterly power. It is composed of five graceful and pleasing human figures, besides the bull rampant and a dog, and other sculpture, and if cut out of one block of marble, would seem to be a miracle of art. Why it should have been removed from Rome to Naples I am not aware. But the Museum at Naples is very spacious and extensive, and may have afforded better accommodation than any place in Rome. Some of the rooms are filled with articles of domestic use recovered from the ruins of Herculaneum and Pompeii; and, what is very curious, in one room loaves of bread, grain of various sorts, dates, and other edibles 1800 years old are exhibited. Many of the curious frescoes found upon the walls of Pompeii have been removed to the Museum and built bodily into its walls. The colours of these frescoes are considerably faded, but copying them seems to afford employment to a number of artists, who, however, impart to their copies the supposed original brightness of the pictures, and one seldom sees an original Pompeian fresco possessing that vividness of colouring which representations of them usually manifest. One room is fitted up as a reproduction of a Pompeian bedroom, and gives a greater idea of luxurious comfort than one would imagine possible from the appearance of the rooms, now in ruins, which we afterwards saw in Pompeii itself.

The afternoon is the time for seeing the Chiaja, for then

all the private carriages of Naples may be witnessed driving about; and on one occasion we had the good fortune to pass the Princess Margherita, now the Queen of Italy. Girls are on the watch to sell large and beautiful bouquets of flowers at marvellously cheap prices. An aquarium has been built near the centre of the Chiaja gardens, which we visited the morning of the day following, before going to Castellamare. It is not nearly so large as that at Brighton, but it is interesting enough. It contained, *inter alia*, a good many octopi, which repulsive fish is said to be sold and eaten in Naples, and, in all probability, occasionally appears under some disguised name at the hotel dinners.

Naples is a great place for the sale of photographs and articles of bijouterie in lava, and of coral and tortoiseshell. At Mr. Sommer's Fine Art Establishment near the Chiaja, a large collection of beautiful photographs of almost all places in Italy is to be found. These are very moderate in price—the cheapest in Italy—as well as good, and in number exceed five thousand. I laid in a good stock, and only wish I had taken more. Any of them can be at once procured by reference to the number they bear. They are best kept flat, but if rolling be preferred, they should always be rolled up with the photograph side outwards. Why it is that photographs of a size which cost a shilling at Naples should be charged five shillings or six shillings, or even more, at home, I don't know. But the consequence is that people buy the Italian photographs by the hundred, whereas at home, if they buy at all, it is by the unit. Our dealers plainly miss the market by their high prices. Mr. Sommer might do well to extend his operations to the towns of France and to Switzerland, where photographs are expensive.

Among other shops we also visited Squadrilli's, which is recommended in Bædeker. Here we found a well-stocked store of articles in lava and coral, but owing, I suppose, to the thieving which exists in Naples, and from which, no doubt, they have sometimes suffered, we were rather unpleasantly watched by three persons, a circumstance of which others who had been there also complained. The articles, however, seemed to be good, while the prices are fixed, though a discount of five per cent. was allowed for cash. The gold used in Naples for bijouterie is considered to be inferior to the standard quality of England, and even of Rome, which professes to be, like England, of eighteen carats. Squadrilli allowed that their gold was only fourteen carats, and perhaps his estimate might not apply to all his articles. There are many imitations, however, even of this inferior gold, and some articles, possibly 'job lots,' are sold in Naples at astonishingly low prices. The articles supposed to be of lava are, I believe, in reality cut out of the limestone rocks of Somma, one of the peaks of Vesuvius.

We were anxious to make our stay in Naples as short as possible, as so much is heard of its insalubrity. After the general survey we had thus made of it, we took train to Castellamare, the railway passing Mount Vesuvius on the one side and the coast on the other, so that we were in view of the bay nearly all the way. Castellamare is a convenient halting-place for seeing Pompeii, which, however, may be visited from Naples itself, either by hiring a carriage from Naples,—making a pretty long drive, and, I believe, of little interest, the road being a continuous street of houses,—or by taking the train as far as Torre dell' Annunciata, and a carriage thence to Pompeii, which is not two miles off. Castellamare is one of those populous unclean towns which lie upon the bay. Friends had said it was a remarkably nice place to stop at, and the Hotel Quisisana, on the height above the town, is a fairly comfortable one, commanding a splendid view of the bay, of Vesuvius, and of Naples beyond. Perhaps we did not remain long enough to acquire a knowledge of its beauties, but we were not taken with the dirty town; while the garden of the hotel, which might have been laid out to great advantage, and thus have helped to reconcile us to the place, was no better than such Italian gardens usually are. I suppose that Nature has been so lavish of her bounties when the sun shines, that the Italians think it unnecessary to supplement her labours. Yet I have sometimes thought that the time of waiters, who between meals in foreign places have often little to do, might, not unprofitably to the hotels, and with some advantage in health to themselves, be occupied in trimming the hotel gardens. Our bedrooms looked towards the bay, and therefore were, I presume, considered more choice; but being a northern or north-western exposure, we found them extremely cold at night. It was, however, intensely interesting to look across to Vesuvius, which I had seen emitting a red light on our second evening at Naples, without being aware, unfortunately, till afterwards that this light was unusual, and that had I watched it for half an hour longer I should have seen it become more intensely bright. People were then in full expectation of an eruption, and even the very day had been predicted, although the premonitory symptoms of streams drying up had not appeared; but expectation was not gratified.

We arranged the following morning to drive to Pompeii, which is about three miles distant.

Pompeii on being approached seems like a huge mound, somewhat akin in the distance to a fortified place. The excavated town itself is not visible from the road. The visitor is deposited at the door of what appears to be a sort of tavern or place of refreshment, through which, threading one's way among tables, entrance is had to the excavations. We found the tavern filled with people taking an early dinner, or rather breakfast, rendering the access by no means an agreeable one. Here leaving with the *cameriere* our wraps,—not without some misgivings, fortunately not realized, that we should never see them again,—we passed up a stair, and through a magazine for sale of lava ornaments, etc., the prices asked for which, as usual in show places, were exorbitantly and forbiddingly high. Outside the magazine we paid two francs each for admission and for the assistance of a guide (children being charged only a half-franc each), and procured a little French-speaking guide in smart uniform and side arms, whom we found very obliging and attentive. These guides are necessary, and must be taken, though sometimes respectable people who have been there before are allowed to go without them; perhaps not always with advantage to the ruins, as it is a very common trick with people who should know better, and who might not be expected to do such a thing, to pocket stones which can be of no use whatever to themselves, but the abstraction of which is detrimental to the place whence they are taken. On one occasion in Italy, a lady of a party in which I was—who acknowledged to being in the habit of bringing away a stone from every place to which she had been—quietly pocketed a piece of marble lying on the ground, when the custodier, who was keeping a sharp look-out, went up to her and desired her to replace it. It was a numbered piece, and he would, he said, be responsible for it to the authorities. The practice of chipping stones from a building of note, or taking up loose pieces, cannot be too severely reprehended, and ought sometimes to be punished. The guides at Pompeii are not allowed to receive any gratuity from the visitors, but they make a little by an accorded permission to sell photographs of the ruins.

Passing through an old gateway, we were ushered into a museum, the contents of which are not numerous, as the bulk of the articles found is sent to the large Museum of Naples. It contains, however, some things of great interest, particularly the casts of men and women found in Pompeii who had perished in the great overthrow, and whose bodies had been so curiously enveloped with the scoriæ as to form a close-fitting, indurated mould, and a cast from it, when the dust is blown out, reproduces every line of the body or of the clothing of the suffocated person. Some of the casts so taken give a clear representation of the form of the features; and I noticed that the dress of the men seemed to be very similar to what is still worn by those in the vicinity, particularly in the tight-fitting, wrought woollen jacket covering the body. If I was right in this supposition, it is another instance of the manner in which the people cling to ancient habits and modes of dress.

We were then taken to the excavations which are being systematically carried on, and our examination commenced with the forum, a large open space, containing the remains of the pillars by which it was surrounded. From these remains and the remains of other public buildings, it is evident that Pompeii was a very elegantly adorned city. It had temples, no less than nine being marked upon the plan, but they are all in ruins; only fragments exist, the pillars and superincumbent building having been almost everywhere thrown down. In some of them, such as the temple of Venus and temple of Isis, a few columns, with their entablature, stand, to indicate the beauty of their construction. Besides temples there have been excavated two theatres and a large amphitheatre, in excellent preservation, capable of accommodating 20,000 persons, and nearly, in length and breadth, as large as that at Nismes; also, as usual in Roman towns, baths, besides other public buildings. But probably the greatest interest attaches to the remains of the private dwellings. It is rarely that private houses exhibit, after a lapse of nearly 2000 years, even in ruins, what they were when in occupation. Here, however, the lava or scoriæ or dust of Vesuvius by hermetical seal closed up these houses, in order that they might be seen by the people of a long-distant age. Many of the houses in Pompeii belonged to men of wealth, and they are all laid out, in the better class at least, upon much the same plan, entering upon a square court, open in the centre to the outer air, in the middle of which a marble fountain played. The rooms were built around or beyond, the principal or public rooms being to the back — a mode of design probably suitable to the climate, at least in summer, and admitting, no doubt, of great elegance of arrangement and design, and of which such houses as those of Marcus Holconius, of the Faun, of Sallust, of the poet, of Meleager, and of Cornelius Rufus afford examples,—all containing beautiful fluted pillars and other decorations, sometimes in marble, still standing, while the walls were tastefully decorated with that peculiar description of painting well known as Pompeian. Some of the houses appear to be only one storey high, but stairs indicate a second storey, and it is even supposed that in some cases there may have been a third. But they had no appearance to the street, while the streets themselves are narrow, so much so that it is impossible to see how in many of them even the smallest carriages could pass each other without encroaching on the equally narrow footway or *trottoir* (discovery of the remains of it here revealing its use in ancient times); but the large stones or slabs forming the street pavement are in some places marked with a deep rut, indicating a good deal of carriage traffic. The shops on the streets are small, and are sometimes built into the dwellings, so that shop floors then were probably as remunerative as they seem to be now with ourselves, although persons now in similar rank of life in Great Britain would little like to allow a portion of their mansions to be so occupied. As, however, the streets were so confined, there could have been no view from the house itself upon the front facing the street; yet, no doubt, from some windows in the upper apartments behind there might be fine glimpses of the bay and of Vesuvius, as well as of the surrounding country. At all events, we obtained excellent views from the ruins, especially from the walls. Vesuvius appears close at hand, and one feels astonished at the foolhardiness of people building towns and houses so close under the fiery mountain after the tremendous warnings received in the destruction of Pompeii and Herculaneum. We were shown at one place in the 'House of Diomede' a long vault or cellar, in which the remains were found of seventeen unfortunate persons who had taken refuge there during the awful time when they knew not where to flee, and supposed that the walls of the house would cover them from calamity. We could not look upon such places without thinking what an appalling time it must have been, and what heartrending agonies must then have been endured. Notwithstanding all the elegance of the public portions of the houses, and perhaps even of the private chambers, it seemed as if the actual comfort of the inhabitants could not be great, and especially in the matter of bedroom accommodation, for I imagine the sleeping-rooms were of the smallest dimensions—mere closets, not such as people of the present day in good circumstances would approve.

It would, however, be impossible, in small compass, to give any adequate idea of these houses or of their decorations. Books have been written upon the subject, and an excellent recent account of Pompeii, its history, buildings, and antiquities, containing nearly 300 illustrations, has been written by Dr. Thomas H. Dyer. Nothing, indeed, but a visit to Pompeii itself can convey a sufficient idea of the resuscitated city; but a study of Mr. Dyer's book before going, as well as after a visit, will help materially to an understanding of it. Pompeii is a place of engrossing interest entirely unique, and in some respects it offers, I think, more attractions to a visitor than any other in Italy, and well merits more than one visit. The excavations are still proceeding, and it will probably be many years before they are completed, as there is still a large piece of ground, probably as much again as has already been opened, on which to operate.

Having seen Pompeii, we did not care to stay longer at Castellamare, and next day, taking a carriage with three horses, the bells jingling cheerily all the way, drove to Sorrento. The drive occupied an hour and a half, and is considered to be one of the finest to be had in Italy. The road borders the bay, and passes through several large Italian villages most picturesquely situated, and across a deep ravine, evidently the result of an earthquake, by a beautiful bridge. Sorrento is a long town, and the road through its suburbs is shut in by lofty and most objectionable garden walls. As we drove down the road towards it, from the height to the eastward the place looked very charming, surrounded by hills on every side except the north, which is open to the sea. Turning down a long narrow lane, we arrived at the Tramontano Hotel (kept by an Irish landlady, an active and most obliging woman), where everything is remarkably comfortable, and the accommodation is ample. It is situated on classic ground, Tasso having resided in a house which, or its site, is now part of the hotel. A garden, where, no doubt, Tasso often meditated, encloses the hotel upon the south, while the north windows and terraces command magnificent views of the bay, of the islands, of Naples lying opposite, and of Vesuvius, whose smoke, always ascending, is an excellent indicator of the direction of the wind. The garden extends away to the eastward, where a dependence or additional house is kept for the accommodation of the guests. A large public room, with windows to the bay, was being added to the main house, so that now both *salon* and *salle-à-manger* are large rooms. Having had experience of the cold of northerly chambers at Castellamare, we chose cheerful rooms on the south side overlooking the hotel yard, with all its enlivening bustle, and the garden and green hills behind.

Sorrento lies upon a platform or broad level space of land, the seaward side being high perpendicular cliffs, so that one looks sheer down from the hotel windows on the north to the water far below, which is reached from the hotel by a winding tunnel cut into the rock. It is placed, like Mentone, under the guard of a semicircle of hills, although these are both nearer and much lower than those at Mentone; but as the town faces the north, instead of the south as at Mentone, it is rather a summer than a winter residence. We had it very cold there during the night, but in the glowing mid-day sun it was charming to look out upon the water and land, and see everything bathed in an atmosphere of light, while vegetation was now beginning to advance, lending an additional charm to the landscape. We were not, however, altogether without rain. One night was particularly stormy and wet.

There are excursions from Sorrento upon the hills which can be accomplished by aid of donkeys, and it is also possible to cross over the hills to Amalfi, though this was not reckoned altogether safe from bandits. Boats can be had for boating, but the main excursions are by steamboat to Capri, and driving to Massa, a picturesque town a few miles westward; the road to it by the coast being a continuation of that from Castellamare, and affording lovely views at every turn. The excursion to Capri is made by steamboat, and every fine morning two rival steamers (a paddle and a screw boat) from Naples approached Sorrento to take excursionists to Capri and its blue grotto. In addition to the fare there and back of 5 francs, innumerable other little charges for boats, etc. make the expense up to 8 francs each. When the sea is stormy, the boats do not

SORRENTO FROM THE WEST.

go, as it is impossible to enter the grotto when there is the least swell upon the water. This is annoying to unlucky persons who are left on the island, as it sometimes happens in consequence that the boats may not leave Naples for weeks together. I met on board the steamer two American friends who had come from Naples, were to sleep a night at Capri and return the next day, having taken their passage for the day following in a steamer for Genoa. The next day, however, proved stormy, and the steamboats did not make their appearance for several days afterwards, so that our friends must have been kept prisoners on the island and lost their passage besides. We had, however, a very beautiful day for the trip, the steamboat taking about two hours to reach Capri from Sorrento, and it was most enjoyable. The views from the deck are enchanting. When we arrived off the grotto, the vessel was surrounded by a multitude of little boats; and as three persons only are allowed to each, it took a long time for all the visitors to get off. The sea where the steamer stopped was of a most lovely blue colour, perhaps due to some great local saltness of the ocean. On approaching the entrance to the grotto, all were desired to lie down on the bottom of the boat, otherwise, by catching the crest of a wave, we might have broken our heads against the rocks of the entrance, which is very low,—although it might, one would think, be enlarged,—while the boatmen carefully pushed the boat inside. Once we were in, however, there was space enough for several boats to paddle about. We found everything bathed in the blue light of the sea reflected on the walls of the cavern. It is this which gives the name to the grotto. The rocks themselves are just ordinary colour, and do not, as might from the name be supposed, consist, like those of the blue John Cavern of Derbyshire, of actual blue spar.

When all had seen the grotto, the steamboats took us to the town of Capri, which, with another on the hill, is picturesque. There are good hotels near the landing-place. A long ascent leads to the high town, near which the palace of Tiberius once stood. From the height I had a view of the southern coast of Italy; but the day was hot, and the atmosphere therefore hazy, so that we could not see far. We returned to Sorrento in the afternoon.

Sorrento is a great place—in fact, the chief place—for the manufacture of articles of inlaid wood. It is the industry of the town, and everywhere we found workshops for its manufacture, having attached to them shops for its sale, although, I presume, the larger part of the manufacture is for export or transmission elsewhere. As may be supposed, there is considerable diversity of skill among the workmen, and many articles exhibit inferiority; but I soon found out in which shops the best workmanship prevailed, and in particular considered the articles manufactured by M. Grandville were both well finished and wrought in good taste. Garguilo also, who has a more imposing establishment, had some very fine specimens of work. Every visitor buys more or less, principally, doubtless, to take home as gifts to friends, and I did not escape the contagion. Some of the articles are extremely beautiful; and one I secured, which seemed to be one of the finest examples, was so delicately inlaid that at first sight it seemed as if it were a painting on the wood. I saw, however, the process by which the inlaying is effected, which satisfied me with the reality of the inlaying. A picture is drawn on paper, and little pieces, corresponding in colour to the pattern, are cut out of larger coloured pieces with an extremely slender steel saw—almost a thread for fineness. These are glued down upon the pattern so closely that the joinings are invisible, and it is in the comparative skill with which this nice operation is conducted I presume the difference of quality and effect is mainly found. In purchasing these articles, however, one has not to lose sight of the fact that the transaction is taking place in the South of Italy, and sometimes a considerably higher price is asked than the seller is prepared to take. I had the specimens purchased put in a box, carefully packed, to send from Naples home by sea, and found on entering Naples that *octroi* duty upon it was exacted, and this not according to value, but to weight. The wood shops are among the best in Sorrento, but I was struck with the marvellous likeness there was, in size at least, in the common small shops of Sorrento to what had been shops in Pompeii.

We led a quiet life very pleasantly among friends and acquaintances at the hotel in Sorrento for about a fortnight, glad of rest after so much previous sight-seeing; but the hotel was always full, and the constant jingling of horses' bells, denoting the arrival or departure of carriages, kept it lively, while, among other diversions, we witnessed the Tarantala dancing entertainment, to which I have elsewhere alluded (p. 72). We had at first thought of going to Cava, with a view to taking trips thence to Amalfi and Pæstum; but preferring rest, left that, like many other excursions, to another opportunity, which might never come. We returned to Naples on 11th April, having a glorious day for the return drive to Castellamare. The trees were only budding, so that we did not see things in perfection. As we drove out of the hotel yard, a man, neither clothed in plush and fine linen nor recently washed, jumped up and sat on the luggage behind, an undesirable-looking and unengaged lackey. The driver explained it was to guard the luggage, which sometimes, I believe, is, by the nimble-fingered inhabitants of the bay, quietly abstracted if not well roped. It was only, however, a genteel method of begging for 30 centimes, with which at Castellamare he was well satisfied. The beggars of Sorrento are certainly industrious in their calling. I stayed a few minutes at one place to make a little sketch, and was immediately surrounded by half-a-dozen women, and at least as many children, all wanting copper. One regular beggar, a man, old to appearance, who was constantly sauntering about, stick in hand, amused me much. His address was, as you approached him, arrestively and decisively, 'Signor!' You proceeded a yard farther, and it was more decisively, or rather imperatively, 'Signor!' You passed him, and it was 'Signor! Signor!' (weepingly) 'povero vecc. he he per amor di Dio,' a phrase generally employed by the Italian beggars. It is, however, but fair to add, that begging in Italy is not nearly so bad as it once was, for the authorities are setting their face against it. Still, in some places, it is a great annoyance that one cannot walk along the streets of a small town like Sorrento without being assailed by the same everlasting beggar, giving to whom only encourages to ask again.

We were anxious upon our return to Naples to have ascended Vesuvius, at least as far as the Observatory, but unfortunately a heavy cloud hung over the mountain, and reluctantly we had to give it up. Instead, we took a drive to Puteoli, or, as it is now called, Pozzuoli, about two hours distant. Our way lay through the grotto of Posilipo, which is lighted up with gas, and is about a third of a mile long, about 21 feet wide, and varies in height from 70 to 25 feet; thence along an uninteresting road till again we reached the sea, when the islands and Puteoli looked very picturesque. One could hardly imagine from its appearance that it was formerly a great Roman port; but it has been subjected to many changes, and bears evidence of the forces below agitating the ground, by which some parts have been alternately submerged and upheaved, and the recurrence of such events would be sufficient of themselves to account for its desertion. Here we drove over the southern termination of the Appian Way, paved with the large old Roman stones; and our coachman pointed out the part of the old Roman pier (now in fragments, like a row of giant stepping-stones lifting their heads above water) at which he alleged the

Apostle Paul had landed. There are some ruined temples in Puteoli and its neighbourhood, and the ruins of a large amphitheatre, which the guide said had held 45,000, but, as is more credibly stated by others, 25,000 spectators, for it is not so large or so imposing as that at Nismes, while the measurements are considerably less, — Nismes exceeding it in length by 75 feet, and in breadth by 120 feet. Chambers underneath were discovered in 1838, and are very interesting. They contained dens for the confinement of the wild beasts, and rooms where the gladiators were trained to fight. We had, previous to entering Puteoli, taken a side road to Solfatara. This is a scarcely extinct crater, supposed to have a direct communication underground with Vesuvius, twelve miles distant. However, there has been no eruption since 1198, when it sent forth a current of lava. A man who appeared as guide threw a heavy stone upon the probably thin crust of sulphurous matter constituting the ground over which we were treading; the reverberation from the fall indicated that it was hollow below, and in all likelihood a slender protection from a fiery furnace which it might not be safe to expose to the air and light of day. And as Solfatara is quiescent when Vesuvius is active, and active when Vesuvius is quiescent, which it then was, the thought, as we were intruding upon the domains of these angry forces of nature, that some sudden impulse might burst the earthy covering and blow us all up into the air, like Paul Pry peering about the steamboat when the boiler burst, was not comfortable. The guide took us to a hole from which sulphurous fumes were issuing, and for a few coppers entered it at some risk of suffocation, and by means of a long stick pulled out some pieces of hot sulphur from the boiling natural caldron, which we carried off as souvenirs of our visit to a place which some day may become the scene of a terrible disaster.

Taking a different route on returning, we passed the

supposed tomb of Virgil; and crossing over the hill, came again in sight at some distance of Naples, and the continuous stretch of houses along the coast to the southward. Altogether it was a very interesting drive. Had we had time for it, we should have gone farther, as far as to Baiæ, which is a few miles beyond Puteoli.

As illustrative of the method of selling and clutching at a profit, however small, I may here mention that, going out with a friend from the hotel, we were waylaid by boys offering walking-sticks for sale. The first boy asked 2 francs for a cane, my friend offered 1 franc, and it was at once taken. Thereupon another with much better canes came up. My friend picked out five of the best, for which he was asked 15 francs, and they were really very cheap at the money. He offered 5 francs and then 6, and to throw in the stick he had just bought of the other boy. The offer was at once closed with, so that he got for 7 francs five beautiful canes, which, judging from prices asked in the shops, were worth 20 francs at least.

We had still a good deal to see in Naples; but, not feeling very well, we were anxious to leave a place the reputation of which for salubrity is by no means assuring, and departed for Rome by a morning train, leaving at 7 o'clock and arriving before 2 P.M.

XIV.

FLORENCE, BOLOGNA.

FLORENCE.

WE stayed in Rome until 27th April, when we left for Florence. We had intended going round by the attractive town of Perugia, but the morning of the 26th was wet, and, delaying our departure for a day, we gave up Perugia, partly because to have gone upon a Friday would have involved spending a Sunday there. The latter part of our journey was interesting. On arriving at the outskirts of the town the railway circumnavigates it, so that we had an opportunity from the very first of seeing the cathedral dome and campanile, and the other towers and spires of Florence, which lies beautifully situated in a luxuriantly verdant valley, enclosed by the Apennines and other hills, and intersected by the river Arno, which, seeing for the first time in the soft moonlight in the course of the evening, looked so lovely.

The Lung' Arno, or bank of the river, where most of the principal hotels are placed, is considered the best situation, at least for winter residence. Some of the hotels are unpleasantly near a waterfall or wear stretching across the river, the incessant din of which is troublesome at night. We spent a few nights at one of the hotels there, and afterwards a fortnight at the Pension Molini Barbensi,[1] on the left bank of the river, where we found pleasant society and some former travelling acquaintances. The house is a good one, and the rooms are large, but a very little expenditure on sanitary arrangements would improve it as a residence. Living seems not to be expensive at Florence, and lodgings can be procured at a moderate rate.

Florence lies upon the same river as Pisa, but I suppose fifty or sixty miles farther up, and the town bears some resemblance to it, but is far more picturesque and far more lively and populous. In fact, Pisa is quite a dull, quiet, dead-alive town beside it. The population of Florence, at present about 170,000, is four times as great as that of Pisa, and it has been a royal town as well as a provincial capital. The river is crossed by six bridges (three, or rather four of them, of very old date) connecting the north and south portions of the city, which, however, lies mainly upon the north shore. Of these bridges (all strongly buttressed against the force of the river, which no doubt occasionally descends in floods with great power), the Ponte Vecchio is peculiar and picturesque, and a remnant of old times, being covered on each side with houses, and on one side, on the top floor, by the long gallery which connects the Uffizi and Pitti Palaces. These houses on the bridge are very curious. Next the street they present to view on both sides small booths or stalls, principally occupied by goldsmiths or jewellers, which very likely much resemble what the shops of Old London were, but at the present day do not, for jewellers' wares, inspire confidence. On the other or river sides, all manner of chambers in or on the wall project, jut out, and overhang the river, very

---

[1] So named after the present proprietrix, Mme. Barbensi. It seems quite a foreign or at least an Italian practice to call houses after the name of the proprietor. Molini was either her maiden name or the name of the previous proprietor.

PONTE VECCHIO,—FLORENCE.

perilous to behold, and suggestive of *oubliettes* through which murdered travellers on the bridge might be quietly dropped into the river below, but conferring a quaintness of appearance precious in the sight of the artist. Equally striking in effect is an adjoining range of buildings on the left bank—also flanking the river, and with their projecting chambers overhanging it. In the centre of the bridge large arched openings enable the passer-by to look up and down the river, and take in the prospect beyond.

Nearly all along both sides of the Arno (protected by parapet walls) a wide street runs, and the buildings lining it are some of them stately and handsome, others are old or massive or peculiar, while the line is diversified here and there by a spire or a curious tower. The remarkable lofty old tower of the Palazzo Vecchio, and the dome and campanile of the cathedral,—all such notable objects in the pictures of Florence,—are prominent from almost every part, but especially from the south side of the river. There are, however, certain points of view from which Florence can be commanded. One of these is the terrace of the church of San Miniato, which stands upon a hill to the south-east, and is reached by a very delightful winding road bordered by villas, which were all at the time of our visit looking very charming in their new drapery of spring foliage. The church is an old one, finely decorated with marble and mosaics and marble pillars, and possessing a large crypt below. In itself it is well worth seeing, but it is principally visited for the sake of the prospect. Looking down from the terrace in front, Florence, with dome and towers, is seen lying away below very compactly in the centre of a long, large, flat plain, cut in two by the river, and surrounded by hills. It has here a fresher and cleaner look than most Italian towns. Immediately below San Miniato the piazza named after Michael Angelo lies, adorned in the centre by that artist's famous colossal statue of David.

The smart terraces of this nicely laid-out piazza command views similar to those from San Miniato, but from a lower elevation. A different winding road, as pleasant as the other, conducts down to the town.

Another fine drive is to the very ancient town of Fiesole, which stands on a hill upon the north side, and is about three miles out of town. There is here a curious old church or cathedral, with pillars said to be of the first century. Ascending a hill a little higher, and probably 1000 feet above the sea, the view from the top is more commanding than that of San Miniato, and one sees the Arno winding its way for a long distance down the valley, and the Carrara Mountains in the distance. These and other drives about the suburbs of Florence give the impression of a very charming place for a spring residence; but Florence is hot in summer and often very cold in winter time, fierce winds blowing from the hills, which I suppose are frequently covered with snow. The older portions of the city are similar to most Italian towns, full of narrow, tortuous streets; but adjoining the river and in the newer portions, and in the outskirts, the streets are regular and comparatively wide, with piazzas or open spaces in several parts. There are wide, handsome boulevards or *viales* encircling the city. In the Piazza Cavour there is a graceful triumphal arch akin to that in the Tuileries of Paris. At the west end, and adjoining the Arno, a large public park extends, called the Cascine, in which are long avenues bordered by trees, affording room for delightful drives and walks, one portion being also laid out as a racecourse. In the quarter south of the Arno the Boboli Gardens attached to the Royal Pitti Palace are also extensive, but open to the public only on Sundays and Thursdays.

Florence, historically, is a place of great interest, and is associated with many great names. It is the birthplace of, among others, Dante, Boccaccio, Machiavelli, Galileo, Michael Angelo Buonarotti, Cimabue, Fra Angelico, Leonardo da Vinci, Carlo Dolci, and others eminent in art. The houses of some of these celebrities are pointed out.

I can imagine that to those who spend a winter in Florence it must be exceedingly interesting to study the history of the place, and read on the spot such entertaining books as the remarkable life of that most remarkable man, Benvenuto Cellini, giving, as it does, such an insight into Italian life in the sixteenth century. Machiavelli, who died in 1527, brings his history down only to the year 1492; but after reading Trollope's history, in four vols., Napier's in six (leaving off at the year 1824) will afford for a whole winter a sufficiently tough *pièce de résistance*, the perusal whereof one's physician would no doubt recommend should be diversified occasionally by a chapter in Mrs. Oliphant's *Makers of Florence*, or by George Eliot's *Romola*, which it is to be hoped was not drawn from the life.

Florence, although in itself a more desirable place of residence than Rome, has no Roman ruins. It possesses, however, very many objects of great interest. There are within it about ninety churches, not a few of which are attractive.

The cathedral, commenced about six hundred years ago, and in its façade not yet finished, is immense, being 556 feet long by 342 feet wide. The spirit in which it was originated was lofty, the Florentine Republic desiring 'that an edifice should be constructed so magnificent in its height and beauty that it shall surpass everything of the kind produced in the time of their greatest power by the Greeks and Romans.' It is, at least in external covering, composed of marble—white, black, and green—with many sculptures and carvings in the marble, especially about the doorways. The stones are laid on a species of panelling consisting of upright parallelograms broken by large, formal, circular openings. Though it be somewhat stiff in pattern, and may be objected to as piebald, a certain richness of effect is produced. But the interior is not correspondent with the exterior; it is vast, but too bare and empty, and dark and dingy—perhaps, therefore, the more sublime! Looking up from below into the magnificent dome, it seems an enormous height to the lantern; as it no doubt is, being 352 feet—so high, in fact, that the dome itself is higher than that of St. Peter's, although the highest pinnacle is not. In design and general effect, as a whole, the cathedral will not compare with the great temple of Rome. The campanile or bell tower which adjoins, but is separated from it, is of marvellous beauty, and stands nearly 300 feet high. It is a perpendicular square tower, built of every kind of coloured marble, adorned by statuary and covered with rich alto-relievos (of which photographs can be procured); also by the graceful windows, very charmingly decorated in a species of suitable tracery. There is a completeness about this tower, even though it lacks the spire with which Giotto intended it to be crowned, combined with an exuberant affluence of decoration, which renders it a delightful object of contemplation, or rather, I should say, a choice object of study.

On the side of the piazza opposite to the west front the baptistery stands, an octagonal building 94 feet in diameter, and in one of the entrances the celebrated bronze gates are placed. We often availed ourselves of opportunities to examine these beautiful embodiments in bronze of Scripture subjects. Being exposed to the street, they are laden with dust, which to a certain extent reduces their apparent sharpness. Over this entrance gate there is a representation of the baptism of Jesus in three sculptured figures—our Lord, John the Baptist, and an attendant angel. Inside the baptistery, besides its oriental granite columns and its mosaics, there is nothing very remarkable.

On the south side of the cathedral, in the piazza, we found the little church of the Misericordia, belonging to that peculiar body of monks who, dressed in long black cloaks, with black masks over their faces pierced by eyeholes, are to be occasionally seen going about Florence and elsewhere in procession with the dead, which they bury, taking thus the place of the relations, who, in some parts of Italy, seem to abandon their friends when they die, and appear regardless of what becomes of their remains. We saw the chapel upon Ascension Day, which was a great holiday, or, to speak more exactly, *holy* day in Florence. On that occasion it was, like other churches, crammed to the door with a changing audience, and, after pushing our way in, we were as glad to push our way out again.

The churches of Santa Croce, S.S. Annunciata, Santa Maria Novella, and San Lorenzo are among the finest. They contain beautiful marble monuments, altar paintings, and other decorations which it would be endless to mention. The large church of Santa Croce has a fine white and black marble façade—rather straight and angular, however, in its lines. It measures nearly 500 feet long, and the interior, besides being adorned, as usual, with pictures, is the great receptacle of monuments to illustrious Florentine men, such as Michael Angelo, Galileo, and Machiavelli. The cloisters adjoining the church are well worthy of a visit. Most of the important churches in Florence have the advantage of a large open piazza in front. The vacant space surrounding the cathedral, unfortunately, is comparatively insignificant, and it were well if it could be enlarged. That in front of Santa Croce is large, and is adorned by a colossal marble statue of Dante in classic robe, attended by an eagle and guarded by four lions placed at the corners of a suitable pedestal.

From the church of San Lorenzo, founded in the fourth century, and one of the oldest churches in Italy, we were conducted by a touting guide to the adjacent chapel of the Medici,—the princes of Florence,—and the tombs of these princes, erected at a cost of nearly £900,000. The chapel contains Michael Angelo's masterpieces in sculpture — Lorenzo de Medici as a warrior resting, but ready, while Day and Night personified recline below, and on the opposite side Julian de Medici sits pondering over recumbent Dawn and Twilight. Opinions, however, have differed as to which is Lorenzo and which is Julian, and I am afraid the visitor has, like the little boy, to 'take his choice.'

The monastery, formerly of the Silvestrine, afterwards the Dominican monks, now the Museum of San Marco, is close to the church of San Marco. Here are to be seen a great many paintings by the pure-minded Fra (Giovanni) Angelico, who resided in the monastery during the first half of the fifteenth century. All his works, wrought out in prayer, are distinguished by the beautiful though smooth painting of the faces, many of which, here and elsewhere in Florence, are angelic, or, as we might more correctly designate them, of a saintly, soft beauty, and composed, devout inexpressiveness of any passion, but peculiar both in attire and employment. It would be a mistake, however, to set down all Angelo's faces as of this description, as in some of his paintings there is great diversity of contour and of expression, although the drawing is often singular and in the pre-Raphaelite style. I suppose it is generally correct, although not always. In one instance I noticed that a neck seemed to be a linked sweetness rather long drawn out. There is likewise shown in this museum, which is in reality a range of monkish cells, the little cell in which Savonarola, the illustrious, eloquent prior of the order, lived, —a man of great force of character, a precursor of Luther, fearless as Knox, and a saviour of Florence, whose people, when they burnt him at the stake, put to death their greatest benefactor. In a large room were exhibited an immense collection of the flags, banners, and colours of all the towns and corporations of Italy which were represented at the Dante festival in 1865.

On the south side of the river, with the exception of Minesota, the churches do not appear to be so fine; but there is one, the church of San Spirito, which is large and attractive, and contains no less than thirty-eight chapels encircling it—by far the largest number of side chapels attached to a church I have seen anywhere.

The visitor, however, is at first most attracted by the Piazza della Signoria, which—the centre of business—is a large open space, wherein, or in its neighbourhood, some of the most important buildings are congregated. On the south side of this piazza there is a lofty, covered, arcaded hall, called the Loggia dei Lanzi, open on two sides to the street by arches resting upon high ornamental pillars. Here are arranged some of the most beautiful modern statues in Florence, including the Rape of the Sabines in marble, by Giovanni da Bologna—a spirited work, which, like some of the others, is constantly being copied on a small scale in marble and alabaster, for sale in the shops ; and Perseus, a bronze statue by Benvenuto Cellini, a master of whose works there are various specimens to be seen in Florence. Both these stand in line with the front of the Loggia. Behind them are several other groups, including the Rape of Polyxena, Hercules slaying the Centaur, and one supposed to represent Ajax dragging along the body of Patroclus or of Achilles, all in fine powerful action. Tall, massive buildings have been erected on another side of the square, and opposite them, sentinelled by statues, the Palazzo Vecchio rises grandly but grimly, with its conspicuous campanile towering over everything around. This palace is well worthy of a visit. Immediately within the doorway we found, in contrast with the exterior, a graceful entrance court, encircled by an arcade supported by rows of columns florid in arabesques, each differing from the others, and a small fountain in the centre giving life to the whole. Ascending a long stair, we were ushered into an enormous hall, ornamented by six huge fresco paintings representing events in the history of Italy. On a floor above we were shown a chapel and several small rooms, in one of which there was a model of the proposed façade of the cathedral. I suspect it will be a long time before the façade itself be an accomplished fact. It appears strange that it should be allowed to remain in its present condition, a blemish upon the building, and a reflection upon the spirit in which the erection was commenced.

The house of Michael Angelo is not far from the Piazza. It has been converted into a museum, and contains, besides a series of paintings representative of events in his life, with some of his drawings and models in wax, and a small collection of works of art, a closet or studio in which he wrought, and a portrait and statue of this extraordinary artist and fiery independent man, conscious of a genius as versatile as it was unrivalled. The high estimate in which he has been held by those qualified to judge may be seen by referring to Sir Joshua Reynolds' *Discourses*.[1] In another street an inscription upon a stone in the wall denotes a house in which Benvenuto Cellini at one time lived.

But the greatest sources of attraction in Florence are the Uffizi and Pitti Galleries. These are open free to the public on Sundays and Thursdays—on other days on payment of a franc. The Uffizi Gallery occupies the upper

---

[1] 'Were I now to begin the world again, I would tread in the steps of that great master; to kiss the hem of his garment, to catch the slightest of his perfections, would be glory and distinction enough for an ambitious man.'—15th Discourse.

floor of the three sides of a long narrow street or court or *cul de sac*, I believe 450 feet long—the fourth being open to the Piazza della Signoria. The building has a handsome elevation, scarcely visible in the narrow street, and is adorned by nearly thirty marble statues of celebrated Tuscans, such as Dante, Petrarch, Michael Angelo, Lorenzo il Magnifico, evidencing the wealth of Florence in illustrious men. The gallery itself is reached by a long staircase, and through vestibules embellished by busts and statues. On entering we find ourselves in a long corridor, which is carried round the whole length of the three sides of the building; in fact, making three long galleries, not particularly high, though high enough for the purpose, and lighted from the top and by windows looking into the court. In these corridors, besides a good many pictures interspersed upon the walls, the greater part of the sculpture of the collection is assembled—embracing some choice specimens of ancient art, but in number very small compared with the vast treasures of the Vatican. Doors open all round into suites of rooms containing an immense assemblage of paintings, principally Italian, and among them many of the choicest works of the great masters. Besides the many chambers devoted to works of art of various nations, among which Britain seems to be nowhere and Italy to predominate, there are some small rooms containing collections of gems, medals, and bronzes. Two of the larger galleries exhibit several hundred portraits of artists, one of the most pleasingly beautiful among them being a sweet likeness by Mme. Le Brun of herself, a very favourite subject of copy, and with herself a not uncommon subject of her brush, as may be noticed in the Louvre. A very large room is likewise set apart mainly for the exhibition of seventeen most painfully-expressive statues of the famous Niobe group. But of all the rooms in this great gathering of art, the Tribune is the one which displays the choicest specimens. It is a comparatively small room, but is said to have cost £20,000 in its construction. Here are chef-d'œuvres of Raphael, Titian, Guido Reni, Correggio, and various others; while the chamber also contains the famous Venus de Medici, the Wrestlers, the Dancing Faun, the Whetter—all masterpieces of ancient sculpture.

Descending by a stair, the visitor proceeds by an almost interminably long corridor, which stretches out to the Ponte Vecchio, and across that bridge away to the Pitti Palace on the south side of the Arno—I suppose scarcely less than half a mile between the two places. This corridor, being lined with engravings, with drawings of the masters, and with tapestries,—a collection of things in themselves valuable,—would take a long time to examine, but in presence of so much else more attractive, scarcely succeeds in alluring the passing visitor to any lengthened scrutiny. Away and away it stretches, till after a weary walk it comes to a termination, and ascending by another stair into the Pitti Palace, we find ourselves in a collection of upwards of five hundred paintings and a few sculptures, occupying about fifteen different beautiful large rooms. It may truly be said there is hardly a painting in these rooms which is not good, while there are among them some of the choicest works of the great masters, as, for example,—for it is but one of very many which might be named,—Raphael's Madonna della Sedia, the beauty of which painting is something wonderful. No engraving and no copy that I have seen approaches the lovely expressiveness of the original. I was several times in these galleries, in which one could spend many days with the greatest enjoyment. But to endeavour to write a description would be not merely fruitlessly to seek to realize the works, but would be to attempt a disquisition on the great in art, which, even with capacity for the undertaking, would here be out of place. I suppose there is not an Italian painter of eminence who is not represented in the gallery, though beyond native art I think the only other nations whose artists' works appear are the Dutch and Spanish. Photographs and engravings can be procured of many of the pictures in the shops.

At all times artists are engaged, in both the Uffizi and Pitti Galleries, making copies of the more celebrated or most attractive pictures—occasionally two upon the same picture; and they do proceed with most wonderful patience and infinite pains, copying to the minutest hair, and laying on coat after coat with the greatest delicacy, some of them attaining to great excellence. A *permesso* is necessary to copy, and for some of the more celebrated paintings the artists, I was told, had sometimes to wait their turn for years. When they have, after elaborate painstaking, made a good copy, I fancy they manufacture other copies from it. I was fortunate enough, among others, to secure a copy of the lovely Madonna del Cordellina by Raphael, so perfect that it might almost vie with the original. It was obviously a copy direct from, and inspired by, the original. Beside it stood in the same shop another copy, but oh! how different! I believe that some of the copiers attach themselves more particularly to given masters,—for example, one in general copies Titians, another Murillos, another Raphaels. To protect against the abstraction of pictures from the galleries, no one is allowed to take a picture, not even a copy, out of Italy without a *permesso*. I bought a small copy of a Titian in the galleries, and the artist (Adolphe Boschi) accompanied me with it to the town, because, he said, they would not have allowed me to pass with it myself.

There is one little inconvenience attendant upon the extreme length of the galleries. Upon occasion of my first visit, I had unfortunately taken an umbrella, which I was obliged to leave at the door of the Uffizi Gallery. After wandering to the extreme end of the Pitti Gallery, I had to retrace all my steps to regain this umbrella. It is better, therefore, if anything must be left at the door, to confine a visit to one or other of the palaces, and there is abundance in either to engage a whole forenoon.

Not far from the Piazza della Signoria is what is called the National Museum, contained in the old Palazzo del Podesta, rich, but severely rich, in its architecture. The ground floor is occupied with ancient and modern armour and arms. Above there is a gallery of statues, some of them by Michael Angelo, a room full of majolica, another of ivory carvings, two of bronzes, two of tapestry, and two of sculpture; but the collection, though interesting, looks small after experiencing the extent of the Uffizi and Pitti Galleries, and seems hardly deserving to be dignified with the name of National.

The Corsini Palace, on the Lung Arno, is open three days in the week to the public, and contains in twelve rooms a large collection of paintings, many of which are by the great masters.

The Academia delle Belle Arti contains a large collection of pre-Raphaelites, commencing with Cimabue, and comprising among others some fine Peruginos. It is accordingly interesting. In an upper floor several rooms exhibit paintings by modern Italian artists, principally battle-pieces. I paid a visit also to the rooms of the Association for the Encouragement of the Fine Arts, which seems to be founded somewhat on the same principles as similar associations in Great Britain; but from such opportunities as I have had of forming an opinion, I cannot say that the mantle of their great predecessors—whose works are constantly before them, and might be thought calculated to inspire—has fallen upon the modern Florentine artists.

Florence, besides being a great place for the sale of copies of paintings, and for the manufacture of the well-known massive and tastefully-decorated picture-frames, all carved out of the solid wood, upon which the gilding is laid without any mixture of composition, is the place of all others for the manufacture and sale of marble and alabaster sculpture, and of the beautiful Florentine mosaic jewellery. It is filled with shops for the sale of these various articles, which are to be had at moderate prices, and strangers seldom leave without more or less extensively making purchases.

The streets of Florence are always full of life. Occasionally of an evening a body of men, perhaps twenty or thirty, would form themselves in a ring, and with deep, rich, melodious voices sing Italian songs. The power of voice or strength of lungs which the Italians sometimes possess is indeed often exhibited in a surprising manner. All of a sudden, walking along a street, it may be meditatively, a vendor of smallwares will abruptly at your very ear, and without apparent effort, discharge a sharp, stentorian cry, piercing and startling as with the shock of a nine-pounder, and nearly knocking you down breathless and affrighted. The markets, too, are noisy,—bargain-making being a serious operation, in which success is supposed to attend the most vociferous and energetic,—but sometimes they are more quietly conducted. Having once penetrated them, and found myself in the press of a great crowd in very narrow passages, and in odious proximity to heaps of most unpleasant-looking fish, it was with no little satisfaction I made my escape as soon as escape was practicable.

There are many other places in Florence to be seen besides those I have specially mentioned. We did see a good deal in the time we were there, but not all by any means, and what we did see was in a very general way. We remained not quite three weeks, and could with pleasure have stayed much longer. It is a place which, like Rome, though not to the same extent, requires a long stay, and is full of objects meriting careful study and worthy of repeated examination. It is not, however, without its drawbacks, chief among them being the not uncommon practice in Italian towns of making air-holes from the drains to the streets, from which unsavoury whiffs occasionally come, not pleasant to contemplate. The authorities plainly want in sanitary arrangements some teaching.

BOLOGNA.

We left Florence for Bologna by train at 7.50 A.M. As we were about to enter a railway carriage, a pleasant-looking English lady looked out and cried to us deterringly, 'This is not a smoking carriage.' 'Thank you, madam,' I replied; 'that is just what we want.' So, as the two parties filled the compartment, we were not troubled with any selfish smoker, and, as we were all English, with no needless exclusion of the views by lowering the blinds. We reached Bologna at noon. The railway passes through many tunnels, and in some places at a great elevation. The views from it are fine.

Bologna is a singular old university town, very compact within the walls, so as to accommodate its population of 109,000. From the twelve or thirteen gates in the walls, leading streets converge to the centre, constructed with arcades at the sides, under which the pavements and shops are placed. The object of the arcading is probably to afford shelter from the snow in winter and the rain in summer. The town itself is dull, and the shops entering from the arcades are dark and second-rate. Photographs of Bologna can be procured at Florence, and perhaps in some as yet undiscovered region in Bologna itself. The Hotel Brun (the principal one) is an old-fashioned house. Like many of the Italian hotels, the *salons* are entered direct from the court-yard.

As soon as possible, as we were only to stay one night, we went out for a drive of some hours, and were taken first to the two leaning towers, which stand together. These are long, lanky, and square, dark with age and long exposure to the weather, often, I suspect, of a humid character. One of them—the *Torre Asinelli*—said by Bædeker to be 272, and in other authorities 320 feet high, was originally 476 feet, or 40 feet higher than the top of the cross of St. Peter's. It was shortened in 1416 after an earthquake. It now lies 3 ft. 5 in. off the perpendicular. The other, that of Garisenda, is, according to Bædeker, 138 feet high, and upwards of 8 feet out of the perpendicular, and by no means assuring to look at. They are neither of them imposing architecturally, although noted features viewed from outside the city. From this point we went to the Etruscan Museum, in which a variety of antiquities are exhibited, and, among other things, several skeletons of an old date discovered in neighbouring excavations. Under the same roof there is also a large library, comprising upwards of 100,000 volumes. I believe the museum and library are connected with the University, 760 years old. Close by is the large church of San Petronio, 384 feet long by 154 feet wide, intended to have been a vast deal larger. Here Charles V. was crowned emperor in 1530. There are various other large churches interesting to see, but, after those in Rome and Florence, they have, with all their grandeur, rather a provincial look. We then drove beyond the walls to the Villa Reale, one of the royal palaces. It stands upon a height, and commands admirable views of the town, out of which rise a good many towers, domes, and spires, relieving its otherwise spiritless level. One also sees far into the surrounding country, which, for the most part, is very flat. The villa contains some long corridors, one of them 500 feet long, adorned by statues. The church of the monastery is entered from the galleries.

From this we drove (still outside the walls) to the Campo Santo, which is much larger, is more ramified, and is older than that at Genoa, but it is by no means equal to it either in arrangement or in monuments. Some of the monuments are good, but many are paltry. On our way back to town we entered the churches of San Domenico and San Pietro, both large, and containing greater objects of interest than San Petronio.

Cab fares in Bologna are moderate. I paid the cabman half a franc more than his fare, and, wonderful to say, he thanked me. It was the first and only time in Italy. The usual course is to take all that is offered and beg for more. Do the cabmen of Bologna graduate at the University?

Rain fell heavily the following morning, and as we were to leave for Venice at twelve o'clock, we had not much time, but I could scarcely leave Bologna without taking a hurried glimpse of the Academia delle Belle Arti. An hour in this large gallery was, of course, far too brief a space for seeing its contents, and in the galleries there are many great paintings of more or less merit; among others, Raphael's celebrated and beautiful picture of St. Cecilia listening to heavenly music, in which, however (such are the exigencies of art), six solid angels, securely seated on a cloud, obtain their words and their time, somewhat inconveniently, from two stout music-books, perhaps purchased in the Via outside—a profane remark; but irreverent thoughts will intrude even in the presence of the most wonderful works. It was a change to pass from the well-favoured countenance of St. Cecilia to Guido Reni's Crucifixion. There are indeed two Crucifixions by Guido, but the smaller one seems to me the grander effort of genius. The effect of the darkness in the painting is truly sublime.

XV.

VENICE AND VERONA.

VENICE.

THE rain continued while we proceeded to Venice, but cleared off shortly before we arrived at our journey's end, about five o'clock. The country for some distance from Bologna is very flat, and was then full of water, but rich and verdant. We passed the towns of Ferrara, Rovigo, and Padua. In approaching the old city Padua, the country becomes hilly. 'This university town arrests attention by its domes and towers, and seemed to invite a visit; but one cannot see everything in a single tour. Venice is only twenty-two miles distant from Padua, but the railway takes nearly two hours to reach it. At last we arrived at a broad lagune, separating the mainland from the island city, and crossed by a railway viaduct apparently about two miles long. From this bridge, gazing from the carriage windows, we saw lying before us at a little distance, like fairyland, Venice, as if floating on the water, a strange sight! On arriving at the station, which is real stone and lime, resting on veritable ground, and very much like railway stations elsewhere, except that no omnibuses or cabs wait arrival, the exit is to the banks of the Grand Canal. We were met outside by the *commissionaire* of the Hotel Danieli (Royal), who gave us in charge of a boatman; and leaving the *commissionaire* to bring the luggage afterwards, we had our first experience—a new and curious one—of a gondola on the canals of Venice. The boatman took us a certain length along the Grand Canal, and then, as I found the post office could be reached on the way, we turned aside into a narrow canal to a place which it would have required infinite trouble to discover, secured our letters, and an early ingiving of our address, and thence went on to the hotel, which is nicely situated on the Riva degli Chiavoni,—a broad quay recently formed along the Great Canal di San Marco from the Piazzetta at the Doge's Palace, eastward, I suppose, about 1000 yards, while a continuation of the walk westward from the Piazzetta has been made in the Royal Gardens fronting the Royal Palace. This situation is decidedly the best in Venice. It faces the south, and the views from it are open and surpass others. The hotel is within a stone-throw of the Doge's Palace, and people can at once get out from it to the open fresh air, walk freely about, and visit many of the objects of greatest interest without stepping into a gondola, or picking their way along the numerous narrow and tortuous streets or lanes intersecting Venice, which are extremely perplexing to a stranger. Most of the other hotels are situated upon the canals,—sometimes in sunless interior parts,— with communications behind by these narrow lanes with the landward parts of the town; and they want the advantage of the quay in front, which with the shipping always affords a lively, interesting promenade.

Rain fell during the evening, but next morning we sallied out to see a little of this wonderful place. It is a curious sensation to see for the first time a town like Venice, whose leading features by means of pictures have been familiar to us from childhood; but no pictures ever come up to the reality. We stood for a little upon the pretty bridge which crosses a narrow canal, and looked up to the renowned Bridge of Sighs, which, at a considerable elevation over this small canal, connects the east side of the Doge's Palace with the prison. The façade of the palace upon this side exhibits a combination of elegance with an appearance of massive strength, to which the lower tiers of masonry, formed of rows of tooth-shaped or square diamond-pointed bosses (they perhaps have a technical name), similar to the enrichments on Crichton Castle (Midlothian), very much contribute. Then we passed the well-known south front of the Doge's Palace to the Piazzetta separating the Doge's from the Royal Palace—a wide, open space, wherein stand the two red granite pillars one sees in every representation of this part of Venice; the one surmounted by the winged lion, and the other by the former patron of the Republic, San Teodoro, who was turned out by the mundane authorities and succeeded in office by San Marco, such patrons having no will of their own in the bestowal or withdrawal of their patronage. Then walking up by the west side of the Palace, we entered the large open square called the Piazza di San Marco, nearly 600 feet long, by, at the east end, 270 feet wide, narrowing to 180 feet at the west end, and presenting on each side a handsome façade in the Italian style, the lower floor being occupied with shops and cafés under arcades. The Church of St. Mark forms the east side of this Piazza. Near to it, on the south-east of the Piazza, its lofty campanile rises; while opposite the famous clock tower and clock form a portion of the north side.

But the eye is first arrested by the cathedral. There is in St. Mark's a mixture of styles, but its predominating Byzantine style of architecture, so different from what one is ordinarily accustomed to,—its façade, so beautifully ornamented by pictorial representations in mosaic, bright and vivid in their colouring; its mosque-like domes; its pierced pinnacles; its graceful lines and cresting statues; its numerous rich, and all differing, marble columns (500 outside and in),—give to the whole a magnificence of effect which fixed us to the spot, gazing in admiration from beside the noticeable and noted flagstaffs planted in front. The pause was fatal to peace. We were immediately surrounded by a small swarm of touters, quick to scent fresh blood, and eager to be employed to show the way into St. Mark's and give imperfect or perhaps altogether unintelligible accounts of the edifice. Brushing them aside, on entering our first impression of the interior was of darkness and dirt. The place is 900 years old, and the sun was at the time under a cloud. The floor is very uneven, having sunk at many places in a series of waves, as if it had once rested on the Adriatic, and the traces of its motion had been left behind. The mosaics, which cover many thousand square feet, and are very old, are cracked, and have given way in several parts; but it was a very curious, peculiar church, and it grew upon one the longer it was looked at. On this occasion we contented ourselves with a general view of the interior, spending more than an hour in doing so, and in seeing the 'Presbyterio,' which was shown by the sacristan. The choir of the church is raised above the ground floor of the main body, and is railed off by a parapet or screen, adorned by eight columns and surmounted by fourteen statues and a large central crucifix. It is reached by a few steps, and there hangs in front of it, suspended from the ceiling, a massive silver lamp—a peculiar adornment. Here are the high altars with their costly ornaments, and the principal curiosities and valuables (some of them very ancient) of the church; among others, two pillars said to be from Solomon's temple. These, with the Pala d'Oro (an elaborately-wrought gold screen), the bronze bas-reliefs, the statues, all contribute to the interest. But other people are waiting, and we are hurried through.

By this time it was nearly twelve o'clock, and we went outside to see the clock strike. The clock tower is a large broad building six storeys high, topped by a short central tower forming an additional storey. On the façade, a large dial marks the hours up to twenty-four, according to old Italian time, and some other astronomical mutations. Over the dial there is a statue of the Virgin, and on the top of the tower, surmounted by a golden lion, two bronze giants with sledge-hammers strike the hours, whereupon, by means of machinery, three puppet kings, preceded by an angel, stagger out at a door on one side of the Virgin, and passing jerkily along, each in turn, as it arrives opposite her, bows to her stiffly with puppet grace, marches on, and with a twitch disappears at another door, both doors closing after all have done their duty. A crowd watched the performance, which we were in luck to see, as after Whitsunday the show does not take place for some length of time.

This important event witnessed, we walked round the Piazza, which at night is a gay scene—lights blazing, a band of music performing, and the whole square filled with people. In the day-time it is comparatively quiet. Here and in an adjoining street the shops of Venice are concentrated. They are small boxes resembling very much the little shops in the Palais Royal in Paris, though not so rich in jewellery or so well stocked with merchandise. In many of them there are always for sale little models of gondolas in all kinds of material, from silver to leather and wood. In others photographs are sold, the photos of Venice being noted as remarkably good; and they are printed, I think, on rather thicker paper than elsewhere, but they are slightly dearer than those in the South of Italy. There are also shops in which the famous Venetian glass is sold. The manufacture of glass is a great trade in Venice, and one sees among them very beautiful samples of the work, embracing articles in iridescent glass;

but as the manufacturers have agents in London, it is not very desirable to purchase such frail commodities to take so far home. People, however, do so, and probably they would not purchase at home; while it is certainly true that purchases made in distant places of what is peculiar to the place acquire a value which never attaches to the same things procured in one's own country. On a subsequent day we visited one of the glass and mosaic works, which our gondoliers (for some unaccountable reason, if we put aside personal motives and small commissions which the brave gondolier must assuredly be above accepting) were always pressing we should stop at. The manufacture is interesting, but one feels under an obligation to purchase in requital for attention, and really the prices asked were forbiddingly high.

In the afternoon of this our first day, we had our first real experience of going about in a gondola. The gondolas are all, by order of the authorities, to prevent expensive rivalry in colours, painted black, and they have therefore a very funereal look. One would think that, as it is merely uniformity which is desired, a brighter colour might have been chosen, and for this everybody would plead. Just fancy all our street cabs of the colour of funeral carriages! Some of the gondolas, perhaps all of them, have wooden removable covers, analogous to waggonette covers, which for wet weather may be very useful; but, generally speaking, they have, at least in warm weather, white or light-coloured linen canopies stretched on rods for protection from the sun, which was very hot during our stay. These canopies, however, interfere with the view, and as we had not the Continental dread of the sun, we used at once to desire them to be taken down. It is marvellous how one rower, who rows upon one side of the boat, manages to propel it steadily along. On one occasion, however, we had a gondolier who shook the boat from stem to stern at every step, owing to some awkwardness he had in managing his foot or his oar, rendering the shaking motion most unpleasant; but with this exception (and we took care to avoid this man again), sailing in the gondolas we found to be one of the most delightful ways of going about, gliding noiselessly through the water, and continually passing others similarly engaged. The dexterity with which the boatman steers is somewhat marvellous. He will, for instance, approach a rope stretched from a ship, and pass under it, the high prow clearing it by an inch. Again, on entering the narrow canals (in doing which the men always sing out a peculiar warning cry), or making a turn in one of them, these long boats were managed most adroitly. The fares for the gondolas are very moderate, being with one gondolier 1 franc (lira) for the first hour, and half a franc for every other. If two men be employed, the fare is doubled. The boatmen, however, generally seem to expect more than their fare, and even on giving more, as we always did, we never were thanked. Whenever a gondola stops at a place, and we had continual stoppages, there is an officious man waiting to hook the boat with his stick, for which he expects a soldo, value one halfpenny.

On occasion of our first trip we crossed the Canal di San Marco (really an arm of the sea) to the island di San Georgio Maggiore, on which has been built the church of that name, which, with its dome and columned front, and its high, conspicuous campanile, is a boldly prominent and graceful object from the town. The main attraction inside the church is its beautiful carved wooden choir, representing the life of St. Benedict, executed by Alberto di Bruli, of Flanders. It is likewise filled with marbles, bronzes, and paintings; after examining which we ascended the campanile and had a splendid view of Venice and of all the islands. The view from it, indeed, is somewhat better than that which we subsequently had from the campanile of San Marco, which looks rather directly down upon Venice.

From this island we rowed across to another long island called La Guidica, forming one side of the canal of the same name; and on this island is the church of Il Redentore, which contains some fine marbles, and in the sacristy some paintings by Bellini.

But it would be almost endless to describe the various churches which in the course of our short stay we visited. Most of them are adorned by pictures by Titian or by other great masters, by monumental sculptures, and by every other species of ornamentation. I shall only mention the names of some, with a remark.

The church of San Sebastian, containing the tomb of Paul Veronese, and some of the finest specimens of that artist's works. Santa Maria della Salute, nearly opposite the Royal Palace, and at the entrance to the Grand Canal—a vast church, which with its domes forms a striking leading feature of Venice. It was erected after the plague of 1630, and the only wonder is that there is not an annual plague in Venice, the smells are so atrocious. The old church of San Stephano, with its statues, monuments, and bronzes. When we visited it, a grand funeral service was being performed; the singers led by a man with a baton,—very unlike real mourning. The church of Santa Maria dei Frari, full of monuments, paintings, and statues, but its main attractions are the magnificent marble monuments to the memory of Titian and Canova, in two very different styles of art. The church of the Scalzi, or barefooted friars, gorgeously ornamented with marbles from all parts of the world, some of the marbles being cut in curious imitation of drapery and cushions. The church of the Jesuits, decorated in a strange, florid style with black and white marble—in imitation of damask patterns, I presume, inlaid somewhat like mosaics —pillars and pilasters and other parts being all so covered, as if with cloth, in black and white damask. It is elaborate and peculiar, and looks like a freak in architecture. The church of San Giovanni et Paolo, a grand old place, full of magnificent altars, fine columns, and gorgeous monuments, most of them to Doges, very many of whom are buried here. This church is therefore regarded as the Venetian Westminster Abbey. The chapel del Rosario was an adjunct to it, and when entire must have been of exquisite beauty, as is evident from the remains of the sculpture. It was, unhappily, set on fire by an incendiary in 1867, whereby many fine paintings were destroyed, including a grand one by Titian. The keeper of the chapel had photographs of the sculpture for sale; but, as usual when offered at show places, asked extravagant prices.

The palaces, however, of Venice are among its main attractions. They line almost continuously the Grand Canal, and are to be found occasionally in the side canals. Formerly the abodes of the old nobility, probably few of them are now occupied by private proprietors. To appearance, the majority of them are diverted to other uses—some as government offices, others as hotels, others as museums, and, I suspect, even in some cases for purposes of trade and manufacture. For any one to attempt to describe them in few pages would be vain, and they require the aid of the pictorial art to realize them. Fortunately, good photographs of many of them can be procured. They are imposing, and not infrequently very beautiful buildings. Their design is in some cases a species of fanciful Gothic, and in others the heavier style of the Renaissance; but a character of their own pervades them, denoting them Venetian. Our architects at home occasionally reproduce them in our public buildings, with variations. No two are alike. Their variety is pleasing, and age has in many imparted a rich colouring to the stone or marble of which they are built. In nearly all the balcony is a prominent feature; and no doubt on many grand occasions their balconies were crowded by the fairest of the fair, decked in their best attire, and many bright and loving eyes have peered over balustrades gaily decorated with brilliant hangings on sumptuous pageants passing beneath, and darted captivating glances on favoured gallants taking their part in the spectacles. Long poles stuck into the canal in front of many of the palaces indicate the nobility of the families to which they now or at one time belonged. Some of the rooms in these palaces are very spacious, as, for example, those in the Palazzo Pesaro, a large edifice in the style of the Renaissance, where there was one great hall the whole depth of the house, from the front facing the canal to the back. This room was filled with pictures, some for sale; and, as usual, balconies overlooked the canal, from which we had a charming view of all the life afloat. In the Palazzo Emo-Treves we were shown the two last works of Canova—statues of Hector and Ajax. They are gigantic, and seem rather out of place in a comparatively small room. In other palaces the visitors are conducted through suites of rooms hung with paintings.

So numerous are the palaces, that I see eighty-nine are mentioned in a small but useful guide-book, called *A Week in Venice*,[1] the churches being about as many in number. The grand palace of all, however, is the Doge's. This is a magnificent building both inside and out. The admission is by ticket, costing a franc each for the palace itself, with extra tickets for the Bridge of Sighs and the Museum, a small collection. The palace is a square or oblong building, with a large court-yard in the centre, and both externally and on the walls of the court is highly decorated; but there is a heaviness in the upper part of the west and south exterior façades, and a dumpiness about the windows with which these parts are pierced, which could never reconcile

---

[1] A large valuable work in small folio, copiously illustrated—veritable volumes *de luxe*—has recently been published: '*Venise: Histoire, Art, Industrie, la Ville, la Vie.* Par Charles Yriarte.'

me to them. Even the lower part in its arcading wants relief. Thirty-four Gothic arches in a row, and all monotonously alike in size and figure, however beautiful individually, without a break loses in effect. The entrance from the Piazzetta is by a beautiful Gothic doorway closely adjoining St. Mark's, richly sculptured. After examining and passing through it, we find ourselves at the foot of the Giant's Staircase; but the large central square court round which the palace extends arrests the eye, and we enter it to admire the interior façades, particularly those on the east and north. The north side is short and broken, and more diversified than the others, not merely by statues and a peculiar rich ornamentation, but by the domes of St. Mark, which tower over it and claim to be a portion of the structure. But after lingering about this handsome court, and taking a look at the carved bronze wells which are placed in it, and from which water is obtained, ascent is made by the Giant's Staircase to the first floor, where admission is gained to the portions of the building shown to the public. The arrangement of the rooms is somewhat perplexing to the visitor, requiring a plan which is not anywhere given to guide him through. But we find our way through some immense halls, all decorated by huge pictures principally representing scenes in the history of Venice—real 'gallery pictures' in point of extent of canvas, but highly suitable to the noble proportions of the rooms. One picture, not by any means a pleasing one, is the largest in the world, and occupies the whole breadth of an immense room— 'Paradise,' by Tintoretto, who seemed fond of enormous canvases; his chef-d'œuvre, the Crucifixion, in the Scola di S. Rocco, being also huge. The ceilings of the rooms in the palace, some of them lofty, are also, according to Italian practice, embellished with paintings and massive gilding; but labour and expense seem greatly thrown away, it is such a strain to look up to them. In one large room, just below the ceiling, in a running row, portraits are seen of all the Doges, 120 in number, commencing in the year 697 and ending 1797, a period of exactly 1100 years. One of them, however, as a traitor to Venice, is painted under veil. These portraits in all likelihood are, at least among the earlier Doges, as reliable as are those of the early kings of Scotland in the gallery of Holyrood Palace, or of those of the earlier popes in certain churches in Rome. The rooms, however, of greatest interest are those in which the Doge and his council assembled in conclave; and one cannot help, when in such rooms, endeavouring to conjure up old scenes happening there, and thinking how the glory of Venice has departed.

When in the library we were asked to go into a small room off it, where we were shown some old MSS., and a fine old unique breviary, with most beautiful illuminated illustrations. It has been or is being photographed, and I presume copies will be for sale.

The dungeons, which are seen by crossing the Bridge of Sighs, are, so far as shown, small, but sufficiently repellent.

The Doge's Palace abuts upon the church of St. Mark, which we rarely passed without entering. On Whitsunday (20th May 1877) a grand service was held in the church. The singing was performed by about from twelve to twenty choristers in the organ gallery, with a leader. The voices were splendid, and the music very fine. On another occasion we walked round the gallery of the church under guidance of an attendant, and examined the mosaics, of which one thus gets a nearer view. They are imposing, but unfortunately are giving way in many places. At a west window we were taken outside to see the four fine bronze horses over the portal, which form a feature in the ornamentation of the façade. The horses are, however, in size small, and apparently not sufficiently gigantic for the situation.

In the Piazza di San Marco immense flocks of pigeons are always to be seen; they are kept under the protection of the city, the law being that to kill or ill-treat them is a punishable offence. Every day at two o'clock they are regularly fed with grain, and they are said to know the time so exactly as to arrive for their dinner from all quarters at the precise hour. It is certainly remarkable to see how tame they are, being quite devoid of the fear and dread of man, perching all over any stranger who will feed them, with as much confidence as if they were with Adam or Eve in the Garden of Eden.

After we had seen a good deal of Venice we ascended the campanile of St. Mark. This is a wide square tower, and by a commodious sloping internal ascent the belfry is attained, where we get among the bells. The hours are struck by a man stationed to pull the ropes and watch for fires, which, when he discovers, he notifies to the proper quarter—a useful, but, I fear, a rare species of precaution against this species of calamity. The view from this tower (which is 322 feet high to the hair of the angel's head, an altitude which I need scarcely say we did not attempt) is commanding, ranging over the city and lagunes, looking, however, as I have already said, a little too directly down upon the roofs of the houses below. However, one gets a pretty clear idea of the map of Venice, with its multifarious canals, islands, and narrow streets. As stated by Bædeker, the '15,000 houses and palaces of Venice (population, 128,901) are situated on 3 large and 114 small islands, formed by 147 canals, connected by 378 bridges (most of them stone), and altogether about 7 miles in circumference.' I occasionally endeavoured to thread my way through the narrow streets of Venice, and considered it rather an achievement the first time I managed to pioneer through all the intricacies of the passage from the Piazza San Marco to the Ponte Rialto and back again. This famous bridge is a graceful marble arch, of one span of 74 feet, across the Grand Canal. An elegant marble balustrade protects each side, the space on the bridge being divided into three footways by two covered arched or arcaded buildings used as shabby little shops, which one would gladly see abolished, being so little in keeping with the handsome character of the bridge. Here at the Rialto there are also markets on either side of the canal, for the sale of fruit and other things.

Situated on the Grand Canal, but nearer to the railway station, is the Museo Correr, in which we found a collection of pictures, armour, and curiosities, of no great extent, but said to be valuable. The Palazzo Marcello (proprietor, Richetti) contains a quantity of 'antiquities,' curiosities, bronzes, and other things manufactured for sale, some of them curiously designed.

Nearer to the principal part of the town the Academia delle Belle Arti lies—a very extensive collection of paintings in twenty large halls, besides smaller rooms, the pictures numbering in all 679. These are all, with the exception of a few of the Dutch school, if I am not mistaken, the works of Italian artists, most of them by the great masters, and many on a large scale. Among others is what is considered Titian's masterpiece—'The Assumption of the Virgin,' a clear and brilliant, a glorious work in point of drawing and colour. In fact, the colour is perhaps rather too strong in reds and blues. One great canvas, a grand picture by Paul Veronese of the banquet in Levi's house, occupies the entire breadth of the largest hall. The banquet is represented as held under a remarkably Venetian-looking light colonnade, open to the outer air, and peopled by characters evidently clothed in Venetian attire of the painter's era. But it scarcely does to scan such works of art with too much regard to accessories. What appears to be the favourite picture is another Veronese — a Virgin with a young, naked, little St. John the Baptist standing on a pedestal, with legs to appearance (it may be merely the effect of shade) of unequal lengths. There were half a dozen painters when we were there, engaged in copying the chubby St. John. Copies of it may be seen in many of the shops of Venice. They are, I fancy, favourites with the ladies. We paid only one visit to the Academy, but it would take several visits to do its galleries justice.

The arsenal of Venice, dating back to the year 1104, is well worthy of a visit for the sake of its museum, an interesting collection of arms and models of ships, particularly of the grand state gondolas; nothing but the museum is apparently shown to the ordinary visitor. The arsenal is not so extensive as it once was. Admission is had by simply entering one's name in the visitors' book, and, as usual at all these show places where admission is not by payment, giving a small fee to the *custodes*, one being stationed in each hall.

A steamboat, large enough for the traffic, sailed every hour from the quay in front of our hotel to the island of Lido, about two miles distant. We crossed in it one afternoon; and the sail is interesting, as the vessel passes the other islands, and fine views are had from it of the town, and, in the distance, of the mountains of the Tyrol. The island of Lido is long and narrow. Upon landing we walked across to the other side, about half a mile of road. Here we were on the borders of the Adriatic. The island is a bright little spot with a few buildings on it. Returning, we got on board just in time to escape, under cover of its awning, a thunder-shower which came pelting down very heavily, and lasted all the time we were on board.

We had now been eight days in Venice, and had been

constantly going about seeing much that was to be seen, but yet only seeing it in a superficial way. There was no place in Italy which was more attractive. Its gorgeous palaces and churches, its strange, unique kind of life, the multitudinous canals teeming with gondolas, and the pleasure of moving about in them, was something we never could forget. We saw Venice usually in brilliant sunshine, with everything sparkling in light, although nearly every afternoon, with a severe punctuality which enabled us generally to be prepared for it, black clouds gathered, and a thunderstorm emptied them quickly. But perhaps the most beautiful sight of all was to see Venice in moonlight. One is familiar with photographs of the fair city, tinted with a deep blue in imitation of moonlight effect, a white spot being picked out for the moon herself (as, of course, the photographs are taken during the day), and I can hardly say that there is in these pictures much, if any, exaggeration. The blueness of the sky, and of everything with which the light is tinged in moonlight, is something remarkable and very lovely, while the effect is increased when the moon, getting behind a cloud, gives to the cloud a luminous edging of silver.

We were exceedingly unwilling to leave this bright fairyland, but became afraid to stay longer. The fact is, that with all its attractiveness Venice has not, at least to a stranger, the feeling of healthiness. It drains into the canals, where the tide rises and falls only 2 feet, and has not force sufficient to carry off the drainage. The effluvium from the narrow canals is sometimes overpowering, and yet it is said, as it is said of so many other places one might imagine insalubrious, that Venice is naturally so healthy that the people are notedly long-lived; and, indeed, one instance of this occurs in the case of Titian, who lived to the patriarchal age of ninety-nine. How this comes, 'let doctors tell.'

We left on 23d May, pursuing our way up the Grand Canal and under the Ponte Rialto, and on to the railway station,—a long pull, but one we always enjoyed. In fact, if a visitor do nothing but obtain a sail along this canal, he sees the greater part of Venice; just as, though much less completely, a stranger sees much of London by a sail upon the Thames, and would see more were the main buildings, as at Venice, placed upon its banks; which henceforth, perhaps, there is a hope they may be. The canal is, I think, about two miles in length, and on an average not less than 100 feet wide, and is lined by palaces, churches, and houses, in the utmost irregularity of height and diversity of character and style, many of them beautiful, while the canal itself is alive with gondolas; and the *tout ensemble* is so picturesque, that when the sun shines, as it generally did, everything looks engaging to the eye. One by one we passed and gazed at the palaces (which had become, as it were, old friends) with many a lingering look, as if resolved we never should forget them. But the vision came to an end as we entered the modern and disenchanting railway station, whence we shortly after proceeded on our journey to Verona, the scene of *Romeo and Juliet*. Romance was not, therefore, to be quite at an end, and as the train issued out of the railway station the curtain was raised for a momentary glimpse; and slowly wending our way over the lagune by the long viaduct of 222 arches, we looked intently on the floating city, wondering if ever we should see it again. Losing sight of it lying on the one side, attention was forthwith drawn to the other by the line of the Tyrolese mountains, which at some distance were in view, and flanking us nearly the whole way. We passed Padua and Vicenza, and through a country which is flat, but was smiling in the greens of early summer, and after a journey of about seventy miles in four hours reached our destination.

VERONA.

We had proposed spending two nights at Verona, but American friends who came with us from Venice were anxious to get on to Milan, so that we had just two hours the following morning for a drive about the town. We regretted afterwards that our opportunity was not greater, for it is indeed a place at which one may stay for a few days with advantage. It is very picturesquely situated on the river Adige, and contains a good deal that is interesting. We first drove through the old market-place, where people were busy selling fruit, vegetables, and other things in a piazza surrounded by curious old houses. Then into the Piazza dei Signori, where are some very fine buildings, old and new, and adjoining it a small open space or square closely surrounded by houses, in which the noted and highly decorated tombs of the Scaligers, enclosed within a wall and railing, are seen. Then on to the Arena, which is not so imposing as the Colosseum or even the Arena at Nismes, and although covering more ground than the latter, was seated for fewer spectators; but it is in a very perfect condition—the most perfect, I think, of any we saw in Italy, the large marble slabs of which it is built being nearly all in place. We mounted to the top row, and had an excellent view of the country round about. From this we drove to the church of San Zenone Maggiore, a thousand years old, and very curious. The portal is peculiar, and adorned by rich marble reliefs. Within are some fine old pillars, said to be of single pieces of marble, a crypt, and cloisters—altogether a place of great interest and of striking conformation. We were only sorry we had so little time to examine it minutely, for we could take but a rapid walk round. Returning to town we entered two other churches,—San Fermo Maggiore, with an open ceiling in walnut wood, and the Duomo, which is

TOMB OF JULIET,–VERONA.

quaintly ornamented; but we had seen so many Italian churches elsewhere that we were rather attracted to a little building at the end of a garden, said to be the tomb of Juliet. One is fain to believe in it, but as matter of fact it is discredited. This tomb so-called Juliet's is an elegant, small, open, three-arched vault, or recessed covered place with slender double columns, containing within a sarcophagus. More certainty is attached to what is shown at a different part of the town as Juliet's window; but, alas for the romance! the window looks into the street, and it has no balcony.

So rapid a survey was not doing justice to fair Verona. There was much more to be seen in the town, while the river and its bridges and surroundings, and the neighbouring country, all looked so picturesque and inviting, that I have no doubt it is a favourite halting-place for the artist, and it may well repay a visit of some days.

XVI.

MILAN AND THE ITALIAN LAKES.

MILAN.

We left Verona at mid-day for Milan. The scenery was fine, and for some miles we had Lake Garda, the largest of the Italian lakes, in view, at one part as near as only a mile off. Here we passed over the field of the battle of Solferino, which took place on 24th June 1859. An interest naturally attaches to ground where not many years previously a great battle was fought, and so many events were being enacted terrible to the actors, but there is nothing specially to mark it out. The day had been clear when we started, but before we got to Milan the clouds began to gather, the sky became very black, and we unluckily arrived at four o'clock in a thunderstorm. However, we had not far to drive down the wide Corso to the Hôtel de Ville, which is well situated near the Cathedral, in the principal street of Milan.

We were out betimes next morning to see the glorious cathedral. It is certainly a magnificent church, inside and out, built of white marble, and of great size and height, being only inferior in size or extent to St.

Peter's.[1] It was not a little refreshing to see a Gothic church of any sort, after having had so much elsewhere in other styles. It is not divided into or surrounded by chapels, so that it wants the aid which these accessories afford for decoration; and therefore, in contrast with many less pretentious churches, there is a feeling of vacancy about it, although it is devoid of the gloom of the large, empty, dark Duomo of Florence. Fault, no doubt, has been found with the windows that they do not throw down the light sufficiently from above, but the windows themselves are traceried and filled with beautiful stained glass. Upon entering by the great portal at the west, the eye is caught in the far distance by the glimmering colours of the grand east window, whose dimensions are colossal, as may be gathered from the fact that its traceried compartments comprise no fewer than 350 pictures in glass, copies, in many instances, of known paintings. Then the eye is arrested by four long rows of lofty clustered columns—upwards of 50 in number in all—each 8 feet in diameter and 90 feet high, their comparative slenderness giving an airy character to the great interior, which rises in graceful pointed arches in the nave to the height of 152 feet. These pillars are most peculiarly adorned by a sort of double capital, between which are placed in canopied niches sculptured figures or statues in white marble, evincing that herein Milan is master; but somehow they do not attain the effect of a grand capital. The roof is painted in imitation fretwork or open carving, a species of deception which, however well done, is hardly to be expected, or even tolerated, where no cost has otherwise been spared.

The exterior has so light and fairy-like an appearance that one can hardly believe it to be of stone, and yet all

---

[1] Here, as in other things, measurements differ, one authority having it 443 feet long, another 477 feet, interior measurement. Though it may be shorter than St. Paul's of London, it is no doubt considerably wider, and covers, therefore, a greater area.

the parts which look so light and delicate are in reality massive and substantial marble. The mass or quantity of statues is really surprising. Niches innumerable contain them, studded at every conceivable spot over the huge building. Every one of the countless pinnacles, besides being adorned in successive courses by them, is surmounted by a statue, a mute mast-headed man, patiently and uncomplainingly remaining where he has been ordered to do duty, and so aiding to adorn the magnificent edifice. The number of marble statues inside and outside has been variously computed, but cannot be less than 4000. The central tower may be objected to as fully too small or too light for the size of the building, but it is in style in harmony with the numberless spirelets which rise like a forest around it, sometimes in clusters, and spanned by flying buttresses in lace-like decoration, which give strength and stability to a structure which, if it were not irreverent to say so, has a good deal of the look, in its white purity, of a most gigantic and beautiful bride-cake.

We lingered about the cathedral on our first visit for a long time. It was grand to hear the great organ pealing through the vast chamber, although the music was not so fine as it had been at St. Mark's on the Sunday.

The following morning (for while at Milan we never missed seeing it every day) we again entered the church, and found an important service proceeding, apparently either a levée, or, more likely, a consecration of priests. An old bishop wearing a large mitre sat on his throne, and one after another young men ascended and knelt before him, when he placed his paternal hands on the head of each successively, and apparently kissed him. The string of those who thus went up for consecration seemed, like Paddy's rope, to have had the other end cut off—we thought it would never terminate. But what struck me much was the remarkable want of intelligence in the faces of the old priests, particularly those who wore the grandest dresses; they had such a stupid, stolid look, reminding one very much of a 'donnered auld Hieland porter.' After witnessing enough of this ceremony, we ascended the stair leading to the summit, admission to which costs a small fee. The cathedral is 360 feet high, if not higher to the topmost point, for here also authorities differ; but the point I reached might not exceed 300 feet, and, if I am not mistaken, there did not seem to be open access to the public to a higher elevation. There are many breaks of the ascent by the way, where one can halt and look around and have a near view of the sculpture, which is by no means coarsely executed; the figures, however, upon the top of these long needle-shaped pinnacles convey a nervous dread of their stability, though, no doubt, securely fastened. About many of them lightning conductors are placed, without which they might only be points of attraction for the electric fluid. The roof of the building is composed of slabs of white marble in neat layers or courses overlapping each other upon a slope of moderate angle, giving a remarkably clean finish to the whole. It was glorious to think of this being a work of man. One could envy the feelings of the architect who had the honour to design and commence it, but did not live to see it completed. It was begun in 1385; the main body was finished thirty-three years later, but the central spire not till the year 1440. It may be said, therefore, that it is 450 years old, and yet it has such a freshness about it that one could readily suppose it is hardly a generation old. They are, however, always making additions to and repairing it. Standing upon the high tower, and surrounded by a forest of marble pinnacles and statues, and by rich sculpture at every point, the eye is yet attracted to the distant view from the summit, which is very magnificent. The country, which for miles from Milan is very flat but verdant, lies spread out in panorama, from Turin, 80 miles distant, to Venice, 150 miles off;

but Venice, at least, is too distant to be visible, and I doubt if Turin, even by aid of a glass, can be descried. Right in front to the north, and thence west and east, within a radius of from 80 to 100 miles, the grand mountain ranges of Switzerland lie. We saw some of the snowy peaks, but unfortunately the sky was clouded, and the view of most of them was obscured. But we took note of where Mont Blanc, the Matterhorn, Monte Rosa, and other old friends might have been seen on a clear day, though it would require a good telescope to distinguish the different mountain celebrities. The Italian lakes are, with the exception of Lake Garda, between 30 and 40 miles distant, but, shut in by the mountains, they are not visible, although we imagined we could make out their situation. The city of Milan lay compactly spread out all around just under us, the cathedral standing very much in the centre of all.

We were fortunate in getting a tolerably clear day for this ascent. I had intended to go up again on the following Monday, but found it too cloudy to be of any use. Another rather interesting sight, however, was in progress that day within the church; for an immense number of young children—boys and girls—were all seated in long rows round a vacant space, wherein were priests with candles, and an archbishop or some other dignitary, who was going round them. The girls were all dressed in white with white veils, the boys in their best attire, many of them with white ties and some with white waistcoats. The children seemed to be from seven to fifteen years of age, and by all it was evidently regarded as a grand gala-day—something like a public school examination-day in Scotland, before breaking up for the summer holidays. They were perhaps receiving confirmation. The procession of priests stopped at each child in rotation. The old bishop performed motions with his hands over each—I suppose making the form of the cross over them, and mumbling something inaudibly. It must have taken a long time so to go over them all, as there were several hundreds.

The people of Milan have wisely left a large vacant space or piazza in front of the cathedral, upon its west side, so that one can admire, without intervening interruption, its beauty from a sufficient distance. On the south side of the piazza, or rather of the cathedral, the Royal Palace, a plain building, is situated. The piazza itself is surrounded on three sides by new and very handsome commercial buildings, which are quite an ornament to the place; and out of it, upon the north side, there has been built, at an expense of no less than £320,000, the Galleria Vittorio Emanuele—a splendid arcade, or rather street or streets of stone buildings, laid out in the shape of a cross, covered over by an iron and glass vaulted roof, upon the Crystal Palace model. The main gallery is nearly 1000 feet long, about 50 feet wide, and 94 feet high; and it is occupied in the lower floor by shops, and the upper floors apparently by warehouses or other places of business, the façades being of an elegant style adorned by sculpture. The central dome is particularly graceful, and at night is lighted up by a circle of gas jets placed round the top. These, with the other lights, produce a most brilliant effect, and it is scarcely surprising to find that in the evening the gallery is crowded by the townspeople and strangers, so that passage through it is rather difficult. This gallery—really the most perfect thing of the kind I have seen anywhere—leads out at the other end to another piazza, in the centre of which a very fine marble monument to Leonardo da Vinci has been erected. He stands surrounded by four of his pupils, all of white marble. In another part of the town is the famous picture by that artist of the Last Supper, a fresco which is almost obliterated. The charge for admission to see this celebrated work is at the exorbitant rate of 1 franc per person.

There may be seen gratuitously on the streets of Milan a picture of a different kind in the elaborately made-up head-dress of the women. In a pad of hair at the back of the head a dozen or two of long pins, of more or less magnificence, are stuck, in arrangements to suit the fancy of the wearer, but most commonly in a fan shape. It is not for man to pry into the hidden mysteries of the toilet, but it seems scarcely possible for any woman to effect this elaborate tire unaided, nor is it probable that the effect is achieved by a daily effort. The amount of nightly torture by acupressure to which the Milanese women may therefore subject themselves, in obedience to a law of fashion, is not agreeable to contemplate. We can only be grateful.

In order to see a little of the town, we took a carriage one afternoon and drove out in the direction of the Piazza d'Armi, a large open space about 2000 feet square, outside the inhabited part of the city. The castle or barracks occupies one side of the square. The noble Arco della Pace, begun by Napoleon in 1804 as a termination to the Simplon route, faces the castle on the west side. It is of the same character as the triumphal arches of the Tuileries at Paris, and the Piazza Cavour at Florence, and is a beautiful three-arched gateway of white marble, Corinthian columns supporting an entablature, on the top of which a hero drives six fiery horses abreast, in utmost peril to himself and them (were they living), while a man on horseback at each of the four top corners, in equal peril and in violent action, holds up a conqueror's wreath. These figures, being in bronze, will not, it is supposed, readily commit an act of self-destruction.

On the north side of the piazza there is a large, modern, oval amphitheatre of wood, and without cover, within which races are held, and capable of accommodating 30,000 spectators.

From the piazza we proceeded to visit some of the churches, and *inter alia* the church of San Ambrogio, founded by Saint Ambrose in the fourth century. It is entered by passing through a large arcaded court or *atrium* in front, dating back a thousand years. The church, associated with various events in history, is ancient evidently, and peculiar in its interesting decoration, but not to be compared with that of San Zeno in Verona. On Sundays mass is celebrated, accompanied by the old Ambrogian music, but this we did not hear. The church of San Lorenzo was not far off—also a very ancient building, said, in part at least, to have been built in the fourth century. It is octagonal in form and surmounted by a dome. A colonnade of sixteen large Corinthian columns stands close by, and is thought to have formed part of a Roman building or temple, of which the church may at first have been also a part. All the churches, at the time of our visit, were being decorated for Trinity Sunday.

The picture gallery (the Pinacoteca) was unfortunately closed while we were in Milan, so that we missed seeing its frescoes and examples of the great masters. There is apparently not much more to be seen in Milan than what I have mentioned; but it contains some good streets and a public park—not of great extent—embracing within it in a zoological garden a small and not very valuable collection of animals. This park is no doubt a very nice retreat in hot weather. We spent an hour in it one afternoon, and while there witnessed a very novel method of watering the road. Attached to a water-barrel drawn on a cart, was a flexible pipe about five or six feet long and about six inches in diameter, with a bulb at the end perforated with holes. A man walked behind with a rope attached to the bulb, by which he jerked it about so as to spread the water from side to side all across the road. This man, who was endowed with a pair of five-o'clock legs, was, notwithstanding his deformity,—which seemed, indeed, to contribute to his power of dispersing the water,—somewhat of a wag, and with a wicked leer quietly contrived to bestow an amicable sprinkling on the laughing nurserymaids as he passed. The method of watering, however, was both novel and ingenious, and answered its purpose remarkably well. But there was little dust to lay in this rainy quarter; and indeed it never was, while we were in Milan, particularly hot, and perhaps it never is; while in winter-time, especially in December, it is sometimes a place of excessive cold.[1]

ITALIAN LAKES.

We left Milan for Baveno on Monday, 28th May, at noon. It was a slow train to Arona, where passengers embark on board the steamer on Lago Maggiore. Unfortunately, just before arrival at Arona, the rain began to fall heavily, so that we not only had to walk on board in the rain, but we did not see the lake to advantage. For although the rain shortly ceased, the clouds remained and no sunshine succeeded, and a haze hung over the lake, which then assumed very much the appearance of one of our Highland lochs in similar condition, except for the Italian character and bright colouring of the houses on the margin. On a sunny day the lake would, no doubt, wear a different aspect. Fortunately it continued fair till we got housed in the large, comfortable Hotel Belle Vue at Baveno, which, lying at the point of a jutting promontory upon the border of the lake, looks out right upon it. Soon afterwards, however, the rain again began, and it fell in torrents, to our great disappointment, and continued almost without intermission till the Friday afternoon, when it cleared up, and in the evening of that day we had a beautiful sunset, with the sun shining brightly upon the

---

[1] It is stated in one book that in December 1845 the thermometer registered as low as — 82·90°, equal to about — 185° Fahr. This was incredible; and on looking the Austrian official records I found it should have been — 2·9°, showing with what caution such statements in non-official books should be taken.

Simplon, to see which effect all the people in the hotel turned out upon a balcony commanding it. In consequence of the clouds we hardly ever could see across the lake, so much so that I could only finish on the Friday evening a sketch of it which I began on the Monday afternoon upon arrival, the mountains being invisible or under a gloomy pall nearly the whole intervening time. When we could catch the view it was very beautiful. The lake is here just sufficiently broad to form a fine picture, the bold, well-marked, conical mountains on the other or east side,—one of the peaks, I believe, rising to about 6000 feet,—the neighbouring town of Pallanza on the north, and the mountains behind it composing the background to the lake, studded by the charming Borromean Islands, lying so picturesquely near, with their curious houses and their trees; Isola Bella, with its strange gardens, being an especial feature. These islands are the great attraction to Baveno; but unfortunately we had not the opportunity of seeing them, except from the steamboat in passing, as the days were never fair sufficiently long to permit of our venturing in a boat to land upon them. If there be anything else to see in the neighbourhood of Baveno, as doubtless there was, we had little means of becoming acquainted with it, for usually upon venturing out for a walk we were speedily driven back again by warning drops. The town itself is a mere village, although the houses are capacious—bulky, barrack-looking—and the church on the slope above is large, with a high, square, ugly campanile. Luckily, the windows of our rooms, as well as of the public rooms, all looked over the lake; and there was a library of books for visitors' use, which, in this unpropitious condition of the atmosphere, received marked attention from all; but it was the dreariest time we had spent since we left home, reminding us rather too much of Loch Lomond in its normal condition.

When the Saturday morning came with bright sunshine

we were glad to avail ourselves of it, lest we might become prisoners for another week, and to be off accordingly for Lugano, which is situated on a portion of outlying Swiss territory overlapping Italy, so that one has to cross an odd nook of Switzerland to get from Maggiore to Lake Como. The trip in the steamboat is pleasant, and in crossing from Baveno to Pallanza, which is probably about three miles distant by water, we had the good fortune to see both the Simplon and Monte Rosa through a gap in the mountains — the latter raising its snowy head in the distance. Pallanza is a place which some people prefer to Baveno for stopping at in order to see Lago Maggiore. It is much more of a town, and, commanding the view of Monte Rosa, has a finer outlook, while it is not very much farther from Isola Bella and the other islands, a pull to which must be most enjoyable. From Pallanza the steamer crossed to the other side of the lake, then went up to Luino, where we disembarked, and on our leaving it proceeded to the northern extremity with those *en route* for the St. Gothard Pass. It was a glorious sail in the bright sunshine, with Monte Rosa, the Simplon, and also, in the upper portion, St. Gothard, all appearing snow-clad in view. The porter of the hotel had asked us to allow him to telegraph for a carriage to be waiting us at Luino, and willing to oblige him we consented, but we should have been better to have chosen one for ourselves upon arrival. However, it was a lovely drive of above two hours and a half to Lugano, part of the way being by the banks of a river, which was greatly swollen by the five days' previous rain. The Hotel du Parc at Lugano is nicely situated near the lake at the entrance to the town, and has a small garden attached to it. It was formerly a monastery, and is built as a large square house, with a courtyard in the middle. Bædeker recommends Lugano as a very pleasant place for a lengthened stay; and it may be so, but we were anxious to get on to Lake Como to rest there, and remained only three nights.

Hot sunny weather succeeded the week of rain, so that we enjoyed walks by the banks of the gleaming lake, plucking the wild-flowers, which were abundant, though not of many kinds. The town of Lugano looks very well in the distance —a mile off—at the head or north end of the lake; but it is not particularly enticing in itself, and it lies too much on the level of the water, so that the road was, when we arrived, half covered, the lake having, in consequence of the continued rain, overflowed its banks. The Lake of Lugano looks bold, and in a storm would look angry, from the fact that except at the north end the mountains appear to dip almost sheer down upon it. I believe the sail from the other end to Lugano (which is what those who purchase circular tickets from Milan obtain a coupon for) is very grand, but a gentleman I subsequently met told me he had experienced a terrific storm upon it, in which the vessel was in the greatest danger, as the sailors could not see where they were being driven to, by reason of a dense fog.

Upon the Monday we walked in a broiling sun, from which we could not always obtain shelter, about two miles up the road leading to the top of San Salvatore, which, 3000 feet high, is the great ascent here, and to those in good health and active, the exercise is rewarded by an extensive prospect, while a hotel offers refreshment on the summit. Choosing shady places where to rest, we spent a charming day upon this road, which everywhere commanded fine views, particularly down upon the lake and up to the snowy mountains of the St. Gothard range.

In the old church adjoining the hotel there are three frescoes by Luini, a pupil of Leonardo da Vinci. The principal fresco, that of the Crucifixion, is a curious large picture, containing within it, expressively depicted and cleverly arranged, all the different scenes connected with the death of our Saviour, from His trial to His ascension. But the three crosses are lengthened to what represents 20 feet at least, in order to admit of use being made of the background. Many angels are ministering to our Lord, while one angel is on the cross of the repentant thief, and a devil crawling along the other cross has charge of his sinful fellow. A skull and cross-bones at the foot of the central cross indicate the place to be Golgotha. The picture is quite a study.

We left Lugano for Bellaggio on the Monday morning by steamer for Porlezza, at the east end of the lake, about ten miles distant. Before reaching it we crossed the invisible line which here separates Italy from Switzerland, and the steamer was boarded by an Italian custom-house officer. Upon arrival at Porlezza our luggage underwent the formality of examination, and we the reality of detention for a considerable time until the examination was concluded. From this town to Menaggio, on Lake Como, the drive was in an omnibus, and we regretted much afterwards not having had a carriage to ourselves, as we could see little from the omnibus windows. The distance is about six or seven miles, and inclines gradually to the shoulder of a hill overlooking Lake Como; and in such a bright, sunny day as we were favoured with, the drive in an open carriage would have been delightful, especially on approaching Lake Como from the high ground, where it is seen lying magnificently below. One advantage of a private carriage is that it may be stopped at the will of the party, and the scene viewed at leisure. Coach and omnibus fares here were quite after Highland rates. At Menaggio, finding the steamboat would not arrive for an hour and a half, we took a boat (charge, 3 fr.), and were in three-quarters of an hour rowed across the lake to the Hotel Grand Bretagne, which is nicely situated away to the south end of Bellaggio, and outside the small town. It was hot, broiling sunshine, and this, our first experience of a boat upon Como, was exceedingly charming. Blinds were all down, and nobody observed our arrival, so our boatman had to shout from the quay

BELLAGGIO.—LAKE COMO.

across the garden to the hotel porter. We found very comfortable quarters in this hotel, which is a large, long building, with many bedrooms looking to the lake; for, if I am not mistaken, there were upwards of 100 bedroom windows overlooking it. The ground floor is entirely occupied by a suite of public rooms, terminating at one end in a large, airy dining-hall, and on the other in a superb, similarly large drawing-room, both with suitably lofty ceilings. Other public rooms on this floor are occupied as *salles à manger* and *salons de conversation, de concert et de lecture, de billiard*, etc. In one of the reading-rooms there was a small library for the use of the visitors. I do not think we had found anywhere such ample public accommodation within doors, while in front a large garden extended the whole length of the house, reaching up into grounds and a wood behind, with shady seats under the trees, where one could sit and read, or look out upon the lovely views, or watch the passing steamers and pleasure-boats, or observe the countless green lizards which at Bellaggio, as elsewhere in these warm regions, were constantly making rapid runs over the paths.

Here we remained for about a fortnight, resting and enjoying our rest. From our windows we looked across to lofty mountains on the opposite shore, with Cadenabbia and Menaggio lying at their foot, while away to the north end of the lake a range of snowy peaks rose as if barricading exit in that direction, and forming a fine, important feature in the landscape. The Lake of Como is in fact completely hemmed in by high, steep, bare mountains, which fall with considerable abruptness down upon it, leaving but a small border of land for cultivation and habitation. The principal mountain opposite Bellaggio is San Crucione, which rises to a sharp peak, taking six or seven hours to ascend; but it is stated to command striking views of the snowy Alps, and especially of the Monte Rosa chain, 'une armée de géants.' The mountain itself is no doubt a study for the geologist, as it offers a most extraordinary exhibition of upheaval of strata, the face of it showing in a great waving line, commencing near the margin of the lake and sloping up the face to near the top, a huge stratum of rock, which in the distance appears to be of sandstone, but more likely is of limestone formation, uplifted probably nearly 3000 feet.

The borders of Lake Como are fringed with trees, in some places a few hundred feet up, and dotted with those small, picturesque Italian villages, each with its church and campanile, which always give such a charm to the landscape.

The town of Bellaggio is small but rather curious. Where it borders the lake an arcade has been formed, with terraces projecting from the houses and covering the roadway. In this arcade and elsewhere a few small shops offer articles for sale, and particularly small things in olive wood, the manufacture of which is an industry of the place. The wood is more darkly marked than at Sorrento or in the south of France, sometimes to the extent of being blotchy. Photographs, principally of the lake scenes and sculptures in the neighbourhood, can be procured, but, though good, they are dear for Italy.

Half-way up the hill at the foot of which Bellaggio stands, reached by a steep road, is the Villa Serbelloni. This is now a dependance of the 'Grande Bretagne,' and in the season is said to be always full. It is a *pension* for protracted stay, not for a passing night. What the comforts of the house itself may be, whether the *pension* be good or not, I do not know; but the house is most charmingly situated, surrounded by the extensive grounds of the place, nicely laid out with long terrace walks winding up the hill, crowned on the top by the ruin of what was probably an old castle. The hill is covered with trees, affording delicious shade from the sun, while the roses climb about them to a height of 50 or 60 feet, and with the other flowers make it a sort of enchanted land. From the top of the hill, views are had all round and up the lake to the snowy mountains of the Splugen Pass, and down the lake, which here is forked, one prong running in the direction of Como, and the other of Lecco.

It was hot sunshine all the time we were at Bellaggio, diversified by two grand thunderstorms, accompanied by vivid flashes of lightning, sheet and forked, one of which flashes set fire to a tree or a church on the opposite shore. It was a dreamy life, too hot to do very much; but there was always a little excitement at the departure and arrival of the steamboats, which go up and down the lake, and to and from Lecco, several times a day; and if we had no better amusement, it was great fun to feed the fishes abounding in the lake; the water being so clear one could see their every motion, and watch the caution with which, proportioned to their age and consequent experience, they would approach the bread. When a piece was thrown in, there would be a general assembly to the spot. The young ones would at once dart at it, trying to seize it, but, being much too big for their little mouths, ineffectually. Then, after a little, larger ones would come snuffing at it without touching; by and by, perceiving no symptom of hook or line, would get bolder, and, thinking all safe, would venture to the attack. Then still larger ones would come and swim in large circles round and round it, thinking, thinking, till possibly the piece was gobbled up by younger ones before their thoughts were matured. But generally there would be quite a scramble and a splutter, twenty fishes together, after a single piece, which got less and less by successive dabs, till a big fellow made a dart and swallowed it whole. But sometimes the piece was too large for even his throat; it was speedily disgorged, and then another scramble took place, till it wholly disappeared among them.

A charming variety in our life was to take one of the small pleasure-boats, always lying at the hotel quay for engagement, and pull about on the lake, although at noon it was fully too hot even for that. Still we had several delightful sails upon the lake. One of these was across to the Villa Carlotta. This residence contains some exquisite sculptures, particularly the 'Cupid and Psyche' by Canova, which, by means of photographs, and sometimes in alabaster copies, is so well known. Also 'Innocence,' a winged youth or maiden holding a pair of doves, by Bien Aimé; and a large frieze, with reliefs, by Thorwaldsen, which cost £15,000. The hall in which this beautiful collection of sculptures is placed does not seem worthy of it. It looks rather like a receptacle or storage room till the proper hall be ready; but one would almost wish that such gems of art could be seen in a less inaccessible place. The grounds of the villa are delightful; the vegetation is quite tropical, while the views are superb, especially looking across to Bellaggio and the lofty mountains bordering the other side of Lake Lecco, which tower like a huge wall of rock behind the Serbelloni Hill. Returning to our boat, we rowed round the coast, which contains very many luxuriant spots; one of the most lovely of these was a little summer-house by the banks of the lake, filled with graceful drooping acacias and brilliant summer flowers—one of those 'juicy bits' which artists so much prize.

On another occasion we visited the Villa Melzi, lying upon the Bellaggio side. It contains some good sculptures, but not equal to those in the Villa Carlotta. The gardens, however, were fascinating—shady walks with sloping grass banks, lofty trees, and all by the margin of the smiling lake. One could hardly imagine a more romantic residence, but the proprietor occupies it only two months in the year—September and October. We did long for the power of transplanting such places, with all their sunshine and clear blue sky, to our native land.

The sail in the steamboat to Como takes about two hours, and is a very charming excursion. The lake winds about among the mountains, and the boat, crossing from side to side, touches every now and then at one of those picturesque Italian villages which adorn the lake and form such admirable subjects for the painter's brush. At the south end, where the town of Como lies, the mountains dwindle down to insignificant hills, and the town is built for the most part on a large level plain, which probably has been gained from the lake by deposit. The town is one of some size, its principal ornament being the cathedral, a large and imposing church with a dome built of white marble, and finely ornamented within by sculpture. This and the adjoining Broletto, or Town Hall, built in alternate courses of black and white marble, with an open arcade below, and an old tower by its side, are, with the cathedral, the attractions of the ancient city of Como.

The sail in the other direction, towards the snowy mountains, is much grander, and also takes about two hours, stopping at Colico. The sail upon Lake Lecco we did not take.

It was too hot to walk to any distance, but one forenoon two of us ventured exploringly as far as St. Giovanni, a small fishing village with two churches, about a mile or more to the south of Bellaggio. Here quantities of the fish caught in the lake by means of nets were hanging up to dry and be baked in the sun. On our way we passed a monument in course of erection to some Principe, whose name I did not gather, curiously composed of a combination of red brick, granite, and marble; and not far off the ruins of a church, whose tall square campanile, remaining standing, was an object in the landscape.

In one of our walks, we found lying on the road one after another three small snakes, which had been killed and left there. They were probably about 15 inches in length and ⅝ths of an inch thick.

We had a continuance of hot weather, and in those glorious days this was generally the even tenor of our way. In the early morning, too soon to rise and dress, but tempted to look out at window, we could see that the sun was illuminating the snowy peaks of the Splugen range, and casting a brilliant light on San Crucione and all the hills on that, the other side of the lake. By nine o'clock the sun had obtained power; but it was a great joy to go out after breakfast and stroll under the shade of the trees by the banks of the limpid blue water, and look across its lustrous expanse to the opposite shore, fringed with verdure, out of which rose the giant mountains circling the lake, and over all to the clear blue Italian sky, making, with the broad snowy range of peaks in the north, one of the loveliest pictures we had seen in Italy. Then, when the sun came round to the south, the air, heated as by a furnace, trembled with the sultry glow, and all blinds were drawn down, and the houses looked asleep. Everything was still, save when at given hours the steamboat paddles beat upon the water, or the bell announced arrival or departure. We would return to the hotel for shade and coolness, have lunch, read our letters or answer them, dip into the newspapers, say good-bye to those who were leaving, or sometimes be gladdened by meeting old travelling friends just come; or, failing any more important occupation, take up a book and withdraw to a sofa in the great cool *salon*, to obtain a quiet read. Then in time the dressing-bell would ring, and we would shortly after assemble at dinner, and enjoy pleasant intercourse with those around. Dinner over, some of the visitors, especially among those just arrived, would embark in pleasure-boats upon the lake; and others (ladies throwing a shawl over the shoulders, and a hat upon the head) would sit out in the garden a good while, conversing and looking upon the fair prospect and the boats gliding along, their oars gently touching and turning the silver water and leaving a ripple behind; and, by and by, the sun would retire and set behind the mountains; and though the lesser orb, being then in its infancy, could not afford us the resplendent spectacle of full moon on the lake, the stars were on the *qui vive*, and, stealthily sending their pale twinkling scouts to peep timidly out and reconnoitre, would all, the moment the enemy disappeared, with bold face rise, each in its appointed position, and, as they slowly and silently, but steadily, pursued the sun in his flight, hang out their far-shining lamps, radiant in green and gold, to light up the beauteous scene. The very rapture of the frogs, as they maintained, agreeably to themselves, an incessant 'wrack-wrack,' seemed not out of place; while the glow-worm, with greater humanity, and in greater keeping with all around, would turn upon the garden paths its glittering tail. But as it became dark, and visitors had one by one retreated to the house, it would happen that either from our shore or from the Cadenabbia shore, the hotelkeepers began to burn coloured lights, ignite fireworks, and send rockets blazing and bursting high up into the air; and, this show being over, it was time to retire to rest, and, if the heat would admit of sleep, perchance to repeat our experience of the day in visions of the night, and wake on the morrow for another such day. And so, like many others similarly placed, we dreamed away this blissful fortnight.

But we were now in the middle of June, and the season seemed to be drawing to a close, and probably a month later, when the sun's heat would be intolerable, Bellaggio might become altogether deserted. The numbers at the hotel lessened day by day, so that for a week I was at the head of the table as the oldest inhabitant. It was warning we must move on. We must leave this land of Beulah; bid adieu for a time to the sunny soil and sky of Italy, where we had now spent nearly four months, and proceed to the cooler regions of Switzerland by the neighbouring Splugen Pass.

SWITZERLAND—FRANCE.

XVII.

THE SPLUGEN PASS, SWITZERLAND.

THE SPLUGEN PASS.

VETTURINI are always hanging about the hotels at Bellaggio, to be engaged either by the landlords or directly by travellers, although their usual course is to refer the inquirer to the landlord, to arrange with whom no doubt they have an understanding. But one labours under the disadvantage, by hiring at Bellaggio, of not seeing either the carriage or the cattle which are to convey you over the mountain — perhaps, too, in a thunderstorm. Therefore, and because of the high charge at the hotels, I took, before travelling, the steamer to Colico at the head of the lake, and arranged for a carriage thence to be waiting the arrival of the boat on the following Monday; and an English gentleman and his wife agreed to accompany us.

Monday proved a fine day, without too much sun, and we left Bellaggio by steamer at half-past ten with not a little regret. The sail up the lake, amongst the bold mountains with which it is enclosed, and by the nine little Italian villages on its margin, to visit which the steamer crosses from side to side, giving thus alternately the view from each side at different points, is very enjoyable, although it was trying to think we were so soon to bid adieu to it all. At Colico the mountains are rugged and bare, and the lake gets very marshy, so that the locality is unhealthy. Here the carriage was ready for us, and it took about three hours' drive to reach Chiavenna, the road winding for a long way by the Lagunes of the lake. Upon leaving Colico we were immediately among the mountains, the road gradually ascending. The drive was beautiful, but extremely dusty.

Chiavenna is an Italian and old Roman village town about 1100 feet above the level of the sea, very picturesquely buried among the bluff high mountains which closely hem it in on every side, and upon the heights of some of which patches of snow were visible in many places. It lies at the foot of the Splugen Pass, and on the river Maira, which, crossed by a good stone bridge, pours a torrent of water down from the snowy heights. We had time, both before dinner and after, to stroll about and see the little that was to be seen. Chiavenna is celebrated for its beer, and we thought it our duty to try it as the wine of the country, expecting to get it in perfection, but found it very flat. We had had it better at Bellaggio.

Soon after seven o'clock the following morning, we left the hotel, and had three hours of a most laborious ascent to Campo Dolcino, only eight miles distant. The three horses with which we started, afterwards supplemented by a fourth, toiled up innumerable zigzags, getting higher and higher at every turn, but making very little onward progress; so that generally some of us would get out of the carriage, and by climbing up at the end of one zigzag to the end of the next, meet its slow arrival there. The distant views as we proceeded were fine, and improved the higher we mounted; while in the narrow valley beneath,—farther and farther beneath as we got higher and higher,—the river was seen wending its foamy course, augmented at little intervals by every fresh rivulet which rushed to embrace it from the lovely waterfalls descending in long, silver-grey, horse-tail streams from the mountains opposite, in bright white contrast with the brown rocks over which they dashed and fell. There is not much to be seen at Campo Dolcino. It is a small village in a bleak-looking district; but, stopping for three hours to rest the horses, look about, and obtain lunch at the little inn, we proceeded on our way up the pass. Soon afterwards we reached the Madesimo waterfall, which is near to the road; and all turned out to see this famous cascade from a small stone gallery above it, whence the water is observed rolling over and tumbling and sinking in one grand heap 700 feet down, scattering, by the mere force of the descent, into a cloud of spray below. Little by little we continued ascending, passing in the way through three long tunnels (one of them 1530 feet in length), built to protect from the avalanches, which at certain seasons would otherwise bury the road; and at last we reached the region of perpetual snow, where the inaccessible Alpine roses bloom, and amidst blue gentians springing from the banks on the roadside. Mile after mile we passed along the road cut through the snow, not pure or clean, standing consolidated on each side, like the Red Sea when the Israelites passed over its channel and the waters were divided and became 'a wall unto them on their right hand and on their left;' very possibly by the action of frost upon the sea as it fled from the pressure of the fierce east wind which made the sea dry land. But though there was no fear of our experiencing the fate of Pharaoh's host, our walls were slowly melting away in little trickling streamlets at every part, under the influence of the hot sun, no doubt to be made good again by a snowstorm from the next moisture in the air. As we approached the top of the pass, the scene became wild and dreary. Immense fields of snow lay spread out in a melting condition, sending down innumerable streams, all converging on the river which descends to Chiavenna, and by whose side, though generally at a great elevation above, our road had all along lain, the large roaring torrent at Chiavenna being here but a small turbid stream. But the cold-looking, slushy snow-field afforded an admirable notion of how these rivers are fed.

We reached the summit, which is 6945 feet high, and is surrounded by lofty mountains, one of them 9925 feet, and another 10,748 feet high, covered with their white mantle, and, by an optical illusion, looking nearer and lower than they really were. The feeling (perhaps arising out of our having been so lately in the midst of all that was suggestive of heat) was strange upon finding ourselves in the vicinity of such cold peaks, and very much as if we had been suddenly tumbled into the arctic regions—desolate, barren, impassable retreats for man, and yet not altogether so; for the boundary line between Switzerland and Italy lies at the top of the pass, and not far below this great altitude the Italian *douane* station has been built. One would imagine the position hardly tenable by the poor custom-house men in winter months. The traveller into Switzerland, however, is not troubled by any *douanier*.

Here two of the horses were liberated, and dashing down with the remaining two along many zigzags, we gradually came in sight of the village of Splugen, 2200 feet below, and about five miles distant from the summit, passing by on the way a river which gradually got larger and larger, and proved to be the source, or one of the sources, of the Rhine. We arrived about half-past five, making it a journey of fully ten hours to traverse a distance, between Chiavenna and Splugen, at least as the crow flies, of not more than sixteen miles.

SWITZERLAND.

We remained in Switzerland from the 19th June to the 11th September, nearly three months; and as I wish to notice our movements in it, for the most part in well-beaten paths, merely by way of connection, I shall do so very briefly. We had decided to spend another winter in the Riviera, and with a view to this to pass the remainder of the summer in Switzerland, and thereafter cross over France to Pau and Biarritz, to spend there the period intervening, till it should be time to move onwards to Mentone.

The Swiss village of Splugen has a southern exposure, and lies very picturesquely with its church on the slope and top of a little eminence, at an altitude of 4757 feet above the sea, overlooking a valley out of which lofty mountains raise their heads, one of them to the north behind the village itself. Pine forests are planted on the slopes, affording, no doubt, a little shelter from the cold north winds. Like all such places, it looks best at a little distance; and, approaching it from the opposite hill, it seemed a pretty village of wooden houses, built in the Swiss chalet style, and therefore quite a change from the Italian houses to which our eyes had been for the last few months accustomed. The accommodation was primitive. We were lodged in a large wooden hotel. The temperature, too, and the aspect of everything was changed. We had bidden adieu to the heat of Italy, and found it much colder upon the northern side of the mountains. This produced an accident which was annoying to me, and created a good deal of after trouble, as in winding up my watch at night the chain gave way, I presume, owing to the jump from great heat to frosty cold to which it had been subjected. The attempt I afterwards made in Switzerland to get it repaired only made matters worse, and the ultimate repair at home costly. One would almost require to carry a spare watch in travelling among these localities. We had time to see a little of Splugen in the evening. The fields were literally covered with bright flowers, tempting us to pluck many handfuls. Although standing so high, the valley does not give one the impression of its great elevation.

Before eight o'clock next morning, we started for Coire. Down and down we drove by the banks of the roaring and foaming Rhine, the road and river being beautifully wooded. The drive was most charming. At every mile the river got larger, while the mountains reared their heads above, to heights varying from 8000 to 11,000 feet. In about two hours' time we reached the Via Mala, where the mountains or rocks converge, and the river dashes far below, in some places nearly hidden by the pines thickly set upon the precipitous banks, wherever they can obtain a footing. At one time the pass may have been a dangerous one; but now, although it be still impressive, the road is good, and there is nothing to fear, notwithstanding the cliffs rise perpendicularly to a great height, higher even than they appear to do. Yet, were a mass of rock to loosen and fall, and block up the road or tear it away, it would be decidedly awkward for persons passing. The gorge, at which you look straight up and straight down, is well seen from a bridge, where a man was ready to plump a big stone into the torrent far down in the depths below. Everybody walks through the pass; the most indifferent to grand effects could hardly sit still in his carriage. I suppose it is possible to get to some safe place near the water, as photographs have been taken looking up to the bridge; and so seen, it appears perched high above, over steep and even impending rocks, which, save for a tree here and there, are smooth and bare, and form a narrow, ugly, perilous cleft, through which the river flows at the bottom.

Emerging from the pass, and just out of it, we reached the clean and tidy but shadeless village of Thusis, which lay basking in the hot sun, though not so hot as we had had it at Lake Como. There is a good hotel here, but one might well dispense in such places with men-waiters, black coats, and white ties. From the garden of the hotel, an excellent view is had of the entrance to the pass. Here we rested two and a half hours, and then drove on to Coire by the banks of the Rhine, looking up to the lofty mountains with their snowy tops, and across a well-wooded landscape. At Coire there is a railway to Zurich, by which we had intended to proceed; but, arranging with the driver, he took us on to Ragatz, about two hours farther, where we arrived at half-past five, the last half hour being in a thunderstorm. It had been down hill the whole way since we left Splugen in the morning, and the horses, notwithstanding the fatigues of the preceding day, went briskly along, and apparently returned next morning; for it is not the habit of the owners of these Swiss conveyances, if they can help it, to give their horses a day's rest after excessive fatigue. We enjoyed our three days' drive amazingly, through scenery alternately grand, wild and desolate, or beautiful and romantic. A more pleasant excursion could not be planned; but to be enjoyed, it requires to be taken in the way we did. One has not the same freedom in travelling by diligence, and besides it goes on night and day, and passes through the best of the scenery in the dark.

Ragatz lies a little beyond the range of the usual tourists' track, and we had not ourselves visited it before. It is very charmingly situated, at the entrance of the Gorge of Pfäffers, in a valley up from that of the Rhine flow, and hemmed in by high, bold mountains, which, from the Ragatz side, look like immense walls, on whose higher slopes some patches of snow were then visible. The village is small and spotlessly clean, externally at least, and the

Hotel Quellenhoff, a large new comfortable house, has grounds attached to it which afford pleasant retreats and walks. It is, however, a somewhat noisy establishment, being one of those Continental watering-places where a band of music, paid for by a daily tax on each visitor, plays morning and night to the accompaniment of out-door drinking. We found the house full of Germans, and having one or two distinguished visitors, among whom were the King of Saxony and Count Arnim. In the public breakfast room we found one morning four Germans smoking at a table—a disgusting piece of rudeness which is sometimes experienced in Switzerland. In the grounds there are a kursaal, where the band plays, a newsroom, and a bookseller's stall—all under one roof; and in another neat range of buildings, shops for the sale of Swiss and other articles, a fountain flowing with Pfäffers water, and baths of the same.

The walk up the Pfäffers Gorge is very interesting. Crossing a rustic wooden bridge over a deep rapid torrent, not very wide, however, the road at once begins to lead into a confined valley, the rocks or hills on either side rising steeply, and leaving room only for the river and the road by its side, with an occasional widening. It is well wooded all along, the pine trees affording shelter to some extent from the sun when it penetrates, as it does in certain positions. The seclusion is alluring, but it is not altogether free from danger. At one place my daughter ran up a bank, and came flying back to say that she had found a snake moving in the grass at her feet. An older person, less observant, would in all likelihood have trod upon it.[1] As we proceeded, the mountains seemed to rise higher and higher overhead; and, about two and a half miles from

---

[1] Afterwards, at Interlachen, when standing on a rustic bridge, she saw a small snake crawling on the path, and called to me. It was about 15 to 18 inches long. I went and pitched it into the stream.

Ragatz, the rocks approach still closer, and a large hotel, seemingly very much out of place, greets the eye. Here tickets are procured for entrance to the gorge itself. It is effected through the hotel to a wooden gallery resting on a ledge cut out of the rock, which impends at a by no means assuring acute angle immediately overhead, and even some way beyond the shaky platform. Looking down the abyss, the water is seen below flowing still and deep and fast through the narrow cleft; and this cleft rises high, as we can see the rocks appearing to all but touch above, while one side inclines to the other with an apparent appalling desire to embrace. It looks as if an earthquake had split up the rock, and as if another shock might at once and for ever close it up again. It is a damp, gloomy sort of cavern, till one reaches the part where the hot spring escapes from the rocks, one half of it flowing into the river in a huge spout, and the remainder being carried in a long pipe to Ragatz to supply the baths there. We entered by a door into a cave in the rock, a distance of probably 50 or 60 feet, pitch dark, hot, and vaporous, where we had given us a little of the hot water to drink, not disagreeable to the taste. Afraid of chill, we left in time to get back to Ragatz ere the road should be in shade.

We should have stayed at Ragatz with pleasure for at least a week, but, expecting letters at Lucerne, remained only three nights. Leaving the hotel at half-past eight, we had a tedious journey, as we did not arrive at Lucerne (only about 76 miles distant by rail) till four o'clock, the railway passing through a very pretty country, well wooded and watered, stopping at every station by the way, and for an hour at the town of Zurich. Leaving in sunshine, we were again unfortunate enough to arrive at Lucerne in heavy rain, which, with previous falls, had caused the lake to overflow its banks.

We spent three nights at Lucerne, and had rain great part of the time. We were fortunate, however, to obtain, on the Tuesday, a charming sunny day to cross the lake and proceed by diligence to Interlachen by the Brunig Pass. The steamboat left the quay at Lucerne at 10.10 for Alpnacht, and we did not get to Interlachen till about 8 P.M., having had, however, two long halts by the way to enable the passengers to dine or obtain refreshment and to rest the horses. We had the interior of the diligence to ourselves, and, though objecting at first to the closeness, it afforded cover from the sun, then in full power. The other passengers were accommodated in other and open carriages. The sail and drive are both beautiful; the sunset upon the Jungfrau awaiting our arrival was one of the finest we enjoyed while at Interlachen, tinting the snow with a shining glow of bright red light, which gradually left the lower parts till the shade ascended to the summit; and then the whole mountain was as if dead, but it shortly after returned to life in the like ruddy hue of the after-glow,—a beautiful effect we did not often afterwards witness.

We had several times visited Interlachen before. It was at this time very empty. We had arrived in the German season, and there were few but Germans there. The English do not generally begin to come to Switzerland until the middle or end of July, when Interlachen becomes crowded, and it is difficult to secure good accommodation. We found little change in the place since we were last there (five years previously), but the prices of the Swiss carvings on wood exhibited in the shops had risen very considerably.

Interlachen, with which we had many associations, is a charming spot at which to remain for some time, and I arranged for my family to stay at the Jungfrau Hotel *en pension*, which they did for above two months, and during part of this time I went home on a flying visit. It is an admirable centre for excursions, while the place itself is, especially in the height of the season, exceedingly attractive. The hotels are for the most part situated on the north side of the high road conducting in one direction to Thun and Berne, and in the other to Brienz, Meyringen, and Lucerne, always full of life. Though the hotels are large, they retreat from the road, and have not the towny look which large hotels generally have. The trees, and the flowers, and the pretty chalets, and the wood-carving shops, and the background of mountains—all confer a rustic look, as seen from the highway, which is greatly enhanced by the large open field so properly kept open upon the south side of the road, lined by fine old trees, between which one catches sight of the picturesque church and the equally picturesque houses at some distance, and behind them the ranges of green mountains and the conical tree-covered hill called the Jungfraublick; but beyond all, the grand view of the majestic snow-clad Jungfrau itself, fifteen miles off, seen at the termination of the magnificent vista afforded by the gap in the mountains which lie between it and Interlachen; by a road through which Grindelwald, Lauterbrunnen, the Wengern Alp, and the Murren are reached—all glorious excursions.

Then there are the Lakes of Thun and Brienz, both affording delightful steamboat trips, and in the locality round about innumerable walks. However, like most places among the mountains, great changes in the weather often take place, and frequent thunderstorms with drenching rain, intermingled with glowing hot days, are experienced. We had a fair share of both.

When I thought to make a run to Scotland, I found that leaving by a train to Berne at 9.50 A.M., and proceeding by Neufchatel and Dijon, I could get to Paris by 5.35 next morning, stopping two hours by the way at Berne.

On the return journey, leaving Paris at 7.40 evening, I did not get to Interlachen till near dinner-time next day, being compelled to spend four hours again at Berne. These stoppages are annoying to those who have been at Berne before, and, as a train leaves just immediately antecedent to the arrival of the train from the north, they might at least in that case easily be avoided. But probably the intention is to compel a short stay at Berne.

We had heard Chateau d'Œx highly spoken of as a pleasant, cool retreat, where we might be invigorated by Highland breezes for the coming winter.

Having engaged a carriage for this rather long drive, we left Interlachen on 28th August about 7.30 A.M., and had a splendid but cruelly hot day. The distance, I should imagine, might possibly be fifty miles, if so much; for certainly we did not go on an average at a greater speed than five miles per hour,—considerable part of the way being indeed just crawling up the hill. After leaving Interlachen by the south bank of Lake Thun, we soon got into the shade of the hill, and it was chilly, causing all wraps to be in requisition. Reaching high ground over Spiez, we took our last view of Interlachen in the distance, with the smoke of morning fires hanging over it. From this point the road lay in a long valley between two ranges of hills, which, after those we had been so long looking upon, did not appear high. Everything was now in bright sunshine, and the valley and the slopes were so verdant and luxuriant as to make the drive lovely, though scarcely, except at one or two parts, could it be called grand. We passed many little villages, all looking so sleepy in the sun, but evidently prosperous. Soon after twelve we stopped at the little town of Boltigen, to rest the horses for two hours and dine at the hotel with the sign, life-size, of the gilded bear, kept by a pleasant young woman, who strove to make us comfortable. The road after Boltigen was still up hill till we reached a point whence descent is made to Sarnen, the centre of the famous Gruyère cheese district, and soon after we came in sight of Chateau d'Œx, with its picturesque church, formerly a castle, on the top of an isolated conical hill, from which the small town takes its name. This chateau or church at once arrests the eye, and gives character to the place; but the town itself lies at the foot of the eminence, and is 3260 feet above the sea. Bold mountains, well wooded, rise on every side, and are probably, some of them, 5000 or 6000 feet high—all contributing to fill a considerable river in the valley a good way below. There are several hotels in the town, and chalet pensions on the slopes above, the pension in all being amazingly moderate, somewhat upon the scale which formerly prevailed throughout Switzerland. The Hotel Berthod, at which we stopped, accommodates about eighty people, and is built of wood, the appointments being somewhat rough, though clean. The season is short, but the hotel is for part of the time full. As it is so much out of the beaten track, the society is probably more select than it sometimes is in other parts of Switzerland. For the active, there are abundance of nice walks in the immediate neighbourhood. The air, though in day-time hot, was invigorating; but as we were getting near the end of the season, it had a tendency at night at this elevation to get cold. We therefore only spent eight days there, though very pleasantly.

On leaving Chateau d'Œx, we took the diligence to the pretty large town of Aigle, and to reach it had slowly to ascend the mountains to an altitude of between 5000 and 6000 feet. It was a most charming ride or walk, and I got out and walked several miles ahead of the lumbering conveyance. The descent from the summit of the pass continues to Sepey, a village where we halted for lunch, and said to be another charming centre, with pension upon the same moderate scale as we had just experienced. The views here were very fine, but the place itself did not strike me as so desirable as Chateau d'Œx, although it has the advantage of being more accessible. From Sepey we descended to Aigle, where there is a large hotel or hydropathic establishment just out of the town. The diligence deposited us at the railway station nearly an hour previous to the train to Montreux on the Lake of Geneva being due.

From its comparatively sheltered situation, Montreux is much frequented during winter months, and it is a little warmer than Geneva or Lausanne; but during part of the winter the temperature of Montreux is, I believe, lower than that of London and Edinburgh, so that possibly it may therefore not be suitable as a winter resort for those having delicate constitutions. The picturesque and interesting Castle of Chillon lies about two miles off, nearer the upper end of the lake. Our bedroom windows commanded the view of the lake, together with the Dent du Midi in the distance, so that the prospect was always pleasing. Montreux is rather too much of a town, and the walls and houses shut out almost completely the sight of the lake from the road or street. The adjoining town of Clarens, nearly united to it, appears to be, on the whole, nicer for summer residence.

After being at Montreux for a few days, we left by the steamboat, and had a lovely sail to Geneva, where, in the afternoon, just before dinner, we obtained a good glimpse of Mont Blanc in the distance unveiled. Resting one night, we proceeded to Lyons by train next day, and were once more in France.

XVIII.

BIARRITZ.

I HAD thought it might have been possible to arrange for proceeding across country from Lyons to Biarritz by a westerly line, say by Clermont, instead of by the Mediterranean line, which we had already travelled. But although there are lines in that direction, it seemed extremely difficult to make them fit in so that we could, upon stopping at any place, obtain next day a train at a suitable hour for prosecuting the journey. Not only so, but being quite out of the ordinary beat of tourists, and especially of English tourists, one could not possibly rely on getting such hotel accommodation by the way as is desirable and is procurable on the beaten tracks. I therefore gave up this thought, though not till after some laborious studies of the *Livret Chaix*, and after consulting Cook's agent at Geneva, who, I found, did not issue tickets towards Biarritz. There seemed no alternative, therefore, but to go by the Chemin de Fer du Midi, the Paris and Marseilles Railway. We had hoped, it being the 12th September, to have seen the Rhone in all its summer beauty, but were disappointed. The day was dull and misty when we started, and soon after it began to rain; so that we could see little, and everything looked dismal, whereas in summer sunshine the prospect is no doubt very lovely. Before we reached Avignon (in six hours ten minutes) the rain ceased. We stopped a night there (see p. 135), and had fortunately good weather. Next afternoon brought us to Nismes, two hours distant from Avignon by rail; and after another night in our old quarters there, and seeing places this time in sunshine instead of shrouded by the mistral, which prevailed during our visit in the previous year, we left at mid-day for Toulouse, arriving at this large city about eleven o'clock at night. There is not another train by which we could have proceeded from Nismes to Toulouse during day, nor is there any place nearer Toulouse where it is desirable to stop except Montpellier; but Montpellier is only an hour distant from Nismes, and better adapted, therefore, for stoppage coming from Toulouse on the return journey, and on our return journey we accordingly spent a night there. Cette, where we changed carriages and were long detained for no apparent good reason, and where there are extensive salines or manufactories of salt, lies very low and is marshy. It is therefore considered a most unhealthy spot, not to be thought of for sleeping at. The journey to Cette is not particularly interesting. Beyond it to Toulouse the country is more inviting. The distance is about 136 miles, and the train most tiresomely stopped several minutes at every little station, twenty-nine or thirty in all, with an extra halt at Narbonne, amounting to twenty minutes, where a hasty though acceptable dinner waited the arrival of the train. The more interesting part of the road was passed in the dark.

We had been recommended by fellow-passengers to the Hotel Sacaron at Toulouse, and found it remarkably comfortable; but to all appearance it was then out of season, as we seemed to be the only guests, except it might be our old friends the mosquitoes, who, paying nothing but penalties, were unceasing in their attentions, and from whom we might have suffered more than we did had we not been well protected by the snowy-white mosquito curtains. Our daughter, however, had a long watch, and discovered in the morning her forehead was jewelled in thirty-two holes.

Leaving next morning for Pau by the 11 o'clock train, we had no opportunity of getting more than a glimpse at this important provincial town. The houses are large, and the streets—such of them as we saw—are wide. The railway station is handsome and tidy. We arrived at Pau about 5 P.M., by a quick or express train, having only stopped at eleven out of thirty-four stations. Notwithstanding it took us six hours to go little more than 130 miles, being at the rate of 22 miles per hour. However, it was an improvement upon the previous day's travelling. The only other trains by which we could have gone from Toulouse to Pau were two,—one which left at midnight, getting in at 10 o'clock next morning; and another which left at 5.20 A.M., getting to Pau at half-past 1. I mention these facts just to show that every consideration is not paid here, and elsewhere (and it is better here than elsewhere) on French lines, to the convenience of travellers. Apart from the disagreeableness of starting at such inhuman hours, to travel by the midnight train would be to miss for great part of the way the view of the most interesting scenery along the railway route, which skirts the Pyrenees.

These grand mountains we saw now for the first time. Near to Lourdes the railway approaches them closely, and the church of Lourdes, to which it has been customary of recent years to make pilgrimages, is not far from the railway. It rises loftily from the ground far below. A crowd of pilgrims was marching towards its supposed miraculous shrines. The scenery about Lourdes is very picturesque, and the railway to Pau for a great part of the way runs parallel to and overlooks a mountain river, apparently the Adour, very much resembling at this part such rivers as the Garry in Perthshire; a clear-flowing stream, descending through a rocky bed, with many a rushing fall or rapid between converging rocks.

We arrived at Pau on the Saturday afternoon, and left it on the following Tuesday morning—just having time to rest. I reserve, therefore, any observations regarding Pau till our return journey, when we spent a longer time there. The railway ride (between sixty and seventy miles) from Pau to Bayonne is very beautiful, part of the way being by the banks of the Adour, which, as it approaches Bayonne, becomes wide, and is, indeed, navigable for forty miles up. We were advised to book to Bayonne, and hire thence to Biarritz; but I found the fares asked for the drive so excessive, occasioned, as we afterwards learnt, by races being then held at Bayonne, that we took the train just about to start on to Biarritz. The station La Negresse proved, however, to be two miles out of Biarritz, and only one carriage was waiting disengaged. For this short distance I was charged 8 francs; certainly exorbitant, but during the season at Biarritz everything is very high, and the races had then taken off the usual supply of vehicles, so that we were at the mercy of the gorgeously-attired coachman, who drove us in by a pretty rural road between trees and hedges. In all likelihood he had driven a party to join the train we had just left, so that we may have been indebted even to this chance for finding any conveyance waiting. I do not know why the railway company laid their line so far away from the town, unless it was that they did not appreciate the importance of the station. As an attempt to remedy the evil, a short line intended to connect Bayonne specially with Biarritz has been made; but though the Biarritz terminus is tolerably near the centre of the town, the other terminus does not enter Bayonne, and is a long way from the general railway terminus. It may be useful for excursionists, but it is useless for other traffic, and I should hardly think it would pay.

We had been recommended to the Hotel de Paris, near the rocks, and, with some difficulty, the town being then very full, got accommodation in it; rough enough at the first, but after two nights we obtained a change to first-floor rooms, fairly good. The hotel is situated in a public square planted with trees, the north end being open, overlooking the sea. Here the band played every evening, Sunday included, from half-past 8 till 10 o'clock during the season, making our rooms for the time very noisy; but as our windows looked right down upon the seated enclosure, brightly lighted up with numerous lamps, it was a little variety and divertisement to watch the gay crowd with whom it was at first filled, who paid for admission half a franc each. The charges in the hotels and for lodgings at Biarritz are said to be, during the summer season, immoderately high, and to cost in some cases as much as £5 per day. I cannot help thinking, however, that there must be a little exaggeration in these statements, or some extravagance on the part of the visitor so charged. We were ourselves charged at no excessive rate. The Angleterre and Grand Hotels, with superior arrangements, I believe, charged a good deal more. But there are other and more moderate hotels, such as the Hotel de France and the Hotel des Ambassadeurs, which, however, are both in the town itself, and not so well situated as those I have already named.

We remained at Biarritz till 13th October, nearly four weeks, and enjoyed it very much, although for a considerable part of the time, particularly during the earlier part, east and north-east winds, said to be unusual, prevailed, rendering the place for the time being cold, and giving us a taste of what winter weather is there, a visitor informing us that he had not found it colder in winter. If, however, it be no colder on winter days than what we did experience, it could hardly be described as trying for persons in good, strong health; but the prevailing winds are west and south-west, both mild and salubrious, though sometimes the south wind blows, and brings with it, in the hot months, the parching heat of the sirocco.

Biarritz is a place of very recent growth. Formerly nobody but English people, for the sake of the bathing it afforded, frequented it. Afterwards the civil war of succession in Spain brought many of the best Spanish families to live in it as a frontier town, and among others the Countess de Montijo and her two daughters, one of whom became the wife of Napoleon III. Her fondness for the place induced the Emperor to build the Villa Eugenie as a marine residence, and so, practically, made this delightful watering-place.

There may be said to be two bays, one north and one south; the first lying between the lighthouse and the pier, and the second upon the Basque beach. In the centre of the north bay the Villa Eugenie reposes on a rocky eminence, 40 or 50 feet above the shore to the east of the town, and is seen from many points. East and west of it, the sloping beach, a fine sandy one, stretches away on the right hand to the steep rocks, about 70 feet high, under the lighthouse, resting on a jutting promontory forming the eastern enclosing arm, to the rocks on the west, among which, looking down the small harbour, may be seen the town lying above and back from them. Westward from the Villa Eugenie, perhaps about half a mile distant, an imposing range of lofty hotels—the Grand Hotel and the Angleterre, with the Casino between them, all towering many storeys high—meets the view, and beyond them we see the spire of a large town church; and then still beyond, outward to the sea, running to a point, a range of high rocks or small hills which enclose the bay on the west. Some of the hilly rocks are surmounted by houses, and one prominent one by a semaphore or signal station. The rocks afford some shelter to the beach from the fury of the waves, but are

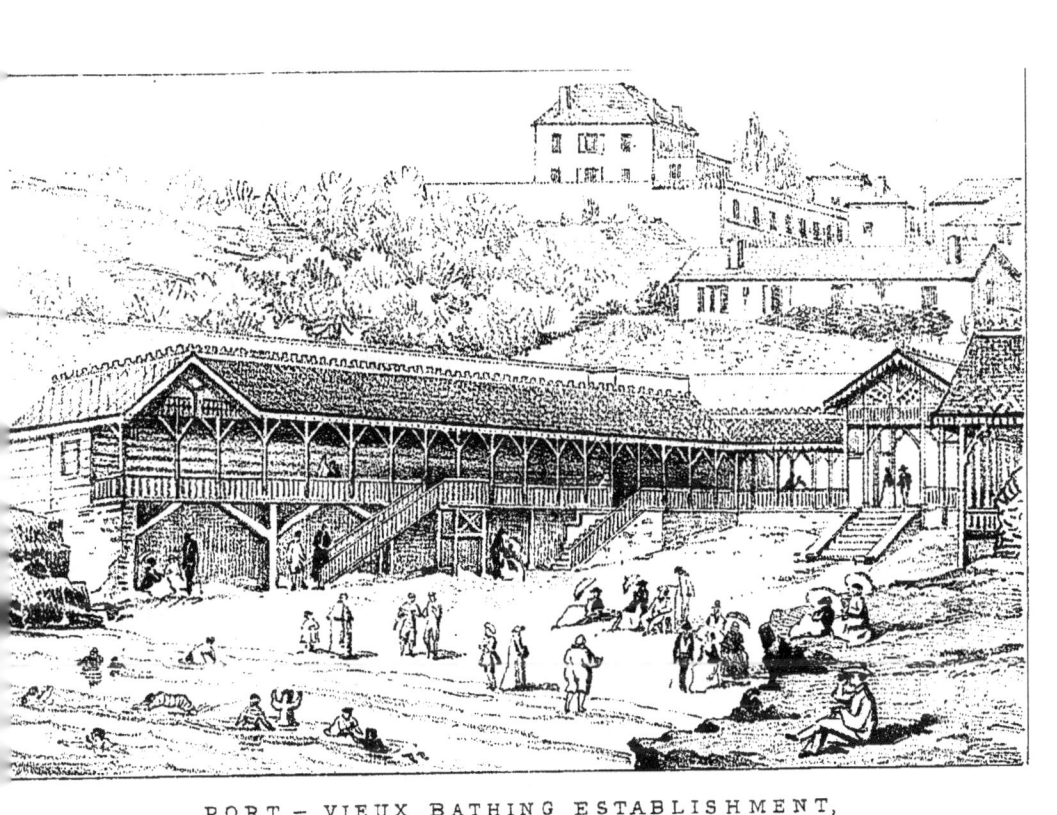

PORT – VIEUX BATHING ESTABLISHMENT, BIARRITZ.

themselves gradually giving way. No doubt at one time they formed a strong natural breakwater and better barrier, and extended well out into the ocean; but year by year they are succumbing to the force of the Atlantic and the storms which visit the Bay of Biscay.

In the centre of the north bay, and to the westward of the Villa Eugenie, a short promenade has been formed, on or adjoining which the great bathing establishment has been erected, the beach here being called the Grande Plage, in contradistinction to the other beaches. From the west end of it the road winds up below the Casino and past the Angleterre, and along by the top of the rocks overlooking the harbour, and through a tunnel under one of the hills to what was intended to be a breakwater, but is now a sort of pier, at which no vessels ever lie, becoming, therefore, only a place people stroll to in moderately calm weather, to watch the waves dashing upon and over the rocks in wild beauty. In rough weather no one dare venture. From this pier the road winds back towards the town and southward round the Port-Vieux, and through a gap in the rocks to the sandy Basque beach, which extends away southward for miles, the rocks rising perpendicularly from it, perhaps 80 feet high, the curve of the rocks forming the south bay. From any of the heights about the Port-Vieux or the Basque, one can see along the coast 20 miles to the entrance of the Bidassoa (the boundary there between France and Spain), and then on from that to the coast-line of Spanish mountains (offering a strong barrier against the aggression of the sea) for at least 40 miles farther, some even saying, though I should doubt it, seen 100 miles altogether. Southward the range of the Pyrenees bounds the horizon, the eye being caught by the Trois Couronnes or three-cornered or peaked mountain, rising boldly as commander of this battalion of the great guardian mountain chain.

The town of Biarritz bears every mark of its rapid construction. The streets are very irregular, the houses having been placed just any way and according to any plan, at the mere caprice of the builders. One leading street, lined by trees, passes through it to the Port-Vieux. In the centre of the town this widens to what may be called a large square or place, whence the omnibuses or diligences start, and where carriages can be had for hire. The Hotel de Ville has been built at one end of this place, which, in the height of the season, must be full of life. The principal shops are in its neighbourhood, some of them exhibiting in their windows articles of lace worn by the Spanish ladies, and Spanish shawls, sword-sticks, stilettoes, as well as other things of a more agreeable use. Itinerant vendors, too, of Spanish goods are always going about during the season, sometimes gaily dressed in a sort of showy fancy Spanish costume; but when the summer season is over, they migrate to Pau, and even to Cannes, Mentone, and other winter-season places, where we frequently saw the same men and women so occupied we had previously noticed at Biarritz. Some shopkeepers from Nice open establishments during the season at Biarritz, and close them when it is over. Besides many good shops, there is a regular market, though of small size. The town covers a considerable extent of ground, and new houses are being constantly built. The ordinary population now exceeds 4000. The English church had been found too small for its occupants, and a large new one was, while we were there, in course of completion.

Many nice-looking villas have been planted on the outskirts of the town, particularly upon and in the direction of the road to Bayonne. The heights above the Basque beach are likewise studded by various distinctive houses; and about a mile from town, isolated from everything about, there is a house belonging to Lord Ernest Bruce, built in the Moorish style with a glass dome, and surrounded by a garden.

The French and Spanish form the bulk of the visitors during August and September, these months constituting, *par excellence,* what is called the season, while during the winter months the English take possession. In the winter months the hotel charges undergo great modification, and *pension* can then be had in some of the best hotels at 7 francs per day.[1] It is noteworthy that *pension* at Biarritz and Pau, and elsewhere in the south of France, includes wine. House accommodation, too, in the winter months is correspondingly cheap. The best months for enjoying Biarritz, we were informed, are the months of April and May, when the heat is sufficient but not oppressive. The month of July is sometimes unbearably hot. A family who had been there during July told us that they could hardly venture out in that month till late in the evening; and if the sirocco prevailed, they were even obliged to close the windows, the hot sand percolating through every crevice. The band of music, I understood, plays only during the two months of the season, and removes at its close, when the enclosure is dismantled.

But the great attractions of Biarritz consist in its beach, its rocks, its grand seas, and in its capacities for good bathing. We were never fortunate enough to witness a storm in the bay, although there was occasionally enough of swell upon the water to show what a storm could be. Our landlord, speaking of the appearance of a storm on the ocean, described it as 'terreeble;' and no doubt it is, and not very safe, too, as sometimes people are washed away by an unexpected dash and sweep of the ocean. But a standing evidence of the force of the waves is exhibited by the remains or ruins of the breakwater, begun in view of here affording a port of refuge and pier. Regarding this scheme Count Russell says (p. 13):—

[1] I am told the winter season is now becoming very gay and very dear too.

'Napoleon III. suggested it, meaning to connect by a breakwater several of the detached rocks scattered on the north-western side of the Porte Vieux, and thus to form a small harbour, only open to the north. A clever engineer, M. Palaà, was entrusted with this almost superhuman undertaking, but the only result has been, after years of labour and more than one sacrifice of life, to accumulate a shapeless and useless mass of ruins along the intended harbour. The breakwater (or what is left of it) was built with concrete; artificial square blocks weighing 36 tons (some of them 48) were sunk by hundreds at random and just where they liked to fall! But the tremendous surf has been playing with them as if they were pebbles, and in 1868 one of them was carried right over the pier (22 feet above low-water mark) like a toy or a feather! For these and for financial reasons the works are now suspended. They have already cost £120,000, and all to no purpose. In fact, nothing human can resist such a sea as the Sea of Biscay, except, perhaps, at St. Jean de Luz, where nature has half made a harbour.'

The sea is by far too treacherous and violent to make boating safe, and we seldom, if ever, saw pleasure-boats out, although they were lying in the harbour.

Some isolated rocks stand out in the water, separated from the mainland, with which, I fancy, they have at one time been connected. They are rough, and rugged, and bare, and honeycombed, and even, occasionally, altogether perforated by the water; bearing witness in their haggard condition to the violence of the waves by which they are continually assailed, undermined, broken up, and thrown down. It is, indeed, very beautiful to see, during a swell, the water lashing the rocks and dashing over in clouds of white spray, or sometimes through the perforations or over and down the rocks in streams of white foam. During the day we used to stand and observe the swell surging into the large cavities formed by continual action, and tossed out again, as if the rocks had said with Phineas, 'Friend, thee isn't wanted here;' while the whole water around, nothing daunted, was boiling and excited, dancing and glancing and sparkling in the sun as if in glee, or in the spirit of fun and mischief. This, too, in calm weather. But at night we used to hear the boom of the waves as they tumbled into these caverns and were as promptly turned out again, as if it had been guns firing — for which, indeed, at first we were inclined to mistake the sound.

Unlike the Mediterranean Sea, the tide has the usual ebb and flow of the Atlantic, consequently not only is the beach more interesting, but the town is kept more healthy. The sands afford the usual occupation and delight to children, but shells and seaweed are rare. A good many jelly-fish are thrown up; some gelatinous animals of a large size perhaps were octopi. We used often to sit by the beach and watch the sea, especially under the Basque Rocks, where the waves, with the slightest breath of wind, would come charging gallantly in, high and crested, and turn gracefully over in long lines when they neared the shore. Over the rocks the inhabitants would seem to have the odious habit of running their drains or dirty water, both unsightly to the eye and leaving disagreeable black pools below. This surely might be remedied. It does create a drawback to this most enjoyable beach. Equally objectionable, if not more so, is the practice, so offensive at Cannes, of putting the outlets of the town drains close to each of the bathing-places. The tide, no doubt, is such at Biarritz as to remove the stuff carried down, but there could or should be no difficulty in carrying the pipes away to some distance from parts where people enter the water to bathe, and at all events in not making them so obnoxiously near and prominent.

There are three bathing establishments at Biarritz. One, and the largest, is on the Grande Plage, between the Villa Eugenie and the hotels, though much closer to the latter. It is a large wooden building of one storey, in the Moorish style, and opening from the promenade, three or four steps leading down at each end to the sands. When the tide is low there is a long space of sand to traverse. At the west side, where the rocks are, a rope for the use of the bathers is stretched between two rocks running seaward. The second is on the Port-Vieux, a creek perhaps 400 or 500 feet long by 100 to 150 feet wide. The wooden building forming the bathing establishment, of very neat design, with a balcony running all round, and a red-tiled roof, is built on three sides of the square down to the usual high-water mark. The fourth and open side is to the sea, which for a good way out is hemmed in by rocks, between which a rope, slack but strong, is stretched across the creek, hanging, in very low tide, considerably above water, but in high tide having the middle part submerged. One side of the house is devoted to the dressing-rooms of the ladies and the other to those of the gentlemen, and long wooden stairs on each side enable the bathers to reach the sands. A few yards brings into sufficient depth for bathing, but at low water the sea goes back so as to land one among the rocks, especially in spring tides, and bathing is then not so pleasant, especially to non-swimmers; but this condition does not last above an hour. When the wind is in the west, even when hardly perceptible, there is more or less surf at the edge, and in strong west or north-west winds the swell must be such as to prevent bathing altogether at the Port-Vieux. But in this case more shelter will no doubt be had at the Grande Plage, which is to a small extent protected on the west by rocks. In stormy weather it must be altogether impossible to bathe anywhere. The third bathing establishment is at (though raised some feet above) the Basque beach, and is intended for the convenience of those residing in that neighbourhood on the plateau above. It is smaller considerably than either of the other two, and can be reached from the sands by ascending a ladder or stair of steps, or from the town by descending a zigzag path from the top of the nearly perpendicular rock against which it is placed. The arrangements of all are, I suppose, on exactly the same principles: little boxes under cover of the establishment for undressing and dressing, towels, and the usual appliances, including a tub of hot water to take the sand out of the feet.

The establishment at the Grande Plage is much the largest, but we always gave the preference to the Port-Vieux, where the Empress formerly used to sit and watch the bathers if she did not bathe herself. The town and road are high above it, and descending by a handsome stone staircase, one is confronted at the bottom by the ticket office, where (those not bathing can without charge go down to the beach) those intending to bathe pay according to their requirements, usually from half a franc to a franc each, the assistance of a bathing man being charged half a franc additional. No gratuities are expected, but a box at the dressing-room entrance-door modestly appears, into which those who choose may in passing drop a coin now and then. Bathers can be supplied with a bathing dress, and have it washed, but most people naturally prefer to have their own habiliments.

Bathing is the great occupation of the visitors. Many bathe twice a day, and some, I believe, all the year round, wind and weather permitting. The sea is full of saline particles, and is usually warm, while the atmosphere is also warm and salubrious, so that bathing is even advantageous to those who dare not venture on it in the British Isles. Unless the wind be blowing, say, from the north-west, it is almost always possible to obtain a dip. To call a bathe there a dip, however, would be exceedingly inappropriate. It is a steady, serious occupation of some duration, and more or less protracted according to the heat of the weather and the enthusiasm of the bather. The times for bathing are in the morning before breakfast, after breakfast between ten and twelve, and in the afternoon between three and six. During the bathing hours spectators in crowds, perhaps not so numerous and certainly not so noisy as at Ramsgate on a forenoon, but stationed upon every available point, or quietly standing or sitting on rocks, sands, or chairs, or on the steps or balconies of the establishments, amusedly watch the performances, which are extremely interesting, and to British eyes peculiar. At the Port-Vieux special vantage-ground is gained by the road, which, like a gallery, envelopes the three sides, and being higher than the roof of the building, enables the passers-by to peer down from perhaps 50 feet above on the aquatic sport below.

For ladies and gentlemen array themselves in bathing costume, in which they march down to the water from the establishment—the ladies in general wearing over all a cloak or shawl, which they drop ere they reach the edge, and it is taken charge of by a friend or a bathing man. The ladies' habit, of which the fanciful patterns (possibly imagined and engraved in far-away Paris) exhibited in dressmakers' shop windows afford but a faint and incorrect idea (as, for example, in representing ladies appearing in lace frills, and trig, tight, little laced boots), usually consists of a short tunic with equally short sleeves, not reaching to the elbows, and knee-breeches reaching barely to the knees, the tunic girt at the waste by a girdle, to which is attached in the majority of cases, *à la* John Gilpin, two empty yellow gourds as floats. Then very often a straw hat is stuck upon the head, and tied by a ribbon over the crown and broad brim and under the chin, giving the appearance of a frightful 'ugly;' while on the feet are generally worn a pair of local shoes made of canvas, with thick hemp soles, which, decorated with devices in worsted, are very commonly worn by the residents, and even for walking about the beach by many of the visitors, and are sold for 2 or 3 francs per pair. The bathing dresses vary in pattern and shape, and are of all colours. White is seldom worn. Bright colours —red, scarlet, green, light blue, yellow, amber—are often seen; in short, the aim with many is apparently at something stunning, suitable for the adornment of a pretty

BIARRITZ BATHERS.

BATHING COSTUME—THE SCENE. 429

mermaid. To add to the effect, smart young ladies will also have their dresses embroidered, and otherwise made attractive and bewitching, in the way only a graceful girl knows how; and really it must be confessed that this bloomer costume is exceedingly becoming, at all events to the younger ladies. Stout old ladies cut a figure in it sometimes remarkable.

The gentlemen, on the other hand, look like harlequins, for their costume in general consists of a somewhat tight-fitting dress either of cotton or woollen, and most commonly in stripes of two colours, and of all colours and shades, though white and blue stripes are the most common. Their dress costs from 6f. to 20f. (a very good woollen one in red and black stripes cost me 13f.). Some of the old gentlemen wear a straw hat loose on their heads, so that occasionally it is seen floating away from the wearer by reason of an accidental wave or submersion. I suppose the object of the straw hat is to obtain protection against the beams of the sun, but it suggests the uncomfortable idea that the wearer never plunges his or her head under water, the doing of which would, I doubt not, afford equal protection against the sun's heat, and is in any view always necessary to prevent a flow of blood to the brain in bathing.[1]

In these varied and brightly-coloured costumes, the bathers cut gay figures. But the picture is composed and completed when they enter into action. At the edge of the water, the gentlemen bathers, sometimes portly and rotund, having threaded in bare feet their way down through the ladies sitting on the stairs, and through the crowd of spectators on the sand, wait with patience in their brilliant, tight, and unusual attire, the observed of all observers, the arrival of their lady friends, if they any have, and on

---

[1] The accompanying illustration, depicting three gentlemen and seven ladies in bathing costume, was taken (tell it not in Gath) from jottings made at a safe distance. The stout lady in the centre was doubtless a Spaniard.

their arrival, taking their hand, accompany them into the water; or the ladies take the hand of a bathing man engaged to attend them, and march in under their charge, and presently they are in the clear salt water, alive with bathers in every colour and in every form of movement practised by those who go down to the sea to bathe. Some rush from the shore wildly and inhumanly into the water, and, wickedly regardless of frightening the small fishes, dive head foremost with a splash, and strike out. Others stalk in majestically, and either quietly push far out, or paddle about pretending or attempting to swim in shallow water. Then other gentlemen are giving encouragement to their little boys or girls, or to their wives, or possibly their lovers, or improbably their sisters, either dipping them, or helping them to swim, or teaching them to float, or joining in other usual maritime gyrations. Others catch hold of the rope stretched out if the water be low, and dance about in a mad and profitless way, or if the tide be high, the swimmers catch at it as they pass and take a rest; and sometimes, if at a proper height, an adventurous one will sit upon the rope, like a sparrow on a telegraph wire, when (perhaps beholding admiringly from the treacherous seat some fat lady floating on her back on the surface, her bathing integuments undulating in the water like the tentacular folds of a jelly-fish) of a sudden somebody else, perhaps waggishly, perhaps innocently, clutches at the slack rope, and with unexpected shock upsets the unwary, abstracted philosopher, who with a whirl capsizes heels in the air, and head making discoveries through eyegate, nosegate, and mouthgate in the brine below. Or two recently arrived English young ladies will walk in, hand in hand, scorning the aid of a bathing man, and perform together, with all the regularity of clockwork, an endless series of curtsey ducks in the water without stirring from the safely selected spot. Other ladies, to vary the programme, are carried out by a bathing man and dipped horizontally in the wave, so that head and feet obtain ablution simultaneously; or a stout matron will take hold of a bathing man, who swims out with her on his back apparently, so that she enjoys the luxury of being buoyed up and drawn through the water, and can say, 'I'm afloat.' But these sham swimmers are notably the exceptions. The great matter of observation is that the vast majority of the ladies, young and old, swim about as easily as the gentlemen, though they are in doing so generally accompanied by a man swimming behind or beside them in case of accident; and, indeed, one important occupation of those employed as bathing men is to teach the young idea how to swim, an accomplishment which, after a few lessons, they are usually able to master, and young girls are constantly seen swimming about among the others, like minnows among the tritons. Some ladies, after long practice, are very adventurous; two of them will go out together in a boat a considerable distance, when, throwing off their cloaks, they will dive head foremost from the side of the boat and swim ashore, the boat following. One little girl was most clever. She would go out to what looks like the vestige of an old pier, and, jumping high, perform a somersault, and, diving under the water, 'come up smiling,' swim about, and do it again and again. I have, however, seen many older diving belles jumping from the same pier. In fact, bathing in all its forms is here carried by the ladies to an enviable perfection altogether unknown at home; and while it not merely affords a most invigorating exercise, it becomes a most valuable branch of education, tending to lessen the risk of casualties at sea. It were well that at home the good example could be followed.

The late King of Hanover was at Biarritz while we were there. Being blind, he was carried into the water upon a *chaise-à-porteur* by four men, his suite bathing with him. His daughter was said to bathe at an early hour in the morning, and many ladies, we were told, bathed as early as six o'clock. During the time we were there, and the weather being cold, forenoon and afternoon were preferable.

The bathing men will never dip one's head unless expressly desired to do so, and never propose it—a great mistake. The bathing dress is not at all inconvenient or uncomfortable while in the water, but it is heavy out of it, especially if of woollen material (decidedly the best kind), because it absorbs and retains a great deal of water.

Away from the beach all the walks are on the high roads, which are principally three,—to the railway station, to Bayonne, and to the lighthouse. The distance to the lighthouse by the road is considerably farther than by the beach, from which to the platform on the top of the rocks whereon it stands, access is had by a steep path. From the top of the lighthouse, 220 feet from the level of the sea to the lantern, a most extensive view is had northward up the west coast of France, bordered by the Landes—a low sandy coast, now planted with pine trees to guard against the incursions of the sea—stretching 100 miles towards Bordeaux; and in the other direction along the Spanish coast, bounded by a chain of mountains far as the eye can see; while inland the view extends towards the Pyrenees. A steep path leads from the lighthouse to a small recessed platform half-way down the rock, where in calm weather one can behold the swelling and surging sea below ever and anon dashing against the rocks, and where men repair with long rods and lines to fish. But in stormy weather it is dangerous even to stand on the ground above; people are exposed to be swept away by unexpected rushes of the sea, and many have been drowned there in consequence. The fish caught at this platform, so far as we know, were small. Indeed, at Biarritz there are not many caught, though the table is always supplied from neighbouring fishing stations. Lobsters, however, seem to be plentiful.

THE VILLA EUGENIE.

The Villa Eugenie, between the lighthouse and the town, is an object of interest to every one visiting Biarritz. It is shown to the public on Mondays. Entrance is had by the west approach, where there is a lodge and large but not elegant stabling accommodation. The grounds are not extensive (about thirty acres in all), but sufficient for a marine residence of the kind; nor do they exhibit much attention to horticulture, though perhaps it is hardly fair to judge of them in present circumstances. The house, of three storeys, commenced in the year 1854, forms three sides of a square, with an *annexe* (I presume, offices) on the east side. It still belongs to the Empress, who, of course, never occupies it now, and she will not sell or let it. Ringing the bell, an old servant (who expects a small fee from each party for his trouble) opens the door and shows visitors through the house. Our troop consisted of several distinct parties, mustering probably above a dozen persons in all. The rooms are of comfortable size, and compose just what an Empress would consider to be a snuggery. The dining-room is the largest room in the house, the windows facing on one side the west to the town and sea, on another northward to the sea and lighthouse. On a rough guess, and speaking from recollection, it is probably from 40 to 50 feet long and from 20 to 25 feet wide, the ceiling lofty. The reception-room is comparatively small. The bedrooms of the Emperor, Empress, and Prince are just of a comfortable size. There are many small bedrooms, very nicely decorated, for use of the suite or for visitors. The floors are polished, and the staircase is so slippery that people are cautioned to take great care in descending, the steps not being carpeted. It was melancholy to think it was no longer possible for poor Eugenie to occupy this delightful residence.[1] Perhaps it is the only place in France where

[1] As this is passing through the press, the sad news has come which has sent a thrill of sympathy through every British breast for the heartbroken bereaved mother. Any objection on the part of France which might formerly

the Imperial arms remain, and one sees upon it also the touching monogram ⋺Ν⋶, which reads up or down. The place would to our Queen be objectionable as being so close to a town; but to a French lady this, no doubt, would give it additional attraction, and it must be recollected that Biarritz in reality largely owes its existence to the Empress having built her villa there. For this the French people should be grateful, although it looks a little unlike it, because in the grounds two pillars in front of a small unfinished chapel for the Imperial family use have been much broken. This, however, may merely have been the result of accident.

It is a pleasant drive to Bayonne, which lies about five miles off. Like many other roads in France, such as at Pau, the road proceeds a long way in a straight line, flanked by regimental rows of trees, which, affording shade from the sun, have a peculiarly stiff effect. Here, as elsewhere, too, contrary to the Roman beau-ideal of a road that it should be level, this one, though straight, yields to the inequalties of the ground, and is alternately in hollows and on elevations. But people ought to be thankful the road is so good, for, speaking of a time about forty years ago or more, Dr. Taylor (*Climate of Pau*) says:—

> 'There was no carriage road from Bayonne to Biarritz, the only conveyance being *en cacolet*, which contrivance consisted of a pair of panniers laid on the back of a horse or mule, into each of which a traveller of equal weight, if possible, had to perch himself at the same instant with his fellow, and to preserve their position as best they could. In the event of one being lighter than the other, there was a make-weight of stones put along with him in the pannier to adjust the equilibrium.'

Judging from the specimens of comfortable Spanish ladies

have prevailed against her return to Biarritz, if she should desire it, can no longer possibly exist. Let us hope that a generous kindly feeling will pervade all parties in France towards one who once filled a place so high among so great a people, and upon whom such overwhelming sorrows have fallen.

we saw at Biarritz, I should pity the horse or the mule which had to carry two of them.

About half way to Biarritz, a very elegant white stone villa in the Moorish style is passed—the Villa Sophia. There is something very unique in the appearance of this building, which is covered with arabesques, inducing me to go out one day and take a rough sketch of it. On approaching Bayonne, the road lies through a wood—I suppose, a suburban park. Then on entering the town we see a long many-arched stone bridge spanning the Adour,— here very wide,—and beyond it the fortifications, built by Vauban. These may at one time have been considered strong, but at the present day cannot be thought so, and they are overlooked by neighbouring heights. The fort lacks the picturesquely-imposing appearance of stone wall castles. A good deal of historical interest attaches to Bayonne and its fortifications. The town itself is not remarkable for much save its four bridges, crossing very close to each other the river Nive, which here joins the Adour. The cathedral, above seven hundred years old, is large and handsome, and is in course of restoration. The spires (one of them only is completed, the other being in course of completion) are very beautiful, tapering gradually, with spirelets around; but the church is like too many others abroad, rather hemmed in by the houses around.

There are other good drives about Biarritz, and particularly to the Bois de Boulogne and to the old historical maritime town of St. Jean de Luz, about ten miles distant, and not far from the Spanish border. It was here Louis XIV. had a residence and was married. His house, in the French style, with square towers at the four corners, stands now in the centre of the town upon the main street, and in its ground floor is occupied with shops and cafés. St. Jean is also a bathing place, but is not so popular, and is certainly not so attractive, as Biarritz.

There is a fine drive to Cambo, at the base of the Pyrenees, but during the first part of the period of our stay at Biarritz the weather was too cold to take it, and in the latter part the days were getting rather too short, the distance being about eighteen miles.[1]

Few people visit Biarritz without making an excursion by railway to St. Sebastian to see a little of Spain. It is thirty-seven miles distant by rail, and can be easily managed in a day—in fact, going by morning train, one is left rather too much time in St. Sebastian. Crossing the river Bidassoa, the picturesque town of Fuenterrabia is the first object catching the eye on the Spanish border. A halt of an hour is made at Irun for examination of the luggage, and it is possible, though a risk, to drive off and return in time for the train after a hurried examination of this interesting old town, which from the railway has an appearance of being deserted. Leaving Irun, the railway winds its way through the mountains, and reaches St. Sebastian, which is a tidy-looking town standing at the mouth of a river crossed by a handsome bridge, with view out to the Bay of Biscay and to the fortress of St. Sebastian on a hill next the sea. The town lies on the landward side of this hill, the more modern part of it, at least, consisting of wide streets and lofty square houses with nothing redeeming about their aspect. Passing along the main wide street from the bridge, we arrive at an enclosed natural harbour, a tract of sea, like a bag contracted at the neck, through which communication is had with the bay without. The shipping is not extensive; the harbour proper, lying on the side nearest the sea, being small. On the south side, next the newer portion of the town and the railway, the grand *plage* bathing-place, with a wooden bathing-house, is found.

[1] Some additional information, particularly regarding places in the vicinity, will be found in *Biarritz and Basque Countries*, by Count Henry Russell, though the chapter on Biarritz itself is brief and scanty.

Behind it the mountains rise picturesquely. It requires an order to see the fortress, which is mainly of earthen ramparts. The town itself has little of interest in it. Close by the railway station, however, there is a very large wooden amphitheatre for bull-fights. Bills containing announcements of one of these savage entertainments were placarded on the building and the railway stations and elsewhere. The dwellings on the line of railway are similar to those about Biarritz, principally of the Basque style; many of them have on the top little glazed houses, sort of huts, no doubt designated, according to the taste of the occupants, as observatories, retreats, or smoking-rooms. Except for seeing a little of Spain, I believe it is better rather to stop and see the curious old town of Fuenterrabia.

After 1st October a very marked change came over the appearance of Biarritz. Nearly all of the Spanish and French visitors (coming no doubt for the gaiety) then left, while the English influx for the winter season had scarcely begun. During the first fortnight of this month the town wore a deserted look, and this was greatly aggravated by many of the shops commencing to pack up for migration to other places, and one after another closing. I daresay, a month later, there would be more life in the place.

We had all experienced the greatest benefit from our short residence of about a month in Biarritz, and although the weather was, during the greater part of the time, especially at first, very cold, in consequence of the north-easterly winds, we felt that our invalid especially had derived great good from the ' soothing and invigorating air;' so much so that we fondly thought, owing to this and the former changes, she was now in recovered health, and that it only wanted another winter in the Riviera to set her completely up. Biarritz is considered too cold a place for delicate persons to winter in, and the approach of its winter season would in any view have warned us away. But we did feel extremely reluctant to leave; for this agreeable watering-place had quite taken our fancy, and perhaps we felt the leaving all the more that we had not seen it in its stern grandeur of a storm, or even in its wild grandeur of a cloudy sunset, while, under the influence of a gentle wind blowing from the south, the day upon which we left was one of the finest and sunniest we had had while there. Having a good hour before departure, we visited all the beaches and rocks, and lingered sorrowfully upon the scenes now so radiant in sunshine and so genial in their warmth, where we had spent pleasant times, and thence looked out upon the bright sparkling ocean gleaming below us, and the waves gently kissing the shore and bidding us adieu, and with unwilling steps returned to our hotel to leave for Pau. This leave-taking is one of the penalties to be paid for the pleasure of travelling in bright spots where everything has combined to make one happy—where the scenes are new and pleasing, where the object of travel seems to have been secured, and where hearts in perfect harmony and with congenial likings are able to appreciate the blessings they have thus been privileged together to enjoy.

XIX.

PAU.

ENGAGING a small omnibus for 8 francs to Bayonne, five miles distant, we left Biarritz at 12.25 for the 1.45 train to Pau. The station at Bayonne for Pau in one direction, and Bordeaux in another, is on the north side of the Adour, so that we had to cross the long bridge over that river. The day was glorious, and the Adour, by whose banks we proceeded part of the way, was looking very fine.

The traveller arrives at Pau by railway, in a station down in the depths on the banks of the river Gave, a tributary of the Adour. But the town itself mainly lies on a level platform, about 150 feet higher, and almost immediately above, the rise being sharp, and the road whereby it is reached very steep. The best advantage has been taken of the situation to erect in front line a series of imposing edifices near to the edge of this almost perpendicular height, so that on issuing from the railway station the *coup d'œil* is extremely impressive. Commencing at the west end, the chateau or castle, with its ivy-clad old tower or donjon, is the first object arresting the attention—a large symmetrical building in the chateau style. Then the eye runs along to the great new Hotel Gassion, with its corner projections (which are neither towers nor turrets), surmounted by clumsy extinguisher pointed roofs, and then the white Church of St. Martin's, with its lofty graceful needle spire, and on to the Hotel de France and other imposing houses in the Place Royale—the whole producing an effect which gives to the stranger the idea of a magnificent city behind. But the truth is (all honour to those who did it), that the grenadiers have here all been brought to the front rank; for the stately group assembles in this commanding spot nearly all the buildings which are noteworthy in Pau, the only other, if I am not mistaken, being the white Church of St. Jacques, with its fine double spires, and perhaps the adjoining Palais de Justice, both at a little distance from the Place Royale.

We had been recommended on our first visit to apply for quarters at the Pension Colbert, near the termination of the Rue Montpensier, at the north or rural side of the town, kept by English ladies (Misses Finch). It was at first a steep pull up the hill for the horses, but the hill conquered, the road was thereafter level. We had been made not merely so comfortable, but so much at home, at this house that we engaged rooms in it on our return from Biarritz. On our first visit in September, it was before the season commenced, and we were accordingly the only guests; on the second, the house was nearly full, and we experienced similar kind attention. It is recommended, with a view to getting gradually accustomed to the climate before winter sets in, that invalids should come in September, and there seems no reason in the shape of excessive heat or the presence of mosquitoes to prevent it; the weather, indeed, was cool during our first visit. But the season does not really begin before the end of October, and it is even the first week of November before Pau becomes tolerably full. We accordingly found it upon our second visit, in the middle of October, still comparatively empty.

The climate of Pau is not what suits every one. As compared with Biarritz in the months from October to March inclusive, the mean temperature is, according to the month, from one to five degrees lower. Whether it was owing to our experiencing a difference of temperature, or to the fact of our having had a good deal of rain while in Pau, or whether due to accidental circumstances, such as neglect to shut a bedroom window one evening, we all caught colds there, and lost much of the good we had got at Biarritz. The fact suggests some notice of what has been said on the subject of the climate of Pau as a health resort.

Dr., afterwards Sir Alexander Taylor, who wrote a special book on the climate of Pau and other places,[1] divides climates into three classes: *exciting*, *sedative*, and *relaxing*, and he gives us examples (p. 21)—

1. Of exciting climates—Nice, Naples, Montpellier, and Florence.
2. Of sedative climates—Rome and, *par excellence*, Pau.
3. Of relaxing climates—Pisa and Madeira.

'In the sedative climate we have a more neutral state of the atmosphere—a remarkable freedom from dryness on the one hand, and from communicable humidity on the other, and in Pau particularly, great stillness of the atmosphere.'

It is therefore only in cases where a sedative climate would be beneficial that Dr. Taylor recommends Pau, and in a subsequent chapter (p. 100) he mentions the kind of cases for which the climate of Pau is specially beneficial.

Among the characteristics of the climate, he mentions that while more rain falls in Pau than in London and some other situations in England, yet from the absorbent nature of the soil, and from some peculiar electric state of the

---

[1] I have his third edition, published in 1861. It is possible there may be a later one. Dr. Taylor was knighted, at the request of the Emperor Napoleon III., in recognition of his efforts to develop the resources of Pau as a residence for invalids. He has just (May 1879) died.

atmosphere, there is an absence of 'free communicable humidity;' and that while 27 inches of rain fall annually in London, and from 40 to 50 inches in Pau, the number of rainy days is only 109 against 178 in London. Further, a very important advantage possessed by Pau is its distinguishing freedom from wind from apparently any quarter, while the malevolent circius, bise, and the mistral are never felt there. Dr. Taylor contrasts in tables the difference of temperature between Greenwich and Pau—as, for example, in the mean temperature of each for the months between October and May, showing them to vary, according to the month, from 3 to 7 degrees in favour of Pau. The mean moisture of the air is also shown to be generally about one-twelfth less at Pau; while a further circumstance is that there is more sunshine at Pau, imparting greater cheerfulness to the winter climate. A very curious additional fact is thus stated (p. 80) :—

'From an examination of the mean distribution of the winds, according to the cardinal points of the compass, indicated by carefully-kept registers for a considerable series of years, we find that they show northerly winds prevailed in summer, southerly in winter, easterly in autumn and winter, and westerly in spring and early summer; and when we recall to the reader what has before been said with regard to the usual want of force of the winds at all times at Pau, he can easily figure to himself how the heats of summer being modified by the northerly wind, the cold of winter shorn of its intensity by the southerly, and the usual biting keenness of spring softened by the prevalence of westerly winds, the climate should act beneficially on the irritable air passages and on the lungs of invalids either predisposed to active disease or which are already a prey to it.'

At another place Dr. Taylor gives a table of death-rates, from which Pau would seem to be at the top of the list for least mortality—as, for example, while in Pau 1 in 45 died annually, in London it was 1 in 40, in Nice 1 in 31, Rome 1 in 25, Vienna 1 in $22\frac{1}{2}$, etc.; and he adds this important statement (p. 94) :—

'In the department of the Basses Pyrénées, in a period of seventeen years, 1777 persons died from 90 to 95, 649 from 95 to 100, and 168 above 100 years of age. In Pau itself, during a period of twenty years, 390 persons died from 80 to 85, 161 from 85 to 90, and 103 from 90 to 100 and upwards. By the last census, there were in Pau several persons ranging from 100 to 104 years of age, and in the department also several *centenaires* who are described as being still very healthy.'

But I must refer to Dr. Taylor's work for more information on this and other matters relating to Pau. Besides containing general information relative to the town itself, it deals in its last half with the climate of other places, and particularly affords information relative to the different places of resort in the Pyrenees.

Another book (already referred to, p. 53), by Dr. Frederick H. Johnson, entitled, *A Winter's Sketches in the South of France and the Pyrenees*, is similarly devoted to Pau and the Pyrenees, and is written in an interesting, graphic manner.

Mr. C. Home Douglas, in his little work called *Searches for Summer*, takes a rather different view of the climate of Pau from Dr. Taylor, although opening his observations by saying:

'Passing from Biarritz to Pau, as we did in the beginning of May, seemed almost like returning to the still sunny climate of the south of Spain. The fresh strong Atlantic breeze—invigorating, doubtless, to many constitutions—gave place to such gentle and balmy air as we used to open our windows to at Malaga.'

Mr. Douglas, not confining comparison to London, compares the temperature of Pau with that also of other places in Great Britain, showing that the sunny temperature of Pau is $4°·1$ below that of Helstone in Cornwall, and is under that of Torquay in Devonshire and Valentia in Ireland during the same winter months, and quotes Dr. Otley to the effect that there is greater daily range of temperature at Pau than in England, adding that the nights must be colder at Pau than in the west coasts of Britain, and expresses the opinion that 'no one who cannot stand severe cold ought to think of going to Pau for the winter; better go to Easdale in Argyllshire. No one so constituted should think of going till March at soonest; April, in my opinion, is early enough.'

Mr. Douglas writes as a meteorologist, and his little volume is a valuable contribution to the consideration of the temperature of the various places of health resort therein mentioned; but the facts stated by Dr. Taylor, even though one is inclined to look with suspicion on medical advocates of special places, show that the value of a place for an invalid may not wholly depend on the records of the thermometer.

We made Pau only a halting-place for nine days, *en route* for the Riviera, and to form some opinion as to its suitability for a longer stay at another time. Coming from the ever-changing ocean, and from Biarritz, which had so captivated our fancy, perhaps we did not take so kindly to Pau, a large inland rural town, as we might otherwise have done; while, in consequence of the season not having fairly commenced, the strangers encountered in the streets were few, and the town consequently was more dull than it would have been later on. The weather also was such that we had not much opportunity of seeing the environs.

Before 1840, Pau apparently was a place of no repute. I presume Dr. Taylor's recommendation gave it its great stimulus. But in twenty years after 1840 it had largely increased, evidences of which were, that the octroi duty had in 1860 realized nearly double, that the British visitors had amounted to 1000 in number in the year, and that its population had augmented to 21,000. It has gone on increasing since, and is now so well frequented as to require no less than three English churches and one Scotch church, with resident ministers, while the population is reckoned to amount to 30,000.

The town itself is regularly built, with good leading streets, and possesses a large market-place, where goods of all kinds, even broadcloths, are sold in open stalls; and as Pau is the centre of a very large rural population, it is on market days a busy place; but there are many good shops in some of the best streets, and the wares are, I think, cheaper than in Nice and elsewhere in the Riviera. The two town churches, St. Martin's and St. Jacques, are new and of white stone, and with their fine tapering spires are externally handsome, but internally, except for their stained-glass windows, want the richness of ornamentation we had seen in so many other Roman Catholic churches abroad.

The grand sight at Pau is the chain of the Pyrenees. We had only to go a short way along the country road, in which the Pension Colbert is, to see them. But a more uninterrupted prospect is had from the Boulevard du Midi, or terrace of the Place Royale, in front of the prominent buildings I have already mentioned. Leaning upon the parapet wall of this fine terrace, and looking almost straight down upon the valley below, one sees beyond the road and a small outlying portion of the town and the railway station, the river Gave flowing sluggishly along, crossed by a handsome low stone bridge of, I think, five arches, and lined on both sides by rows of tall poplar and other trees, and bordered by straggling houses, which give some character to the scene. Then, on the other side, there rises a range of well-wooded knolls and hills, called the Côteaux of Juraçon and Gelos, the highest about 300 feet in height, and dotted over among the trees by mansions; and then apparently the ground dips behind them, and in the distance (the nearest being twenty miles off) the long range of the Pyrenees stretches out in a continuous line eastward and westward as far as the eye can see, and forming the natural boundary and barrier between the two great countries France and Spain. Rising abruptly and prominently out of the range like two great tusks, are the Pic de Midi d'Ossau, to appearance nearly opposite Pau, and the grandest of the Pyrenees; and away to the eastward, the Pic de Gers; while still farther to the east, but eclipsed by intervening heights scarcely visible from Pau, the Pic du Midi de Bigorre, each of them, or at least the first and last mentioned, from 10,000 to 11,000 feet high. From the upper windows of the hotels on this Boulevard the view must be magnificent. It was very fine from the windows of the Chateau, but they are of a low elevation. This view, perhaps the finest in France, is really the great attraction to the hotels in this quarter, for nowhere else does it seem possible to obtain the prospect from so high a position, and so free from intervening obstructions. When we were at Pau, there was no snow upon the Pyrenees, so that we failed to see them in their best. Even, however, when snow-covered, they cannot bear comparison with the Alps as seen from Turin. But the view may be finer when the mountains are snow-covered and there is a grand sunset, for which Pau is famed. The mountains in the ruddy glow may then resemble the Bernese Alps, as seen from Berne in a brilliant sunset. At Turin, as the mountains lie to the west of the town, the sunset effect must be greatly lost.

The Chateau, which was the residence of the Princes of Bearne in former times, and where Henry IV. of France was born in 1553, is well worthy of inspection, and, of course, any stranger coming to Pau pays it a visit. Three bridges connect it with the town, and at one time it was doubtless a place of strength. Entering on one side through what appears to be a modern screen of three open slender arches embellished by carved work (seemingly rather too delicate for a warlike place), and passing the sentinel, the visitor is at once in the court-yard, the remaining three sides of the nearly square yard forming the castle, pierced by decorated windows. The walls are of great thickness, giving the idea of massive strength and solidity. In some of the rooms the walls are covered with tapestry, and in parts the tapestry is a close imitation in worsted of paintings in oil—

a mistake in art, I think. The ceilings are bold in design, without being either fine or remarkable. The old beds are curious high boxes of carved oak, requiring steps to enable the occupants to get up into them. A lower modern carved bed in one of the rooms, devoid of the canopy of the old ones, seemed vastly preferable. One of the bedrooms was hung with silk of the time of Madame de Maintenon, and, as we understood, manufactured under her superintendence. The most interesting object in the castle was the cradle of Henry IV., made of a large tortoise shell. There is a statue of the great monarch in the grounds, and in the country round about places exist with which he was associated; and, indeed, Pau and its neighbourhood is a place of great historical interest.

A public park closely adjoins the Chateau. It is filled with lofty trees, and continues for a long stretch by the banks of the Gave on a rising ground, through which and under the trees walks have been formed and seats placed, whence charming views of the river and mountains are had. The band plays during the season sometimes in the park and at other times in the Place Royale.

The environs of Pau are said to be beautiful, but we had not much opportunity of exploring them. Mr. Inglis (the traveller), in a passage quoted by Dr. Taylor, says:—

'The Gave serpentines through the charming undulating country that surrounds the town. Grain, meadows, and vines diversify the scenery; and innumerable country-houses are everywhere scattered around. Nothing can exceed the beauty of the promenades in the neighbourhood of Pau. Some lie alongside the Gave, others along the banks of the smaller river.'

The road to Bordeaux and the other roads out of Pau seem to be all lined with regimental rows of poplars, shady perhaps in sunshine, but stiff. Some neat villas in nicely-planted gardens in the outskirts of the town— delightful retreats—are let furnished. I had the pleasure of meeting a very old Scotch friend, who, after having tried many places, has found the climate of Pau to be most suitable, and has accordingly built just out of town an elegant villa for permanent residence.

There are, I believe, many excellent excursions from Pau, such as a drive to Lourdes, 25 miles distant—a long day's work for the horses there and back, but, I was told and can readily believe, most enjoyable. In the summer-time, everybody who can, escapes to the mountains, where so many charming spots, including Eaux-Chaudes and Eaux-Bonnes, are to be found.

We paid a visit to the cemetery, which lies back from the Place d'Armes, and quite out of town, the Protestant ground being, as customary, separate from the Roman Catholic. There are throughout many monuments, including one to Marshal Bosquet, whose name is familiar to us in connection with the Crimean War. After the war he spent his last years in Pau, his native place. One monument to the memory of a Russian lady, representing her in the act of kneeling and praying, in very rich attire, is of white marble, and has no doubt been executed in Italy.

During our stay in Pau, the French General Election took place, and according to French practice was on a Sunday (14th October 1877). Everything was quiet, quieter even than it would have been at home, notwithstanding it was politically a time of great anxiety. Although there were some small crowds of people hanging about the streets on the day of election, and on the following day the newspaper shops at the time of publishing were besieged, all was quite orderly. We had it, of course, for the comfort of the old ladies, that all the Protestants were in bodily fear; and perhaps in former times there might have been some risk, for in some parts of France it was an inconvenient custom, occasionally exercised on a sumptuous scale, to burn, shoot, and otherwise destroy Protestants and other obnoxious heretics. In the present day, however, it would no doubt be considered an economic mistake to slay, or to drive away to other lands, the birds which beneficently lay, in hotels, pensions, furnished villas, shops, and other places, their heart-winning, hate-dissipating golden eggs; and instead of a display of unpleasant engines of extirpation, there is great kindliness of feeling towards Protestants, and every provision is made for alluring strangers to Pau, and detaining them there by means of cricket and golf grounds, skating-rinks, fox-hunting, lawn tennis, libraries, museums, and the like active and passive means of enjoyment.

XX.

SECOND WINTER IN THE RIVIERA.

WE left Pau for Toulouse on 23d October 1877. The journey occupied upwards of eight hours, or two hours longer than the same journey from Toulouse. At every little station there is a stoppage for an apparently endless length of time, although I suppose the delay is partly attributable to the necessities of the careful system of registration of luggage. One tunnel was shored up, and we went slowly through it and over the ground before and after. When we approached Toulouse, and had to cross the rivers, the train proceeded with the utmost caution. The bridges had evidently been washed away, and what we passed over seemed either unfinished or temporary. It was here, it may be recollected, that in the year 1875 such disastrous floods took place. But whether the condition of the bridges in 1877 was attributable to this or to a more recent flooding, we could not tell. The journey, though long, was agreeable, the rivers resembling our own Scotch rivers, and the Pyrenees clear and crisp, with a slight sprinkling or dusting of snow upon them, though not enough to give them the aspect of snowy mountains. The trees were clothed in their autumn tints of yellow, brown, and red, and the sun was shining. We were accommodated with the rooms we had formerly occupied in the Hotel Sacaron

—clean, tidy, but carpetless; the mosquitoes, however, were gone. A good many persons appeared in the *salle à manger*, but there was no common *table-d'hôte* dinner. Each party dined separately at 5 francs per head. I had, before leaving Pau, calculated on getting a good hour before dinner for a drive through the town; but a change had been recently made,—I suppose about the 16th October, the usual commencement of winter hours,—by which our train, probably to dispense with another, became a slow one, stopping at all stations, and taking two hours longer than before; so that, arriving at six o'clock, there was no time for a drive in daylight. In the evening I had a stroll through a small part of the town, which contains some good wide shop streets. The Church of St. Servan is the finest, and, according to representations, peculiarly constructed, but in the dark I had no opportunity of seeing it. Nor did we see the bridges and other neighbouring public parts. Had we not been anxious to push on towards Marseilles, we might have stopped a day to see a city which has a name, but is a good deal out of the ordinary path of travellers. We also missed seeing the view from it of the Pyrenees, which is said to be there extensive, being about the centre of the chain. It rained through the night, and was damp in the morning; and as our train left at ten o'clock, we could not obtain an hour before leaving for Montpellier.

The scenery between Toulouse and Cette, great part of which we had missed on our former journey in the dark or twilight, was not equal to that of the previous day. We passed field after field of vineyards, where they were lading large carts with the grapes. About Biarritz and other places in the south-west of France, the carts are generally drawn by oxen. In Italy, the equally patient buffalo, with its meek eyes, is used. Here the carts seen from the railway were drawn by two horses. Grapes were charged at the railway station of Narbonne, in the centre of this vine district, 5d. per lb. We had paid elsewhere from $1\frac{1}{2}$d.

(15 centimes) to 3d. (30 centimes) per lb., but at railway stations prices are usually increased. For oranges at railway stations, 20 centimes apiece were sometimes demanded. The sun went down as we got into Cette, but not before gaining, as we approached that port, a glimpse now and then of our old friend the Mediterranean. A cup of coffee at the station was refreshing, but the waiter, who calculated in sous, was very confused in his reckoning. We arrived at Montpellier in the dark at 6.44, and found the omnibus of the Hotel Nevet waiting; but it would not start till all luggage was got out, so that we might as well have taken our luggage with us instead of leaving it, as we usually did on such journeys, for the night at the station. This hotel, recommended as the best, is rather old-fashioned both in accommodation and furnishing, giving an idea of the comforts enjoyed there in former times when Montpellier was in vogue, and its name was a synonym for any place where the air was peculiarly pure and salubrious. Now I suspect it has lost favour, and more modern localities, such as Cannes and Mentone, have supplanted it, as railways have brought their previously-hidden virtues to light, and rendered them more easy of access, probably to yield in turn to others better spoken of. Dr. Taylor (p. 7) thus adverts to its climate:—

'The climate of the south-east of France, of which Montpellier may be considered as the centre, is, on the contrary' (to Pau), 'highly electric and dry, subject, particularly during the spring, to severe cutting and irritating winds, loaded with impalpable dust, exciting in its qualities, and productive of inflammatory diseases of an acute character. To prove these latter assertions, we shall produce the following unbiassed evidence. We find in a work on the medical topography of Montpellier, the following statistical results of diseases treated during a year in the public hospital of that town. The number of patients admitted in one year was 2756; the proportion of deaths was 154; and of that number, 53—that is, more than a third—were caused by diseases of the chest. Again, we find the following opinion from a work full of valuable observations on the effect of the winds of the south-east of France: "One ought to have a chest sound and well constituted to resist such impressions." Matthews also, in his *Diary of an Invalid*, says " that every mouthful of the air irritates weak lungs and sets them coughing."'

After a late dinner, I walked out, but could see little.

The town seemed full of cafés. In the morning, before the train started, we had an hour to look about. It would be unfair to judge of any place with such slender opportunities, but it did not appear to offer great attractions. In the centre of the town, surrounded by lofty buildings, there is a large open place, adorned by a handsome fountain. Out of this place a Boulevard runs, leading to the Place d'Armes, where people walk and drive, and it is said there are fine views of the Pyrenees and Alps to be had; but the morning was hazy, and any prospect was hid. It was also cold, and wraps became advisable.

We had to change carriages twice between Montpellier and Marseilles—viz., at Tarascon, and again, in little more than an hour, at Arles. The second change was aggravating, because we could not see why the carriages might not have gone on to Marseilles; while those into which, after some detention and trouble, we were shifted, were antiquated, narrow, and confined. Fortunately no rain fell during the change, for Arles station is not under cover.

I have already, in mentioning our first visit to the Riviera, taken note of Marseilles. We were glad to meet some old Scotch friends unexpectedly at the Hotel Noailles. The weather was cold, which of itself would have rendered it advisable to push on; so, after a drive through the town next day, we left for Hyères, about fifty miles distant, by the 1.20 train, but found by another of those changes made just a few days previously, we could only book to Toulon, the train in connection from Toulon to Hyères by a branch line having been discontinued, although the Hyères season was just commencing—a rather odd way of accommodating the coming visitors. On arrival at Toulon, we had accordingly upwards of three hours before a train would start for Hyères, and we availed ourselves of the time to explore a little about this noted naval station.

The town of Toulon itself is uninteresting; its streets are

dirty and narrow, the houses high. Near the railway station the ground is more open and the houses more modern. Passing them, we soon came upon the fortifications which surround the town, but retracing our steps, walked down to the docks and along the public quay. There are two large docks communicating with each other —the Port Marchand and the Port Militaire. The latter is one of the great arsenals of France; but we could not see it, an order of admission being required, only procurable in the morning. It extends to 35 acres and is said to be capable of receiving 200 ships of the line. The other dock is probably of about the same extent. Both docks are highly fortified. On looking from the quay, we saw many of the old men-of-war laid up like invalids, dismasted and dismantled and put under cover, apparently as hospital ships. At one time convicts were kept in some of them. A little beyond, some serviceable men-of-war lay, and the quays were crowded with boats which, with men and officers, were passing to and fro, making it a lively, gay scene. Some civilians were evidently going out in the boats to see the ships or their friends on board. A bronze statue has been erected upon the public quay, to the memory of the many eminent men who have been connected by birth or otherwise with Toulon and its history, and whose names are engraved on the sides. After our stroll, we were glad to return and have, in the railway station refreshment room, dinner (supplied at $3\frac{1}{2}$ francs a head, the usual station tariff), and at 6.50 left in the dark for Hyères, arriving at eight o'clock. Nine omnibuses in a semicircle were waiting the arrival of the train, but we were the only passengers requiring conveyance. We took that of the Hotel d'Orient, recommended in Bradshaw and also by Murray for its beautiful situation. It is a comfortable hotel, the hotelkeeper is attentive, and the situation is more sheltered from the mistral than others; but it seems a mistake to speak of it as 'beautiful,' as any view it may have commanded at one time is shut out by the trees of the garden on the opposite side of the road. The Hotel des Îles d'Or is the principal hotel in Hyères. It commands a fine view, but has a west or south-west exposure. The Hesperides Hotel is near to it. This and the Hotel des Ambassadeurs, in the centre of the small town, are considered comfortable and more moderate.

Hyères is considered less costly than any of the other important places in the Riviera, regarding it as within the Riviera, which perhaps, strictly speaking, it is not. I believe it may be considered to be about 2 francs per day less than Mentone for corresponding accommodation and pension, and in all probability the reason for this is that it is not usually thought so attractive. The town itself is most uninviting. The original and older part of it, lying upon the hill slope, is so very dirty that I could not bring myself to visit it a second time. The drains there run down the middle of the streets, and no regard seems to be paid to cleanliness. It speaks well, doubtless, for its healthiness, that the inhabitants can survive its pestilential odours. The newer part of the town consists mainly of a long street, in which most of the hotels are, and a few poor shops, some of which were not, at this early period of the winter, opened. The Rue des Palmiers, in which the English church is situated, is the best street. It is flanked by gardens attached to the houses, and by a row of palm trees on each side, which grow better in Hyères than they do in some other parts where they are more exposed to dust and sea air. This Rue has quite the look of a retired row in the suburbs of a large city. Outside the town, which is altogether very small, there are a number of pretty villas. Behind the town a hill rises steeply to a height of 650 feet, whereon the château, an old castle, stands. The view from this hill is very fine, looking down upon the plains below, and the surrounding mountains, and the Mediterranean three miles off—the long, low, but picturesque islands of Hyères, called the Îles d'Or, the nearest being to appearance about two to three miles from the shore, or six miles off, but as distance on water is deceptive, probably rather more. These islands, formerly productive, now barren, but said to be salubrious, are four in number, the largest being four miles long by two miles broad, and (speaking from distant recollection of a visit to Ireland) slightly resembling from Hyères, though larger, Spike Island at Queenstown, Cork.

There are a number of very nice walks at Hyères. About a mile out of town, a piece of ground has been recently laid out as a Jardin d'Acclimation; but as yet it is mainly occupied by an immense number of ducks of all kinds. The great drawback to Hyères is, that it is not sufficiently sheltered from the mistral, which blows during spring from the west and unprotected side. It is also far from the sea-shore, and is therefore deprived of the life and interest always found at the sea-side. Its climate, though warm, is, I believe, changeable. On the 1st November it was as hot there as it is any day in July in London; but it may suit some invalids who require to be at a distance from the sea. We did not like it, but were perhaps spoiled for fully appreciating it by having been previously at other and, as we thought, more attractive places. This, however, has to be said, that our visit to Hyères took place before the season had fairly commenced, and to be in a season place out of season is always dreary. We were very nearly the only persons in our hotel. There was one family there, whom we met in very painful circumstances. They had brought with them a daughter who had been given up in London by her physicians, who said her only chance of life was going to the south of France. With great difficulty she was brought so far. She survived about five or six weeks from the time of leaving home, but died a few days after reaching Hyères. We attended her funeral, conducted by the English clergyman, and it was gratifying to see that it created an apparent sympathy among the native population, who assembled in considerable numbers in the burying-ground.

Hyères is no doubt interesting to other persons; indeed, we have met with those who have spoken very highly of it. La Plage, the nearest point on the coast, is about three miles distant, and the railway has been extended to it and to the salines beyond. We took the train to it one day, and found a few villas had been built in the hope of making it a seaside town; but at the time of our visit, at least, the speculation did not seem to look hopeful. There is nothing attractive either about the beach or about the neighbourhood, except a forest of umbrella pines, affording the only shelter it possesses against the winds, which must often blow violently at this part, and were blowing so keenly at the time that we were glad to walk home and not wait three hours for a train.

We were a good deal annoyed by mosquitoes while at Hyères, necessitating recourse to burning pastilles at night, and waging a war of extermination in the morning.

After being eight days at Hyères, we were by no means sorry to leave it for Cannes by the little branch line to Toulon, where we were doomed to wait two hours— one in consequence of the trains not fitting in, and another because the train we were to join (a first-class express from Paris) was an hour behind time. French trains are generally very punctual, but on these long journeys are, especially at the commencement of a season, often late. The engine was, in consequence, urged on at an unusual speed after leaving Toulon, and we had made up a good part of the lost time when we were stopped at Fréjus by a goods train having by some accident got in the way. After all, we were not more than half an hour late at Cannes. We again had much difficulty in getting seat-room, guards affording no manner of assistance; the carriages also were filled with people who had travelled all night from Paris, and perhaps were selfishly unwilling to be disturbed by intruders. On this our second journey to Cannes, the blinds on *both* sides of the carriage were ruthlessly closed by the 'foreigners' sitting next them, so that we had no chance of seeing the lovely views to be had from the windows.

We went to our old quarters at Cannes, where, in spite of mosquitoes and flies, we were, as before, very comfortable. The weather was partly sunny and partly wet during the ten days we sojourned there. On one of the bright days our quondam invalid walked to the top of the Croix de Garde, which she could not attempt on our visit the previous year. It showed how well she then was, and how much cause for thankfulness we then had.

We reached Mentone on 12th November 1877, unfortunately in heavy rain, and, having some time previously secured them, obtained possession of the same bright rooms we had occupied the year before, and there we remained till the end of March.

The weather at Mentone during December and January was unusually cold—such a coldness as had not been experienced for many years. It was penetrating, and hard to withstand, at least during the hours of darkness. When the sun was out, the air was warm; but mornings and evenings were cold, and it was difficult to avoid encountering cold blasts and drafts, especially in passing from hot rooms through cold corridors chilled by open doors, and we did find this year servants very tiresome in leaving doors open which communicated with the outer air. I believe, though not conscious of it at the time, that this cold weather and the cold drafts had reproduced, though it might have then been in a very elementary way, the seeds of disease which we fondly thought had been altogether eradicated.

We found the municipal authorities busy making a continuation of the promenade along the shore for a full additional half-mile or more westward towards Cape Martin, —an addition which has ere this proved a great accession to the place, and will be complete when carried as far as Cape Martin itself, which, with its forest of trees, is one of the most charming haunts about Mentone; but the access to it has hitherto been either by the dusty high road or by the rough stony beach. Builders had also been busy with new houses, but the speculation, I doubt, had not proved profitable, as, owing to the dulness of trade and to the war in the East, many of the villas remained empty, while even the hotels did not fill so rapidly as they had done the previous year. However, when we left in the spring, the builders had not seemed deterred by the want of demand, for building operations were still progressing, and I fear much that in a few years Mentone, if not overbuilt for the number of visitors, will lose a great deal of its charm as a rural town. In other respects it was the same as ever, bright and pleasant; and helping to make it so, we had friends in many of the other hotels, besides meeting old friends in our own.

During the first part of our stay, people were kept in great anxiety about the course of events in France, and we never could tell but that any day a revolution might break out: one result apparently was that newspapers were occasionally stopped, or at least some did not reach us. *Punch* had in one number a certain distinguished gentleman floundering in the mud. This number did not reach us through the usual channels, but the cartoon nevertheless came to the hotel enclosed in a letter to one of the visitors from a friend in Germany. Perhaps the French are a people too easily excited to make it safe to allow such things to be circulated, but it seems strange to our ideas of free discussion.

When these difficulties were overcome, the British portion of the population at least were disquieted by the attitude taken by England in regard to affairs in the East. Before we left home in 1876, Turkish misrule and oppression of the provinces had awakened the attention of the European powers, and a movement for reform was made. The Turkish atrocities in Bulgaria had also come to light, and Mr. Gladstone, with all the fervour of his noble heart, had come to the front, and forced the facts into lively attention, and not without effect. But the firm word from us to the Turk, which would have prevented war, was not spoken, and Russia found herself compelled, single-handed, to have recourse to arms to terminate oppression. Russia did not declare war till April 1877. When she became successful, there was considerable excitement in the south of England, and it seemed as if many good people were not careful of what they fed upon, and for a long time nightly dreamt that the Czar, with one foot on Russia, was putting another on Constantinople, and, like a gigantic Gulliver, was just about to haul India off to St. Petersburg. Into the political causes and consequences of this excitement it would be out of place to enter here. Suffice it to say that they made us uneasy during several months; and had it not been for the extreme moderation and coolness throughout regulating the counsels of Russia (which was no doubt thinking as much of taking Jupiter or Georgium Sidus as of taking India, or even Constantinople, and was perhaps amused, though displeased, at our fright), joined to the restraining good sense of the country at home generally, we should have been involved in war, all Europe would have been ablaze, and—selfish thought —what would those have had to do who found a foreign residence necessary?

Among other delicious canards to which we were treated from time to time during the war in the little French newspapers, was the astounding information that our beloved Queen had resolved to resign.

Two important events, however, did happen during our stay at Mentone—first, the somewhat sudden or unlooked-for death of Victor Emmanuel in January 1878; and, within a month afterwards, the long-expected death of Pope Pius IX. On both these occasions a special service was held in the Cathedral of Mentone, and I suppose 2000 persons must have been crammed into its body and recesses. Although the church is a pretty large one, the odour with which it was filled was by no means that of sanctity, and it was a relief, when the service was over, in little more than an hour, to get out to the fresh air. Besides black drapery hung throughout the church, a grand catafalque was in each case erected in the centre of the cathedral, in front of which a space was reserved and seated for the grandees of Mentone. The altar at the back was denuded, perhaps to afford space, and the singers and players on instruments were placed between it and the catafalque, out of sight of the audience. The harsh sounds of the brass instruments as they blew their trumpet-blasts thus in our ears seemed vastly inappropriate. The singing had quite a provincial mediocrity; but on the whole, for a small country town, I believe it may be said the arrangements, according to Romanist notions of how such things should be conducted, were fairly good.

The death of the Pope, while it prevented the celebration of the Carnival in Rome, had no influence in preventing its observance in Mentone and Nice, and scenes similar to those of last year were enacted, with a difference—not to the better—in the pageant. At Nice the Carnival was, I believe, grander than ever, and many of the Mentone visitors made a day of it there. The Carnival time brought with it rather appropriately, though probably accidentally, some fancy balls in Mentone, for which gay and elaborate costumes were, I believe, procured at Nice. We were kindly invited to one of these entertainments, but for reasons declined.

The tendency towards such gaieties seemed this winter rather on the increase. They suit some, but to those desirous of quiet evenings it is disturbing to have frequent routs, and concerts, and other diversions in the drawing-rooms of the hotels.

We were treated, however, to a different description of pleasure, in the shape of an exhibition at New Year's time of a large collection of water-colour paintings of views in Mentone, Cannes, Corsica, etc., by Mr. Van der Weldt, a skilful artist. The pictures were for sale, but the admission money went to the funds of Helvetia.

The orange and lemon trees this winter bore scantily, and we could not help feeling regret to see how few and far between were the bunches of golden fruit. To what cause this failure of the crop was to be attributed I do not know, but I believe that the trees do not bear largely for two successive years.

We again, on leaving Mentone, took a carriage to San Remo, and fortunately had a quiet and warm sunny day for the drive. The dust lay thick on the road, but there was no wind to raise it. The loveliness of the ride was the one atoning circumstance to put against all the pain of parting with friends, and leaving a place with which so many happy recollections were associated. We little thought we were bearing away from it one—then in apparent good health, and, fond of travel, thoroughly appreciating all that she saw—who would never see it again; for the regret of leaving was tempered with the hope that it might be our privilege, though it might not be absolutely needful, to return in a future year to this bright land of the olive and fig tree, the lemon and orange—this land of cloudless sky and cheering sun.

After leaving Ventimiglia, we looked out for the Roman amphitheatre which had been discovered and was being excavated, but could not find the place, and our driver was unable to render us any information or assistance. We were now in the heart of the scenery forming the *locale* of that deeply-interesting story, *Dr. Antonio*; and on the previous occasion our driver, I believe, pointed out to us the veritable house in which Sir John Davenne and his heavenly daughter had their abode. After paying a passing visit to friends in Bordighera, we soon afterwards were again in San Remo.

We remained three weeks at San Remo, and during our stay had a good deal of wind blowing from the west, and cold air with heavy rain, and consoled ourselves by thinking that the wind being in that direction, was probably more felt at Mentone. On leaving, we proceeded by train to Alassio, about twenty-eight miles along the coast eastward. We had heard Alassio a good deal spoken of, and wished to see it. It is as yet only visited by casual travellers, and it has not become a place of common winter resort for invalids. Had we not written for rooms, we might not have found any carriage waiting to take us to the Hotel de Rome, which was at the time the only hotel, I believe, to which English people could go. It was a drive of about a mile from the station (principally through the long narrow streets of the town) to the hotel, which fronts the beach, just out of and to the west of the town. It is a comparatively new house, and the accommodation is fairly good and clean. Another hotel, 'The Grand,' on a much larger scale, has been built, also fronting the sea, but about the middle of the town. It was not, however, then opened, and the situation did not seem so desirable, though nearer the station.

We found Alassio to be one of those little Italian coast towns in the Riviera which are by no means attractive in themselves. The population is said to be 5500, so that it is of some extent. It is dirty and disagreeable, and unfortunately, like some others, is not shelved away upon an avoidable eminence, but is stuck down upon the very best part of the shore. The towers of the cathedral and other churches, and the structure of the houses, combine to give it, at a little distance, a picturesque appearance. A sandy beach forms the shore, on which, opposite the town, many fishing boats lay. The sands, of a pale yellow or white, though they may afford good bathing, are not interesting, shells and sea-weed being scarce. The town lies at the head or in the centre of a bay formed by two projecting capes or protecting arms, the Capo della Melle on the west and the Capo S. Croce on the east. Between these two points the distance may, I suppose, be about three miles. A semicircular cordon of hills runs back from their termini, and with an inner circle surrounds and hems in Alassio lying in the basin below. The slopes of most of the hills, at least of the inner circle, are covered with olive, carroube, and other trees, giving them a richly-wooded aspect; but the hills themselves do not rise to any great altitude. They are sufficiently high and close upon the town to give much—perhaps, in summer, too much—shelter to Alassio, and to afford room for supposing that it might become, on a smaller scale, another Mentone for winter residence. Possibly if no old Italian town had existed there, and everything could be laid out anew, Alassio might be made a good place and suitable for strangers; but the great drawbacks to it for residence, and not regarding it from a medical point of view, are the existence of this old dirty town, which usurps nearly the whole of the shore space, and is far from attractive, and the confined or limited situation. I believe that many fine walks may be found about it, but the mountains lack the height and picturesque grandeur of those of Mentone, and there seem to be no valleys and rivers to offer variety. Some English families, however, have been so pleased with it as to have built houses there, for permanent occupation, on the slopes of the hills. One of these we visited—that of Mr. Gibb, a Scotch gentleman. Its position is commanding, and derives shelter from the hills behind; and from the terraces overlooking the town, the views were fine. The ground was laid out in the style of hanging gardens, full of orange trees. At leaving, Mr. Gibb kindly caused a basketful of oranges to be plucked and given to us, and they were of the most delicious flavour; indeed, I believe the Alassio oranges are noted for their excellent quality. Although a little society is to be found at Alassio, it struck me as a dull place of residence except to those who are fond of retirement. A great improvement to the town would be the formation of a promenade along the shore, as at Mentone, Cannes, and Nice. Were this done, it would help to draw strangers, and if strangers came, other improvements would follow.

On the first afternoon, we had, after arrival, time to take a walk westward along the beach for about a mile to a small village Laigueglia, which, as usual, possesses a church with a campanile; other large buildings like granaries fronted the sea. We took, the following day, a much more interesting walk up the height of Santa Croce to the eastward, encountering unexpectedly by the way a smart shower, from which some protection was afforded by the trees. Upon leaving the town, a paved donkey-path leads up the hillside, skirted by woods (the carroube trees here growing luxuriantly), to the ruins of an old chapel, whence an extensive panorama spreads out on one side, back over the hills behind the town, and down on the town and ocean below; while eastward the rockbound coast stretches away, visible as far, I believe, on a clear day, as Genoa and beyond it. But the day was not sufficiently clear to see so far.

Dr. Giuseppe Schneer has published a pamphlet of about eighty pages on Alassio, titled, *Alassio ed il suo clima confrontato con quello di S. Remo, Mentone, Nizza, e Cannes.* It is in Italian, unfortunately, and consists of three parts. The first and largest part contains medical advice, leading up, of course, to approval of Alassio. The second part gives some information about the town, its population, schools, hotels, etc.; and in reference to its healthiness, adduces a table of mortality from which it would appear that during nine years the average was about 100 deaths per annum in a population assumed to be now and throughout 5500, or 1 in 55, which would certainly be extraordinarily low. Another table is given to show the duration of life, evidencing considerable longevity. The third part deals with the meteorology of Alassio, and contains some tables, from which it would appear, if the observations be correctly taken, Alassio stands well, and, on the whole, obtains a higher temperature than places on the Riviera with which it is compared—a result which may be accounted for by its being more shut in. I take the liberty of quoting an excerpt from one of these tables (p. 74):—

'*Media della Temperatura delle Singole Stazioni della Riviera.*

Stazioni.	Gennaio.	Febraio.	Marzo.	Aprile.	Novembre.	Decembre.	Media de 5 Mesi. piu freddi.
Alassio, . .	9·18	10·	13·45	14·05	11·86	10·80	11·05
San Remo, .	8·97	11·44	11·22	13·83	12·41	10·43	10·25
Mentone, .	9·3	9·5	11·6	14·6	12·2	9·5	10·04
Nizza, . .	8·1	9·5	11·2	14·5	12·6	9·2	9·83
Cannes, . .	8·6	9·8	13·4	17·3	13·5	9·9	10·45'

Dr. Schneer also states that in the five months from November to March there are 79 days all bright, 37·5 half so, 36 cloudy, and 20 bad.

It may be, therefore, that the climate of Alassio is one suitable for invalids, and living is moderate, as pension can be had at the Hotel de Rome for 7 and 8 francs per day *tout compris.*

After being two nights there, we left for Genoa. The day was fine, and having a compartment to ourselves, we had full opportunity of looking about and enjoying the scenery. The distance is about fifty-seven miles, and as the train took nearly four hours to arrive quietly at Genoa, we moved leisurely. I paced one of our bedrooms at the Hotel de Gênes, and it seemed to be 27 feet long by 21 feet wide, and probably it was 20 feet high. In the afternoon we drove out again to see the Campo Santo, and found little change since last year. On the following day we visited most of the places we had seen the previous year, and some others, including some additional palaces already noticed. With a little difficulty we made discovery of the Via Orifici (a narrow street in the heart of the town, not far from the hotel), where the filigree shops are, and made a few purchases. The shops are on both sides of the street, and contain sometimes beautiful specimens of this delicate work in silver and gold; perhaps the shop of Salvi exhibited the largest collection of choice handiwork. In buying, it is well to remember one is transacting in Italy. Genoa has a Galleria, but not nearly so handsome as that at Milan, although equally suitable for its purpose. Last year we had seen it in course of construction, but it was now completed, and some of the best shops in Genoa were opened in it. But at the time of our visit it was not fully occupied. At night it was, as at Milan, crowded by the townspeople and visitors. A long, wide, lofty arcade like this, covered over by a glass roof, and brilliantly lighted up, is naturally an attraction, and something of the kind in our large towns might induce a withdrawal of many from the gin-palaces and drinking-shops, the glare and comfort of which seem to be so great an inducement and temptation to certain classes. But, like the Italian galleries, they require to be thoroughfares in good central situations—not *cul-de-sacs*.

In the afternoon of the third day we left by train for Turin. A few drops fell as we left, augmenting as we proceeded under inky clouds to heavy rain. We obtained our last glimpse of our old friend the Mediterranean just after leaving Genoa. The railway stations, not improved by the rain, looked all so dirty—filthy, indeed. At Alessandria, where we had an hour to wait, affording time to dine, the whole platform was most disagreeable, from the abominable habit (elsewhere alluded to) the Italians have of defiling every place, even the floors of churches, so that it is not uncommon to see a notice up in the churches requesting that it be not practised. However, good service is done by the women, who trail their gowns over the floors, and thus, with a thoughtful consideration for others and an unselfish disregard for themselves, keep them cleaner than they would otherwise be.

We arrived at Turin about eight o'clock in the evening, and found quarters in the Ligurie, a large, new, first-class hotel, not far from the station. The double windows, thick shutters, and the cloth curtains outside the bedroom doors, were suggestive of what descent in temperature there may sometimes be in Turin; but except a little cold and damp in the evening, resulting from the rain which had fallen before our arrival, we had it warm and sunny during the three days we remained there. The following forenoon we devoted to a long drive in and about Turin. The streets are exceedingly regular and wide, and the houses being lofty and the town of considerable extent and full of handsome public buildings and monuments, Turin has all the appearance of a capital; but though a city upwards of 2000 years old, there is about it quite a modern air. The view along several of the streets is terminated by a grand vista of snowy mountains, and one of the sights of Turin—indeed, its great sight—is the view obtained from it of the Alps. To witness this in perfection, it should be seen from a commanding height early in the morning of a clear day. We accordingly, soon after breakfast, driving past the public park and gardens, and round an imposing quadrangular building called the Castel di Valentino, and crossing the river Po by a stone bridge of five arches, were deposited at the foot of the steep hill on which the Capuchin Monastery is built. Here, by a road winding round the hill, we walked to the top, and from the plateau beheld the most magnificent mountain prospect I had ever seen, or which I suppose is visible in Europe. Right in front of us, against a sky all but clear, rose the great range of the snowy Alps, stretching far as the eye could reach to right and left, the nearest being only about fifteen miles distant, but seeming much nearer as seen through a transparent atmosphere over a range of low hills lying in front of them. Monte Viso, conical in shape, about forty-five miles to the south-west, in which the river Po finds its source, rises prominently like a huge tusk, the rest like an enormous jaw, in wavy line of peaks or serrated folds. Between the river Po, flowing below, and the mountains, the ground appears one vast level plain, on which the city rests in regular lines of lofty houses, the monotony being broken by the numerous towers and domes of the public buildings; and conspicuous among them is the great ugly peculiar square dome of the Jewish Synagogue, a far from pleasing object. In a different direction, away to the north-east, we saw the Superga or Royal Mausoleum, built on the crest of a hill much higher than the monastery, and commanding a fully better view. To visit it and the royal tombs is a day's excursion, and we gave it up. The royal palace was among the places in town which we visited.

Its magnificent rooms are reached by a truly regal staircase of marble adorned by sculpture. The armoury, an interesting exhibition, is not far from the palace. A long room in it is filled with figures of men-at-arms on horseback clad with the armour of different periods.

The streets of Turin are to a large extent lined by arcades, and no doubt in bad weather, and especially in snowstorms, such a method of construction must be useful, the shops, however, being generally placed under them.

Turin possesses many fine monuments. One of the finest is that to Cavour, inscribed, 'A Camillo Cavour nato a Torino il x. Agosto MDCCCX., morto il vi. Giugno MDCCCLXI.' A kneeling female figure, representing doubtless Italia, is presenting him with a garland; while below, the base is adorned by emblematical figures at least life-size, and, like the statue, of white marble—all very tasteful. Another and very singular monument is that to the Duke of Genoa. His horse falls to the ground on its knees wounded, and the rider, the Duke, sitting on the horse, is resting one foot on the ground and waving his sword.

We had a Sunday in Turin, and in the morning went into the cathedral. It is a large building, not very imposing; but inside it is dark, and the dirtiest church we had seen in Italy, which is saying a good deal. To Protestants, the Waldensian Church is a place of great interest. Unfortunately we had been informed at the hotel that the Italian service was in the morning, and the French service in the afternoon; and we therefore attended service in the morning, in the English Church in the yard immediately behind it. Returning in the afternoon, we found our informant was mistaken; the French service had been in the morning, the afternoon service was in Italian. The church, which is a large one, was scantily attended by a shifting congregation of the poorer classes of Italians. Many, apparently Roman Catholics, just entered to see what was doing, and after a few minutes went out again, to be replaced by others. As we understood little of what was said, we did not stay the service out. We learned at dinner from a lady who had been there in the forenoon, that the morning service had been in French, that the church was crowded by a most respectable congregation, and that the whole service was most interesting.

Turin is a place in which a few days can be well spent, and an excursion is not unfrequently made from it to the Waldensian valleys, part of the way to which is by railway.

We had a beautiful day on which to leave for Aix-les-Bains by the Mont Cenis Tunnel. The view of the snowy mountains was brilliantly clear as we approached them. In about six miles we reached the first or low hills. Thenceforth the scenery along the line of railway was at some parts wild and grand, and at others the hills were surmounted by structures which gave a picturesque character to them. At last we reached and passed through the Mont Cenis Tunnel. The time taken in passing through was about twenty-eight minutes. It was long to be boxed up in the dark, but it did not feel so long as I anticipated. Once or twice I put down a window; the air felt slightly damp, not cold. On issuing from it on the French side, the railway makes a long detour to reach the lower level of Modane, where luggage is examined by the French *douaniers*, and we changed into French carriages, which were superior in comfort to those of the Italian line. The scenery all along to Chambery and Aix-les-Bains was among the mountains, some of them capped with snow.

We stayed, as we had planned, a week at Aix-les-Bains, and we should have enjoyed it but that great part of the time we had rain, and the air, though warm, was moist. A range of low hills separates Aix from Lake Bourget, enclosed on the other side by steep rugged mountains, their summits visible over the hills. A short walk takes one to the top of these hills, whence an excellent view is had of the lake, upon which a steamer plies during the summer. The lake is reached by the road at a part fringed by tall poplars about one and a half to two miles distant, offering a pleasant stroll on a fine afternoon such as we had to walk to it.

We left by a morning train for Dijon, and shortly after the sky got black, and we were obliged to change carriages at Culoz in drenching rain, the station being destitute of cover so necessary at a junction like this, or indeed at every railway station. As we passed along, the whole country seemed to be inundated. Both at Dijon and Fontainebleau we were caught in showers unexpectedly. At Paris, where we rested for a few days, we had rain, but principally through the night. At Boulogne we had a shower. Crossing thence, we landed, after a beautiful passage, at Folkestone in May 1878, and proceeded by Bristol to Stoke Bishop. Here, instead of the sunshine with which the neighbourhood of Clifton is usually favoured at this season, and to which we had looked forward, we were still pursued by almost daily rain. After remaining six weeks looking constantly for better weather, we got back to Scotland.

And here with a sad heart I must close. I had written most of these pages at a time when we had every belief that the changes experienced had effected cure—at least to the extent of allowing us to go home for the summer. And we had been so much longer away than we had proposed when we left, that not unnaturally we were the more anxious to be back. The last change was destined to be fatal. Looking to second causes, it is probable that the unforeseen and unusual moisture to which we had been exposed everywhere after leaving Italy, succeeding so long a residence in a dry climate, had developed latent seeds of disease, and weakness had latterly been increased by exposure to a cold draft inducing cough. Whatever was the cause, she for whose benefit we had taken this prolonged tour in sunny lands, and who we had fondly hoped had been restored to health, sank within a few months from the time of touching her native shore. It was when hopes were beginning to revive, and she herself had thought the crisis was past, a sudden change for the worse took place. After a restless night, the morning light, for which she had anxiously longed, only arrived to bear her soul peacefully away from weakness and solicitude to a land brighter than any she had looked on here. Though gentle and unpresuming, her cheerful and unselfish disposition, joined to other graces, and to good sense born of a well-balanced and well-informed mind, soon made her acquaintance valued wherever she went; and, scattered as so many are, perhaps it is only through this little record some may chance to learn that they have lost an esteemed friend.

THE END.

APRIL 1879.

GENERAL LISTS OF NEW WORKS

PUBLISHED BY

Messrs. LONGMANS, GREEN & CO.

PATERNOSTER ROW, LONDON.

HISTORY, POLITICS, HISTORICAL MEMOIRS &c.

Armitage's Childhood of the English Nation. Fcp. 8vo. 2s. 6d.
Arnold's Lectures on Modern History. 8vo. 7s. 6d.
Bagehot's Literary Studies. 2 vols. 8vo. 28s.
Buckle's History of Civilisation. 3 vols. crown 8vo. 24s.
Chesney's Indian Polity. 8vo. 21s.
— Waterloo Lectures. 8vo. 10s. 6d.
Digby's Famine Campaign in India. 2 vols. 8vo. 32s.
Durand's First Afghan War. Crown 8vo.

Epochs of Ancient History :—
    Beesly's Gracchi, Marius, and Sulla, 2s. 6d.
    Capes's Age of the Antonines, 2s. 6d.
    — Early Roman Empire, 2s. 6d.
    Cox's Athenian Empire, 2s. 6d.
    — Greeks and Persians, 2s. 6d.
    Curteis's Rise of the Macedonian Empire, 2s. 6d.
    Ihne's Rome to its Capture by the Gauls, 2s. 6d.
    Merivale's Roman Triumvirates, 2s. 6d.
    Sankey's Spartan and Theban Supremacies, 2s. 6d.

Epochs of English History :—
    Creighton's Shilling History of England (Introductory Volume). Fcp. 8vo. 1s.
    Browning's Modern England, 1820-1875, 9d.
    Cordery's Struggle against Absolute Monarchy, 1603-1688, 9d.
    Creighton's (Mrs.) England a Continental Power, 1066-1216, 9d.
    Creighton's (Rev. M.) Tudors and the Reformation, 1485-1603, 9d.
    Rowley's Rise of the People, 1215-1485, 9d.
    Rowley's Settlement of the Constitution, 1688-1778, 9d.
    Tancock's England during the American & European Wars, 1778-1820, 9d.
    York-Powell's Early England to the Conquest, 1s.

Epochs of Modern History :—
    Church's Beginning of the Middle Ages, 2s. 6d.
    Cox's Crusades, 2s. 6d.
    Creighton's Age of Elizabeth, 2s. 6d.
    Gairdner's Houses of Lancaster and York, 2s. 6d.
    Gardiner's Puritan Revolution, 2s. 6d.
    — Thirty Years' War, 2s. 6d.
    Hale's Fall of the Stuarts, 2s. 6d.
    Johnson's Normans in Europe, 2s. 6d.

London, LONGMANS & CO.

Epochs of Modern History—*continued*.
>Ludlow's War of American Independence, 2*s*. 6*d*.
>Morris's Age of Queen Anne, 2*s*. 6*d*.
>Seebohm's Protestant Revolution, 2*s*. 6*d*.
>Stubbs's Early Plantagenets, 2*s*. 6*d*.
>Warburton's Edward III., 2*s*. 6*d*.

Froude's English in Ireland in the 18th Century. 3 vols. 8vo. 48*s*.
— History of England. 12 vols. 8vo. £8. 18*s*. 12 vols. crown 8vo. 72*s*.
— Julius Cæsar, a Sketch. 8vo. 16*s*.
Gairdner's Richard III. and Perkin Warbeck. Crown 8vo. 10*s*. 6*d*.
Gardiner's England under Buckingham and Charles I., 1624-1628. 2 vols. 8vo. 24*s*.
— Personal Government of Charles I., 1628-1637. 2 vols. 8vo. 24*s*.
Greville's Journal of the Reigns of George IV. & William IV. 3 vols. 8vo. 36*s*.
Hayward's Selected Essays. 2 vols. crown 8vo. 12*s*.
Hearn's Aryan Household. 8vo. 16*s*.
Howorth's History of the Mongols. Vol. I. Royal 8vo. 28*s*.
Ihne's History of Rome. 3 vols. 8vo. 45*s*.
Lecky's History of England. Vols. I. & II., 1700-1760. 8vo. 36*s*.
— — — European Morals. 2 vols. crown 8vo. 16*s*.
— Spirit of Rationalism in Europe. 2 vols. crown 8vo. 16*s*.
Lewes's History of Philosophy. 2 vols. 8vo. 32*s*.
Longman's Lectures on the History of England. 8vo. 15*s*.
— Life and Times of Edward III. 2 vols. 8vo. 28*s*.
Macaulay's Complete Works. 8 vols. 8vo. £5. 5*s*.
— History of England :—
>Student's Edition. 2 vols. cr. 8vo. 12*s*. | Cabinet Edition. 8 vols. post 8vo. 48*s*.
>People's Edition. 4 vols. cr. 8vo. 16*s*. | Library Edition. 5 vols. 8vo. £4.

Macaulay's Critical and Historical Essays. Cheap Edition. Crown 8vo. 3*s*. 6*d*.
>Cabinet Edition. 4 vols. post 8vo. 24*s*. | Library Edition. 3 vols. 8vo. 36*s*.
>People's Edition. 2 vols. cr. 8vo. 8*s*. | Student's Edition. 1 vol. cr. 8vo. 6*s*.

May's Constitutional History of England. 3 vols. crown 8vo. 18*s*.
— Democracy in Europe. 2 vols. 8vo. 32*s*.
Merivale's Fall of the Roman Republic. 12mo. 7*s*. 6*d*.
— General History of Rome, B.C. 753—A.D. 476. Crown 8vo. 7*s*. 6*d*.
— History of the Romans under the Empire. 8 vols. post 8vo. 48*s*.
Phillips's Civil War in Wales and the Marches, 1642-1649. 8vo. 16*s*.
Prothero's Life of Simon de Montfort. Crown 8vo. 9*s*.
Rawlinson's Seventh Great Oriental Monarchy—The Sassanians. 8vo. 28*s*.
— Sixth Oriental Monarchy—Parthia. 8vo. 16*s*.
Seebohm's Oxford Reformers—Colet, Erasmus, & More. 8vo. 14*s*.
Sewell's Popular History of France. Crown 8vo. 7*s*. 6*d*.
Short's History of the Church of England. Crown 8vo. 7*s*. 6*d*.
Smith's Carthage and the Carthaginians. Crown 8vo. 10*s*. 6*d*.
Taylor's Manual of the History of India. Crown 8vo. 7*s*. 6*d*.
Todd's Parliamentary Government in England. 2 vols. 8vo. 37*s*.
Trench's Realities of Irish Life. Crown 8vo. 2*s*. 6*d*.
Walpole's History of England. Vols. I. & II. 8vo. 36*s*.

BIOGRAPHICAL WORKS.

Burke's Vicissitudes of Families. 2 vols. crown 8vo. 21*s*.
Cates's Dictionary of General Biography. Medium 8vo. 25*s*.

London, LONGMANS & CO.

General Lists of New Works.

Gleig's Life of the Duke of Wellington. Crown 8vo. 6s.
Jerrold's Life of Napoleon III. Vols. I. to III, 8vo. price 18s. each.
Jones's Life of Admiral Frobisher. Crown 8vo. 6s.
Lecky's Leaders of Public Opinion in Ireland. Crown 8vo. 7s. 6d.
Life (The) of Sir William Fairbairn. Crown 8vo. 18s.
Life (The) of Bishop Frampton. Crown 8vo. 10s. 6d.
Life (The) and Letters of Lord Macaulay. By his Nephew, G. Otto Trevelyan, M.P. Cabinet Edition, 2 vols. post 8vo. 12s. Library Edition, 2 vols. 8vo. 36s.
Marshman's Memoirs of Havelock. Crown 8vo. 3s. 6d.
Memoirs of Anna Jameson, by Gerardine Macpherson. 8vo. 12s. 6d.
Memorials of Charlotte Williams-Wynn. Crown 8vo. 10s. 6d.
Mendelssohn's Letters. Translated by Lady Wallace. 2 vols. cr. 8vo. 5s. each.
Mill's (John Stuart) Autobiography. 8vo. 7s. 6d.
Newman's Apologia pro Vita Sua. Crown 8vo. 6s.
Nohl's Life of Mozart. Translated by Lady Wallace. 2 vols. crown 8vo. 21s.
Pattison's Life of Casaubon. 8vo. 18s.
Spedding's Letters and Life of Francis Bacon. 7 vols. 8vo. £4. 4s.
Stephen's Essays in Ecclesiastical Biography. Crown 8vo. 7s. 6d.
Stigand's Life, Works &c. of Heinrich Heine. 2 vols. 8vo. 28s.
Zimmern's Life and Works of Lessing. Crown 8vo. 10s. 6d.

CRITICISM, PHILOSOPHY POLITY &c.

Amos's View of the Science of Jurisprudence. 8vo. 18s.
— Primer of the English Constitution. Crown 8vo. 6s.
Arnold's Manual of English Literature. Crown 8vo. 7s. 6d.
Bacon's Essays, with Annotations by Whately. 8vo. 10s. 6d.
— Works, edited by Spedding. 7 vols. 8vo. 73s. 6d.
Bain's Logic, Deductive and Inductive. Crown 8vo. 10s. 6d.
    PART I. Deduction, 4s. | PART II. Induction, 6s. 6d.
Blackley's German and English Dictionary. Post 8vo. 7s. 6d.
Bolland & Lang's Aristotle's Politics. Crown 8vo. 7s. 6d.
Bullinger's Lexicon and Concordance to the New Testament. Medium 8vo. 30s.
Comte's System of Positive Polity, or Treatise upon Sociology, translated:—
 VOL. I. General View of Positivism and its Introductory Principles. 8vo. 21s.
 VOL. II. Social Statics, or the Abstract Laws of Human Order. 14s.
 VOL. III. Social Dynamics, or General Laws of Human Progress. 21s.
 VOL. IV. Theory of the Future of Man; with Early Essays. 24s.
Congreve's Politics of Aristotle; Greek Text, English Notes. 8vo. 18s.
Contanseau's Practical French & English Dictionary. Post 8vo. 7s. 6d.
 — Pocket French and English Dictionary. Square 18mo. 3s. 6d.
Dowell's Sketch of Taxes in England. VOL. I. to 1642. 8vo. 10s. 6d.
Farrar's Language and Languages. Crown 8vo. 6s.
Grant's Ethics of Aristotle, Greek Text, English Notes. 2 vols. 8vo. 32s.
Hodgson's Philosophy of Reflection. 2 vols. 8vo. 21s.
Kalisch's Historical and Critical Commentary on the Old Testament; with a New Translation. Vol. I. *Genesis*, 8vo. 18s. or adapted for the General Reader, 12s. Vol. II. *Exodus*, 15s. or adapted for the General Reader, 12s. Vol. III. *Leviticus*, Part I. 15s. or adapted for the General Reader, 8s. Vol. IV. *Leviticus*, Part II. 15s. or adapted for the General Reader, 8s.

London, LONGMANS & CO.

Latham's Handbook of the English Language. Crown 8vo. 6s.
— English Dictionary. 1 vol. medium 8vo. 24s. 4 vols. 4to. £7.
Lewis on Authority in Matters of Opinion. 8vo. 14s.
Liddell & Scott's Greek-English Lexicon. Crown 4to. 36s.
— — —. Abridged Greek-English Lexicon. Square 12mo. 7s. 6d.
Longman's Pocket German and English Dictionary. 18mo. 5s.
Macaulay's Speeches corrected by Himself. Crown 8vo. 3s. 6d.
Macleod's Economical Philosophy. Vol. I. 8vo. 15s. Vol. II. Part I. 12s.
Mill on Representative Government. Crown 8vo. 2s.
— — Liberty. Post 8vo. 7s. 6d. Crown 8vo. 1s. 4d.
Mill's Dissertations and Discussions. 4 vols. 8vo. 46s. 6d.
— Essays on Unsettled Questions of Political Economy. 8vo. 6s. 6d.
— Examination of Hamilton's Philosophy. 8vo. 16s.
— Logic, Ratiocinative and Inductive. 2 vols. 8vo. 25s.
— Phenomena of the Human Mind. 2 vols. 8vo. 28s.
— Principles of Political Economy. 2 vols. 8vo. 30s. 1 vol. cr. 8vo. 5s.
— Subjection of Women. Crown 8vo. 6s.
— Utilitarianism. 8vo. 5s.
Morell's Philosophical Fragments. Crown 8vo. 5s.
Müller's (Max) Lectures on the Science of Language. 2 vols. crown 8vo. 16s.
— Hibbert Lectures on the Origin and Growth of Religion. 8vo. 10s. 6d.
Noiré on Max Müller's Philosophy of Language. 8vo. 6s.
Rich's Dictionary of Roman and Greek Antiquities. Crown 8vo. 7s. 6d.
Roget's Thesaurus of English Words and Phrases. Crown 8vo. 10s. 6d.
Sandars's Institutes of Justinian, with English Notes. 8vo. 18s.
Swinbourne's Picture Logic. Post 8vo. 5s.
Thomson's Outline of Necessary Laws of Thought. Crown 8vo. 6s.
Tocqueville's Democracy in America, translated by Reeve. 2 vols. crown 8vo. 16s.
Twiss's Law of Nations, 8vo. in Time of Peace, 12s. in Time of War, 21s.
Whately's Elements of Logic. 8vo. 10s. 6d. Crown 8vo. 4s. 6d.
— — — Rhetoric. 8vo. 10s. 6d. Crown 8vo. 4s. 6d.
— English Synonymes. Fcp. 8vo. 3s.
White & Riddle's Large Latin-English Dictionary. 4to. 28s.
White's College Latin-English Dictionary. Medium 8vo. 15s.
— Junior Student's Complete Latin-English and English-Latin Dictionary. Square 12mo. 12s.

Separately { The English-Latin Dictionary, 5s. 6d.
{ The Latin-English Dictionary, 7s. 6d.

White's Middle-Class Latin-English Dictionary. Fcp. 8vo. 3s.
Williams's Nicomachean Ethics of Aristotle translated. Crown 8vo. 7s. 6d
Yonge's Abridged English-Greek Lexicon. Square 12mo. 8s. 6d.
— Large English-Greek Lexicon. 4to. 21s.
Zeller's Socrates and the Socratic Schools. Crown 8vo. 10s. 6d.
— Stoics, Epicureans, and Sceptics. Crown 8vo. 14s.
— Plato and the Older Academy. Crown 8vo. 18s.

MISCELLANEOUS WORKS & POPULAR METAPHYSICS.

Arnold's (Dr. Thomas) Miscellaneous Works. 8vo. 7s. 6d.
Bain's Emotions and the Will. 8vo. 15s.

London, LONGMANS & CO.

General Lists of New Works.

Bain's Mental and Moral Science. Crown 8vo. 10s. 6d. Or separately: Part I. Mental Science, 6s. 6d. Part II. Moral Science, 4s. 6d.
— Senses and the Intellect. 8vo. 15s.
Buckle's Miscellaneous and Posthumous Works. 3 vols. 8vo. 52s. 6d.
Conington's Miscellaneous Writings. 2 vols. 8vo. 28s.
Edwards's Specimens of English Prose. 16mo. 2s. 6d.
Froude's Short Studies on Great Subjects. 3 vols. crown 8vo. 18s.
German Home Life, reprinted from *Fraser's Magazine*. Crown 8vo. 6s.
Hume's Essays, edited by Green & Grose. 2 vols. 8vo. 28s.
— Treatise of Human Nature, edited by Green & Grose. 2 vols. 8vo. 28s.
Macaulay's Miscellaneous Writings. 2 vols. 8vo. 21s. 1 vol. crown 8vo. 4s. 6d.
— Writings and Speeches. Crown 8vo. 6s.
Mill's Analysis of the Phenomena of the Human Mind. 2 vols. 8vo. 28s.
Müller's (Max) Chips from a German Workshop. 4 vols. 8vo. 58s.
Mullinger's Schools of Charles the Great. 8vo. 7s. 6d.
Rogers's Defence of the Eclipse of Faith. Fcp. 8vo. 3s. 6d.
— Eclipse of Faith. Fcp. 8vo. 5s.
Selections from the Writings of Lord Macaulay. Crown 8vo. 6s.
The Essays and Contributions of A. K. H. B. Crown 8vo.

> Autumn Holidays of a Country Parson. 3s. 6d.
> Changed Aspects of Unchanged Truths. 3s. 6d.
> Common-place Philosopher in Town and Country. 3s. 6d.
> Counsel and Comfort spoken from a City Pulpit. 3s. 6d.
> Critical Essays of a Country Parson. 3s. 6d.
> Graver Thoughts of a Country Parson. Three Series, 3s. 6d. each.
> Landscapes, Churches, and Moralities. 3s. 6d.
> Leisure Hours in Town. 3s. 6d.
> Lessons of Middle Age. 3s. 6d.
> Present-day Thoughts. 3s. 6d.
> Recreations of a Country Parson. Three Series, 3s. 6d. each.
> Seaside Musings on Sundays and Week-Days. 3s. 6d.
> Sunday Afternoons in the Parish Church of a University City. 3s. 6d.

Wit and Wisdom of the Rev. Sydney Smith. 16mo. 3s. 6d.

ASTRONOMY, METEOROLOGY, POPULAR GEOGRAPHY &c.

Dove's Law of Storms, translated by Scott. 8vo. 10s. 6d.
Herschel's Outlines of Astronomy. Square crown 8vo. 12s.
Keith Johnston's Dictionary of Geography, or Gazetteer. 8vo. 42s.
Nelson's Work on the Moon. Medium 8vo. 31s. 6d.
Proctor's Essays on Astronomy. 8vo. 12s.
— Larger Star Atlas. Folio, 15s. or Maps only, 12s. 6d.
— Moon. Crown 8vo. 10s. 6d.
— New Star Atlas. Crown 8vo. 5s.
— Orbs Around Us. Crown 8vo. 7s. 6d.
— Other Worlds than Ours. Crown 8vo. 10s. 6d.
— Saturn and its System. 8vo. 14s.
— Sun. Crown 8vo. 14s.
— Transits of Venus, Past and Coming. Crown 8vo. 8s. 6d.
— Treatise on the Cycloid and Cycloidal Curves. Crown 8vo. 10s. 6d.

London, LONGMANS & CO.

Proctor's Universe of Stars. 8vo. 10s. 6d.
Schellen's Spectrum Analysis. 8vo. 28s.
Smith's Air and Rain. 8vo. 24s.
The Public Schools Atlas of Ancient Geography. Imperial 8vo. 7s. 6d.
— — — Atlas of Modern Geography. Imperial 8vo. 5s.
Webb's Celestial Objects for Common Telescopes. New Edition in preparation.

NATURAL HISTORY & POPULAR SCIENCE.

Arnott's Elements of Physics or Natural Philosophy. Crown 8vo. 12s. 6d.
Brande's Dictionary of Science, Literature, and Art. 3 vols. medium 8vo. 63s.
Decaisne and Le Maout's General System of Botany. Imperial 8vo. 31s. 6d.
Evans's Ancient Stone Implements of Great Britain. 8vo. 28s.
Ganot's Elementary Treatise on Physics, by Atkinson. Large crown 8vo. 15s.
— Natural Philosophy, by Atkinson. Crown 8vo. 7s. 6d.
Gore's Art of Scientific Discovery. Crown 8vo. 15s.
Grove's Correlation of Physical Forces. 8vo. 15s.
Hartwig's Aerial World. 8vo. 10s. 6d.
— Polar World. 8vo. 10s. 6d.
— Sea and its Living Wonders. 8vo. 10s. 6d.
— Subterranean World. 8vo. 10s. 6d.
— Tropical World. 8vo. 10s. 6d.
Haughton's Principles of Animal Mechanics. 8vo. 21s.
Heer's Primæval World of Switzerland. 2 vols. 8vo. 16s.
Helmholtz's Lectures on Scientific Subjects. 8vo. 12s. 6d.
Helmholtz on the Sensations of Tone, by Ellis. 8vo. 36s.
Hemsley's Handbook of Trees, Shrubs, & Herbaceous Plants. Medium 8vo. 12s.
Hullah's Lectures on the History of Modern Music. 8vo. 8s. 6d.
— Transition Period of Musical History. 8vo. 10s. 6d.
Keller's Lake Dwellings of Switzerland, by Lee. 2 vols. royal 8vo. 42s.
Kirby and Spence's Introduction to Entomology. Crown 8vo. 5s.
Lloyd's Treatise on Magnetism. 8vo. 10s. 6d.
— — on the Wave-Theory of Light. 8vo. 10s. 6d.
Loudon's Encyclopædia of Plants. 8vo. 42s.
Lubbock on the Origin of Civilisation & Primitive Condition of Man. 8vo. 18s.
Macalister's Zoology and Morphology of Vertebrate Animals. 8vo. 10s. 6d.
Nicols' Puzzle of Life. Crown 8vo. 3s. 6d.
Owen's Comparative Anatomy and Physiology of the Vertebrate Animals. 3 vols. 8vo. 73s. 6d.
Proctor's Light Science for Leisure Hours. 2 vols. crown 8vo. 7s. 6d. each.
Rivers's Rose Amateur's Guide. Fcp. 8vo. 4s. 6d.
Stanley's Familiar History of Birds. Fcp. 8vo. 3s. 6d.
Text-Books of Science, Mechanical and Physical.
    Abney's Photography, small 8vo. 3s. 6d.
    Anderson's (Sir John) Strength of Materials, 3s. 6d.
    Armstrong's Organic Chemistry, 3s. 6d.
    Barry's Railway Appliances, 3s. 6d.
    Bloxam's Metals, 3s. 6d.
    Goodeve's Elements of Mechanism, 3s. 6d.
    — Principles of Mechanics, 3s. 6d.
    Gore's Electro-Metallurgy, 6s.
    Griffin's Algebra and Trigonometry, 3s. 6d.

London, LONGMANS & CO.

General Lists of New Works.

Text-Books of Science—*continued*.
  Jenkin's Electricity and Magnetism, 3*s*. 6*d*.
  Maxwell's Theory of Heat, 3*s*. 6*d*.
  Merrifield's Technical Arithmetic and Mensuration, 3*s*. 6*d*.
  Miller's Inorganic Chemistry, 3*s*. 6*d*.
  Preece & Sivewright's Telegraphy, 3*s*. 6*d*.
  Rutley's Study of Rocks, 4*s*. 6*d*.
  Shelley's Workshop Appliances, 3*s*. 6*d*.
  Thomé's Structural and Physiological Botany, 6*s*.
  Thorpe's Quantitative Chemical Analysis, 4*s*. 6*d*.
  Thorpe & Muir's Qualitative Analysis, 3*s*. 6*d*.
  Tilden's Chemical Philosophy, 3*s*. 6*d*.
  Unwin's Machine Design, 3*s*. 6*d*.
  Watson's Plane and Solid Geometry, 3*s*. 6*d*.
Tyndall on Sound. Crown 8vo. 10*s*. 6*d*.
 — Contributions to Molecular Physics. 8vo. 16*s*.
 — Fragments of Science. New Edit. 2 vols. crown 8vo. [*In the press.*
 — Heat a Mode of Motion. Crown 8vo.
 — Lectures on Electrical Phenomena. Crown 8vo. 1*s*. sewed, 1*s*. 6*d*. cloth.
 — Lectures on Light. Crown 8vo. 1*s*. sewed, 1*s*. 6*d*. cloth.
 — Lectures on Light delivered in America. Crown 8vo. 7*s*. 6*d*.
 — Lessons in Electricity. Crown 8vo. 2*s*. 6*d*.
Von Cotta on Rocks, by Lawrence. Post 8vo. 14*s*.
Woodward's Geology of England and Wales. Crown 8vo. 14*s*.
Wood's Bible Animals. With 112 Vignettes. 8vo. 14*s*.
 — Homes Without Hands. 8vo. 14*s*.
 — Insects Abroad. 8vo. 14*s*.
 — Insects at Home. With 700 Illustrations. 8vo. 14*s*.
 — Out of Doors, or Articles on Natural History. Crown 8vo. 7*s*. 6*d*.
 — Strange Dwellings. With 60 Woodcuts. Crown 8vo. 7*s*. 6*d*.

CHEMISTRY & PHYSIOLOGY.

Auerbach's Anthracen, translated by W. Crookes, F.R.S. 8vo. 12*s*.
Buckton's Health in the House; Lectures on Elementary Physiology. Fcp. 8vo. 2*s*.
Crookes's Handbook of Dyeing and Calico Printing. 8vo. 42*s*.
 — Select Methods in Chemical Analysis. Crown 8vo. 12*s*. 6*d*.
Kingzett's Animal Chemistry. 8vo. 18*s*.
 — History, Products and Processes of the Alkali Trade. 8vo. 12*s*.
Miller's Elements of Chemistry, Theoretical and Practical. 3 vols. 8vo. Part I. Chemical Physics, 16*s*. Part II. Inorganic Chemistry, 24*s*. Part III. Organic Chemistry, New Edition in the press.
Watts's Dictionary of Chemistry. 7 vols. medium 8vo. £10. 16*s*. 6*d*.
 — Third Supplementary Volume, in Two Parts. PART I. 36*s*.

THE FINE ARTS & ILLUSTRATED EDITIONS.

Bewick's Select Fables of Æsop and others. Crown 8vo. 7*s*. 6*d*. demy 8vo. 18*s*.
Doyle's Fairyland; Pictures from the Elf-World. Folio, 15*s*.
Jameson's Sacred and Legendary Art. 6 vols. square crown 8vo.
  Legends of the Madonna. 1 vol. 21*s*.
  — — — Monastic Orders. 1 vol. 21*s*.
  — — — Saints and Martyrs. 2 vols. 31*s*. 6*d*.
  — — — Saviour. Completed by Lady Eastlake. 2 vols. 42*s*.

London, LONGMANS & CO.

Longman's Three Cathedrals Dedicated to St. Paul. Square crown 8vo. 21s.
Macaulay's Lays of Ancient Rome. With 90 Illustrations. Fcp. 4to. 21s.
Macfarren's Lectures on Harmony. 8vo. 12s.
Miniature Edition of Macaulay's Lays of Ancient Rome. Imp. 16mo. 10s. 6d.
Moore's Irish Melodies. With 161 Plates by D. Maclise, R.A. Super-royal 8vo. 21s.
— Lalla Rookh. Tenniel's Edition. With 68 Illustrations. Fcp. 4to. 21s.
Northcote and Brownlow's Roma Sotterranea. PART I. 8vo. 24s.
Perry on Greek and Roman Sculpture. 8vo. [*In preparation.*
Redgrave's Dictionary of Artists of the English School. 8vo. 16s.

THE USEFUL ARTS, MANUFACTURES &c.

Bourne's Catechism of the Steam Engine. Fcp. 8vo. 6s.
— Examples of Steam, Air, and Gas Engines. 4to. 70s.
— Handbook of the Steam Engine. Fcp. 8vo. 9s.
— Recent Improvements in the Steam Engine. Fcp. 8vo. 6s.
— Treatise on the Steam Engine. 4to. 42s.
Cresy's Encyclopædia of Civil Engineering. 8vo. 42s.
Culley's Handbook of Practical Telegraphy. 8vo. 16s.
Eastlake's Household Taste in Furniture, &c. Square crown 8vo. 14s.
Fairbairn's Useful Information for Engineers. 3 vols. crown 8vo. 31s. 6d.
— Applications of Cast and Wrought Iron. 8vo. 16s.
— Mills and Millwork. 1 vol. 8vo. 25s.
Gwilt's Encyclopædia of Architecture. 8vo. 52s. 6d.
Hobson's Amateur Mechanics Practical Handbook. Crown 8vo. 2s. 6d.
Hoskold's Engineer's Valuing Assistant. 8vo. 31s. 6d.
Kerl's Metallurgy, adapted by Crookes and Röhrig. 3 vols. 8vo. £4. 19s.
Loudon's Encyclopædia of Agriculture. 8vo. 21s.
— — — Gardening. 8vo. 21s.
Mitchell's Manual of Practical Assaying. 8vo. 31s. 6d.
Northcott's Lathes and Turning. 8vo. 18s.
Payen's Industrial Chemistry, translated from Stohmann and Engler's German Edition, by Dr. J. D. Barry. Edited by B. H. Paul, Ph.D. 8vo. 42s.
Stoney's Theory of Strains in Girders. Roy. 8vo. 36s.
Thomas on Coal, Mine-Gases and Ventilation. Crown 8vo. 10s. 6d.
Ure's Dictionary of Arts, Manufactures, & Mines. 4 vols. medium 8vo. £7. 7s.

RELIGIOUS & MORAL WORKS.

Abbey & Overton's English Church in the Eighteenth Century. 2 vols. 8vo. 36s.
Arnold's (Rev. Dr. Thomas) Sermons. 6 vols. crown 8vo. 5s. each.
Bishop Jeremy Taylor's Entire Works. With Life by Bishop Heber. Edited by the Rev. C. P. Eden. 10 vols. 8vo. £5. 5s.
Boultbee's Commentary on the 39 Articles. Crown 8vo. 6s.
Browne's (Bishop) Exposition of the 39 Articles. 8vo. 16s.
Conybeare & Howson's Life and Letters of St. Paul:—
  Library Edition, with all the Original Illustrations, Maps, Landscapes on Steel, Woodcuts, &c. 2 vols. 4to. 42s.
  Intermediate Edition, with a Selection of Maps, Plates, and Woodcuts. 2 vols. square crown 8vo. 21s.
  Student's Edition, revised and condensed, with 46 Illustrations and Maps. 1 vol. crown 8vo. 9s.
Colenso's Lectures on the Pentateuch and the Moabite Stone. 8vo. 12s.

London, LONGMANS & CO.

Colenso on the Pentateuch and Book of Joshua. Crown 8vo. 6s.
— — PART VII. completion of the larger Work. 8vo. 24s.
D'Aubigné's Reformation in Europe in the Time of Calvin. 8 vols. 8vo. £6.12s.
Drummond's Jewish Messiah. 8vo. 15s.
Ellicott's (Bishop) Commentary on St. Paul's Epistles. 8vo. Galatians, 8s. 6d. Ephesians, 8s. 6d. Pastoral Epistles, 10s. 6d. Philippians, Colossians, and Philemon, 10s. 6d. Thessalonians, 7s. 6d.
Ellicott's Lectures on the Life of our Lord. 8vo. 12s.
Ewald's History of Israel, translated by Carpenter. 5 vols. 8vo. 63s.
— Antiquities of Israel, translated by Solly. 8vo. 12s. 6d.
Goldziher's Mythology among the Hebrews. 8vo. 16s.
Jukes's Types of Genesis. Crown 8vo. 7s. 6d.
— Second Death and the Restitution of all Things. Crown 8vo. 3s. 6d.
Kalisch's Bible Studies. PART I. the Prophecies of Balaam. 8vo. 10s. 6d.
— — — PART II. the Book of Jonah. 8vo. 10s. 6d.
Keith's Evidence of the Truth of the Christian Religion derived from the Fulfilment of Prophecy. Square 8vo. 12s. 6d. Post 8vo. 6s.
Kuenen on the Prophets and Prophecy in Israel. 8vo. 21s.
Lyra Germanica. Hymns translated by Miss Winkworth. Fcp. 8vo. 5s.
Manning's Temporal Mission of the Holy Ghost. 8vo. 8s. 6d.
Martineau's Endeavours after the Christian Life. Crown 8vo. 7s. 6d.
— Hymns of Praise and Prayer. Crown 8vo. 4s. 6d. 32mo. 1s. 6d.
— Sermons; Hours of Thought on Sacred Things. Crown 8vo. 7s. 6d.
Merivale's (Dean) Lectures on Early Church History. Crown 8vo.
Mill's Three Essays on Religion. 8vo. 10s. 6d.
Monsell's Spiritual Songs for Sundays and Holidays. Fcp. 8vo. 5s. 18mo. 2s.
Müller's (Max) Lectures on the Science of Religion. Crown 8vo. 10s. 6d.
Newman's Apologia pro Vita Sua. Crown 8vo. 6s.
O'Conor's New Testament Commentaries. Crown 8vo. Epistle to the Romans, 3s. 6d. Epistle to the Hebrews, 4s. 6d. St. John's Gospel, 10s. 6d.
One Hundred Holy Songs, &c. Square fcp. 8vo. 2s. 6d.
Passing Thoughts on Religion. By Miss Sewell. Fcp. 8vo. 3s. 6d.
Sewell's (Miss) Preparation for the Holy Communion. 32mo. 3s.
Shipley's Ritual of the Altar. Imperial 8vo. 42s.
Supernatural Religion. 3 vols. 8vo. 38s.
Thoughts for the Age. By Miss Sewell. Fcp. 8vo. 3s. 6d.
Vaughan's Trident, Crescent, and Cross; the Religious History of India. 8vo. 9s. 6d.
Whately's Lessons on the Christian Evidences. 18mo. 6d.
White's Four Gospels in Greek, with Greek-English Lexicon. 32mo. 5s.

TRAVELS, VOYAGES &c.

Ball's Alpine Guide. 3 vols. post 8vo. with Maps and Illustrations :—I. Western Alps, 6s. 6d. II. Central Alps, 7s. 6d. III. Eastern Alps, 10s. 6d.
Ball on Alpine Travelling, and on the Geology of the Alps, 1s.
Baker's Rifle and the Hound in Ceylon. Crown 8vo. 7s. 6d.
— Eight Years in Ceylon. Crown 8vo. 7s. 6d.
Bent's Freak of Freedom, or the Republic of San Marino. Crown 8vo.
Brassey's Voyage in the Yacht 'Sunbeam.' Crown 8vo. 7s. 6d. 8vo. 21s.
Edwards's (A. B.) Thousand Miles up the Nile. Imperial 8vo. 42s.

London, LONGMANS & CO.

Evans's Illyrian Letters. Post 8vo. 7s. 6d.
Grohman's Tyrol and the Tyrolese. Crown 8vo. 6s.
Indian Alps (The). By a Lady Pioneer. Imperial 8vo. 42s.
Lefroy's Discovery and Early Settlement of the Bermuda Islands. 2 vols. royal 8vo. 60s.
Miller and Skertchley's Fenland Past and Present. Royal 8vo. 31s. 6d. Large Paper, 50s.
Noble's Cape and South Africa. Fcp. 8vo. 3s. 6d.
Packe's Guide to the Pyrenees, for Mountaineers. Crown 8vo. 7s. 6d.
The Alpine Club Map of Switzerland. In four sheets. 42s.
Wood's Discoveries at Ephesus. Imperial 8vo. 63s.

WORKS OF FICTION.

Becker's Charicles; Private Life among the Ancient Greeks. Post 8vo. 7s. 6d.
— Gallus; Roman Scenes of the Time of Augustus. Post 8vo. 7s. 6d.

Cabinet Edition of Stories and Tales by Miss Sewell:—
- Amy Herbert, 2s. 6d.
- Cleve Hall, 2s. 6d.
- The Earl's Daughter, 2s. 6d.
- Experience of Life, 2s. 6d.
- Gertrude, 2s. 6d.
- Ivors, 2s. 6d.
- Katharine Ashton, 2s. 6d.
- Laneton Parsonage, 3s. 6d.
- Margaret Percival, 3s. 6d.
- Ursula, 3s. 6d.

Novels and Tales by the Right Hon. the Earl of Beaconsfield, K.G. Cabinet Edition, complete in Ten Volumes, crown 8vo. price £3.
- Lothair, 6s.
- Coningsby, 6s.
- Sybil, 6s.
- Tancred, 6s.
- Venetia, 6s.
- Henrietta Temple, 6s.
- Contarini Fleming, 6s.
- Alroy, Ixion, &c. 6s.
- The Young Duke, &c. 6s.
- Vivian Grey, 6s.

The Modern Novelist's Library. Each Work in crown 8vo. A Single Volume, complete in itself, price 2s. boards, or 2s. 6d. cloth:—

By the Earl of Beaconsfield, K.G.
- Lothair.
- Coningsby.
- Sybil.
- Tancred.
- Venetia.
- Henrietta Temple.
- Contarini Fleming.
- Alroy, Ixion, &c.
- The Young Duke, &c.
- Vivian Grey.

By Anthony Trollope.
- Barchester Towers.
- The Warden.

By the Author of 'the Rose Garden.'
- Unawares.

By Major Whyte-Melville.
- Digby Grand.
- General Bounce.
- Kate Coventry.
- The Gladiators.
- Good for Nothing.
- Holmby House.
- The Interpreter.
- The Queen's Maries.

By the Author of 'the Atelier du Lys.'
- Mademoiselle Mori.
- The Atelier du Lys.

By Various Writers.
- Atherstone Priory.
- The Burgomaster's Family.
- Elsa and her Vulture.
- The Six Sisters of the Valley.

Lord Beaconsfield's Novels and Tales. 10 vols. cloth extra, gilt edges, 30s.

Whispers from Fairy Land. By the Right Hon. E. H. Knatchbull-Hugessen M.P. With Nine Illustrations. Crown 8vo. 3s. 6d.

Higgledy-Piggledy; or, Stories for Everybody and Everybody's Children. By the Right Hon. E. M. Knatchbull-Hugessen, M.P. With Nine Illustrations from Designs by R. Doyle. Crown 8vo. 3s. 6d.

London, LONGMANS & CO.

POETRY & THE DRAMA.

Bailey's Festus, a Poem. Crown 8vo. 12s. 6d.
Bowdler's Family Shakspeare. Medium 8vo. 14s. 6 vols. fcp. 8vo. 21s.
Brian Boru, a Tragedy, by J. T. B. Crown 8vo. 6s.
Cayley's Iliad of Homer, Homometrically translated. 8vo. 12s. 6d.
Conington's Æneid of Virgil, translated into English Verse. Crown 8vo. 9s.
Cooper's Tales from Euripides. Small 8vo.
Edwards's Poetry-Book of Elder Poets. 16mo. 2s. 6d.
— Poetry-Book of Modern Poets. 16mo. 2s. 6d.
Ingelow's Poems. First Series. Illustrated Edition. Fcp. 4to. 21s.
Macaulay's Lays of Ancient Rome, with Ivry and the Armada. 16mo. 3s. 6d.
Petrarch's Sonnets and Stanzas, translated by C. B. Cayley, B.A. Crown 8vo. 10s. 6d.
Poems. By Jean Ingelow. 2 vols. fcp. 8vo. 10s.
    First Series. 'Divided,' 'The Star's Monument,' &c. 5s.
    Second Series. 'A Story of Doom,' 'Gladys and her Island,' &c. 5s.
Southey's Poetical Works. Medium 8vo. 14s.
Yonge's Horatii Opera, Library Edition. 8vo. 21s.

RURAL SPORTS, HORSE & CATTLE MANAGEMENT &c.

Blaine's Encyclopædia of Rural Sports. 8vo. 21s.
Dobson on the Ox, his Diseases and their Treatment. Crown 8vo. 7s. 6d.
Fitzwygram's Horses and Stables. 8vo. 10s. 6d.
Francis's Book on Angling, or Treatise on Fishing. Post 8vo. 15s.
Malet's Annals of the Road, and Nimrod's Essays on the Road. Medium 8vo. 21s.
Miles's Horse's Foot, and How to Keep it Sound. Imperial 8vo. 12s. 6d.
— Plain Treatise on Horse-Shoeing. Post 8vo. 2s. 6d.
— Stables and Stable-Fittings. Imperial 8vo. 15s.
— Remarks on Horses' Teeth. Post 8vo. 1s. 6d.
Nevile's Horses and Riding. Crown 8vo. 6s.
Reynardson's Down the Road. Medium 8vo. 21s.
Ronalds's Fly-Fisher's Entomology. 8vo. 14s.
Stonehenge's Dog in Health and Disease. Square crown 8vo. 7s. 6d.
— Greyhound. Square crown 8vo. 15s.
Youatt's Work on the Dog. 8vo. 12s. 6d.
— — — — Horse. 8vo. 6s.
Wilcocks's Sea-Fisherman. Post 8vo. 12s. 6d.

WORKS OF UTILITY & GENERAL INFORMATION.

Acton's Modern Cookery for Private Families. Fcp. 8vo. 6s.
Black's Practical Treatise on Brewing. 8vo. 10s. 6d.
Buckton's Food and Home Cookery. Crown 8vo. 2s.
Bull on the Maternal Management of Children. Fcp. 8vo. 2s. 6d.
Bull's Hints to Mothers on the Management of their Health during the Period of Pregnancy and in the Lying-in Room. Fcp. 8vo. 2s. 6d.
Campbell-Walker's Correct Card, or How to Play at Whist. 32mo. 2s. 6d.
Crump's English Manual of Banking. 8vo. 15s.
Cunningham's Conditions of Social Well-Being. 8vo. 10s. 6d.
Handbook of Gold and Silver, by an Indian Official. 8vo. 12s. 6d.
Johnson's (W. & J. H.) Patentee's Manual. Fourth Edition. 8vo. 10s. 6d.
Longman's Chess Openings. Fcp. 8vo. 2s. 6d.

London, LONGMANS & CO.

General Lists of New Works.

Macleod's Economics for Beginners. Small crown 8vo. 2s. 6d.
— Theory and Practice of Banking. 2 vols. 8vo. 26s.
— Elements of Banking. Fourth Edition. Crown 8vo. 5s.
M'Culloch's Dictionary of Commerce and Commercial Navigation. 8vo. 63s.
Maunder's Biographical Treasury. Fcp. 8vo. 6s.
— Historical Treasury. Fcp. 8vo. 6s.
— Scientific and Literary Treasury. Fcp. 8vo. 6s.
— Treasury of Bible Knowledge. Edited by the Rev. J. Ayre, M.A. Fcp. 8vo. 6s.
— Treasury of Botany. Edited by J. Lindley, F.R.S. and T. Moore, F.L.S. Two Parts, fcp. 8vo. 12s.
— Treasury of Geography. Fcp. 8vo. 6s.
— Treasury of Knowledge and Library of Reference. Fcp. 8vo. 6s.
— Treasury of Natural History. Fcp. 8vo. 6s.
Pereira's Materia Medica, by Bentley and Redwood. 8vo. 25s.
Pewtner's Comprehensive Specifier; Building-Artificers' Work. Conditions and Agreements. Crown 8vo. 6s.
Pierce's Three Hundred Chess Problems and Studies. Fcp. 8vo. 7s. 6d.
Pole's Theory of the Modern Scientific Game of Whist. Fcp. 8vo. 2s. 6d.
Scott's Farm Valuer. Crown 8vo. 5s.
Smith's Handbook for Midwives. Crown 8vo. 5s.
The Cabinet Lawyer, a Popular Digest of the Laws of England. Fcp. 8vo. 9s.
West on the Diseases of Infancy and Childhood. 8vo. 18s.
Willich's Popular Tables for ascertaining the Value of Property. Post 8vo. 10s.
Wilson on Banking Reform. 8vo. 7s. 6d.
— on the Resources of Modern Countries 2 vols. 8vo. 24s.

MUSICAL WORKS BY JOHN HULLAH, LL.D.

Chromatic Scale, with the Inflected Syllables, on Large Sheet. 1s. 6d.
Card of Chromatic Scale. 1d.
Exercises for the Cultivation of the Voice. For Soprano or Tenor, 2s. 6d.
Grammar of Musical Harmony. Royal 8vo. 2 Parts, each 1s. 6d.
Exercises to Grammar of Musical Harmony. 1s.
Grammar of Counterpoint. Part I. super-royal 8vo. 2s. 6d.
Hullah's Manual of Singing. Parts I. & II. 2s. 6d.; or together, 5s.
Exercises and Figures contained in Parts I. and II. of the Manual. Books I. & II. each 8d.
Large Sheets, containing the Figures in Part I. of the Manual. Nos. 1 to 8 in a Parcel. 6s.
Large Sheets, containing the Exercises in Part I. of the Manual. Nos. 9 to 40, in Four Parcels of Eight Nos. each, per Parcel. 6s.
Large Sheets, the Figures in Part II. Nos. 41 to 52 in a Parcel, 9s.
Hymns for the Young, set to Music. Royal 8vo. 8d.
Infant School Songs. 6d.
Notation, the Musical Alphabet. Crown 8vo. 6d.
Old English Songs for Schools, Harmonised. 6d.
Rudiments of Musical Grammar. Royal 8vo. 3s.
School Songs for 2 and 3 Voices. 2 Books, 8vo. each 6d.
Time and Tune in the Elementary School. Crown 8vo. 2s. 6d.
Exercises and Figures in the same. Crown 8vo. 1s. or 2 Parts, 6d each.

London, LONGMANS & CO.

www.ingramcontent.com/pod-product-compliance
Lightning Source LLC
Chambersburg PA
CBHW071705230426
43670CB00008B/918